Going GAS
From VBA to Google Apps Script

Bruce Mcpherson

Beijing · Boston · Farnham · Sebastopol · Tokyo

Going GAS

by Bruce Mcpherson

Printed in the United States of America.

Published by O'Reilly Media, Inc., 1005 Gravenstein Highway North, Sebastopol, CA 95472.

O'Reilly books may be purchased for educational, business, or sales promotional use. Online editions are also available for most titles (*http://safaribooksonline.com*). For more information, contact our corporate/institutional sales department: 800-998-9938 or *corporate@oreilly.com*.

Editor: Meg Foley
Production Editor: Colleen Lobner
Copyeditor: Rachel Monaghan
Proofreader: Jasmine Kwityn

Indexer: Judith McConville
Interior Designer: David Futato
Cover Designer: Randy Comer
Illustrator: Rebecca Demarest

February 2016: First Edition

Revision History for the First Edition
2016-02-08: First Release

See *http://oreilly.com/catalog/errata.csp?isbn=9781491940464* for release details.

978-1-491-94046-4

[LSI]

Table of Contents

Preface

Why Read This Book?

Perhaps you already use VBA to extend Office, but are considering alternatives. You may have already "gone Google," or you might be looking at Microsoft's Apps for Office options. In particular, you're wondering what to do with all the VBA code built up over the years that you consider essential to enabling your business processes.

This book will show you how to transition from VBA with minimal effort. Even if you are not a VBA user, you will learn how to use Apps Script and its ecosystem to automate processes in the Google Apps platform.

Why Transition from VBA?

In many ways, VBA has been a victim of its own success. Its tight integration with Office and very usable and immediate development environment make it hard to beat. However, it's been with us since 1991, the same year that Tim Berners-Lee created the first website, which is still running today (*http://bit.ly/uw-first*), but for historical rather any aesthetic or functional reasons.

Although VBA is as far removed from its 1991 forefather as today's HTML5 sites are from that first website, every version of Office for as long as I can remember has come with a threat that perhaps VBA will not be supported. Office 2008 for Mac did not support VBA, but it was back again by public demand in Office 2011. Office 2016 has just been released, and we can all breathe a sigh of relief to see that VBA is still there. But Microsoft's focus is shifting to Office 365 from Office for the desktop. According to Satya Nadella of Microsoft, "the most strategic developer surface for us is Office 365."

With incompatibilities between 32-bit and 64-bit versions and between Office for Mac and Windows, and with a reliance on references to libraries that are no longer shipped with Windows, VBA becomes harder for Microsoft to support and for us to use.

I'm a longtime proponent and fan of VBA. I'm not alone, considering the Office development section of my website still generates almost a million annual page views, and there are still many active VBA communities and forums around. VBA continues to enjoy immense popularity, but (sadly) it's probably time to move on, as one of these days it really will no longer be shipped with Office.

This book will show you by example how to do some of the same things you do today in VBA, but in Apps Script. The examples will use the Google Apps platform, but we'll also look at the Microsoft JavaScript API.

Intended Audience

You are probably already a VBA or .NET developer. You might even already be an Apps Script developer who needs to understand something about VBA to assist with a migration, or perhaps you simply want to learn Apps Script. This is not intended to be a book for beginners, and best fits those who are already comfortable with one or more development languages.

It's not necessary to already know JavaScript, but things will move faster if you do. This is not a JavaScript tutorial, but this book will introduce the language components and syntax and provide enough examples to enable the proficient use of Apps Script.

For add-ins and add-ons (extending Docs and Office with client-side web apps), and the HtmlService sections of the book, you'll need some understanding of HTML, CSS, and the DOM.

The VBA Library

The overall objective of this book is to demonstrate how to apply Apps Script services best practices to solve problems common across Office automation platforms. A key output is a library that emulates many built-in VBA functions in JavaScript. This will allow you to port some of your VBA code and structure to Apps Script with minimal changes, while concentrating on the Apps Script services capabilities.

Reading Order

The first part of the book compares the capabilities of each platform, then moves on to the fundamentals of the JavaScript language, emphasizing how it differs from VBA. That is followed by a long reference section containing an implementation in

JavaScript of each of the main VBA built-in functions, as well as some of the utility objects.

If you decide to use this library, it means that you can still write VBA-style code that calls VBA built-in function names, instead of using the native JavaScript equivalent. Alternatively, you can refer to the translations and implement those when you port your applications.

The rest of the book deals with each Google Apps Script service that has an equivalent in VBA (and a few that don't), and will generally show you the contrast in navigating and interfacing between the respective object models.

There are both tutorials and reference material, and the order in which you read them is not especially important, although some of the examples refer back to previous chapters and concepts. It is likely that you already have experience in some of the subjects (or don't plan to use some of the services covered). It's not really required that you read the content sequentially.

In summary, the scope of the material is not only the contrast between how to do things in Apps Script and VBA, but also how to get things done in the Google universe. This will ease the transition to Google Apps, regardless of where you are coming from.

Apps Script is both young and versatile, with new capabilities being added (and old ones being deprecated) regularly, and unlike with VBA, you don't have the option to get stuck on an old version (even if you want to).

The Examples

The code illustrations are a mixture of snippets and longer projects, but they quickly become challenging, using the kind of patterns found in real-world scenarios. This is by design. After all, you are probably already an accomplished developer and "Hello, World"–level tutorials are not going to be much help for quickly porting VBA applications that have already benefited from significant investment in intellectual and financial capital.

All examples (VBA and Apps Script) are publicly available on GitHub, the details of which you'll find in Appendix A, but I encourage you to try to create some of the code in the Apps Script IDE to build up familiarity with the environment. Some of the VBA examples are more appropriate for Office for Windows and may not be fully compatible with Office for Mac. Of course, the Apps Script examples are platform independent.

All code will be in monospace font and accompanied by the appropriate icon, like this for VBA:

VB `Dim someVBA as string`

and this for JavaScript:

JS `var someJavaScript;`

I've omitted much of the exception handling that would normally need to be built in, simply so that the code can remain as focused as possible on the explanation of the topic in hand. If you do reuse any of the code in real applications, don't forget to extend the error handling to your house standard.

Once you have mastered the techniques demonstrated, you should be in a good position to port all your legacy applications over to Apps Script with minimal effort.

Good luck!

Conventions Used in This Book

The following typographical conventions are used in this book:

Italic
> Indicates new terms, URLs, email addresses, filenames, and file extensions.

`Constant width`
> Used for program listings, as well as within paragraphs to refer to program elements such as variable or function names, databases, data types, environment variables, statements, and keywords.

`Constant width bold`
> Shows commands or other text that should be typed literally by the user.

`Constant width italic`
> Shows text that should be replaced with user-supplied values or by values determined by context.

> This icon signifies a tip, suggestion, or general note.

> This icon indicates a warning or caution.

Using Code Examples

Supplemental material for this book is available for download at *https://github.com/brucemcpherson/GoingGas*.

This book is here to help you get your job done. In general, you may use the code in this book in your programs and documentation. You do not need to contact us for permission unless you're reproducing a significant portion of the code. For example, writing a program that uses several chunks of code from this book does not require permission. Selling or distributing a CD-ROM of examples from O'Reilly books does require permission. Answering a question by citing this book and quoting example code does not require permission. Incorporating a significant amount of example code from this book into your product's documentation does require permission.

We appreciate, but do not require, attribution. An attribution usually includes the title, author, publisher, and ISBN. For example: "*Going GAS* by Bruce Mcpherson (O'Reilly). Copyright 2016 Pepada limited, 978-1-4919-4046-4."

If you feel your use of code examples falls outside fair use or the permission given above, feel free to contact us at *permissions@oreilly.com*.

Safari® Books Online

 *Safari Books Online* is an on-demand digital library that delivers expert content in both book and video form from the world's leading authors in technology and business.

Technology professionals, software developers, web designers, and business and creative professionals use Safari Books Online as their primary resource for research, problem solving, learning, and certification training.

Safari Books Online offers a range of plans and pricing for enterprise, government, education, and individuals.

Members have access to thousands of books, training videos, and prepublication manuscripts in one fully searchable database from publishers like O'Reilly Media, Prentice Hall Professional, Addison-Wesley Professional, Microsoft Press, Sams, Que, Peachpit Press, Focal Press, Cisco Press, John Wiley & Sons, Syngress, Morgan Kaufmann, IBM Redbooks, Packt, Adobe Press, FT Press, Apress, Manning, New Riders, McGraw-Hill, Jones & Bartlett, Course Technology, and hundreds more. For more information about Safari Books Online, please visit us online.

How to Contact Us

Please address comments and questions concerning this book to the publisher:

O'Reilly Media, Inc.
1005 Gravenstein Highway North
Sebastopol, CA 95472
800-998-9938 (in the United States or Canada)
707-829-0515 (international or local)
707-829-0104 (fax)

We have a web page for this book, where we list errata, examples, and any additional information. You can access this page at *http://bit.ly/going-gas*.

To comment or ask technical questions about this book, send email to *bookquestions@oreilly.com*.

For more information about our books, courses, conferences, and news, see our website at *http://www.oreilly.com*.

Find us on Facebook: *http://facebook.com/oreilly*

Follow us on Twitter: *http://twitter.com/oreillymedia*

Watch us on YouTube: *http://www.youtube.com/oreillymedia*

Acknowledgments

When I started putting together the material for this book, I never realized there was so much I didn't know, nor that it would take so long to find it all out and write it down. Many people have helped me along the way, and I'd like to take a little of your time to thank them.

I owe a great debt of gratitude to my truly international and esteemed group of technical reviewers, who gave generously of their time and knowledge to ruthlessly pick apart everything I wrote. Ian Macro (England) gave me a particularly hard time, pointing out those kinds of errors that are easy to miss as an author.

Fellow GDEs (Google Developer Experts) Martin Hawksey (Scotland), Ivan Kutl (Czech Republic), and Riël Notermans (Netherlands) kept me in line when my prose became too extravagant, my claims lacked foundation, I had missed an important detail, or I was just plain wrong.

Microsoft MVPs (Most Valuable Professionals) Andy Pope (England) and Jordan Goldmeier (USA) ventured over to the Google dark side to help me with the accuracy and relevance of the Office and VBA material, as well as some of the JavaScript content and equivalences, and gave me insight into the appropriateness of the material to VBA experts making the transition.

Special thanks go to my longtime friend (and ex-boss), Ron Roberts, who supported me as I became interested in the APIs that Google was creating with such rapidity, and who so graciously allowed me the latitude to become part of the Google Developer Expert community.

Apologies go to my Cairn terriers, who will be especially pleased that these writings are over (for now). Their thrice-daily walks became a little shorter as my book deadline approached, but now we can get back to normal.

Most importantly, thanks to my wife, Blandine, whose rigorous encouragement inspired me to get typing when I would rather have been eating cheese, drinking wine, playing *Baldurs Gate*, or even washing the car. Without her support and tolerance, I would never have got past the blank page that confronted me on day 1.

Finally, thanks to my editor, Meg Foley, and the team at O'Reilly Media who continue to give ordinary people like us the opportunity to have a voice, and without whose guidance, assistance, and hard work this book would not have been possible.

Without the great products created by both Google and Microsoft, I would have had nothing to write about. The pace of innovation is staggering, the APIs are exciting, and I can't wait to see what's coming up next so I can get started on my next project.

CHAPTER 1

Introduction

Moving from VBA into the world of Google Apps Script (GAS) requires some adjustment of your development and planning approaches. There is not a one-to-one relationship between things you can do in VBA, Apps Script, and JavaScript. Even where one can be articulated, the environmental differences under which they each operate are such that valid approaches in one platform do not necessarily translate into wise or even valid approaches on another.

 With advance apologies to purists, for simplicity I refer to these different environments as "platforms." Even though they don't really qualify for that description, it will do.

I've deliberately divided the code samples into a mixture of languages and extensibility solutions, and of course there is crossover between each item. For example, to write a Google add-on, you have to use Apps Script, which is the JavaScript language with additional Google-specific services. On the other hand, you can write Apps Script without necessarily creating an add-on.

VBA merges similar capabilities to Google Forms, Apps Script, add-on-type user interfaces, and the object model into one platform. You need some or all of the Apps Script–related components to achieve the same thing.

This chapter will describe the platforms covered in this book. Some or all of this material will be evident to those who are already familiar with them, but this foundation will inform future chapters as we contrast the different solutions available on each platform.

What Is VBA?

Because you are probably already a VBA developer, or at least have some problems currently solved by VBA that you want to move to a different platform, I'll keep the definition of VBA fairly brief and focus on its unique attributes (both positive and negative).

VBA applications are the most common way to extend Microsoft Office applications such as Excel, PowerPoint, Word, Visio, Outlook, and Access.

Extending

You can extend VBA's capabilities by adding references to other custom objects held in dynamic link libraries (DLLs) or type libraries created in languages other than VBA. The API for each Office application itself is via a DLL containing the code and data required to manipulate the application object model.

You can make your own classes, create custom functions that can be called from worksheets, define and declare your own events, and access events that are triggerable by built-in and custom objects.

Fragility

VBA's integration and extensibility through library references make it very powerful indeed, but they also make it fragile. Relying on the availability of myriad external shared libraries of a particular version means that transportability from one computer to another is hit and miss for substantial scripts. Furthermore, if DLL providers fail to keep their libraries current you might be unable to move to new versions of Office at will.

Security

The development object model is accessible from VBA, which means that you can write or modify code from code. This powerful capability is one of the serious security holes that has led to VBA being both a desirable and easy target for hackers.

Microsoft's response has been to intensify lockdown with each successive version of Office. Nowadays, by default, you can't run macros (as VBA procedures are known) or even save a document containing VBA. Even the developers' view and access to VBA is hidden.

Asynchronicity

Some operations can be performed asynchronously, although the capability is very limited and somewhat of a science project to implement. An *asynchronous* operation is one that is performed while the main execution flow continues—for example, fetching data from an external website, returning control to the main flow so that it can do something else at the same time, and receiving a callback to be handled when the fetch is finished. VBA does not have good support for asynchronicity, and most operations are processed strictly in sequence. My view is that if you are worried about asynchronicity in VBA you are probably doing it wrong, or using the wrong tool.

Efficiency and Performance

VBA compiles (automatically) into an intermediate language called P-code (pseudo-code). Libraries and controls written in other languages and referenced by VBA are already compiled down to P-code, and their capabilities extend VBA efficiently.

Most applications tend to be small scale, so performance becomes an issue only where memory is scarce and large workbooks are being processed. The garbage collection algorithm in the VBA engine seems to be fairly poor, meaning that you must take care when creating large memory structures with backreferences.

Maintainability

Typically the code is *container-bound*, meaning that it forms part of the spreadsheet or document on which it is supposed to operate. When you make a copy of, for example, a macro-enabled spreadsheet, the code comes with it, which leads to code and version sprawl that's difficult to contain. It is possible, through add-ins, to run code in one spreadsheet that resides in another, but in my view that simply makes a messy situation even worse.

The benefits of P-code (a common intermediate language for libraries) were further diluted when a different standard was introduced for the .NET Framework, complicating things even more.

To be able to support apps written in the .NET Framework, an entirely new runtime and development environment (VSTO) was introduced, again with different versions needed for different versions of Office.

What is VBA good for?

It's clear that writing enterprise-grade, maintainable software using a container-bound platform with difficult-to-control dependencies is challenging.

VBA is great for small, often one-off, computational tasks and for organizing data extracted from other sources.

Despite its age, the integrated development environment (IDE) is a pleasure to work with, and so much has been added over the years you can do almost anything you want with VBA. It also comes with a macro recorder; you can record a series of keyboard actions, and the recorder will generate their VBA equivalent. This functionality seems to have been largely abandoned in later versions, where many actions that operate on the newer additions to the object model are not recorded.

I have mixed feelings about the macro recorder. The positive aspect is that a user can get some insight into how to manipulate the object model. On the negative side, I've seen many dreadful VBA applications based on macros that began life as a series of recorded macros. It's not a good model from which to learn.

Apps Script does not have anything like this, and the type of skills needed to create enduring applications probably cannot be learned from such a tool.

Overall, VBA offers graceful automation coupled with easy implementation. It is a hard act to follow.

What Is JavaScript?

You'll sometimes hear ECMAScript and JavaScript used interchangeably. I'm going to do the same thing, and usually just refer to JavaScript, which is the branded version of ECMAScript controlled by Mozilla. The ECMA organization controls the overall language specification used by all implementations, such as JScript by Microsoft and (of course) Apps Script by Google.

A Quick History

ECMAScript has been around in browsers since 1996. The JavaScript brand was introduced by Netscape for its Navigator browser. JavaScript's main purpose was to enable user interaction and dynamic modification of the document object model (DOM), which was previously created from HTML hosted or created on a server and served up as static content.

JavaScript allowed dynamic manipulation of the DOM from within the client browser, revolutionizing user experience possibilities. The JavaScript name became the property of Sun Microsystems through a Netscape/Sun development alliance, and when Oracle bought Sun, it acquired the JavaScript name, which it still owns today.

Versions

JavaScript continues to evolve, and it is not only a skill much in demand, but also one that many developers learn in addition to their server-side language specialty. With the rise of Node.js (and Apps Script), JavaScript is increasingly being perceived as a viable server-side language too.

Because of the differently branded ECMAScript implementations, it's hard to exactly pin down which features a particular implementation supports. The usual way is to refer to the ECMAScript version specification, the latest of which is version 6, with version 7 under development.

Because there is such a wide variety of browser versions, JavaScript developers have to use various strategies to ensure that their code will run on clients of an unknown vintage or brand. Common strategies are the use of frameworks (e.g., Modernizr and jQuery) that take care of feature detection and use an appropriate JavaScript syntax, or polyfills (code that emulates new features not available in older JavaScript versions when they're required).

In principle, JavaScript tries to always be backward-compatible—meaning that code written using old vanilla JavaScript will still execute in a modern version, and the use of polyfills will attempt to ensure that code written in new versions will run on older JS engines.

JavaScript Is Not Java

The names hint that one should be some kind of subset of the other, but they are not related. JavaScript was originally called Mocha and LiveScript, and only later named JavaScript by Netscape, at the same time that Java was being promoted by Sun Microsystems. Here are some other important distinctions:

- Java is compiled into a universal bytecode language that can (theoretically, anyway) be run on any Java Virtual Machine (JVM). The idea is that a Java binary can be transported between devices with a JVM, whereas JavaScript suffers from different browser implementation inconsistencies.
- JavaScript is interpreted from the original code at runtime. It doesn't go through a compile/build validation process, so coding errors are detected on running.
- Although Java was intended to run on both the server and the browser (as a plug-in), and JavaScript was designed for the browser, these distinctions are becoming blurred. JavaScript is the language of Node.js and Apps Script, both of which are server-based, and the use of Java plug-ins in a browser is increasingly being blocked and falling into disuse.
- Both JavaScript and Java are syntactically based on C, but the languages themselves have fundamental differences—notably, prototypal inheritance as opposed to classes, and dynamic versus explicit typing.

Learning JavaScript

There are probably more generic "get started in JavaScript" tutorials around than for any other language, and it is not my intention to add to their number. An alternative approach that focuses on differences can effectively leverage existing skills and knowledge. Understanding the language fundamentals and built-in capabilities compared to their VBA equivalents is a good way to quickly become operational in JavaScript, irrespective of your current skill levels.

Key things you'll notice about JavaScript, as a newcomer or VBA practitioner, include the following:

- JavaScript is not a typed language.
- Everything is an object, including functions.
- Variables can be "almost equal."
- Key/value pairs and JSON are part of the language.
- Everything is case-sensitive.
- The IDE doesn't help you as much as it should (compared to the VBA one).
- There are always many ways to do the same thing.
- I'm pretty sure you're going to like it—maybe not at first, but soon.

What Is Apps Script?

In the previous section, I covered the difference between ECMAScript and JavaScript. Apps Script is Google's dialect of ECMAScript that runs not in a browser, but on Google's servers. This means that it is essentially browser-independent (but more about that later when we get to running things on the client from Apps Script).

Versions

Apps Script is based on the ECMAScript version 3 specification, and is not directly equivalent to any one version of JavaScript in terms of features. As a baseline it uses JavaScript 1.6, but it also contains features that were implemented in JavaScript 1.7 and 1.8—which we will use heavily in the examples later on.

It Runs on a Server

Because Apps Script does not run in a browser, it does not have access to client-specific objects such as the DOM and Window APIs. Apps Script is server-based, but happens to use a JavaScript variant as its language. Google could have just as easily used Python, PHP, Java, or even some entirely new language, but it decided to use JavaScript (or more precisely, ECMAScript).

It seems counterintuitive that a language originally designed to enable client-side DOM manipulation and user interaction would be a good candidate for a server environment with no DOM and very limited built-in user interaction capabilities. Nevertheless, it turns out that selecting JavaScript as the Apps Script language was a wise choice, not only because it is widely known, but also because HTML service extensions (which allow client-side interaction from Apps Script and run in the browser) are standard web applications with HTML and JavaScript components.

Services

The purpose of Apps Script is to extend Google Apps. This means that it needs access to the object model for Sheets, Docs, Drive, and so on.

At the time of writing, the services in Table 1-1 are all exposed as standard Apps Script services.

Table 1-1. Standard Apps Script services

Service interface	Accesses Google service	VBA counterpart object model
CalendarApp	Calendar	Outlook
ContactsApp	Contacts	Outlook
DocumentApp	Docs	Word
DriveApp	Drive	Local files via Windows.Scripting
FormApp	Forms	Userforms via VBA in Office apps
GmailApp	Gmail	Outlook
GroupsApp	Groups	N/A
LanguageApp	Language translation	N/A
Maps	Geocoding, Directions, and static maps	N/A
SitesApp	Sites	N/A
SpreadsheetApp	Sheets	Excel

A further 18 APIs are exposed as advanced services (e.g., Analytics, BigQuery, Fusion tables, YouTube); another 14 (e.g., Cache, Properties) are available as script services.

Strangely missing from this list are Google Slides and Drawings, and although requested from time to time, scripting implementation for these doesn't seem to have much priority with the Apps Script product team.

Fully Authenticated Environment

OAuth2 APIs are used for both authentication (i.e., that the requestor is who they say they are) and authorization (i.e., that they are allowed to perform the requested operation on the targeted resource). Google's authentication implementation (like those of many others, such as Microsoft and PayPal) is built to the OpenID Connect specification, and its role is to validate identity. Once identity has been verified, confirmation is required to ensure that the validated identity has the authorization to access the resource requested. This combination of operation and resource is known as *scope*.

OAuth2 can be a fairly complex business when you're working from a browser-based client, and generally involves the use of a helper API. In the server environment of

Apps Script, authentication and scope authorization is built in and handled automatically, removing significant complexity barriers to getting started.

Quotas

Because you are running in a shared server environment, Google goes to some lengths to ensure that you don't accidentally create runaway processes, or abuse its service (which is, after all, free) by running processes for hours that really should be run on some of its other (paid) cloud offerings such as App Engine.

A process can run for a maximum of six minutes, and there are various rate and quota limits on what you can do with each service.

Rate limits

Rate limiting is where Google has set a ceiling on how rapidly you can repeat an operation. For example, if you create and publish an Apps Script web app, it will fail if you attempt to execute it more than 30 times a second—even if that is the only time you invoke it in a day.

Quota limits

Quota limiting is where a total number of operations is restricted over the duration of some time period. For example, you cannot send emails to more than 100 different recipients in the course of one day. Although there is clearly a need for such restrictions, they'll be unfamiliar to those accustomed to VBA, and it can be very frustrating and complex to build schemes (such as sleeping between service calls or using exponential backoff for queries[1]) to negotiate these obstacles.

Performance

Just like Office and VBA, Apps Script is best suited to small tasks that extend docs rather than large, resource-intensive systems. It is certainly possible to create complex and sophisticated workflows on the Apps Script platform, but that is the exception.

In addition to the quotas, performance is also controlled, so as a rule of thumb, tasks will take longer on Apps Script than in VBA.

The tradeoff is cloud-based accessibility against client-based complexity.

Various performance aids, such as the caching service, are available (and don't use up any quota), but you need to be extremely careful how you structure your app in order

---

1 Exponential backoff is a technique for progressively slowing down the rate at which an operation is attempted to improve its chances of executing successfully.

to minimize service calls and unnecessary repetition (all good things but less critical in VBA).

A discussion of how to implement these methods of efficiently using Apps Script services will be built into some of the examples in later chapters.

Asynchronicity

In Apps Script, every operation is blocking. There is no asynchronicity, even for fetch operations. This is hard to get accustomed to if you are coming from a regular JavaScript environment, where asynchronicity and event-driven behavior is ingrained. For those coming from VBA, it won't be so much of a culture shock.

Events

There are only a few handleable events in Apps Script, the most useful of which is related to enabling change detection in Sheets data. Like the lack of asynchronicity, this will be frustrating for users already proficient in JavaScript, and a big omission for those accustomed to VBA's extensive portfolio of event interactions.

Triggers

One of the killer features of Apps Script is that it enables you to schedule and run scripts without being logged on. This means you can, say, run regular reports, or summarize data every hour or at 5 a.m. These kinds of scheduled events are called *time-based triggers*.

There are strict quotas on the number of triggers you can have and how much daily runtime they consume, which lessens their usefulness and increases complexity, as the number of workarounds you need to build increases with the more triggers you have.

Web Apps

Another killer feature is the web app. You can publish a web app using the HTML service (to serve up web pages generated by your app), or Content service (to serve up data from your app).

These web apps can service both GET and POST requests by executing Apps Script functions server-side, and provide a convenient way for non–Apps Script apps to get access to docs resources, effectively turning Apps Script into a web server or REST-Query server.

Because these web apps run server-side, fetching data from servers on different domains does not hit the same cross-origin-request restrictions normally faced by client-based JavaScript, and you can even use an Apps Script web app as a proxy to fetch data you could not otherwise reach from your client application.

In VBA terms, this is a little like the difference you'll see between using the xmlHttp object (which is subject to client restrictions similar to a JavaScript app running in a browser), and the serverXmlHttp object (which is similar to an Apps Script running on a Google server).

Maintainability

Previous versions of scripts are maintained for fallback, and there is an extensive library system that you can use to share common code between apps.

You can create both standalone scripts and container-bound scripts—the latter of which reside in a particular document, from which it's clearly more complicated to share code. For this reason, I tend to stick to standalone scripts.

If you are writing custom scripts (i.e., a script accessible from within a formula in a spreadsheet cell), you can do so only from container-bound scripts—which could lead to the kind of code sprawl you see in VBA.

Similarly, templates intended to be used by the HTML service must also be local (although there are ways around this using libraries), which again can lead to code sprawl.

IDE

The development and debug environment for Apps Script is very poor. Autocomplete for services is implemented, and you can use JSDOC (comments in code are marked up to describe the purpose of and arguments to a function) to implement some limited autocomplete from libraries that you have written and reference from your script.

Inexplicably, though, IDE autocomplete is not implemented for functions in the current script, yet it is for custom functions accessed from a worksheet cell.

The debugger has a number of limitations. You can set breakpoints and see the values of variables at those points, but there is no console/immediate mode, and in any case certain kinds of JavaScript constructs cause it to fail.

HTML service apps are especially hard to debug, because they execute dynamically generated code in the browser. Some limited interactive debugging can be done with the browser's Developer Tools, but often the code (as you wrote it) is not visible.

Logging is also fairly limited, as you cannot see any results until the script is finished executing, but the execution transcript, which shows the call details to many Apps Script services, is a useful feature.

It is possible to develop using an add-in for Eclipse, but you have to upload the edited file to be able to run it, and it doesn't improve the debug capabilities.

For me, the IDE is the most disappointing feature of Apps Script, and is a big step backward when you're coming from the more integrated VBA environment.

What Is Apps Script Good For?

As with VBA, if you are writing enterprise-level scalable applications, then Apps Script is probably not the right platform. Apps Script is perfectly suited for connecting to and using other APIs, opening up great integration possibilities for building apps that take data from many places and enrich your docs experience.

The HTML service exposes Apps Script functionality, and allows for the building of much more usable (but harder to achieve) UIs than those you could create with VBA.

Apps Script is very effective for getting something running quickly, whether a production solution or a prototype of a more scalable solution. Because it is part of the Googleverse, authentication to other services is largely built in, so identity and access management are part of the fabric of the platform.

Because it is in the cloud, development across multiple devices is no longer the complexity (and license) problem that it is with VBA, and the platform is always at the most recent version. These benefits allow you to build much more collaborative workflows and manage who is running what more confidently.

Many enterprises are still concerned about the security aspect of running apps and storing their data in the cloud. In many ways, centralizing one version of a document that supports real-time collaboration, and to which access to data and scripts can be finely controlled and monitored, is an extremely secure model.

In a distributed solution using various versions of Windows and Office on files stored on PCs, laptops, and shared network drives, email is often used for collaboration outside the enterprise, leading to externally exposed documents with scripts and data at different revision levels. Having one copy of a document, and being able to control access to it from anywhere, seems a more secure paradigm—at the very least it's cleaner from a version control and document sprawl perspective.

What Are Google Add-Ons?

I've referenced the HTML service a number of times in earlier sections. This is a service that provides a templating system through which you can use HTML and JavaScript to create applications that run on the client browser but can communicate with server-side Apps Script.

With the HTML service, you can create an engaging UX that's responsive (it runs client-side) yet still has (indirect) access to the Google Apps Script services and data.

Types of Add-Ons

There are two types of add-ons:

Sidebar
> These run in a 300-pixel-wide frame on the right of the screen and are best for persistent data related to what's in the main document.

Dialog
> These run in a pop-up dialog box and can be used to collect (or display) one-time data from the user.

Add-ons are added to the applications menu system.

You can also create a "nonpublished" add-on from a container-bound script by adding entries to the applications menu system that execute a container-bound script upon selection. These can display sidebars and dialog boxes too.

The difference is that a real add-on can be published to the Chrome Web Store and is available for installation by any Apps user.

Security

When the HTML service was first introduced, Google was concerned (at least I assume so) that it created security issues by allowing client-based JavaScript and HTML.

As a result, generated code was sanitized through the use of Caja, which had very strict rules about the structure of client-side JavaScript, with the outcome that most JavaScript frameworks were simply blocked and would not run. The performance of sanitized code was also extremely poor compared to its original state.

Nowadays, though, client code is run in an iframe environment, and the restrictive and poorly performing regime has now been removed, paving the way for more responsive add-ons.

The Publishing Process

In order to maintain quality, publishing an add-on to the Chrome Web Store requires an additional step involving a Google add-on review team. This can be a fairly laborious process, with a back-and-forth conversation in which changes requested by the review team are implemented by the developer, who subsequently resubmits the add-on for further review, ad infinitum.

As an alternative, you can publish add-ons within a domain (not public), which is subject to a less vigorous review process.

While it is important to ensure quality items are being published in the store, I believe some changes are needed to streamline the process, along with some kind of publishing option to selected people who don't need this kind of review.

Many developers who are doing this as a hobby or learning experience (you can't yet monetize add-ons) lose interest partway through the current process and their add-ons never see the light of day.

The balance between policing standardization and allowing fresh, innovative approaches is a difficult one.

What Are Google Forms?

Google Forms are a simple way to collect data in a questionnaire format. A link to a form is sent to potential respondents.

Forms are designed using an interactive tool. The main features are as follows:

- Data is automatically stored in a spreadsheet.
- Data validation takes place in form fields.
- Routing can be controlled based on answers to specific questions.
- Forms can be extended through Apps Script.

For a quick solution, using Forms avoids the complexity of creating a UI with the HTML service and Apps Script and is a good compromise for short and simple data collection work, although more complex workflows can also be handled in Forms through Apps Script and add-ons.

What Are Microsoft Add-Ins?

VBA has access to an object called `ScriptControl`, which allows VBA to submit JavaScript (actually JScript) code to the Windows scripting engine for execution and return an answer.

Add-ins can also refer to Office app extensions loaded from separate template files, or from COM or VSTO libraries and managed by the Office app's add-in manager.

Office add-ins have *nothing to do with these capabilities*.

Add-ins are the Office version of Docs add-ons. Microsoft has been playing around with this concept for a few years now: the idea of bringing JavaScript to Office was originally achieved with what they called the "JavaScript API for Office" and "Apps for Office," but this capability has now been renamed to "Office Add-ins."

In principle, an add-in is very similar to an add-on. There are two kinds of add-in:

- The taskpane add-in, which is equivalent to the sidebar add-on
- The content add-in, equivalent to the dialog add-on

Comparison

Microsoft and Google between them have created a complex soup of acronyms that's hard to fathom. Here's a summary:

- Microsoft Office add-ins have been around for a long time and refer to extensions than can be loaded to a document from a separate extension file.
- Microsoft has renamed what was previously known as "Apps for Office" to "Office Add-ins." These are extensions written with the JavaScript API for Office that display in an HTML window, either to the side of the hosting document (*taskpane add-in*) or as a dialog box (*content add-in*).
- Google Apps add-ons are HTML applications that can communicate with server-based Apps Script, but that run in the client browser and present as either a sidebar (equivalent to the Office taskpane add-in) or as a dialog box (equivalent to the Office content add-in).

At first sight, Office add-ins and Apps Script add-ons look similar. They are both HTML- and JavaScript-based apps that run on the client under the control of Office and Apps Script, respectively. However, they are very different in realization.

The Microsoft JavaScript API:

- Has a fixed repertoire of methods and properties that can be used to fetch certain data from the underlying document
- Supports some level of binding (e.g., a client event is triggered if a bound cell changes value)

The Apps Script API:

- Can launch any server-side script from the client and get back a response of your own design
- Does not have any binding, but can emulate binding by periodically calling a server-side script that monitors for changes from the client.

This means that Microsoft add-in capabilities are limited to whatever is implemented in the API, whereas Apps Script can execute any customized script.

I believe we'll see some changes with the Office 365 unified API (currently in preview). This exposes Office 365 services via a REST API, in much the same way as Google APIs expose Google services.

This may lead to a much more open solution for Office services.

CHAPTER 2

Language Basics

JavaScript is the Mozilla-managed version of ECMAScript, and the language of Apps Script is based on JavaScript 1.6, but with some additions from 1.7 and 1.8. The community is looking forward to some of the newer ECMAScript features, but for now we are using a fairly old JavaScript dialect. This book uses Apps Script and JavaScript more or less interchangeably.

There will be some examples in this chapter. If you want to follow along, you'll find how to use the Apps Script integrated development environment (IDE) in the last section.

Style

Although it's not mandatory in either language, style is an important way of communicating information about the variables and functions to yourself and others who might read your code.

Hungarian

If you are a traditional VBA developer, you may be familiar with the convention known as *Hungarian notation*. With this convention, the type of the variable forms part of its name. For example:

```
VB  Dim strInput As String
    Dim intValue As Integer
    Dim varOutput As Variant
```

Nowadays, the use of Hungarian is less popular, even in VBA circles, but nevertheless you'll find it's still very much alive and well in much of the VBA code you'll come across.

I find that its focus on type rather than function distracts from the code objective, and is subject to becoming inaccurate following any refactoring. I never use it, but many others like it. In general, I'll use the JavaScript convention for naming, which will also make language comparison and migration easier.

Camel Case

The JavaScript convention, more or less universally followed, is to use *camel case*, where the first letter of each component of the variable name is capitalized, with the initial component in lowercase. For example:

```
JS   var randomNumber;
     var numberOfColumns;
```

The exception to this is when you create a namespace. For example, the Apps Script services start with a capital letter, but are otherwise camel-cased as usual.

You should follow this simple pattern for your own namespaces and custom objects. Classes, object constructors, and namespaces start with a capital letter, while functions and variables do not. For example:

```
JS   SpreadsheetApp.getRange();
     LanguageApp.translate();
     MyNamespace.init();
     var myObject = new MyObject();
```

Constants do not exist in Apps Script. Just use a variable, but by convention, capitalize the whole name, and use an underscore to separate the components. The difference in styling constants and variables is shown here:

```
JS   var NUMBER_OF_ATTEMPTS = 20;   // constant convention
     var numberOfAttempts = 20;     // variable convention
```

Case Sensitivity

One key difference between VBA and JavaScript is that JavaScript is case-sensitive. In fact, the VBA IDE will automatically fix the case of a variable name to match the previously declared case format.

Copy/Paste Porting

Working through this book, you may be surprised to see just how similar VBA and JavaScript can be in structure (and even in style). It's certainly preferable to stick to the JavaScript style when creating new code (and for me it's not a problem, as I write VBA code in the JavaScript style anyway), but changing the spelling of functions and variables if you are porting from VBA is probably a waste of time (and the case sensitivity will cause time-wasting transcription errors).

I call this kind of translation "copy/paste porting," and the objective is to minimize the code changes needed to create a viable Apps Script port for your VBA functions. Later you'll see most of the VBA built-in functions translated into JavaScript. These will retain the VBA spelling and case, so your original code can work without (much) modification or refactoring.[1]

For example, existing VBA code that looks like this:

```
VB  StrFirst = VBA.Mid(StrName , 1 , 10)
```

could be copied to JavaScript, and would look like this after porting, using the JavaScript VBA library:

```
JS  StrFirst = VBA.Mid (StrName , 1 , 10);
```

From scratch, it would probably look something like this:

```
JS  strFirst = strName.slice (0, 10);
```

Although using the VBA library still leaves that VBA legacy, using it for copy/paste porting means that:

- Indexes (which generally start at 1 in VBA but at 0 in JavaScript) can remain at 1 within the context of library functions.
- Porting changes back to VBA (you'll be running multiple platforms for a while) is easy.
- Initial ports can be done right away, with refactoring over time (maybe when you are completely done with VBA).

Types

JavaScript is not a typed language. There is no need to even define a variable before using it, although you *always should* to avoid unintended scope issues. The JavaScript var keyword introduces a variable definition in much the same way as Dim in VBA, except that you are not able to assign a type to a variable (see Table 2-1).

Table 2-1. VBA and JavaScript types

VBA	JavaScript	Note
Dim a, b	var a,b;	Will be Variants in VBA
Dim i as Long, s as String	var i,s;	Cannot define type in JavaScript

---

1 You'll notice that I've added the VBA prefix to example VBA code. This is optional for built-in functions (it's a default namespace). If you are using the VBA emulation code from a library, you will need to include it. If the emulation code is copied into your script, it is not necessary.

VBA	JavaScript	Note
`Dim t as Boolean, k` `t = True`	`var t=true,k;`	Can assign values at the same time in JavaScript

VBA is implicitly typed. If you don't define a variable, it's assumed to be a `Variant`. In VBA, it is best practice to prevent accidental reference to undefined variables by using:

`VB` `Option Explicit`

It's not exactly equivalent, but I recommend you add this directive at the top of each of your scripts, as it will enhance the detection of common errors by a future version of the IDE (the current version does not yet support this feature, which was added at ECMAScript version 5).

`JS` `'use strict';`

The Apps Script IDE gives a (very) little bit of help in detecting undeclared variables:

`JS`
```
var a;
a = 0;
b = 0;
```

You'll notice that a, which is declared, will be colored green when referenced, whereas b will be black, because it's being used without having been previously declared.

Operators

JavaScript operators and VBA operators are pretty similar, so it should not be a great challenge for the VBA developer to adapt. Sometimes you need a few steps to achieve the same thing in one language or the other, and there are a couple of quirks to be careful of. This section provides a quick reference guide of equivalences.

Mathematical Operators

The operators shown in Table 2-2 are used to perform calculations.

Table 2-2. VBA and JavaScript mathematical operators

Operator	VBA	JavaScript	Note
Addition	`a + b`	`a + b`	
Subtraction	`a - b`	`a - b`	
Multiplication	`a * b`	`a * b`	
Division	`a / b`	`a / b`	
Modulus (remainder)	`a Mod b`	`a % b`	

Operator	VBA	JavaScript	Note
Integer division	a \ b	Math.floor (a / b)	The JavaScript number type is always a real number. Math.floor() truncates anything after the decimal point.
Increment by 1	a = a + 1	a++, ++a	The position of the operators determines the order in which the increment is done; this is useful when incrementing is part of a larger operation.
Decrement by 1	a = a - 1	a--, --a	As with the increment example, the position of the decrement operator determines whether it is executed before or after the expression fragment of which it is part.
Power	a ^ b	Math.pow (a , b)	Raises a to the power of b.

Assignment Operators

The operators shown in Table 2-3 are used to assign values to a variable. For example:

```js
var theAnswerToLife = 42 ;
```

JavaScript has special shortcuts to modify the existing value of a variable. For example:

```js
var counter = 1 ;
counter++ ;          // value 2
counter += 10;       // value 12
counter -= 2;        // value 10
counter *= 5;        // value 50
counter /= 2;        // value 25
counter %= 20;       // value 5
```

Table 2-3. VBA and JavaScript assignment operators

Operator	VBA	JavaScript	Note
Let	a = b	a = b	
Add to	a = a + b	a += b	a += b and a = a+ b are equivalent in JavaScript.
Subtract from	a = a - b	a -= b	a -= b and a = a - b are equivalent.
Multiply by	a = a * b	a *= b	a *= b and a = a * b are equivalent.
Divide by	a = a / b	a /= b	a /= b and a = a / b are equivalent.
Modulus of	a = a Mod b	a %= b	a %= b and a = a % b are equivalent.

String Operators

In JavaScript, string operators are the same as regular assignment operators:

```js
theMeaningOfLife = "try to be nice to people";
```

Table 2-4 compares the string operators in VBA and JavaScript.

Table 2-4. VBA and JavaScript string operators

Operator	VBA	JavaScript	Note
Concatenate	`a & b`	`a + b`	VBA also allows + but it's not recommended.
Append to	`a = a & b`	`a += b`	`a += b` and `a = a + b` are equivalent in JavaScript.
Quotes	`"a quoted string"`	`"a quoted string"` `'another string'`	Either single or double quotes can be used.

Comparison Operators

Comparison operators, which are described in Table 2-5, are used to compare values. For example:

```
var homePlanet;
if ( name === 'Chewbacca') {
    homePlanet = 'Kashyyyk';
}
else {
    homePlanet = 'Alderaan';
}
```

JavaScript has a useful shortcut for the `if {} else {}` pattern:

```
homePlanet = name === 'Chewbacca' ? 'Kashyyyk' : 'Alderaan';
```

This compares to the VBA `Iif` function (sometimes known as a *ternary expression*), which is commonly used directly in the Access UI, but is also available in VBA for all Office applications. However, it should be used with caution.

```
homePlanet = Iif (name = 'Chewbacca', "Kashyyyk" , "Alderaan" )
```

The use of `Iif` can have unintended side effects and differs subtly from both the VBA `If/Then/Else` and the JavaScript `?:` patterns. Because it is a function, it will evaluate both the true and false options, even though the result of only one of them will be assigned.

Using `Iif` in this example, both `getPlanet` functions will always be executed, which is likely not the developer's intention.

```
homePlanet = Iif (name = 'Chewbacca', getPlanet("K") , getPlanet("A" ) )
```

Table 2-5. VBA and JavaScript comparison operators

Operator	VBA	JavaScript	Note
Equals	`a = b`	`a == b`[a]	In this example, JavaScript will do a type conversion. So, for example, `'1' == 1` will be true.
Equals (value and type)	`a = b And TypeName(a) = TypeName(b)`	`a === b`	For example, `'1' === 1` will be false.
Not equal to	`a <> b`	`a != b`	Equivalent to `!(a==b)`.
Not equal to (value and type)	`a <> b OR TypeName(a) <> TypeName(b)`	`a !== b`	Equivalent to `!(a===b)`.
Greater than	`a > b`	`a > b`	
Less than	`a < b`	`a < b`	
Greater than or equal to	`a >= b`	`a >= b`	
Less than or equal to	`a <= b`	`a <= b`	

Conditional	`If (a > b) Then`
	`  c = 'something'`
	`Else`
	`  c = 'something else'`
	`Endif`
	
	`or (use with caution)`
	
	`c = Iif( a > b ,`
	`"something",`
	`"something else")`
		`c = a > b ?`
		`'some`
		`thing' :`
		`'something`
		`else';`
			`if (a>b) {`
			`  c= 'something';`
			`} else {`
			`  c='something else';`
			`}`

[a] A common mistake when you're coming from VBA is to test equality like this: `if (a=b) {...}`. In this case, a will be assigned the value of b, and the result (the original value of b) will be tested for truthiness (not any of `0`, `' '`, `null`, `undefined`, or `false`).

Logical Operators

Logical operators, shown in Table 2-6, are used to construct logical tests on Boolean values.

In VBA, the order of evaluation of expressions is not necessarily the order in which they are written. This means that you may need multiple `If-Then` blocks if the order is important.

The following example would throw an exception if `spaceShip` is undefined:

VB
```
If (Not spaceShip Is Nothing AND spaceShip.isFueled) Then
    takeOff()
    End if
```

And would be better written like this:

```vb
If (Not spaceShip Is Nothing) Then
    If (spaceShip.isFueled) Then
        takeOff()
    End if
End If
```

JavaScript includes the concepts of *truthy* and *falsey*. Values considered to be false are null, 0, false, '', and undefined. Anything else is considered to be true.

Because JavaScript tests conditions in the order specified, you can check that an object is defined and that a property has a particular value in one test as follows:

```js
if(spaceShip && spaceShip.isFueled) {
    takeOff();
}
```

This characteristic can also be used in JavaScript to assign default values:

```js
var homePlanet = planetName || 'Alderaan';
```

Table 2-6. VBA and JavaScript logical operators

Operator	VBA	JavaScript	Note
And	a And b	a && b	
Or	a Or b	a || b	
Not	Not a	!a	
Xor	a Xor b	!a != !b[a]	JavaScript does not have a logical XOR operator.

[a] JavaScript does not have a logical XOR operator, so this equivalence is leveraging truthy and falsey characteristics to emulate one. See if you can figure out how it works.

Bitwise Operators

Note in Table 2-7 that the VBA bitwise operators are the same as the logical ones, but the variables are numeric rather than Boolean.

Table 2-7. VBA and JavaScript bitwise operators

Operator	VBA	JavaScript
And	a And b	a & b
Or	a Or b	a | b
Not	Not a	~ a
Xor	a Xor b	a ^ b

Variables

It's always a good idea to declare all the variables you'll use in a procedure, rather than relying on the fact that neither JavaScript nor VBA insists on it. Experienced VBA developers will already be using `Option Explicit` to avoid unintended variable use.

If you use an undeclared variable in JavaScript, the effect can be worse than in VBA, because the scope or visibility of that variable becomes global (meaning that every function in every script file can see it and potentially change it).

We'll look into that a little more in "Scope" on page 34, but for now always declare the variables inside the function in which you plan to use them. There is a place for global variables (although their use should be minimized), but that place does not include creating them accidentally.

Variable Types

JavaScript is not strongly typed. A variable is dynamically assigned the type of whatever is assigned to it, a little like the `Variant` type in VBA.

The list of JavaScript types is short: `number`, `string`, `null`, `undefined`, `boolean`, and `object`.

Table 2-8 outlines the variable types for VBA and JavaScript.

Table 2-8. VBA and JavaScript variable types

Type	VBA	JavaScript	Note
Integer	`Dim a As Integer` `a = 1`	`var a = 1;`	JavaScript does not have an Integer type. All numbers are held as type number.[a]
Long	`Dim a As Long` `a = 1`	`var a = 1;`	All numbers are held as type number.
Double	`Dim a as Double` `a = 1`	`var a = 1;`	All numbers are held as type number.
Single	`Dim a As Single` `a = 1`	`var a = 1;`	All numbers are held as type number.
Currency[b]	`Dim a As Currency` `a = 1`	`var a = 1;`	All numbers are held as type number.
Byte[c]	`Dim a As Byte` `a = 1`	`var a = 1;`	All numbers are held as type number.

Type	VBA	JavaScript	Note
Date[d]	`Dim a As Date`	`var a = new Date();`	Dates are held as an instance of a `Date` object in JavaScript. There is no date primitive type.
Object	`Dim a As Object` `Set a = anObject`	`var a = anObject`	
Variant	`Dim a` `Dim b As variant`	`var a;` `var b;`	
Boolean	`Dim a As Boolean` `a = TRUE`	`var a = true;`	
String	`Dim a As String` `a = "a string"`	`var a = "a string";` `var a = 'a string';`	Both double and single quotes are acceptable in JavaScript.

[a] JavaScript represents all numbers as 64-bit, double-precision, floating-point: 1 bit is used for the sign, 52 bits for the fraction, and 11 bits for the exponent.

[b] The VBA `Currency` type is a 64-bit whole number, scaled by 10,000, giving an implied four digits after a decimal point. This concept does not exist in JavaScript.

[c] The VBA byte type is an 8-bit unsigned number. Bytes are often used in JavaScript in encryption and Blob processing, but the byte does not exist as a JavaScript primitive type.

[d] VBA represents dates as the floating-point number of days and fractions of days since 1900. The JavaScript `Date` object records the number of milliseconds since 1970, which can be accessed via the `getTime()` method of the `Date` object.

Functions

JavaScript is a prototype-based language, which means that functions play a different kind of role than do procedures (functions and subroutines) in VBA. JavaScript achieves inheritance by cloning properties and behavior through the prototype of other objects. In JavaScript, an instance of an object created with the new keyword and its constructor function can be considered akin to an instance of a class in VBA.

Properties within an instance of a function can themselves be functions, which in turn can be considered the methods of the object instance. We'll look into that a little more in "Classes" on page 37.

As you can see in Table 2-9, there are no subroutines in JavaScript, only functions. Return values from functions and arguments to functions cannot be explicitly typed. This is the same principle by which variables are dynamically assigned types.

Table 2-9. VBA and JavaScript functions and subroutines

Type	VBA	JavaScript

Subroutine	`Sub foo (bar As Integer)`
	`End Sub`
		`function foo(bar) {`
		
		`}`

Function	`Function foo (bar As Integer) As String`
	`    foo = "answer " & bar`
	`End Function`
		`function foo(bar) {`
		`  return 'answer ' + bar;`
		`}`

Use it	`Dim a As String` `a = foo(20)`	`var a = foo (20);`

Assigning Functions to Variables

In JavaScript, a function can be assigned to a variable as follows:

```
JS   var func = function (bar) {
         return 'answer ' + bar;
     };
```

then we can call it:

```
JS   func(20);
```

or pass it to another function:

```
JS   function boo (passedFunction) {
         return passedFunction (20);
     }
```

Anonymous Functions

The ability to pass functions to other functions is a key construct of JavaScript and allows for the abstraction and efficient reuse of code. Anonymous functions are functions that don't have a name or identifier (sometimes called *lambda functions*).

Here's the preceding example, but now defined as an anonymous function:

```
JS   function boo (passedFunction) {
         return passedFunction(20);
     }

     var result = boo ( function (bar) { return 'answer ' + bar; });
```

Functional Programming

In the past, the topic of functional programming was considered more suitable for theoretical discussion than practical application. Nowadays, though, there are even languages (e.g., Haskell, Clojure, and Scala) that are specifically designed to support this approach, and major companies (e.g., Twitter and Facebook) using them. This is not the place to go into the theory and fundamentals of functional programming, but I mention it to introduce some of the good practices that this paradigm encourages.

I'll be covering loops and iterations in the next section, and my advice will be that you avoid the traditional looping mechanisms, which can cause side effects, and instead stick to those that have these functional programming properties:

Statelessness
> The function should be able to stand on its own and be reusable, not relying on outside influence besides the data that is passed to it. Similarly, the effect of a function should be limited to the data it returns.

Immutability
> Data should not be modified by an iteration process. For example, the `map` method creates new data by transforming existing data, and the `reduce` method creates a single result from a list of data. In each case, the original data remains unchanged.

Applying these principles will help create cleaner code that is faster to develop and easier to debug.

Loops and Iteration

Iteration is a key concept in all languages, and JavaScript has a number of looping strategies, the most common of which is the (rather clumsy) `for` pattern: `for (;;) {}`.

JavaScript has a rich collection of array iteration methods (with no VBA equivalent) that take a function as their argument.[2] The function is called for each element of the array with three arguments, as in this example:

```js
var newArray = myArray.map(function (item, index, originalArray) {
    return something;
});
```

The `reduce` method has this pattern:

```js
var reduction = myArray.reduce(function (previous, current) {
    return aModifiedPrevious;
},initialValue);
```

This is cleaner than `for () {...}`, notably because the iterator is not visible outside the loop and therefore avoids unexpected side effects.

---

2 These follow the functional programming principles of statelessness and immutability.

The examples in this book use this form of looping almost exclusively, as they are much better at signaling loop intent than counter-based looping, and they support the functional programming paradigm mentioned earlier. Next, I'll offer a brief tutorial on the most common forms of array iteration methods.

Each example will use an array defined like this:

```js
var theArray = [1,2,3];
```

forEach

The forEach array method can be used for simple iteration through an array. It does not strictly follow the statelessness rule, as there is probably going to be a side effect because it doesn't return anything.

Get the sum of each of the elements in the array (but see the reduce method):

```js
var theSum = 0;
theArray.forEach(function(d) {
    theSum += d;
});
```

reduce

A better way of transforming an array into a single result is to use the reduce method, which carries forward the result of the previous iteration and returns the final result.

Get the sum of each of the elements in the array (0 is passed the initial value):

```js
var theSum = theArray.reduce(function(previous, current) {
    return previous + current;
},0);
```

filter

The filter method returns a new array, containing only the elements that provoked a truthy return from the iteration processing function.

This returns a new array containing the odd numbers from the source array:

```js
var oddNumbers = theArray.filter(function(d) {
    return d % 2;
});
```

map

The map method returns a new array, containing transformed elements from the original array.

This returns a new array containing the squared numbers from the source array:

```js
var squaredNumbers = theArray.map(function(d) {
    return d * d ;
});
```

some

The some method returns a Boolean value indicating whether at least one of the array elements caused the iteration function to return a truthy value.

This code indicates whether the array contains any values greater than 2:

```js
var anyBiggerThan2 = theArray.some(function(d) {
    return d > 2 ;
});
```

every

The every method returns a Boolean value indicating whether every one of the array elements caused the iteration function to return a truthy value.

This code indicates whether the array contains only numbers:

```js
var onlyNumbers = theArray.every(function(d) {
    return typeof d === 'number' ;
});
```

In later versions of JavaScript, there is a whole new set of array iteration methods, but only the ones mentioned in Table 2-10 are supported by Apps Script at the time of writing.

Table 2-10. VBA and JavaScript iteration equivalence

Loop	VBA	JavaScript	Note

for	`For i = 0 To 9`
	`Next i`
		`for(var i=0;i<10;i++) {`
		
		`}`
			In each case, the value of i is visible after the loop.

for in[a]	Not available; if the object is a Dictionary object, can be achieved as follows:
	`For Each key In ob.Keys`
	`Next key`
		`for (key in ob) {`
		`}`
			Returns each key in object ob. Can also be used to iterate arrays (if ob were an array) but order is not guaranteed.

for each[b]	`For Each item In items`
	`Next item`
		`items.forEach(`
		`    function(item,idx,a) {`
		`    }`
		`);`
			In JS, items must be an array. In VBA, it is an array or iterable collection.

Loop	VBA	JavaScript	Note

map	Not available	```var result = items.map (```
		``` function(item,idx,a) {```
		``` return 100*item;```
		``` }```
		```);```
			Creates a new array filled with values returned from function (the example multiplies every array item by 100).

reduce	Not available	```var result = items.reduce (```
		``` function(prev,curr) {```
		``` return prev + curr;```
		``` } , 0```
		```);```
			Returns a single value created from processing each element of an array (the example adds all elements of an array).

filter	Not available	```var result = items.filter (```
		``` function(item,idx,a) {```
		``` return idx % 2;```
		``` }```
		```);```
			Creates a new array of only the items whose anonymous function has returned true (the example returns all items with odd-numbered index).

some	Not available	```var result= items.some (```
		``` function(item,idx,a) {```
		``` return item > 10 ;```
		``` }```
		```);```
			Returns true if any array items return a truthy value (this example will be true if any items of the array are greater than 10).

every	Not available	```var result=items.every (```
		``` function(item,idx,a) {```
		``` return item;```
		``` }```
		```);```
			Returns true if all array items return a truthy value (this example will be true if all items of the array are truthy).

Do While	```x = 10```
	```Do While (x > 0)```
	``` x = x - 1```
	```Loop```
		```var x =10;```
		```while (x > 0) {```
		``` x--;```
		```}```
			In VBA, you can also use While() .. Wend.

Loop	VBA	JavaScript	Note

Do Until	`x = 10`
	`Do Until (x = 0)`
	`  x = x - 1`
	`Loop`
		`var x =10;`
		`while (x != 0) {`
		`  x--;`
		`}`
			Emulated equivalent in JavaScript.

Do While (at least once)	`x = 10`
	`Do`
	`  x = x - 1`
	`Loop While (x > 0)`
		`var x =10;`
		`do {`
		`  x--;`
		`} while (x > 0);`	

Do Until (at least once)	`x = 10`
	`Do`
	`  x = x - 1`
	`Loop Until (x = 0)`
		`var x =10;`
		`do {`
		`  x--;`
		`} while (x != 0);`
			Emulated equivalent in JavaScript.

Object.keys()	Not available; if the object is a Dictionary object, can be achieved as follows:
	`For Each d In ob.Keys`
	`Next d`
		`Object.keys(ob)`
		`.forEach(function(d){`
		`});`
			`Object.keys` can be used to return an array of the keys in an object. Used with `forEach`, this is similar to `for (d in ob) {}`.[a]

[a] `for in {..}` is best avoided, as it will return inherited as well as its own properties. It performs unpredictably in array iteration when dealing with non-explicitly assigned elements. I always use `Object.keys()` for objects and the array loops for arrays instead.

[b] In each of these JavaScript array iteration methods, the input must be an array and the iterators are not visible after the loop (because they are local arguments to the anonymous function called for each element of the array).

Layout

JavaScript and VBA have different rules concerning general layout.

Whitespace and Newlines

While whitespace (spaces and tabs) is not generally significant in VBA, newlines are.

If VBA code is to extend onto a new line, a continuation mark (underscore) is needed to indicate that the line is continued:

```
result = aLongFunctionName("with many arguments", "might mean that", _
        "a continuation mark is needed in VBA")
```

This is also one of the occasions that whitespace is significant. The underscore must have a space before it and must be the last item on the line of code being continued to avoid a syntax error.

JavaScript (usually) treats newlines just like whitespace, so the line can be broken without the need for any continuation sign:

```js
var result = aLongFunctionName("with many arguments", "doesn't mean a thing",
            "to JavaScript");
```

Quoted strings should not be broken. To extend, split the string and concatenate.:

```js
var result = aLongFunctionName("with many arguments", "doesn't mean a " +
            "thing", "to JavaScript");
```

Semicolons

I recommend that you get into the habit of properly punctuating a line of JavaScript with a trailing semicolon. There's a lot of debate about whether one is needed or not. Take a look at the arguments on the Internet for and against and decide, but if you are starting up, just put them in. It will help you understand the language. At first, determining where and where not to put a semicolon can be confusing, but there is really only one rule (of course with a couple of exceptions).

A statement like an assignment or a function execution needs a semicolon:

```js
var a = 1;
return 100;
executeSomeThing();
var myFunction = function () {
  return 'xyz';
};
```

Definitions using curly braces do not:

```js
if (a>b) {
  // do something
}
function abc () {
  return 500;
}
```

Newlines are (usually) treated as whitespace, so the semicolon helps to identify the end of an assignment, and because they have become somewhat optional, some common errors occur. In this example, the developer has assumed that it's OK to put the return value on a newline:

```js
return   // ←- do not do this
    100;
```

This will return undefined, as there will be a semicolon implied after the (potentially complete) return statement, and the 100 will be left dangling (100; is a perfectly legal JavaScript statement on its own, as is return).

Instead, this should be written as:

JS `return 100;`

Another oddity is the `for` loop. Here the `i++` statement should, strictly speaking, have a semicolon, but it will throw an error if one is present.

JS `for (i=0; i < max; i++) { // do something // }`

Curly Braces

Blocks of code are enclosed within curly braces, {}, in JavaScript (see Table 2-11) and within some grammar blocks in VBA. It is possible in both VBA and JavaScript to omit these structures, but I strongly recommend that you never do it, as it can lead to mistakes in the future if the code block needs extending.

Table 2-11. The use of curly braces in JavaScript

VBA	JavaScript	Note

`If (a < b) Then`
`  ' do something`
`Else`
`  ' do something else`
`Endif`
	`if (a < b) {`
	`    // do something`
	`} else {`
	`    // do something else`
	`}`	

`If (a < b) Then doIt()`	`If (a < b) doIt();`	It's best to avoid doing this at all times.

Scope

The *scope* of a variable refers to its visibility and accessibility across components of a project. There are some significant differences between VBA and JavaScript, as outlined in Table 2-12.

Table 2-12. Scope in VBA and JavaScript

Scope	VBA	Apps Script

Global: Variables are visible to all modules and functions in a project.	`'declared before any code`
	`Public bar As String`
		`// declared outside any function`
		`var bar;`
		
		`// accidentally global`
		`function foo() {`
		`  bar = "something"; //`[a]
		`}`

Module: Variables can be seen inside the current module only.	`'declared before any code` `Dim bar As String`	There are no "modules," so the concept of "module-level" variables does not apply.[b]

Scope	VBA	Apps Script

Function: Variables can be seen only inside the current function.	`Function foo ()`
	`  Dim bar As String`
	`End Function`
		`function foo() {`
		`  var bar;`
		`}`

Loops: Variables are visible when a loop has completed.	`For i = 1 To 10`
	`Next i`
	
	`' i is 11`
		`for (var i=1; i <= 10 ; i++) {}`
		
		`// i is 11`

Lexical scoping: Variables at a higher scope are visible inside functions declarations.	No such concept in VBA.	`function foo() {`
		`  var bar = 'bar';`
		`  boo();`
		`  function boo () {`
		`    Logger.log(bar); //`
		`  }`
		`}`

[a] Assigning a value to an undeclared variable without using the `var` keyword makes that variable global.

[b] We'll deal with how to emulate module-level variables in the section "Namespaces" on page 48.

It's important to understand the differences in scope when converting from VBA to Apps Script in order to be able to track down unintended results.

Objects

Unlike in VBA, objects can be created "on the fly" in JavaScript. Complex data structures can be created (and modified) by functions, or even imported from external text representations.

This capability is both a strength and a weakness:

- It's tempting to modify object structures in an uncontrolled way—for example, to return rich data from a function.
- Objects are not immutable, meaning that side effects develop as objects are modified by functions.
- Being able to import objects in JSON (JavaScript Object Notation) format has led to the explosion of REST APIs that we now all enjoy, and JSON is now the standard interchange format for many other languages.

JavaScript Object Notation

JSON can be compared to XML to a certain extent—it's a (much simpler) way of textually representing and exchanging objects between cooperating processes. A key difference is that XML is used by a minority of VBA developers, whereas JSON is used by the vast majority of JavaScript developers. It's part of the language.

Although VBA does not support JSON directly, you can access and create JSON-formatted data from VBA by:

- Using ScriptControl, which allows you to run JScript (Microsoft's JavaScript) using the Windows script engine under the control of VBA.
- Using a custom JSON parser (converts from text to object) and stringifier (from object to text).

In both these cases, however, VBA is not suited to handling the complex data structures that arise. If you use the cJobject JSON library for VBA, you'll see it comes with a comprehensive capability to handle JavaScript-like objects in VBA. Without this kind of functionality, dealing with anything but the simplest JSON in VBA is not very practical. To learn how to get the cJobject library, see "Namespaces" on page 48.

JSON Examples

An object in JavaScript can be created like this:

```
var anObject = {};
```

It doesn't have any properties yet, but we can add them as follows:

```
anObject.owner ="bruce";
anObject.name = "bike";
anObject.type = "transport";
anObject.value = 150;
```

Better still, we can do the whole thing at once:

```
var anObject = {
    owner: "bruce",
    name: "bike",
    type: "transport",
    value:150
};
```

This is not quite JSON yet, but by writing it with double quotes around the property names, we almost have something that can be passed to another process as a piece of text:

```
var anObject = {
    "owner": "bruce",
    "name": "bike",
    "type": "transport",
    "value":150
};
```

```
JS  var jsonString =
        '{"owner": "bruce","name": "bike","type": "transport","value":150}';
```

Normally you'd create JSON strings from an object, rather than encoding them directly as a string. JavaScript provides a function to do that:

```
JS  var jsonString = JSON.stringify (anObject);
```

And the receiver of the string would use the inverse of that function to convert it back into an object:

```
JS  var anObject = JSON.parse (jsonString);
```

Classes

There will be some coding examples in this section. If you don't already know how to use the Apps Script IDE, you may want to flip to "The IDE" on page 51 to see how to get started with it and come back here later.

Because JavaScript is a prototype-based language, there is no such thing as a class. Classes are an important element in properly constructed VBA projects, so let's look at some patterns for creating pseudoclasses (by defining functions) in JavaScript.[3]

Prototypes and Constructors

An *object constructor* is the function that initializes the newly-created object. Here's a constructor for an object that describes common properties of a mammal. The special variable this is a little like Me in VBA and refers to the current target function:

```
JS  var Mammal = function (name) {
        this.vertebrate = true;
        this.milk = true;
        this.blood = 'warm';
        this.legs = 4;
        this.name = name;
    };
```

You can create an instance (a copy) of this object using the new keyword:

```
JS  var camel = new Mammal ('camel');
```

which will give this when stringified:

```
{"vertebrate":true,"milk":true,"blood":"warm","legs":4,"name":"camel"}
```

---

3 In JavaScript, a function is the same as a class.

Inheritance

Creating a new instance of Mammal caused its properties to be inherited in the new object, but it's also possible to create a constructor for a new object from another. The constructor for this new object inherits the properties of Mammal, but changes the legs property to 0.

Using the .call pattern will change the meaning of this in the Mammal constructor to set the properties of SeaMammal rather than the properties of Mammal:

```js
var SeaMammal = function (name) {
    Mammal.call (this, name);
    this.legs = 0;
};
```

Now we need to create a new prototype for this object based on the Mammal prototype and set the constructor to the SeaMammal one just created. The reason that Mammal did not need this step when initially defined is that it inherited the Object prototype by default. SeaMammal needs to inherit everything already defined for Mammal:

```js
SeaMammal.prototype = Object.create(Mammal.prototype);
SeaMammal.prototype.constructor = SeaMammal;
```

And that's it—we can create SeaMammal instances just as if it had been built from scratch:

```js
var whale = new SeaMammal ('whale');
```

When stringified:

```js
Logger.log(JSON.stringify(whale));
```

it gives this:

```
{"vertebrate":true,"milk":true,"blood":"warm","legs":0,"name":"whale"}
```

Methods

There are multiple approaches to add methods (functions assigned to properties) to an object. One of them is to add each method to its prototype, like so:

```js
Mammal.prototype.move = function(fast) {
    return fast ? 'run' : 'walk';
});
```

There is plenty of debate for and against each technique, but I prefer this pattern:

```js
var Mammal = function (name) {
    this.vertebrate = true;
    this.milk = true;
    this.blood = 'warm';
    this.legs = 4;
    this.name = name;
```

```
    this.move = function (fast) {
      return fast ? 'run' : 'walk';
    };
  };
```

which would be used like this:

```
var camel = new Mammal('camel');
Logger.log(camel.move(true));
```

giving this result:

```
run
```

A Note on this

this can change meaning depending on context. I never use this to refer to a target
function (although I may be in the minority) in order to avoid the unnecessary confusion that arises when you use anonymous functions as arguments to another function. In those circumstances, this refers to the passed function, and it's easy to make
unintended references. It's a fairly advanced topic, and one that can confuse even
experienced JavaScript developers. Here's where this can catch you out.

At first glance, these three pieces of code should produce the same result, but the
useThis function returns undefined, whereas the other two return 'Joe'. The reason
is that this in the anonymous function passed to playAround refers not to the Person
function, but to the function itself:

```
function myFunction() {
    var person = new Person();
    Logger.log(person.name);
    Logger.log(person.funcName());
    Logger.log(person.useThis());
}

var Person = function() {

  this.name ='Joe';

  this.funcName = function () {
    return this.name;
  };

  this.useThis = function () {
    return playAround (function () {
      return this.name;     // < -- here, this refers to the passed function
    });
  };

  function playAround (func) {
```

```
        return func();
    }

  };
```

Fixing this to another variable (self) at the beginning of the function helps to avoid this problem later on. This version correctly returns 'Joe':

```
function myFunction() {
    var person = new Person();
    Logger.log(person.useSelf());
}

var Person = function() {

    var self = this;        // <--  fixed the value of self
    this.name ='Joe';

    this.useSelf = function () {
      return playAround (function () {
        return self.name;    // <-- replaced this with self
      });
    };

    function playAround (func) {
      return func();
    }

  };
```

Using self (sometimes people use that) throughout simply avoids the chance of making this kind of unintended mistake.

Rewriting the Mammal constructor as follows, using the convention of self to refer to the target function, removes that confusion because self always refers to the function being defined, irrespective of changes in the reference target of this:

```
var Mammal = function (name) {
    var self = this;

    self.vertebrate = true;
    self.milk = true;
    self.blood = 'warm';
    self.legs = 4;
    self.name = name;

    self.move = function (fast) {
      return fast ? 'run' : 'walk';
    };
  };
```

Getters and Setters

Getters and setters are functions that get or set properties of your object that you don't want to globally expose. In Apps Script services, properties are rarely exposed directly but rather are provided so we can set them. This prevents the accidental compromise of values. In newer versions of ECMAScript, there are specific patterns for getters and setters, but in Apps Script we have traditionally written them as regular methods. Nowadays, Apps Script supports the `Object.defineProperty` style of property definition that was intially specified in ECMAScript v5.1.

In Apps Script services, these functions are normally named `getPropertyName` and `setPropertyName`. By convention (it's my convention and loosely follows the rule in Apps Script that allows hiding of server-side functions from client-side callers), variables considered to be private properties within an object have a trailing underscore. It's not a convention that you need to follow, but I like it.

Here's the `Mammal` function using `self`, and exposing the `legs_` property:

```js
var Mammal = function (name) {
    var self = this;

    var vertebrate_ = true,
      milk_ = true,
      blood_ = 'warm',
      legs_ = 4,
      name_ = name;

    self.getLegs = function () {
      return legs_;
    };

    self.setLegs = function (legs) {
      legs_ = legs;
    };


    self.moveFast = function (fast) {
      return fast ? 'run' : 'walk';
    };
  };
```

And its `SeaMammal` clone:

```js
var SeaMammal = function (name) {
    var self = this;

    Mammal.call (self, name);
    self.setLegs (0);

    self.moveFast = function (fast) {
      return fast ? 'race' : 'swim';
```

```
    };
  };
```

Test the whole thing like this:

```JS
var camel = new Mammal('camel');
Logger.log(camel.moveFast(true));

var whale = new SeaMammal ('whale');
Logger.log(whale.moveFast(false));
```

with these results:

```
run
swim
```

VBA Example

Typically a VBA class will have a constructor, some private variables, some getters and setters, and various methods. Classes in VBA are not much like the prototype approach in JavaScript, so the previous section cannot be exactly mimicked, but here is the final version in VBA for comparison.

It's likely that legs would be defined as a property in VBA, but for easier comparison with the JavaScript version, this code uses getter and setter functions.

The Mammal class

Here is how such a class might look in VBA:

```VB
Option Explicit

Private vertebrate_ As Boolean
Private milk_ As Boolean
Private blood_ As String
Private legs_ As Long
Private name_ As String

Public Function getLegs() As Long
    getLegs= legs_
End Function

Public Function setLegs(legs As Long)
    legs_ = legs
End Function

Public Sub construct(name)
    name_ = name
End Sub

Public Function moveFast(fast As Boolean) As String
    If (fast) Then
```

```
        moveFast = "run"
    Else
        moveFast = "walk"
    End If
End Function

Private Sub Class_Initialize()
    vertebrate_ = True
    milk_ = True
    blood_ = "warm"
    legs_ = 4
End Sub
```

The preceding code would be used like so:

VB
```
Dim camel As Mammal

' can't pass an argument to constructor in VBA
Set camel = New Mammal
camel.construct ("camel")

Debug.Print camel.moveFast(True)
```

The SeaMammal class

Because this kind of inheritance is not possible in VBA, we would have to either build an entirely new class from scratch, or make Mammal a subclass of SeaMammal. Let's take the second option:

VB
```
Option Explicit
Private mammal_ As Mammal

Public Function Get getLegs() As Long
    getLegs = mammal_.getLegs
End Function

Public Function setLegs(legs As Long)
    mammal_.setLegs = legs
End Function

Public Sub construct(name)
    mammal_.construct name
End Sub

Public Function moveFast (fast As Boolean) As String
    If (fast) Then
        moveFast = "race"
    Else
        moveFast = "swim"
    End If
End Function

Private Sub Class_Initialize()
```

```
        Set mammal_ = New Mammal
        mammal_.setLegs = 0
    End Sub
```

Here's the whole test for both:

VB
```
Option Explicit
    Sub tester()
        Dim camel As Mammal, whale As SeaMammal

        ' can't pass an argument to constructor in VBA
        Set camel = New Mammal
        camel.construct ("camel")

        Debug.Print camel.moveFast(True)

        Set whale = New SeaMammal
        whale.construct ("whale")

        Debug.Print whale.moveFast(False)


    End Sub
```

And the result:

VB
```
run
swim
```

Using Object.create

ECMAScript 5 introduced a new way of working with objects and the prototype chain. As you can see from some of the previous examples in this chapter, there are many ways of constructing an object and dealing with inheritance that have developed over time. Object.create and Object.defineProperties were intended to provide a more consistent and understandable approach. These have also been introduced into Apps Script, although most developers have not quite embraced them yet. I would recommend you get to grips with this approach and design your objects using these new methods, although you will still need to know about the older methods as the majority of code will have been written in that style.

An object can be created by specifying a prototype on which to base it, and properties can optionally be defined using the options available to Object.defineProperties, such as the specification of enumerability, writability, and the creation of getters and setters.

An object is created like this:

JS
```
var ob = Object.create (thePrototype , {specific properties});
```

If thePrototype argument is null, the Object prototype will be used.

Redoing a cut-down version of some of the previous examples will demonstrate how clean and powerful this new approach is. First, here's how to create an object that has a couple of properties defined that are common to all mammals, as well as a getter and a function which will be explained later:

```js
var Mammal = Object.create (null, {

    warmBlooded:{
      value:true,
      enumerable:true
    },

    vertebrate:{
      value:true,
      enumerable:true
    },

    introduction:{
      get:function () {
        return 'Im a kind of ' + this.kind +
          ' called a ' + this.name + ' and I eat ' + this.eats +
          '. I' + (this.livesOnLand ? '' : " don't" ) +
          ' live on land and I have ' + this.legs + ' limbs.';
      }
    },

    build: {
      value: function (name, eats) {
        this.name = name;
        this.eats = eats;
        return this;
      }
    }

});
```

Stringifying this object gives this:

```js
Logger.log (JSON.stringify(Mammal));
//{"warmBlooded":true,"vertebrate":true}
```

Now I can use this `Mammal` prototype on which to base a more specific type of mammal—a land mammal:

```js
var LandMammal = Object.create (Mammal, {
    livesOnLand:{
      value: true,
      enumerable:true
    },
    legs:{
      value:4,
      enumerable:true
    },
```

```
      kind:{
        value:'land mammal',
        enumerable:true
      }
    });
```

Stringifying this object (note that the inherited properties are not visible) gives:

```
JS   Logger.log (JSON.stringify(LandMammal));
     //{"livesOnLand":true,"legs":4,"kind":"land mammal"}
```

Next, another mammal with properties specific to a sea mammal:

```
JS   var SeaMammal = Object.create (Mammal, {
       livesOnLand:{
         value: false,
         enumerable:true
       },
       legs:{
         value:0,
         enumerable:true
       },
       kind:{
         value:'sea mammal',
         enumerable:true
       }
     });
```

Stringifying this object gives:

```
JS   Logger.log (JSON.stringify(SeaMammal));
     //{"livesOnLand":false,"legs":0,"kind":"sea mammal"}
```

Creating object instances

Animal specific objects can now be created with the two prototype chains (SeaMammal → Mammal → Object) and (LandMammal → Mammal → Object):

```
JS   var dog = Object.create(LandMammal).build ('dog','meat');
     var rat = Object.create(LandMammal).build ('rat','anything');
```

Using this approach means that there is no need to use the new keyword to create an object instance, but it also means that the constructor function (which is provoked by use of the new keyword) is not executed. The purpose of the constructor function is to set any initialization values (much of which is now done as an argument to Object.create or Object.defineProperties), so in order to still allow the possibility of initialization of an object with some variable values at create time, I generally include a build method at the top of the prototype chain (in this case, in the Mammal object)—which can be used for object initialization.

Stringifying one of these objects gives:

```
JS  Logger.log (JSON.stringify(whale));
    //{"name":"whale","eats":"krill"}
```

Using getters and setters

In Apps Script, there is a convention to use `getPropertyName` and `setPropertyName` to access properties of an object rather than accessing them directly. In ECMAScript 5, it became possible to define getters and setters (these are functions that behave like properties), in a very similar way to `Property Let`, `Get`, and `Set` in VBA.

In the `Mammal` object, there is a `getter` called introduction. It is in fact a function, but can be used as if it were a property (without brackets) as follows:

```
JS  Logger.log(dolphin.introduction);
    //Im a kind of sea mammal called a dolphin and I eat fish.
    //I don't live on land and I have 0 limbs.
    Logger.log(dog.introduction);
    //Im a kind of land mammal called a dog and I eat meat.
    //I live on land and I have 4 limbs.
```

The prototype chain

When a property is referenced in an object, it works its way up the chain of prototypes (e.g., `LandMammal` → `Mammal` → `Object`), looking for the property required until it finds it or reaches the end of the chain. `JSON.stringify` stops at the specific object it is working on and does not pass up the prototype chain. This is exactly the correct behavior, as without this, stringifying any object would not only show the properties of the object, but also of the `Object` prototype.

However, it may be that you want to serialize properties up the chain too. `Object.get PrototypeOf` can be used to return the prototype of an object, which of course can also be stringified. Here's how to get all the properties of an animal specific object, including those of its prototype chain.

```
JS  Logger.log (JSON.stringify(whale));
    //{"name":"whale","eats":"krill"}

    Logger.log (JSON.stringify(Object.getPrototypeOf(whale)));
    //{"livesOnLand":false,"legs":0,"kind":"sea mammal"}

    Logger.log (JSON.stringify(Object.getPrototypeOf(Object.getPrototypeOf(whale))));
    //{"warmBlooded":true,"vertebrate":true}
```

Traversing the prototype chain

When JavaScript is looking for a referenced property it traverses the prototype chain until it finds it or runs out of chain. Here's a generalized function for traversing the chain and creating a new combined object of each property in each prototype. It is of course possible to have the same property name in multiple places in the chain, in which case the lowest level property takes precedence:

```js
function combineChain (ob,obCombined) {
    return ob ?
      combineChain(
        Object.getPrototypeOf(ob),
        Object.keys(ob).reduce(function(p,c) {
          if (!p.hasOwnProperty(c)) p[c] = ob[c];
          return p;
        }, obCombined || {})) : obCombined;
  }
```

It can be used like this:

```js
Logger.log (JSON.stringify(combineChain(whale)));

//{"name":"whale","eats":"krill","livesOnLand":false,"legs":0,
// "kind":"sea mammal","warmBlooded":true,"vertebrate":true}
```

Conclusion

A VBA class can be fairly successfully mimicked using JavaScript functions.

The flexibility of the JavaScript prototypal inheritance system gives us the opportunity to both copy and improve upon the structure of the VBA class approach, while losing some of the safety and structure a class structure can bring.

Namespaces

Apps Script does not include the concept of modules, so this means that eventually some function names have to go in the global variable space. The more there are, the more likely it is that there will be some name collisions.

If you create a function called foo in script file A, and accidentally name another foo in script file B, then the second one will silently overwrite the first—which is clearly not the behavior you would expect. VBA would throw an error if it detected this, but JavaScript will happily replace one with the other.

We've looked at how functions can be used to create pseudoclasses, and how encapsulation of properties and methods can help keep the global namespace uncluttered, thus minimizing the chance of function or variable collisions.

Creating namespaces is another way to unclutter your project and organize code into sensible silos.

Google Services

Each of the Apps Script services is presented as a namespace—for example, methods of the Utilities service are accessed through the `Utilities` class:

```
Utilities.sleep(1000);
```

If the function were simply named `sleep`, there's a good chance that someone somewhere will create a local function called `sleep` that would override the Utilities `sleep` function.

Libraries

Libraries are also presented in their own namespace for the same reason, and you would access functions you created in a library using syntax like this:

```
MyLibrary.someFunction();
```

Creating Your Own Namespace

A namespace is a wrapper into which code and properties can be inserted and referenced (and protected from name collision). In the case of a library, the library code is automatically wrapped in a namespace that corresponds to the name of the library. It is very simple to create your own namespace in Apps Script.

As an example, say we want to create a function for manipulating spreadsheet data, called `SheetData`:

```
var SheetData = (function() {
    var sheetData = {};
        // define methods and properties
        return sheetData;
})();
```

The namespace

1. Assign an anonymous function to a global variable called `SheetData`:

    ```
    var SheetData = function () {...};
    ```

2. But we want this to actually execute when the project is initialized. In other words, `SheetData` should be the result of a function executing. This is easy to achieve by simply executing the anonymous function before the result gets assigned to `SheetData`:

    ```
    var SheetData = (function () {...}) ();
    ```

3. The result should be a new object to which we'll assign properties and methods:

    ```
    var SheetData = (function () {
        var sheetData = {};
    ```

```
//... assign properties and methods to sheetData

    return sheetData;
}) ();
```

Assigning properties and methods

Because we can add new properties to an object, which can themselves be functions, we can encapsulate all methods associated with this namespace in the function that creates it. For example:

```
JS   var SheetData = (function () {
        var sheetData = {};
        sheetData.getDataValues = function (sheet) {
          return sheet.getDataRange().getValues();
        };
        return sheetData;
     }) ();
```

New methods are accessible through the new namespace:

```
JS   var data = SheetData.getDataValues(sheet);
```

Avoiding Namespace Collisions

If you plan to build up your namespace from a series of script files, you wouldn't want to unconditionally create a new SheetData object. Instead, you'd add to an existing one if it exists, or create a new one if it doesn't.

You can achieve this with a small modification. Instead of:

```
JS   var SheetData = (function() {
         var sheetData = {};
         // define methods and properties
         return sheetData;
     })();
```

you'll pass any already defined instance of SheetData as an argument to the anonymous function (which will be added to by this function); otherwise, a new one is created:

```
JS   var SheetData = (function(sheetData) {
         // define methods and properties
         return sheetData;
     })(SheetData || {} );
```

The IDE

If you already know how to use the Apps Script IDE, there's probably nothing of interest to you in this section.

Before getting started with some examples, take a look at the IDE you'll need to use for writing Apps Script code. If you are accustomed to the VBA IDE, you'll be a little disappointed by its capabilities, but it's what we need to use.

Container-Bound Scripts

Container-bound scripts are tied to (and part of) a document, spreadsheet, or form. Normally people start off with these because they want to automate some process associated with a particular document, or perhaps create some custom functions. These are the equivalent of VBA macros you'd find in any Excel spreadsheet or Word document.

Standalone Scripts

Standalone scripts are script files created on Drive, and would typically be more generalized scripts, perhaps in the form of a library, an add-on, or a triggered process that operates on multiple documents.

Code Examples

Some of the code examples will just be snippets. If so, you'll need to enclose them in a test function so you can run them—something like this:

```js
function tester () {

    // ... the code sample
}
```

You can then run `tester` from the IDE.

Accessing the IDE

If you are creating a container-bound script, create a new sheet and select "Script editor..." from the Tools menu, as shown in Figure 2-1.

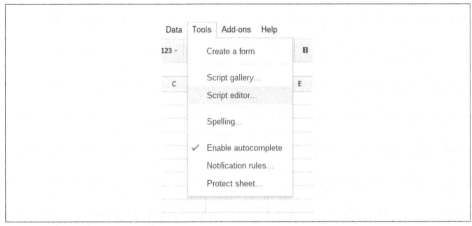

Figure 2-1. Creating a container-bound script

If you are creating a standalone script and this is your first time using the editor, you'll need to connect it to Drive. The simplest way to do this is to visit *script.google.com* and click Start Scripting.

Alternatively, you can connect the scripting app to Drive by selecting "Connect more apps," as shown in Figure 2-2.

Figure 2-2. Creating a standalone script

Then, search for "script," as shown in Figure 2-3.

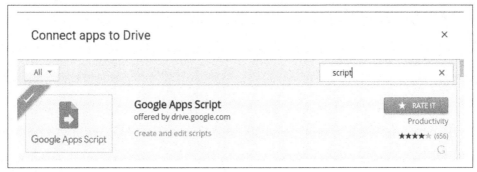

Figure 2-3. *Connecting your script to Drive*

Thereafter, you can create a script file directly from New in Drive.

Create a script for a blank project, as shown in Figure 2-4.

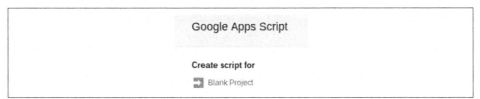

Figure 2-4. *Creating a script for a blank project*

An empty function will be created, as shown in Figure 2-5.

Figure 2-5. *Creating an empty function*

Multiple script files can be created inside a single project, a little like modules in VBA, and within each script file, you create code for your project. It is also possible to create multiple projects within a single container.

One important difference is that VBA includes the concept of private and public scope (procedure and variable visibility) within a module. In Apps Script, the multiple script files are for organizational convenience only. We'll deal with scope and namespace comparisons in a later section.

Running a Function

Select the function you want to run, as shown in Figure 2-6.

Figure 2-6. Selecting a function to run

Examining Results

You can log things from your code using the Logger class:

JS `Logger.log ('something');`

A common pattern is to log an object, which you would first stringify. Logger is able to print the contents of an object, but it's more useful when stringified:

JS `Logger.log (JSON.stringify(someObject));`

You can see the result from Logs in the View menu (Figure 2-7).

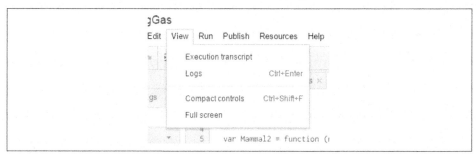

Figure 2-7. Viewing the log results

The execution transcript from the same menu is also very useful, as it shows calls to Google services, and how long they took:

```
[15-09-21 01:50:23:379 PDT] Starting execution
[15-09-21 01:50:23:387 PDT] SpreadsheetApp.getActiveSheet() [0.001 seconds]
[15-09-21 01:50:23:569 PDT] Sheet.getDataRange() [0.181 seconds]
[15-09-21 01:50:23:677 PDT] Range.getValues() [0.108 seconds]
[15-09-21 01:50:23:678 PDT] Execution succeeded [0.293 seconds total runtime]
```

Note that execution transcripts and logs have a limited lifetime. They will disappear after a short time, or upon your exiting from the script.

Libraries

VBA is built on shared libraries already compiled down to P-code. But they have to be compatible in version and architecture, and of course present on the local machine.

Sharing VBA code between local Office documents is challenging. One way is to use the add-in approach, where container- or library-based code from a special kind of document is referenced from another, or you can even open multiple spreadsheets that can access each other's code.

> Confusingly, Apps for Office (HTML-based extensibility for Office) has also been renamed to "Office Add-ins." These are not the same kind of add-ins and are not VBA-based.

There are various tools around to help inject VBA code into workbooks (one example I created is integration with GitHub; you'll find more details in Appendix A), but in principle VBA was designed to be container-based (living inside the document for which it was intended).

All these options add to the fragility of a solution involving VBA shared code.

Libraries in the Cloud

Apps Script libraries are standalone scripts (actually you can publish container-bound scripts as libraries too) whose code has been made available either publicly or to a particular group.

Code in libraries can be used in projects as if the code belonged to the project. As a bonus, libraries come with their own Properties, Lock, and Cache services, which allow cooperating projects to collaborate.

Namespaces and Libraries

Code in a library is encapsulated in a namespace, known as the *library ID*. Just as with your own custom namespaces, this is a way of isolating what might otherwise be conflicting function or variable names.

The pattern for accessing functions in a library is:

```js
LibraryId.function();
```

Managing Library Versions

Apps Script keeps a revision history of managed file versions, which translates into library version numbers. You save a version of a script from the file menu through the dialog shown in Figure 2-8, and manage your versions through the dialog shown in Figure 2-9.

Figure 2-8. Saving a version of a script

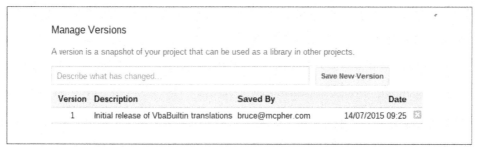

Figure 2-9. Managing versions of a script

When including a library in a project, you specify a particular version number to use with your project. This means that even if the library is updated, your project will still refer to the older version.

Adding Libraries to a Project

To be able to reference a library, you need its project key. To find the key, access the "Project properties" section of the library, as shown in Figure 2-10.

Figure 2-10. Accessing a library's properties to find its project key

Copy this key to use in the project that wants to reference this library, as shown in Figure 2-11.

Figure 2-11. Copying a library's project key

In the Project IDE, under Resources (Figure 2-12), paste the project key to see the library's available versions (Figure 2-13).

Figure 2-12. Accessing a library's resources

Figure 2-13. Pasting the project key to view a library's available versions

Libraries referenced in development mode (Figure 2-14) will always refer to the latest source code (not necessarily the latest saved version, but the latest code).

Figure 2-14. Referencing a library in Development Mode will use the latest code

A popular library may have many projects referencing different versions.

Some Notes on Library Sprawl

Although libraries are very useful, it's easy to create an unmanageable mess with them. You can share libraries using the normal file sharing dialog to control who has access and by providing the library key to potential library users. The more public the library, however, the more likely you are to break something when creating new versions. The following tips should save you some wasted debugging time:

- Development Mode is available only to the library owner (or other collaborators who have edit access). If you release an app that references a library in Development Mode publicly, users will be running the *specified version*, whereas you will have been testing with the *development version*.

- *You must update versions in the correct order* where libraries reference other libraries (starting with the deepest references).
- *Don't cause reference loops.* You won't be able to get the versions properly synchronized.

In general, overcomplicated use of libraries, although tempting, should be avoided.

CHAPTER 3

Translating VBA Functions

The chapter will help you to get started with JavaScript by converting common VBA built-in functions to their JavaScript equivalents. This should do two things:

- Create a useful library of functions that have the same name and operate the same way as the VBA built-in functions. When porting you can choose to simply keep the VBA names, or to refactor in the JavaScript code.

- Demonstrate some everyday JavaScript syntax. The code for these functions is likely to cover most basic manipulation operations.

Conventions

Because these functions will retain their VBA names (and capitalization), we'll be breaking some JavaScript conventions on function names. However, I think it's worth it, as porting will become more of a cut-and-paste operation. By retaining the non-JavaScript-like names, we reduce the risk of a name collision with other, nonported functions.

Library and Namespace

If these functions were to be created locally, I would implement them in their own namespace to isolate them. However, the objective here is to create a reusable library, which will come with its own namespace. All VBA functions will be accessible from other projects using this pattern:

```VB
VBA.builtinFunctionName()
```

For example:

```js
var s = VBA.Trim(aString);
```

It's not very well known, but in VBA, the fully qualified way to call built-in functions is exactly the same. If you enter `VBA.` into the IDE, you'll see a list of all built-in VBA functions, which can then be referenced as `VBA.function()`.

JSDOC

In VBA, the argument type and return value are explicitly called out in the function declaration. Because JavaScript is not typed, there is no way to do that in the language. However, there are a number of different ways of documenting types available based on a language written as part of the comments in the source code. Apps Script has limited support for JSDOC, so we'll use that in the following examples.

Code that includes JSDOC directives is useful for the developer, but Apps Script will also automatically create documentation for a library when you save a new version of its script file.

Unfortunately, the Apps Script JSDOC support is not that great in that it documents only global-level functions and variables (at the time of writing), but it's better to build in full descriptions from the start in case that improves over time.

JSDOC Example

Just before each function, you'll see some JSDOC directives. In this case, the parameter is noted as a number, and the function will return a string:

```js
/**
 * Chr - VBA equivalent - Returns a string given a char code
 * @param {number} code the code to be converted
 * @return {string} the converted string
 */
var Chr = function (code) {
  return String.fromCharCode(code);
};
```

VBA Built-Ins Translated to JavaScript

I won't cover every single VBA built-in function, just the common ones, and they'll be organized into family groups. Their summary definitions are taken from the Visual Studio descriptions.

Helper Functions

Helper functions do not exist in VBA, but there are helper JavaScript functions often used by the VBA equivalents (see Table 3-1). They are in the VBA library if you want to use them directly.

Table 3-1. Helper functions

Name	Code	Note
isObject	```function isObject (obj) {` ` return obj === Object(obj);` `}```	Test if an item is an object.
isArray	```function isArray (arg) {` ` return Array.isArray (arg);` `}```	Test if an item is an array.
isUndefined	```function isUndefined (arg) {` ` return typeof arg === typeof undefined;` `}```	Test if an item is undefined.
fixOptional	```function fixOptional(arg, defaultValue) {` ` return isUndefined(arg) ?` ` defaultValue : arg;` `}```	Apply an optional argument as default if missing.

String Functions

The following section provides an overview of the built-in VBA functions used to manipulate strings.

Asc

The `Asc` function returns an `Integer` value representing the character code corresponding to a character.

Asc (character as string) as Integer

```
/**
 * Asc - VBA equivalent - Returns a numeric Ascii char code given a character
 * @param {string} character Integer value representing the character code
 * @return {number} the converted code
 */
function Asc (character) {
  return character.charCodeAt(0);
}
```

Example: `Asc ("a")`

Result: 97

Implementation notes: The character should be a string of length 1, as only the first character will be converted.

Chr

The Chr function returns the character associated with the specified character code.

Chr (code as Integer) as String

```
/**
 * Chr - VBA equivalent - Returns a string given a char code
 * @param {number} code the code to be converted
 * @return {string} the converted string
 */
function Chr (code) {
  return String.fromCharCode(code);
}
```

Example: Chr (97)

Result: a

Implementation notes: This is the inverse of Asc( ).

InStr

The InStr function returns an integer specifying the start position of the first occurrence of one string within another.

InStr ([start as Integer], [stringToLookIn as String], [stringToLookFor as String], [compareMethod as vbCompareMethod]) as Integer

```
/**
 * InStr - VBA equivalent -
 * Returns the position (starting at 1) of the search string
 * @param {number} [start=1] the start position
 * @param {string} [stringToLookin=""] the string to search
 * @param {string} [stringToLookFor=""] the string to look for
 * @param {number} [compareMethod=0] this is not implemented and ignored
 * @return {number} the start position of the string, or 0 if not found
 */

function InStr  (start, stringToLookin, stringToLookFor, compareMethod ) {
```

```
    // need a hack to identify whether the start argument is actually present
    // see implementation notes for what's going on here
    if (typeof start === 'number') {
      start = start || 1;
      var lookFor = (stringToLookFor || '').toString();
      var lookIn = (stringToLookin || '').toString();
    }
    else {
      // it wasn't so shuffle them along
      var lookFor = (stringToLookin || '').toString();
      var lookIn = (start || '').toString();
      start = 1;
    }

    return (start > 1 ?
      lookIn.slice (start -1) : lookIn ).indexOf(lookFor) + start;
}
```

Example:	InStr (1, 'abcdef' , 'bc')
Result:	2
Implementation notes:	The InStr function is fairly complicated because the VBA version allows for the complete omission of the first argument. Omitting arguments is not something you can do in JavaScript, but to retain compatibility, the first argument is tested for being a number; if it's not a number, then it is assumed that the function has been called with the start position missing.
	Multiple compareMethods are not implemented.

InStrRev

The InStrRev function returns the position of the first occurrence of one string within another, starting from the right side of the string.

InStrRev ([stringToLookIn as String], [stringToLookFor as string], [start as Integer], [compareMethod as vbCompareMethod]) as Integer

```
/**
 * InStrRev - VBA equivalent -
 * the position of the search string, starting right to left
 * @param {string} [stringToLookin=""] the string to search
 * @param {string} [stringToLookFor=""] the string to look for
 * @param {number} [start=-1] the start position -1 means the end
 * @param {number} [compareMethod=0] this is not implemented and ignored
 * @return {number} the start position of the string, or 0 if not found
 */
```

```
function InStrRev (stringToLookin, stringToLookFor, start, compareMethod ) {

  var lookFor = (stringToLookFor || '').toString();
  var lookIn = (stringToLookin || '').toString();
  var start = (start || -1) === -1 ? lookIn.length : start;

  return (start<lookIn.length ?
    lookIn.slice(0,start) : lookIn).lastIndexOf(lookFor)+1;
}
```

Example:	InStrRev ('abcdefbcx' , 'bc')
Result:	7
Implementation notes:	All positions start at 1, and as per VBA, the conversion to strings is done implicitly for the search searchFor arguments. The compareMethod is not implemented.

Join

The Join function returns a string created by joining a number of substrings contained in an array.

Join (sourceArray , [delimiter=" "]) as String

```
/**
 * Join - VBA equivalent - joins an array of values into a single string
 * @param {string[]} sourceArray the array to join
 * @param {string} [delimiter=" "] the item delimiter
 * @return {string} the join array items
 */
function Join (sourceArray , delimiter) {
  return sourceArray.join (fixOptional (delimiter, ' '));
}
```

Example:	Join(['quick','brown','fox'])
Result:	quick brown fox
Implementation notes:	The fixOptional() helper looks like this, and is covered elsewhere:

```
function fixOptional (arg, defaultValue) {
   return isUndefined(arg) ? defaultValue : arg;
}
```

The usual default value pattern, delimiter = delimiter || ' ';, would not work here, as "falsey" values are acceptable delimiters.

LCase

The LCase function returns a string or character converted to lowercase.

LCase (theString as String) as String

```
/**
 * Returns a string converted to lowercase
 * @param {string} theString item to be converted
 * @return {string} item in lowercase
 */
function LCase  (theString) {
  return theString.toString().toLowerCase();
}
```

Example: LCase('HOW THE HIGH AND MIGHTY HAVE FALLEN');

Result: how the high and mighty have fallen

Implementation notes: As with most of these String built-ins, the VBA implicit conversion to a string is emulated.

Left

The Left function returns a string containing the specified number of characters from the left side of a string.

Left (theString as String) as String

```
/**
 * gets the leftmost portion of an item
 * @param {string} theString the item
 * @param {number} length length of result
 * @return {string} The left portion of the string
 */
function Left (theString,length) {
  return theString.toString().slice(0,length);
}
```

Example: Left("Too much agreement kills a chat", 18));

Result: Too much agreement

Implementation notes: As with most of these String built-ins, the VBA implicit conversion to a string is emulated.

Len

The Len function returns an integer containing the number of characters in a string.

Len (theString as String) as Integer

```
/**
 * gets the .toString length
 * @param {string} theString the item
 * @return {number} The length
 */
function Len (theString) {
  return theString.toString().length ;
}
```

Example: `Len('We grow small trying to be great') ;`

Result: 32

Implementation notes: As with most of these String built-ins, the VBA implicit conversion to a string is emulated.

LTrim

LTrim returns a string containing a copy of a specified string with no leading spaces.

LTrim (theString as String) as String

```
/**
 * Removes leading whitespace
 * @param {string} theString the item to be trimmed
 * @return {string} The trimmed result
 */
function LTrim (theString) {
  return theString.toString().replace(/^\s+/, "");
}
```

Example: `LTrim(" I don't do much to keep in trim");`

Result: I don't do much to keep in trim

Implementation notes: Although ECMAScript 7 will have left and right trims built in, the Apps Script version does not.

Regular expressions are available, but not much used in VBA. In JavaScript, they are integral to the language.

This simple regular expression strips whitespace from the beginning of a string.

Mid

Mid returns a string containing a specified number of characters from a string.

Mid (theString as String, start as Integer, [length as Integer]) as String

```
/**
 * gets and extract from a string
 * @param {string} theString the item
 * @param {number} start start position(base 1) of extract
 * @param {number} [length]  Number of characters (default all remaining)
 * @return {string} The extracted string
 */
function Mid (theString,start,length) {
  var s = theString.toString();
  start --;

  length = fixOptional ( length ,  s.length - start );
  return  s.slice ( start, length + start);
}
```

Example:	Mid("I have to take care of the short term, mid term and the long term",40,8);
Result:	mid term
Implementation notes:	As with most of these String built-ins, the VBA implicit conversion to a string is emulated.

Right

The Right function returns a string containing the specified number of characters from the right side of a string.

Right (theString as String, length as Integer) as String

```
/**
 * gets the rightmost portion of an item
 * @param {string|number} theString the item
 * @param {number} [length] length of result
 * @return {string} The right portion of the string
```

```
  */
  function Right (theString,length) {
    return theString.toString().slice(-length);
  }
```

Example:	Right('Too much agreement kills a chat', 12)
Result:	kills a chat
Implementation notes:	As with most of these String built-ins, the VBA implicit conversion to a string is emulated.

RTrim

RTrim returns a string containing a copy of a specified string with no trailing spaces.

RTrim (theString as String) as String

```
/**
 * Removes trailing whitespace
 * @param {string} theString the item to be trimmed
 * @return {string} The trimmed result
 */
function RTrim (theString) {
  return theString.toString().replace(/\s+$/, "");
}
```

Example:	RTrim(" I don't do much to keep in trim ");
Result:	I don't do much to keep in trim
Implementation notes:	Although ECMAScript 7 will have left and right trims built in, the Apps Script version does not.
	Regular expressions are available, but not much used in VBA. In JavaScript, they are integral to the language.
	This simple regex strips whitespace from the end of a string.

Space

The Space function returns a string consisting of the specified number of spaces.

Space (repeatCount as Integer) as String

```
/**
 * Returns a string of ' ' repeated n times
 * @param {number} repeatCount number of times to repeat
 * @return {string} the string of blanks
 */
function Space (repeatCount){
  return repeatCount > 0 ?  Array(repeatCount+1).join(' ') : '' ;
}
```

Example: `Space(5) + "empty space"`

Result: `empty space`

Implementation notes: The Space function uses a little trick by constructing an array with nothing in it, and then joining the elements of that array, creating a string of delimiters, the size of the array – 1. By choosing space as the delimiter, we get the required number of repeated spaces.

Split

The Split function returns a zero-based, one-dimensional array containing a specified number of substrings.

Split (repeatCount as Integer) as String

```
/**
 * Splits an item into an array of strings
 * @param {string} theString the item
 * @param {string} [delimiter] delimiter(default space)
 * @param {number} [limit] max number of splits(default all)
 * @return {string[]} The split arrray of strings
 */
function Split (theString,delimiter,limit) {
  return theString.toString().split(fixOptional(delimiter," "),
     fixOptional(limit,-1));
}
```

Example: `Split("the quick brown fox")`

Result: `["the","quick","brown","fox"]`

Implementation notes: N/A

Trim

The Trim function returns a string containing a copy of a specified string with no leading or trailing spaces.

Split (repeatCount as Integer) as String

```
/**
 * Removes leading and trailing whitespace
 * @param {string} theString the item to be trimmed
 * @return {string} The trimmed result
 */
function Trim (theString) {
  return theString.toString().trim();
}
```

Example: Trim(" I don't do much to keep in trim ");

Result: I don't do much to keep in trim

Implementation notes: N/A

UCase

UCase returns a string containing the specified string converted to uppercase.

UCase (theString as String) as String

```
/**
 * Returns a string converted to uppercase
 * @param {string} theString item to be converted
 * @return {string} item in uppercase
 */
function UCase (theString) {
  return theString.toString().toUpperCase();
}
```

Example: UCase('the peter principle');

Result: THE PETER PRINCIPLE

> **Implementation notes:** As with most of these `String` built-ins, the VBA implicit conversion to a string is emulated.

Conversion Functions

Conversion functions, shown in Table 3-2, are used to convert between one type and another. JavaScript has far fewer types than VBA, and the conversion is trivial.

Table 3-2. Conversion functions

Conversion	Name	Code
To string	CStr	```function CStr (value) {
return value.toString();
}```
To number	CLng	```function CLng (value) {
return parseInt (value , 10);
}```
	CInt	```function CInt (value) {
return parseInt (value, 10);
}```
	CDbl	```function CDbl (value) {
return parseFloat (value);
}```
To Boolean	CBool	```function CBool (value) {
return value ? true : false;
}```
To date	CDate	```function CDate (dateString) {
return new Date (dateString);
}```

Math Functions

JavaScript math functions are found in the Math library, and their names generally correspond to the VBA equivalents. I have included a selection of them in Table 3-3.

Table 3-3. Math functions

VBA name	Code	Note
Abs	```function Abs(value) {
return Math.abs(value);
}```	

VBA name	Code	Note
Cos	```function Cos (value) { return Math.cos(value); }```	
Exp	```function Exp (value) { return Math.exp(value); }```	
Int	```function Int (value) { return Math.floor(value); }```	
Log	```function Log (value) { return Math.log(value); }```	
Rnd	```function Rnd (seed) { return Math.random(); }```	The seed value is ignored in JavaScript.
Round	```function Round (value, places) { return isUndefined(places) ? Math.round (value) : Math.round(values* Math.pow(10,places)) / Math.pow(10,places); }```	Math.round rounds only to a whole number, so this workaround converts to a given number of places.
Sin	```function Sin (value) { return Math.sin (value); }```	
Sqr	```function Sqr (value) { return Math.sqrt(value) ; }```	
Tan	```function Tan (value) { return Math.tan (value); }```	

Informational Functions and Constants

Informational functions, shown in Table 3-4, are used to test the state of a variable. There are also a couple of useful constants included.

Table 3-4. Informational functions

VBA name	Code	Note

IsEmpty	```function IsEmpty (value) {```
	``` return typeof(value) === "string" &&```
	``` value === Empty;```
	```}```
		Not an exact match, but will work for testing if a cell is empty.

Empty	```Empty = "";```	In VBA, IsEmpty("") returns false, but this is the way to test for an empty cell in Apps Script.

IsNull	```function IsNull (value) {```
	``` return value===null ;```
	```}```
		In VBA, null does not occur much.

Null	```Null = null;```	Fixes the case to match VBA.

IsDate	```function IsDate (sDate) {```
	``` var tryDate = new Date(sDate);```
	``` return (tryDate.toString() != "NaN" &&```
	``` tryDate != "Invalid Date") ;```
	```}```
		This just tries the conversion and sees if it works. JavaScript doesn't have a test date.

IsNumeric	```function IsNumeric (theString) {```
	``` return isFinite(parseFloat(theString));```
	```}```	

IsError	```function IsError (value) {```
	``` return isNaN(value);```
	```}```
		There's not a direct equivalent; this will test for an error only in a number conversion.

IsNothing	```function IsNothing (value) {```
	``` return value === null ||```
	``` isUndefined(value) ;```
	```}```
		This is not really a function in VBA. This kind of construct does not exist in JavaScript, but the function given will emulate.

IsMissing	```function IsMissing (value) {```
	``` return isUndefined(value);```
	```}```
		This is normally used in VBA to test if a variant optional argument is present.

TypeName	```function TypeName (value) {```
	
	``` return isObject (value) ?```
	``` (value.constructor ?```
	``` value.constructor.name :```
	``` typeof value)```
	``` : typeof value;```
	```}```
		TypeName in VBA will return the constructor name, whereas typeof in JavaScript would return only object. This emulates the VBA behavior, but will work only for custom objects (not Apps Script built-in classes).

VBA name	Code	Note

VarType	```function VarType (value) {```
	``` return typeof value;```
	```}```
		This is not strictly correct, as VarType should return a type ENUM, but there is no equivalence so this will return the JavaScript type name.

IsArray	```function IsArray (value) {```
	``` return isArray(value) ;```
	```}```	

IsObject	```function IsObject (value) {```
	``` return isObject (value);```
	```}```	

Date and Time Functions

VBA represents dates as the number of days and fractions of days since 1900, so 41011.75 is 6 p.m. (three-fourths of a day), 41,011 days after December 31, 1899.

The JavaScript `Date` object records the number of milliseconds since 1970, a value that can be accessed via the `getTime()` method of the `Date` object.

This different method of handling dates could be a conversion challenge if the VBA app to be converted is using any assumptions about native date format. This example relies on the whole number part of a VBA internal date being the number of days (it works only because of the way dates are stored internally and is poor practice).

VB
```
If (VBA.CDbl(date1) - VBA.CDbl(date2) > 1) Then
        Debug.Print "more than 24 hours have passed - don't do this"
    End If
```

The VBA built-in functions hide the way that dates are stored internally by providing access to their components, such as day, year, second, and so on. It's better to execute date operations using these components rather than by relying on knowledge of the internal VBA representation. The previous example works only because you know that a day is counted as 1 internally in VBA. However, in JavaScript, a day is the number of milliseconds in a day ($24 \times 60 \times 60 \times 1,000$), and the preceding calculation, if ported to JavaScript as is, would consider 1 millisecond to be the same as 1 day.

It's better to use code that works on the extracted date components, because you can transport it to JavaScript using the implementation of `DateDiff` in the VBA library:

VB
```
If (VBA.DateDiff("s", date2, date1) > 24# * 60# * 60#) Then
        Debug.Print "more than 24 hours have passed"
    End If
```

The date implementations shown in this section work with and return the JavaScript representation of a date[1] and do not convert to the VBA internal representation, so any code that relies on specifics of how VBA stores dates will not work properly.

Now

Aside from Now, the functions in Table 3-5 do not have a lot of meaning in JavaScript, although they have been implemented to maintain compatibility with VBA.

Table 3-5. Date and time functions

VBA name	Code	Note

Now	```function Now () {```
	``` return new Date();```
	```}```
		Returns the time and date.

Date	```function DateNow () {```
	``` return DateValue(new Date());```
	```}```
		Returns just the date portion. Note the change in name, as using Date as the function name would conflict with the JavaScript Date object constructor name.

Time	```function Time () {```
	``` return TimeValue(new Date());```
	```}```
		Note that if you format this date, the month and year will be Jan 1970.

Values

The functions in Table 3-6 are used to extract just the date or time parts of a Date.

Usage:

```
var value = VBA.DateValue (theDate);
```

Table 3-6. Date and time values

VBA name	Code	Note

DateValue	```function DateValue (dateTime) {```
	``` return ['Hours','Minutes',```
	``` 'Seconds','Milliseconds']```
	``` .reduce(function(p,c) {```
	``` p['set'+c](0);```
	``` return p;```
	``` },new Date(dateTime));```
	``` }```
		Returns just the date portion, with the time portion set to 12:00 a.m.

---

1 Just like VBA, times and dates returned by these functions are all local time.

VBA name	Code	Note
TimeValue	```function TimeValue (dateTime) {` ` return ['Hours','Minutes',` ` 'Seconds','Milliseconds']` ` .reduce(function(p,c) {` ` p['set'+c](dateTime['get'+c]());` ` return p;` ` },new Date(0));` `}```	Note that if you format this date, the month and year will be Jan 1970.

DatePart

The `DatePart` function in VBA is a single function that gives access to each of the date components. The full call for `DatePart`, implemented in JavaScript, is as follows:

```
/**
 * DatePart - takes an interval and returns the appropriate measure
 * @param {string} interval the interval - e.g., yyyy for year
 * @param {Date} dateTime the date to work on
 * @param {number} [startOfWeek=vbUseSystemDayOfWeek] the day the week starts on
 * @param {number} [startWeekOfYear=vbFirstJan1] the week the year starts on
 * @return {number} the measure
 */
function DatePart (interval , dateTime,startOfWeek,startWeekOfYear) {
    return new DateHelpers(startOfWeek, startWeekOfYear).part(interval, dateTime);
}
```

where `interval` is one of the values in Table 3-7.

Table 3-7. Possible values for interval in the DateTime function

Value	Interval	Example
yyyy	Year	2015
m	Month (starting at 1)	7
d	Day	29
h	Hour	21
n	Minute	50
s	Second	45
q	Quarter	1
y	Day of year	320
w	Day of week	2
ww	Week of year	34

Portions

Portion functions, listed in Table 3-8, return part of the date, using the same base as VBA (e.g., the first day of the month is 1, not 0 as it is in native JavaScript date functions). They are simply aliases for the `DatePart` function. For example:

JS `var years  = VBA.DatePart("yyyy", dateTime);`

is equivalent to:

JS `var years = VBA.Year (dateTime);`

Example usage:

```
var day = VBA.Day (theDate);
```

Table 3-8. Portion functions

VBA name	Code	Note

Year	`function Year (dateTime) {`
	`    return DatePart("yyyy",dateTime);`
	`}`
		DatePart is equivalent to VBA DatePart and will be covered later.

Month	`function Month (dateTime) {`
	`    return DatePart("m",dateTime);`
	`}`
		The JavaScript month number starts at 0. This uses VBA base 1.

Day	`function Day (dateTime) {`
	`    return DatePart("d",dateTime);`
	`}`	

Hour	`function Hour (dateTime) {`
	`    return DatePart("h",dateTime);`
	`}`	

Minute	`function Minute (dateTime) {`
	`    return DatePart("n",dateTime);`
	`}`	

Second	`function Second (dateTime) {`
	`    return DatePart("s",dateTime);`
	`}`	

Weekdays

The weekday function returns the day of the week. By default, 1 is Sunday. There is a little bit of confusion between the worksheet function for both Sheets and Excel and the VBA functions, because VBA allows an optional argument where any day of the week can be specified as the start day, whereas the worksheet function allows only three types of start day.

This function emulates the VBA function and allows any day to be the start day for the week. Some constants corresponding to the VBA ones that identify specific weekdays are also provided.

Example usage:

```
var theDay = VBA.Weekday (theDate);
var theDay = VBA.Weekday (theDate, VBA.vbTuesday);
```

```
JS  /**
     * Weekday - VBA equivalent - Returns the weekday
     * @param {Date} dateTime the date to process
     * @param {number} [startOfWeek=vbUseSystemDayOfWeek] the day the week starts on
     * @return {number} the weekday
     */
    function Weekday (dateTime, startOfWeek) {
      return new DateHelpers(startOfWeek).weekDay(dateTime);
    }
```

Weekday and week number constants

Weekday and week number constants are available in the VBA library:

```
JS  // days of the week
    var vbSunday = 1,
        vbMonday = 2,
        vbTuesday = 3,
        vbWednesday = 4,
        vbThursday = 5,
        vbFriday = 6,
        vbSaturday = 7;

    // default week starts
    var vbUseSystemDayOfWeek = vbSunday;

    var vbFirstJan1     = 1, // Start the week in which January 1 occurs (default)
        vbFirstFourDays = 2, // Start the week with at least 4 days in the new year
        vbFirstFullWeek = 3  //Start with the first full week of the new year

    // change this for the system behavior for week numbers
    var vbUseSystem = vbFirstJan1;
```

Week numbers

The week number of the year is available through the `DatePart` function.

The VBA default is for week numbering to start on the first day of the year, and that is the default adopted by the VBA library implementation. However, the most common week numbering system is the ISO-8601 standard, under which the week starts on Monday. The first week of the year is the week that contains that year's first Thursday.

To get the ISO week number from the VBA library, use this pattern:

```js
var isoWeek = VBA.DatePart ("ww", dateTime , VBA.vbMonday, VBA.vbFirstFourDays);
```

Date calculations

It's best to perform calculations on dates using the functions listed in Table 3-9, as they account for daylight saving time just like their VBA equivalents. They are called like this:

```
var newDate = VBA.DateAdd ("d" , 11 , dateTime);
```

Table 3-9. Date calculation functions

VBA name	Code

DateDiff	`function DateDiff ( interval,date1,date2,startOfWeek,startWeekOfYear ) {`
	    `return new DateHelpers(startOfWeek, startWeekOfYear)`
	          `.dif(interval, date1, date2);`
	`}`

DateAdd	`function DateAdd(interval, measure, dateTime) {`
	    `return new DateHelpers().add (interval , measure , dateTime);`
	  `}`

DateHelpers

The `DateHelpers` namespace contains helper functions and is often referenced throughout the VBA `Date` equivalents. It is in the VBA library, but not directly equivalent to any VBA function. Date and time conversions and comparisons are fairly complex, as JavaScript does not have the richness of VBA in this area. Although it's possible, you needn't use this namespace directly, as the usual interface is via the VBA library equivalent functions already covered.

The code is a little large to be fully included here, but the `DateHelpers` namespace in the VBA library is in the GitHub repository (the reference is in Appendix A), and should help to show the workings involved in translating between native JavaScript and VBA date and time functions.

Optional Arguments

VBA allows for arguments to be optional, with a default value if required.

For example:

```vb
Function someFunction ( _
    requiredArg As String, Optional optionalArg As String = "something") As String
```

Another construct in VBA is named arguments, often used where a function can have a whole string of optional arguments:

VB `anotherSub name:="Han Solo"`

These handy approaches cannot be exactly mimicked in JavaScript.

In some senses, all arguments are optional in JavaScript: nothing will complain if you call a function expecting multiple arguments with less or even none, but you cannot have multiple commas with no argument names in a function call, like you can in VBA.

This would be perfectly valid VBA if the last three arguments were optional:

VB `placeToEat ("pizza",,,"the hut")`

But in JavaScript, you must specify all the intervening arguments in order to avoid invalid syntax errors:

JS `placeToEat ("pizza",undefined,undefined,"the hut");`

Testing for undefined

You can use the `isUndefined` function in the VBA library to test for `undefined`:

VB
```
function placeToEat (food , town , street , shop) {
     if (VBA.isUndefined(town)) {
         //..  do something
         }
     if (VBA.isUndefined(street)) {
         //.. do something else
         }
     if (VBA.isUndefined(shop)) {
         //.. do another thing
         }
 }
```

or you can use straight JavaScript:

JS
```
if (typeof town === typeof undefined) {
    //... do something
    }
```

Applying Default Values

You can emulate this code:

VB
```
Function placeToEat (  food As String, _
    Optional town As String = "london", _
    Optional street As String = "regent street", _
    Optional shop As String ="nandos") As String
```

by using the `fixOptional` function in the VBA library:

```js
function placeToEat (food, town, street, shop)  {
      town   = VBA.fixOptional (town , "london");
      street = VBA.fixOptional (street, "regent street");
      shop   = VBA.fixOptional (shop, "nandos");
}
```

Named Arguments

There is no equivalent to `name:="darth vader"` in JavaScript, but these kind of multiple optional parameters are often dealt with by passing an object to a function with property values defining the default values:

```js
placeToEat ( {
      town:"new york" ,
      street:"broadway"
} );

function placeToEat ( options ) {

    var town = options.town || "london";
    var shop = options.shop || "nandos";
    var street = options.street || "regent street";

}
```

Handling Errors

Dealing with errors in VBA is like stepping back in coding time 20 years (actually that's exactly what it is), as it encourages the developer to do bad things like ignore errors, and forces interruptions to the logic flow by jumping around the code.

VBA error handling will not be duplicated in the VBA library, and we'll just be leaving it all behind, exactly where it deserves to be.

VBA Exception Branching

Exceptions are dealt with on a function-by-function basis. In the function the `On Error` statement is used to define what should happen in the event of an error as follows.

Branch to some other part of the code (yes, really):

```vb
On Error Goto somelabel
```

Just ignore the error and continue (probably the most misused line of code in VBA):

```vb
On Error Resume Next
```

Raise a VBA exception (this is the normal behavior):

VB `On Error Goto 0`

Resuming

Because `On Error Goto` branches off somewhere for handling, we need a way to resume execution. VBA provides the following varieties of `Resume` statement.

Retry the line of code that caused the error (which you've probably now fixed in the exception handler):

VB `Resume`

Resume at the line after the line that raised the error:

VB `Resume Next`

Branch to some other place and resume execution there (yes, really):

VB `Resume someOtherLabel`

Detecting the error

The `Err` object is maintained with the status of the latest error, and you can test `Err.Number` to find out why the error has been raised.

A procedure with error handling could look like this:

VB
```
Private Function someFunction(theExpectedError as long) as boolean

    someFunction = True

    On Error Goto Handler

    somethingThatMightFail()
    codeThatExecutesFailOrNot()

    Exit Function

Handler:
    someFunction = False

    If (Err.Number = theExpectedError) then
      doSomethingWithTheError()
    Else
      reportTheError (Err.Number)
    Endif

    Resume Next

End Function
```

JavaScript try/catch

If there is no handling, then JavaScript will throw an exception. A `try`/`catch` block is used to encapsulate code that might otherwise throw an exception.

An optional `finally` block is available that will run after the `try` (and the `catch` if there was an error) blocks have been executed. The `finally` block is seldom used in most of the code I've seen, but it does allow emulation of the VBA `Resume Next` pattern:

```js
/**
 *demonstrate try/catch
 *@param {string} theExpectedError the name of the error that could be tolerated
 *@return {boolean} whether it executed successfully
 */
function someFunction (theExpectedError)  {
  try {
    somethingThatMightFail();
  }
  catch (err) {
    if (err.name === theExpectedError) {
      doSomethingWithTheError();
    } else {
      reportTheError(err.name);
    }
  }
  finally {
    codeThatExecutesFailOrNot();
  }
}
```

Raising an Error

It is possible in both VBA and JavaScript to raise a custom error—that is, an exception generated by an application.

VBA

In VBA, you use the `Err` object to raise an error, but in order to avoid clashing with built-in VBA errors, you add your homegrown error numbering system to a constant like this:

```vb
Err.Raise vbObjectError + 1003, "some error message"
```

JavaScript

In JavaScript, you can simply throw an error like this:

```js
throw 'some error message';
```

or more correctly:

```js
throw new Error ('some error message');
```

which will (very handily) give you details about where the error occurred:

```js
try {
    throw new Error ("some error message");
}
catch(err) {
    Logger.log (JSON.stringify (err));
}
```

Here's the result:

```
{
  "message":"some error message",
  "fileName":"sheets","lineNumber":27,
  "stack":"\tat sheets:27 (th)\n"
}
```

VBA Built-In Objects

Later on we'll get to the specific interfaces for the Office applications' object models, but VBA has various useful objects in addition to the built-in functions. These can also be emulated in JavaScript, but first let's look at VBA's ability to deal with complex objects that are not instances of classes.

Type

The VBA type is a little like a struct in C and allows you an easy way to define a template for a custom type—a variable that contains properties of varying types.

A custom type definition:

```vb
Type Box
    name As String
    width As Integer
    height As Integer
    color As Long
End Type
```

can be used like this:

```vb
Dim redBox As Box

redBox.color = &HFF0000
redBox.width = 200
redBox.height = 100
redBox.name = "red box"

showBox redBox
```

and displayed like this:

```vb
Private Function showBox(theBox As Box)
    Debug.Print theBox.name, theBox.color, theBox.width, theBox.height
End Function
```

giving this result:

```vb
red box          16711680      200              100
```

JavaScript does not have a type capability, but you can achieve a similar result by simply creating an object on the fly:

```js
var redBox = {};
redBox.color = 0xFF0000;
redBox.width = 200;
redBox.height = 100;
redBox.name = "red box";
showBox (redBox);
```

which is displayed (in Apps Script) like this:

```js
function showBox(theBox) {
    Logger.log(theBox);
}
```

giving this result:

```
{color=1.671168E7, width=200.0, name=red box, height=100.0}
```

The usual way of creating these types of objects (known as *object literals*) is to define them and assign values at the same time:

```js
var yellowBox = {
    color:0xffff00,
    width:200,
    height:100,
    name:"Yellow box"
};
showBox (yellowBox);
```

giving this result:

```
{color=1.677696E7, width=200.0, name=Yellow box, height=100.0}
```

Copying types

Making a duplicate of a custom type instance in VBA is simple:

```vb
blueBox = redBox
blueBox.color = &HFF
blueBox.name = "blue box"

showBox blueBox
showBox redBox
```

and gives this result, as expected:

```
blue box        255            200            100
red box         16711680       200            100
```

But the same thing in JavaScript:

```
var blueBox = redBox;
blueBox.color = 0xFF;
blueBox.name = "blue box";
showBox (blueBox);
showBox (redBox);
```

gives an *unexpected* result:

```
{color=255.0, width=200.0, name=blue box, height=100.0}
{color=255.0, width=200.0, name=blue box, height=100.0}
```

We've changed the contents of both `blueBox` and `redBox` by modifying just one of them. This is because `blueBox` is simply a reference pointer to the address of `redBox`. In other words, they both point to the same object instance. `blueBox` is not a new instance of `Box` and does not occupy its own memory space in the way that a VBA type does.

Cloning objects

Making *deep clones*[2] of objects in JavaScript is not straightforward, and is the subject of another discussion. However, you can easily clone these types of simple objects by stringifying them and parsing them as follows:

```
var blueBox = JSON.parse(JSON.stringify(redBox));
blueBox.color = 0xFF;
blueBox.name = "blue box";
showBox (blueBox);
showBox (redBox);
```

which now gives this result:

```
{color=255.0, width=200, name=blue box, height=100}
{color=1.671168E7, width=200.0, name=red box, height=100.0}
```

Key/Value Pairs

A fundamental construct in JavaScript is *key/value pairs*. An object property name is a key, and its property value is the value. JSON is simply a structured collection of key/value pairs that can map to a JavaScript object when parsed.

---

2 In *deep cloning*, distinct copies of other objects referenced within a source object must be created and referenced in the object clone. *Shallow cloning* simply makes references to the same objects present in the original source object.

VBA has various naive key/value pair constructs such as types and collections. The Scripting Dictionary object provides a slightly more useful version of the same thing (it provides access to its keys as well as its values). Two-dimensional arrays can also be coerced into standing in for key/value pair support.

You can use ScriptControl to delegate the parsing of JSON to JScript, but then it is difficult to navigate and access the resultant object inside VBA.

There are also various XML capabilities that can be used to support JSON-like structures, but there is no really good equivalent to the JavaScript-like object in VBA.

The most popular VBA topic on my Desktop Liberation site (*http://ramblings.mcpher.com*) is Excel/JSON integration. In almost every VBA project I've been involved in for the past few years, I've used a custom class called cJobject either to deal with JSON or simply to provide a useful object to navigate structured data that is more complex than the single-level key/value pairs the Collection and Dictionary objects are designed for.

This is a problem that most VBA developers come across at some point, and there are almost as many different workaround strategies as there are projects that need them.

For this book's examples, I use a class I call KVPairs to deal with multiple-level VBA arrays and objects. It maps fairly well to the JavaScript object, and provides similar capabilities to the Dictionary object for simpler object structures. Hopefully the concepts it uses are recognizable in whatever strategy you have adopted for this purpose.

In order to make the later examples involving KVPairs more comprehensible, Table 3-10 offers a quick comparison of the VBA KVPairs implementation and the equivalent native JavaScript.

Table 3-10. VBA KVPairs implementation versus equivalent native JavaScript

KVPairs	JavaScript

`'create a new object`
`Dim redBox As KVPairs`
`set redBox = new KVPairs`
	`var redBox = {};`
	`//or`
	`var redBox = Object.create();`

`'add a property and value` `redBox .add "name","red box"`	`redBox.name = "red box";`
`'get a value` `name = redBox.getValue("name")`	`var name = redBox.name;`

KVPairs	JavaScript

``
'iterate through values
For Each value In redBox.getPairs()
  Debug.Print value
Next value
``
	``
	for (key in redBox) {
	  Logger.log(redBox[key]);
	}
	// or
	Object.keys(forEach(function(key) {
	  Logger.log(redBox[key]);
	});
	``

``
'iterate through keys
For Each key In redBox.getKeys()
  Debug.Print key
Next key
``
	``
	for (key in redBox) {
	  Logger.log(key);
	}
	// or
	Object.keys(forEach(function(key) {
	  Logger.log(key);
	});
	``

``
' check if a property exists
If (redBox.Exists("name")) Then
  Debug.Print redBox.getValue("name")
End If
``
	``
	if (redBox.hasOwnProperty("name")) {
	  Logger.log(redBox["name"]);
	}
	// or
	if (Object.keys(redBox)
	  .indexOf("name")
	  !== -1) {
	  Logger.log(redBox["name"]);
	}
	// or
	if (typeof redbox["name"] !==
	    typeof undefined) {
	  Logger.log(redBox["name"]);
	}
	``

``` ' replace a value redBox.replace "name", "yellow box" ```	``` redBox.name = "yellow box"; ```

``
' create multiple level objects
Set pos = New KVPairs
pos.add "top", 100
pos.add "left", 200
redBox.add "position", pos
``
	``
	redBox.position = {
	  top:100,
	  left:200
	};
	``

``
'access values from multiple levels
top =
redBox _
  .getValue("position").getValue("top")
``
	``
	var top = redBox.position.top;
	``

``
' get a value by its position-
  (kvpairs can be used as an array..
    starts at 1)
value = redBox.getValue(1)
``
	``
	// if object is an array
	var value=anArray[0];
	// or
	var value=redBox[Object
	  .keys(redBox)[0]];
	``

KVPairs	JavaScript

``
' get the key at a position
key = redBox.getKey(1);
``
	``
	var key = Object.keys(
	    redBox)[0];
	``

You will have your own strategy for dealing with objects already in VBA, so I haven't translated KVPairs to Apps Script. However, the VBA version is available in the Git-Hub repository, details of which are in Appendix A.

Collections

I'm a big user of collections in VBA applications. They provide an iterable, general-purpose way of storing objects (or any variant, for that matter). A collection is the kind of thing you might use an array for in JavaScript, except that it also provides an optional way to index items by some key.

This section shows how to implement a collection in JavaScript for the Apps Script VBA library that will work the same way and take the same arguments as its VBA counterpart.

Some prefer to use the Scripting Dictionary object over the VBA Collection object. They are very similar, except that the Collection object allows access by index (position), and the Dictionary object allows access to its keys.

VBA

Here's an example of everything you can do with collections in VBA:

VB Function collections()

```
        Dim figures As VBA.Collection, figure As Variant
        Set figures = New VBA.Collection

        ' add something
        figures.Add "greedo"

        ' add something with a key
        figures.Add "yoda", "mistake"

        ' add something before something else
        figures.Add "yoda", , 2

        ' add something at the beginning
        figures.Add "luke", "skywalker", 1

        ' iterate
        For Each figure In figures
            Debug.Print figure
        Next figure
```

```vba
    ' get something
    Debug.Print figures.Item(2)

    ' get something by key
    Debug.Print figures.Item("mistake")

    ' how many
    Debug.Print figures.Count

    ' delete something
    figures.Remove 3

        ' iterate
    For Each figure In figures
        Debug.Print figure
    Next figure

    ' how many
    Debug.Print figures.Count

End Function
```

And the result:

```
luke
greedo
yoda
yoda
greedo
yoda
 4
luke
greedo
yoda
 3
```

JavaScript collection

The Apps Script test will look pretty much the same as the VBA version, but with some syntactic adjustments:

```javascript
function collections() {

    var figures = new VBA.Collection();

    //' add something
    figures.Add ("greedo");

    //' add something with a key
    figures.Add ("yoda", "mistake");

    //' add something before something else
```

```
        figures.Add ("yoda", undefined , 2);

        //' add something at the beginning
        figures.Add ("luke", "skywalker", 1);

        //' iterate
        figures.forEach (function (figure) {
            Logger.log ( figure );
        });

        //' get something
        Logger.log ( figures.Item(2));

        //' get something by key
        Logger.log ( figures.Item("mistake"));

        //' how many
        Logger.log ( figures.Count());

        //' delete something
        figures.Remove (3);

        //' iterate
        figures.forEach (function (figure) {
            Logger.log ( figure );
        });

        //' how many
        Logger.log ( figures.Count());

    }
```

The results match the VBA version.

VBA.Collection for JavaScript

The following code is the Collection class implemented in JavaScript and used in the preceding examples, and the results match the VBA version:

```
JS  /**
     * simulate a VBA collection
     * naming case conventions as per VBA
     * indices start at 1
     * @constructor Collection
     * @return {Collection} self
     */
    function Collection() {

      var self = this;
      var collection_ = [];
      var collectionKeys_ = {};
```

```
/**
 * add an item to a collection
 * @param {*} item an item to add to a collection
 * @param {string} [key] the key to retrieve it by later
 * @param {string} [before] the index to insert the item before (starting 1)
 * @param {string} [after] the index to insert the item after (starting 1)
 * @return {*} the item
 */
self.Add = function (item , key , before , after) {

    // check any given args are valid
    if(key && !isUndefined(collectionKeys_[key]) ) {
        throw key + ' already in collection';
    }

    // before and after validity checks
    if (!isUndefined(before) && (before > collection_.length || before < 1)) {
      throw before + ' before index is invalid ';
    }

    if (!isUndefined(after) && (after > collection_.length || after < 1)) {
      throw after + ' after index is invalid ';
    }

    // find position to be inserted at
    var pos = before ? before-1 : ( after || collection_.length );

    // shuffle up keys
    if (pos < collection_.length) {

      Object.keys(collectionKeys_).forEach (function (k) {
        if (collectionKeys_[k] >= pos) collectionKeys_[k]++;
      });
    }

    // insert the item
    collection_.splice(pos,0,item);

    // add the key
    if (key)collectionKeys_[key.toString()] = pos;

    // for chaining
    return item;

};

/**
 * number of items in the collection
 * @return {number} the count
 */
self.Count = function () {
  return collection_.length;
```

```
};

/**
 * get an item from a collection
 * @param {string|number} [key] either a key or a numeric index
 * @return {object} the item, index and key
 */
function getItem_ (key) {

  var index = typeof key === 'number' ? key -1  : collectionKeys_[key];

  return {
    item: collection_[index],
    index: index,
    key: key
  };
}

/**
 * throw an error if item wasn't found
 * @param {object} ob returned from getItem_
 * @return {object} the object
 */
function assertKey_ (ob) {
  if (isUndefined(ob.item)) {
    throw 'key ' + ob.key + ' not in collection';
  }
  return ob;
}

/**
 * get an item from a collection
 * @param {string|number} [key] either a key or a numeric index
 * @return {*} the item
 */
self.Item = function (key) {
  return assertKey_ (getItem_ (key)).item;
};

/**
 * remove an item from a collection
 * @param {string|number} [key] either a key or a numeric index
 * @return {*} the removed item
 */
self.Remove = function (key) {
  var ob = assertKey_ (getItem_ (key));

  // shuffle down
  Object.keys(collectionKeys_).forEach (function (k) {
    if (collectionKeys_[k] > ob.index) collectionKeys_[k]--;
  });
```

```
        // delete the item's key
        if (!isUndefined(ob.key)) delete collectionKeys_[ob.key];

        // and the item from the array
        return collection_.splice(ob.index,1)[0];

    };

    /**
     * a lambda to iterate
     * @param {function} func the iteration function
     * @return void
     */
    self.forEach = function (func) {

        collection_.forEach ( function (d,i,a) {
          return func(d , i , a) ;
        });

    };

    return self;
}
```

The default method

In VBA:

VB `collection.Item(key)`

is equivalent to:

VB `collection(key)`

In JavaScript, the parentheses imply that `collection` is a function that should be executed, but the `Collection` constructor creates an object, not a function:

JS `var collection = new VBA.Collection();`

This will *throw a syntax error* at runtime (because an object cannot be "executed"):

JS `collection(key) ;`

Syntactically, there can be no default method shortcut for the `VBA.Collection` object in JavaScript, and indexing an item must be coded in full:

JS `collection.Item(key);`

CHAPTER 4

Living with the Quotas

One of the daily irritations of Apps Script is being caught by quota limitations that cause scripts to fail. Quotas are imposed on many Apps Script services because they run on shared infrastructure. Runaway processes could have a serious impact on other Apps Script users, and this quota system is intended to protect the Apps Script community as a whole, even though individual users might be occasionally inconvenienced.

Another good reason for quotas is as a signal that an application is no longer suitable for the Apps Script environment, and should be moved to a paid and more scalable environment such as App Engine.

To VBA users, who have free reign over the local PC resources, this can come as somewhat of a culture shock, because these quotas deeply affect the approach to application structure. Although VBA has no direct corollary to this problem, it is important to understand how quotas affect Apps Script development.

The chapter looks at some ways to live with quotas, rate limits, and what Google calls *limitations*.

The Quotas

Many of the underlying APIs used by Apps Script have their own quotas, but Apps Script often has additional restrictions.

Daily Limits

Some services allow you to perform a maximum number of a particular operation per day; that is, when you exhaust this quota, you can no longer perform that specific operation that day. Table 4-1 lists the daily limits from the Apps Script dashboard at the time of writing.

Table 4-1. Daily limits from the Apps Script dashboard

Action	Consumer (gmail.com)	Google Apps for your domain	Google Apps for biz/edu/gov
Calendar events created	5,000	10,000	10,000
Contacts created	1,000	2,000	2,000
Documents created	250	500	1,500
Email recipients per day	100	100	1,500
Gmail read/write (excluding send)	20,000	40,000	50,000
Groups read	2,000	5,000	10,000
JDBC connection	10,000	10,000	50,000
JDBC failed connection	100	100	500
Property GET or SET	50,000	100,000	500,000
SOAP calls	5,000	20,000	20,000
Spreadsheets created	250	500	3,200
Triggers total runtime	1 hours	3 hours	6 hours
URLFetch calls	20,000	50,000	100,000
URLFetch data received	100 MB	100 MB	100 MB

Limitations

Another type of quota is known as a *limitation* by Google. Typically, these are size limitations for an operation's maximum payload. These are hard limits, and there is not much that can be done other than to design applications to avoid hitting them. Table 4-2 lists the limitations at the time of this writing.

Table 4-2. Additional limitations from the Apps Script dashboard

Feature	Consumer (gmail.com)	Google Apps for your domain	Google Apps for biz/edu/gov
Script runtime	6 min/execution	6 min/execution	6 min/execution
Email attachments	250/msg	250/msg	250/msg
Email body size	200 KB/msg	200 KB/msg	400 KB/msg
Email recipients per message	50/msg	50/msg	50/msg
Email total attachments size	25 MB/msg	25 MB/msg	25 MB/msg
Properties value size	9 KB/val	9 KB/val	9 KB/val
Properties total storage	500 KB/property store	500 KB/property store	500 KB/property store
Triggers	20/user/script	20/user/script	20/user/script
URL Fetch headers	100/call	100/call	100/call

Feature	Consumer (gmail.com)	Google Apps for your domain	Google Apps for biz/edu/gov
URL Fetch header size	8 KB/call	8 KB/call	8 KB/call
URL Fetch POST size	10 MB/call	10 MB/call	10 MB/call
URL Fetch URL length	2 KB/call	2 KB/call	2 KB/call

Triggers

Being able to run processes at predetermined times is a great feature of Apps Script.

VBA provides Application.Ontime, and you can also use the Windows scheduler for this purpose, but in both cases, your PC needs to be on, and in the case of Application.Ontime it needs to be running Office.

Apps Script Triggers have some limitations (mentioned in Tables 4-1 and 4-2), but they also are less specifically controllable than their VBA equivalents.

The Trigger dialog is shown in Figure 4-1.

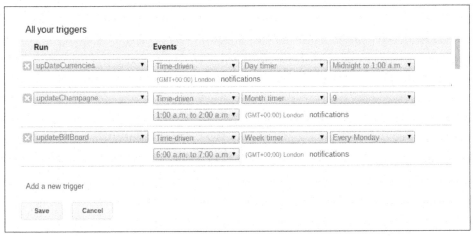

Figure 4-1. The Apps Script Trigger dialog

The times at which these scripts will actually run are only loosely estimated, and as a result they are not predictable enough to be able to use for scheduling dependent processes.

Triggers also run at a reduced priority, so processes that run interactively within the six-minute execution limit may take longer when executed as a trigger.

It's important to remember that the six-minute execution window is *elapsed* time (not *compute* time).

Rate Limits

Rate limits control how rapidly certain operations can be executed, and in some ways are the trickiest to work around. The documentation for exactly which operations are subject to rate limits is hard to track down, but the consequence of hitting one is this error message:

```
Service invoked too many times in a short time
```

Throttling

Throttling is slowing down, or adapting a script's demand profile to operate within the resource's servicing capability.

Sleeping

The simple way to throttle scripts that might be affected by rate limits is simply to sleep after each operation. The examples in the Apps Script documentation are usually based on this approach, and usually show something like this (this example is getting all the messages associated with a Gmail thread):

```js
threads.forEach (function (d) {
    var messages = d.getMessages();
    doSomeThingWith(messages);
    Utilities.sleep(1000);
});
```

Although this is certainly the simplest approach, it could generate a lot of unnecessary waiting. Assuming that the rate limit on getting messages from Gmail is 1 per second, the actual time to return the getMessages and the doSomethingWith functions is going to be affected by the resources available at that time, in addition to their actual execution times.

One second may even already have elapsed by the time the sleep request is executed, meaning that the request might not even be needed. On the other hand, the response could be almost instantaneous, in which case not sleeping between calls risks script failure.

In reality, although it's not documented, the rate doesn't appear to be checked every second, but instead averaged over a longer period of time. This means that short bursts of activity can get away with more rapid operations than the rate limit implies, so there is all the more reason to avoid unnecessary idle time.

Sleeping counts toward the six-minute execution time, so a script that reads 200 threads from Gmail (a typical day's worth of mail) would spend more than half of its available execution time doing nothing.

Exponential Backoff

Exponential backoff attempts the operation, and if it fails, waits a bit, then tries again until it succeeds or gives up. This means that waiting happens only if an error is signaled. The amount of wait time on each attempt:

- Increases exponentially to allow the clearing of any blockage related to infrastructure overload or rate limit averages measured over a period of time.

- Includes a random factor to avoid multiple processes getting locked into the same retry schedule.

Because this is such a common requirement in almost every script that accesses rate-limited resources, it's a good idea to use a common library function for backoff.

It is used like this, with the function to repeatedly attempt being passed anonymously:

```
threads.forEach (function (d) {
    var messages = Utils.rateLimitExpBackoff(function() {
      return d.getMessages();
    };
    doSomeThingWith(messages);
});
```

Exponential backoff waits only if there was a rate limited error signaled, then tries again. This minimizes both idle time and unpredictable failures.

Code for exponential backoff

The error messages can be internationalized for the kinds of errors that should be retried. An example of a quota error is given in Russian in the following snippet. To add your own language, just expand the list with the equivalent Apps Script error message.

These are the errors that have shown to be recoverable on retry:

```
utils.tryAgain = "force backoff anyway";
utils.backoffErrors = [
  "Exception: Service invoked too many times",
  "Exception: Rate Limit Exceeded",
  "Exception: Quota Error: User Rate Limit Exceeded",
  "Service error: Spreadsheets",
  "Exception: User rate limit exceeded",
  "Exception: Internal error. Please try again.",
  "Exception: Cannot execute AddColumn because another task",
  "Service invoked too many times in a short time:",
  "Exception: Internal error.",
  "Exception: Превышен лимит: DriveApp.",
  utils.tryAgain
];
```

```
utils.rateLimitExpBackoff = function ( callBack, sleepFor ,
             maxAttempts, attempts , optLogAttempts , optChecker) {

  // can handle multiple error conditions by expanding this list
  function errorQualifies (errorText) {

    return utils.backoffErrors.some(function(e){
         return  errorText.toString().slice(0,e.length) == e  ;
      });
  }

  // sleep start default is 1 second
  sleepFor = Math.abs(sleepFor || 1000);

  // attempt number
  attempts = Math.abs(attempts || 1);

  // maximum tries before giving up
  maxAttempts = Math.abs(maxAttempts || 5);

  // make sure that the checker is really a function
  if (optChecker && typeof(callBack) !== "function") {
    throw ("if you specify a checker it must be a function");
  }

  // check properly constructed
  if (!callBack || typeof(callBack) !== "function") {
    throw ("you need to specify a function for rateLimitBackoff to execute");
  }

  // try to execute it
  else {

    try {

      var r = callBack();

      // this is to find content based errors that might benefit from a retry
      return optChecker ? optChecker(r) : r;
    }
    catch(err) {

      if(optLogAttempts)Logger.log("backoff " + attempts + ":" +err);
      // failed due to rate limiting?
      if (errorQualifies(err)) {

        //give up?
        if (attempts > maxAttempts) {
          throw (err + " (tried backing off " + (attempts-1) + " times");
        }
        else {
```

```
      // wait for some amount of time based on how many times we've tried
      // plus a small random bit to avoid races
      Utilities.sleep (Math.pow(2,attempts)*sleepFor) +
        (Math.round(Math.random() * sleepFor));

      // try again
      return rateLimitExpBackoff ( callBack, sleepFor ,
        maxAttempts , attempts+1,optLogAttempts);
    }
  }
  else {
    // some other error
    throw (err);
  }
    }
  }
 }
};
```

Splitting

Some limitations apply to scripts rather than to a particular user. This means that by splitting the script in two, you can double the quota.

Libraries

The Properties service is a secure store, rather like the Windows registry. Chapter 5 is dedicated entirely to this service. Scripts each come with their own Properties service. You can mitigate the limitation on overall property size by using the Properties service of a library and passing it to the main script(s) that use it:

JS
```
// library
function getPropertyService() {
  return PropertiesService.getScriptProperties();
}

// main script
function work () {
  var libraryProps = Library.getPropertyService();
  var mainProps = PropertiesService.getScriptProperties();
}
```

Batching

Some scripts can be split so that they work on separate sections of the data being processed. Applying the preceding technique, you can use the Properties service of a common library to exchange progress information between scripts so one can pick up where the other left off.

Parallel Running

Similar to batching, a shared library Properties service can be used to orchestrate cooperating scripts, except in this case the scripts run simultaneously. Often you'll use the trigger service to schedule simultaneous processes, occasionally using MapReduce-type techniques[1] to consolidate and pass data from one phase to another.

Offloading

Apps Script runs on Google Servers, but HTML service tasks can be orchestrated by Apps Script to run on the local client. Generally speaking, compute-intensive tasks will run more quickly when executed locally. The HTML service can asynchronously fire off Apps Script tasks to deal with processes that require interaction with Apps Script services.

Carefully offloading work to the HTML service is a way of completely circumventing many of the server-side limitations, but it's a complex topic that's beyond the VBA/Apps Script scope.

Avoiding Service Calls

Many of the rate-limited services are related to fetching data externally or from Google services or APIs. In some cases, either the data will not have changed from one call to the next, or it is not critical that the very latest data be used. Apps Script provides a Cache service for rapid access to data, enabling the complete avoidance of quota-consuming service calls.

Cache Service

The Cache service allows data to be stored in key/value pairs. It is subject to limitations in data size, but is not constrained by rate limits. As a result, it's often good practice to write service or external data that might be needed by this script to cache, and to first check the cache to see if it's already there. Not only does this avoid service call quota consumption, but also cache is generally faster to access than Apps Script services or external data and doesn't need to be reprocessed.

---

1 MapReduce is a technique where a workload is split into chunks (Map) and processed in parallel. The outputs from each thread are combined (Reduce) into a consolidated result. Examples of Apps Script implementations of MapReduce are covered on the Desktop Liberation site (*http://www.mcpher.com*).

Cache scopes

The selection of which cache to use depends on the data visibility required. The cache visibility is limited to the current script, but within that there are three different caches, described in Table 4-3.

Table 4-3. Cache scopes

Cache	Brief description
DocumentCache	Applies to the current document
ScriptCache	Applies to all users of this script
UserCache	Applies to the current user of this script

A cache is obtained from the Cache service like so:

```js
var cache = CacheService.getScriptCache();
```

Data can be written like this:

```js
var data = getDataFromSomeService();
cache.put("mykey", data);
```

A future call to this same script would first check to see if the data was already in the cache, and if not, make the service call, thus avoiding the service call if there had been one made recently:

```js
var data = cache.get("mykey");
if (!data) {
  data = getDataFromSomeService();
  cache.put("mykey", data);
}
```

Cache data expiry

It's important that cache data expires in order to provoke a refresh from time to time. By default, the cache will expire after 10 minutes, but you can change that like so (where the third parameter is the expiry time in seconds):[2]

```js
cache.put("mykey", data, 1200);
```

Sharing cache

Caches are scoped to a particular script, but there may be occasions when multiple scripts would want to benefit from each other's cached results. You cannot share

---

2 It is not guaranteed that the cache will last that long, as actual cache lifetime can be affected by resource availability in the Google infrastructure.

caches directly, but you can make them accessible through a shared library, using the same technique we used earlier for sharing the Properties services:

```js
// Library
function getCacheService() {
  return CacheService.getScriptCache();
}

// main script
var cache = Library.getCacheService();
var data = cache.get("mykey");
if (!data) {
  data = getDataFromSomeService();
  cache.put("mykey", data);
}
```

CHAPTER 5

The Properties Service

The first few chapters covered the Apps Script language, and how VBA concepts and structures could be translated into their JavaScript equivalents.

VBA becomes useful when the shared libraries that allow access to the Office object model are referenced. In the same way, Apps Script uses Google Apps services to provide access to the object models associated with the apps it can extend. This book will concentrate on those that have Office equivalents, but will also touch on the Google versions of a few additional capabilities that VBA obtains by using other shared libraries. We'll also take a brief look at some services that VBA does not have, but that we need to use Apps Script effectively.

APIs Versus Built-In Services

There are many Google APIs, and only a few of them have been instrumented as built-in services for Apps Script. Many of the services we'll look at here can be accessed from other languages through language-specific APIs, or as JSON REST APIs to be accessed by any language.

Under the hood, these built-in services use these APIs to process translated requests from Apps Script. It is perfectly possible to access them directly from Apps Script through their JSON APIs (if they exist), and in fact in some cases not all of the underlying APIs' capabilities have been exposed in the Apps Script implementation, so there may be some occasions when this is required. The built-in services provide a convenient and well-integrated way of accessing these services, taking care of authentication and other complications behind the scenes.

The scripts family of services, though, are specific to Apps Script and can't generally be accessed through any other API. One such service is the Properties service, which provides a convenient place to store persistent data.

Getting Started with Properties Service

The best way to get started with this service is by example, so this chapter will look at a couple of script services you'll need to become familiar with, starting with the Properties service and its equivalent in VBA.

Uses and Types of Property Stores

Using the Properties service, you can store (and retrieve) persistent data in a property store. Data is stored as a key/value pair:

JS `{"aKey":"some data"}`

in one of three distinct script stores:

DocumentProperties
> Accessible by all users of a document where the script has been published as an add-on

ScriptProperties
> Accessible by all users of a script

UserProperties
> Accessible by the current user of a script

Each script has each of these stores, and which store you select depends on who should be able to access the data stored there. Note that a library has its own stores, which allow properties to be shared between library users but remain hidden from the scripts that use them.

Selecting a Property Store

You select a property store via the `PropertiesService` class, as shown in Table 5-1.

Table 5-1. Selecting a property store

Store	Property store
DocumentProperties	`var prop = PropertiesService.getDocumentProperties();`
ScriptProperties	`var prop = PropertiesService.getScriptProperties();`
UserProperties[a]	`var prop = PropertiesService.getUserProperties();`

[a] When Apps Script first started, UserProperties were accessible by a specific user, and not tied to a particular script. Nowadays, each script has its own UserProperties class that can be accessed only from within that script by a particular user.

The Registry Versus the Property Store

VBA normally uses the Windows registry to store persistent parameters, or more ambitious developers might use custom XML parts in an Office document. Parameters—or *properties* in Google terms—could be keys (e.g., software license keys), application preferences, or some other data that needs to persist across sessions or be embedded in a document.

The problem with the registry approach (and browser cookies too) is that it is specific to a particular machine, while custom XML parts are specific to a particular document. The Apps Script Properties service is in the cloud, and therefore not tied to any particular machine, environment, or operating system.

In VBA there are a few ways to interact with the registry:

- Creating a Windows script shell object and invoking its registry access methods
- Using the Registry API declared as an external function (fairly complicated and subject to version and architecture mismatches)
- Using the VBA `Interaction` namespace

Normally, these kinds of properties would be specific to the current user (`HKEY_CURRENT_USER`), which is all that the `Interaction` namespace allows access to. Typically, the `Interaction` namespace is good enough, so that's what we'll use for this demonstration.

Table 5-2 shows the `VBA.Interaction` registry methods and Apps Script equivalents.

Table 5-2. VBA.Interaction registry methods and Apps Script equivalents

VBA	Apps Script	Notes
`DeleteSetting ( app Name, section, key)`	`prop.deleteProperty(key)`	First set prop to the required store.
`GetSetting ( app Name, section, key)`	`prop.getProperty(key)`	
`SaveSetting ( app Name, section, key , value)`	`prop.setProperty(key,value)`	
`GetAllSettings ( app Name, section)`	`prop.getProperties()`	
Not available	`prop.deleteAllProperties()`	
Not available	`prop.setProperties( properties,delete Others)`	The second argument, if true, first deletes all other properties in the store.
Not available	`prop.getKeys()`	Gets all known keys in the store.

There are a few differences to note here, outlined in Table 5-3.

Table 5-3. VBA versus Apps Script registry interactions

VBA	Apps Script
If you are using the `Interaction` namespace, the "property store" is the `HKEY_CURRENT_USER` branch of the registry.	Choose the property store (`DocumentProperties`, `User Properties`, `ScriptProperties`) as described earlier.
`appName` is used as an argument to each of the VBA methods.	`appName` is implied, as each script has its own set of stores.
`section` is used as an argument to each method to further segregate groups of parameters within the app.	This does not exist in Apps Script, but complex JSON objects can be written as a property value, which can allow multiple sections.

Comparisons

You can achieve similar results using the properties store and the registry.

Writing to the registry

The `VBA.Interaction` namespace provides access to registry access methods. Figure 5-1 shows entries written by the `SaveSetting` method:

```VB
SaveSetting "gogas", "starwars", "yoda", "frank oz"
SaveSetting "gogas", "starwars", "leia", "carrie fisher"
```

Figure 5-1. Registry entries created by SaveSetting

Writing to the property store

The `appName` (in this case, `gogas`) is not needed here, because the properties store already belongs to the script. We use `JSON.stringify` to turn the object into a string first:

```JS
var prop = PropertiesService.getScriptProperties();
prop.setProperty("starwars", JSON.stringify({
    "yoda":"frank oz",
    "leia":"carrie fisher"
}));
```

which looks like Figure 5-2 in the properties store.

Property	Value
starwars	{yoda=frank oz, leia=carrie fisher}

Figure 5-2. Stringified property store entry

Note that this is not exactly the same as the VBA version, as I don't have the `section` parameter. In this case, I've written the whole `starwars` section as a single property.

Adding a single property is a little more complex:

```
var result = JSON.parse(prop.getProperty("starwars")) || {};
result.leia = "carrie fisher";
prop.setProperty ("starwars",JSON.stringify(result));
```

To emulate the VBA `section` so that these can be stored as individual properties, we need a key naming strategy. For example:

```
prop.setProperty("starwars_yoda", "frank oz");
prop.setProperty("starwars_leia", "carrie fisher");
```

which looks like Figure 5-3.

Property	Value
starwars_leia	carrie fisher
starwars_yoda	frank oz

Figure 5-3. Individual property store entries

Reading the registry

Reading by key is straightforward:

```
Debug.Print GetSetting("gogas", "starwars", "yoda")
Debug.Print GetSetting("gogas", "starwars", "leia")
```

and results in:

```
frank oz
carrie fisher
```

Reading all values of a particular section is a little trickier—the data is returned as a two-dimensional string, and VBA has fairly clumsy syntax for that:

```
result = GetAllSettings("gogas", "starwars")
For i = LBound(result, 1) To UBound(result, 1)
  Debug.Print result(i, 0), result(i, 1)
Next i
```

Here's the result:

```vb
yoda          frank oz
leia          carrie fisher
```

Reading the property store

In principle, reading by key is straightforward, but in this example we have to account for the additional section level.

If stored as a single object, this returns the entire section:

```js
Logger.log(prop.getProperty("starwars"));
```

```
{"yoda":"frank oz","leia":"carrie fisher"}
```

Here's how individual keys can be recovered:

```js
var result = JSON.parse(prop.getProperty("starwars"));
Logger.log(result.yoda);
Logger.log(result.leia);
```

```
frank oz
carrie fisher
```

Assuming the items have been stored against individual keys, as in VBA:

```js
Logger.log(prop.getProperty("starwars_yoda"));
Logger.log(prop.getProperty("starwars_leia"));
```

```
frank oz
carrie fisher
```

The properties store also has a method to get all properties:

```js
Logger.log(prop.getProperties());
```

```
{
  starwars_leia=carrie fisher,
  starwars_yoda=frank oz,
  starwars={"yoda":"frank oz","leia":"carrie fisher"}
}
```

Deleting from the registry

Remove a single entry by key in VBA as follows:

```vb
DeleteSetting "gogas", "starwars", "yoda"
```

Deleting from the properties store

Remove a single entry by key like so:

```js
prop.deleteProperty ("starwars_leia");
```

If using the approach of one key per section, you can remove the entire section like this:

```js
prop.deleteProperty ("starwars");
```

Deleting a single property is a little more complex, though:

```js
var result = JSON.parse(prop.getProperty("starwars"));
delete result.leia;
prop.setProperty ('starwars',JSON.stringify(result));
```

CHAPTER 6

The Spreadsheet Service

Google Sheets is the equivalent of Microsoft Excel, and the Spreadsheet service is the interface into its object model. Spreadsheets are the most likely to be extended, for one thing because you can create custom functions that can be accessed directly as formulas from the Excel or Google spreadsheet, using VBA and Apps Script respectively.

Sheet scripts are also the most likely to be (almost certainly in Excel) container-bound, as custom scripts cannot be accessed as a custom formula. In some ways this is a pity, because it continues the tradition of code sprawl and duplication.

Only a subset of the methods available in the Spreadsheet service will be covered here to illustrate the contrast with VBA. The full reference material is available on the Google Developers site, details of which you'll find in Appendix A.

Custom Formulas

Accessing scripts as formulas from a sheet is a long tradition in Excel. The idea is that you can write a script that accepts arguments passed from a formula in a spreadsheet cell, do some processing that you couldn't otherwise do using standard sheet formulas, and return the result to be displayed in the cell.

I'm not a big fan of these kinds of formulas, partly because they introduce a dependency that you can satisfy only by copying code to new sheets, but also because they can be resource-hungry.

Custom sheet formulas generally perform poorly, but we'll cover various techniques to mitigate that—in particular, using array formulas, which are much more usable and understandable than their Excel equivalent.

The main part of this chapter, though, will compare Apps Script spreadsheet tasks to their VBA equivalents, without too much emphasis on how the scripts will be consumed.

Container-Bound Versus Standalone Scripts

Most of the example code in this chapter will be transferable between both container-bound and standalone scripts, but I will create two fairly distinct types of examples in this chapter—namely, functions that:

- Operate on the current spreadsheet
- Access data in spreadsheets

Getting Started with the Spreadsheet Service

For these examples, we'll be working from a container-bound script (i.e., one that is bound to a spreadsheet). Create a new sheet and enter the script editor via the Tools menu.

A Note About Authorization

A script needs authorization to use Google services. A reference to a Google service in a script might prompt a request for scope authorization when you run it. These examples will ask for access to your sheets the first time you run the script, as shown in Figure 6-1.

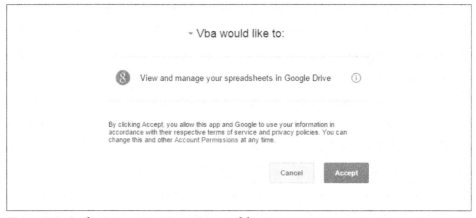

Figure 6-1. Authorizing access to your spreadsheets

Opening the Active Sheet

Table 6-1 compares how to return the sheet object currently active in the spreadsheet in VBA and Apps Script.

Table 6-1. Opening the active sheet

VBA	Apps Script
`Dim sheet As Worksheet` `Set sheet = ActiveSheet`	`var sheet = SpreadsheetApp.getActiveSheet();`

The Range Class

The `Range` class is accessible from the sheet object. The *range* is the most common interface into the data on a sheet, and represents the kind of contiguous cell references used in spreadsheet cells, such as a2:c4. This kind of cell reference is known as *A1 notation*.

Creating a Range

There are a number of ways to create a range in both VBA and Apps Script, the simplest of which is to use A1 notation, as shown in Table 6-2.[1]

Table 6-2. Creating a range using A1 notation

VBA	Apps Script

`Dim range As Range`
`Set range = ActiveSheet.Range("a2:b4")`
`Debug.Print range.Rows.Count`
`Debug.Print range.Columns.Count`
`Debug.Print range.Address`
 	
`results`
`  3`
`  2`
`$A$2:$B$4`
	`var sheet = SpreadsheetApp.getActiveSheet();`
	`var range = sheet.getRange("a2:b4");`
	`Logger.log(range.getNumRows());`
	`Logger.log(range.getNumColumns());`
	`Logger.log(range.getA1Notation());`
	
	`results`
	`  3.0`
	`  2.0`
	`A2:B4`

---

[1] In VBA, it's perfectly OK for the variable name of a class instance to be the same as the class name (`Dim range As Range`), although many tend to avoid it because it confuses the IDE spellchecker, preferring to use variable names like `rng` or `myRange`. Because Apps Script is case-sensitive, `range` is not the same as `Range`, so there's no need to worry. These examples tend to use the Apps Script variable naming paradigm.

All of these are equivalent ways of creating a range from an instance of the Sheet class:

```js
var range = sheet.getRange("a2:b4");
var range = sheet.getRange (2,1,3,2);  // (startRow,startColumn,numRows,numCols)
var range = sheet.getRange(1,1).offset(1,0,3,2); //(offsetRow,Column,rows,Cols)
```

Returning the Data Range

I've seen many different complicated pieces of VBA code for returning the range of cells used in a sheet. The simplest solution is using the UsedRange property, as shown in Table 6-3; assuming there are no trailing blank rows in the sheet, it will work fine.

Table 6-3. Returning the range of cells used in a sheet

VBA	Apps Script
`Set range = ActiveSheet.UsedRange` `Debug.Print range.Address`	`var sheet = SpreadsheetApp.getActiveSheet()` `var range = sheet.getDataRange();` `Logger.log(range.getA1Notation());`
results `$A$2:$B$26`	results `A2:B26`

Getting the Values of a Range

There are multiple ways of processing the values of a range, and VBA quite often iterates through and processes the cells of a range one at a time. A better way is to read all the values into an array at once, process them, and write the results all in one go. This applies to both VBA and Apps Script, except that in Apps Script the performance is greatly reduced (more so than VBA) when the cells in the range are processed one at a time.

I'll show both methods here, but I recommend you generally read the sheet values in one go to improve performance. As a matter of fact, the Apps Script range object lacks the syntax to be able to elegantly iterate in the way that VBA can.

The test data looks like Figure 6-2.

VBA

VBA has good structure for iterating through a range one cell at a time:

```vb
Dim row As Range, cell As Range
For Each row In range.Rows
  For Each cell In row.Cells
    Debug.Print cell.Value
  Next cell
Next row
```

carrier	name
MY	Maya Airways
OZ	Asiana Airlines
OS	Austrian Airlines
UP	Bahamas Air
HG	Niki
HW	North Wright Air
ET	Ethiopian Airlines
MD	Air Madagascar
MK	Air Mauritius
9U	Air Moldova
KL	KLM Airlines
LX	Swiss
UA	United Airlines
US	US Airways
EQ	TAME
EJ	New England Airlines
DB	Brit Air
WP	Island Air
PM	Tropic Air
RE	Aer Arann Express
PX	Air Niugini
SU	Aeroflot Russian Airlines
CZ	China Southern Airlines
LH	Lufthansa Airlines
RJ	Royal Jordanian

Figure 6-2. Getting the values of a range

But you can achieve better performance by reading the data all in one go, even though it's a little clumsy to access the results:

```
Dim data As Variant, rowIndex As Long, cellIndex As Long
data = range.Value
For rowIndex = LBound(data, 1) To UBound(data, 1)
    For cellIndex = LBound(data, 2) To UBound(data, 2)
        Debug.Print data(rowIndex, cellIndex)
    Next cellIndex
Next rowIndex
```

Apps Script

Apps Script lacks the structure to elegantly iterate through a range one cell at a time (and you should avoid doing so in any case):

```
for (var row = 0, nRows = range.getNumRows(), nCols = range.getNumColumns() ;
        row < nRows ; row++) {
    for (var cell = 0; cell < nCols ; cell ++) {
      Logger.log(range.offset(row, cell, 1, 1).getValue());
    }
}
```

Reading all the values at once provides a much more intuitive structure, and is faster:

```js
range.getValues().forEach(function(row) {
    row.forEach(function(cell) {
        Logger.log(cell);
    });
});
```

Writing Values to a Range

It's normal practice (assuming all the data is required) to read in all the values in one go, process them, and write them out again all at once too. In Apps Script, it's both easier and more efficient. Let's add a new column to the sheet that is a concatenation of the first and second columns, using this useful pattern in Apps Script to read, process, and write sheet data:

```js
function readWrite () {

    var sheet = SpreadsheetApp.getActiveSheet();

    // all the data in the sheet
    var range = sheet.getDataRange();

    // get the data
    var data = range.getValues();

    range.offset(0,0,range.getNumRows(), range.getNumColumns() +1)
        .setValues( data.map (function (d) {
            d.push (d[0] + '-' + d[1]);
            return d;
        }));

}
```

Walkthrough

Create a two-dimensional array, one item per row with one cell per column in each row:

```js
var data = range.getValues();
```

setValues writes data against a range that must be the same dimensions as the data array being written.

Because we're adding a column, we can use .offset() to increase the size of the input range by one column:

```js
range.offset(0,0,range.getNumRows(), range.getNumColumns() +1);
```

We can use `Array.map` to modify the structure of each row by adding a new column element to it, which is the concatenation of columns 1 and 2 (index 0 and 1):

```js
data.map (function (d) {
    d.push (d[0] + '-' + d[1]);
    return d;
});
```

Returning Selected Data

The previous example created a new third column by concatenating the first two columns and then rewrote out the entire sheet. Strictly speaking, it needed to write only the third column, as the first two remain unchanged. This better solution is just a very small change to the pattern:

```js
range.offset(0, range.getNumColumns(),range.getNumRows(), 1)
    .setValues( data.map (function (d) {
        return [d[0] + '-' + d[1]];
    }));
```

Walkthrough

Instead of starting at column 0, the single column range starts after the existing final column, and has a width of 1.

Here's the original pattern:

```js
range.offset(0,0,range.getNumRows(), range.getNumColumns() +1);
```

And the new one:

```js
range.offset(0, range.getNumColumns(),range.getNumRows(), 1);
```

Each data row array now contains only the new column, rather than the old columns plus the new. Note that because `setValues()` deals in two-dimensional arrays, the row still needs to be an array of columns, even though there is only one column in that array.

Here is the original pattern:

```js
.setValues( data.map (function (d) {
    d.push (d[0] + '-' + d[1]);
    return d;
}));
```

And the new one:

```js
.setValues( data.map (function (d) {
    return [d[0] + '-' + d[1]];
}));
```

Reading and Writing for Partial Ranges

So far we've applied reading and writing to the entire sheet using the `getDataRange()` method. The previously used pattern also works exactly as written on a section of the sheet, if we simply change the range. For example:

```js
var range = sheet.getRange("B2:E30");
```

Reading Attributes from a Range

Apps Script uses exactly the same method to get the attributes of cells as it does for data, whereas VBA is a little more convoluted.

VBA get background colors

This snippet gets and logs the background RGB colors of a column of a sheet:

```vb
Dim sheet As Worksheet, range As Range, a As Variant, cell As Range, i As Long
Set sheet = ActiveSheet

' get one column
Set range = sheet.UsedRange.Offset(0, 0).Resize(, 1)

' set the array to the right size
ReDim a(1 To range.Rows.Count)

' loop though the cells
i = LBound(a)
For Each cell In range.Cells
    a(i) = cell.Interior.Color
    i = i + 1
Next cell

For i = LBound(a) To UBound(a)
    Debug.Print Hex(a(i))
Next i
```

Apps Script get background colors

The only difference between getting values and the background colors is the range method used (`getBackgrounds` rather than `getValues`):

```js
var sheet = SpreadsheetApp.getActiveSheet();
var range = sheet.getDataRange();

// fill the array with the colors
var a = range.offset(0,0,range.getNumRows(),1).getBackgrounds().map(function(d) {
  return d[0];
});

//loop though the cells
```

```
a.forEach (function(d) {
  Logger.log (d);
});
```

Writing Attributes to a Range

Writing attributes follows exactly the same pattern as writing values, except setValues is replaced by the method for the property being written (e.g., setBackgrounds).

Apps Script and VBA get/set equivalence

The properties shown in Table 6-4 can be read or written (get/set) using this standard approach.

Table 6-4. Apps Script and VBA range methods and properties

Apps Script range method (set/get)	VBA equivalent
BackGrounds	Range.Interior.Color
DataValidations	Range.Validation.Add
FontColors	Range.Font.Color
FontFamilies	Range.Font.Name
FontLines	Range.Font.Strikethrough Range.Font.Underline
FontSizes	Range.Font.Size
FontStyles	Range.Font.Italic
FontWeights	Range.Font.Bold
Formulas	Range.Formula
FormulasR1C1	Range.ForumulaR1C1
HorizontalAlignments	Range.HorizontalAlignment
Notes	Cell.AddComment Cell.Comment.text
NumberFormats	Range.NumberFormat
Values	Range.Value
VerticalAlignments	Range.VerticalAlignment
Wraps	Range.WrapText

Inserting and Deleting Rows and Columns

To insert or delete columns and/or rows in a sheet in VBA, you first construct a range that looks like the one you want to insert. For example, insert two rows at the beginning of a sheet:

```
sheet.range("a1:b2").Insert
```

This kind of operation results in something like Figure 6-3 if there are more columns in the sheet than the number referenced by the insertion range.

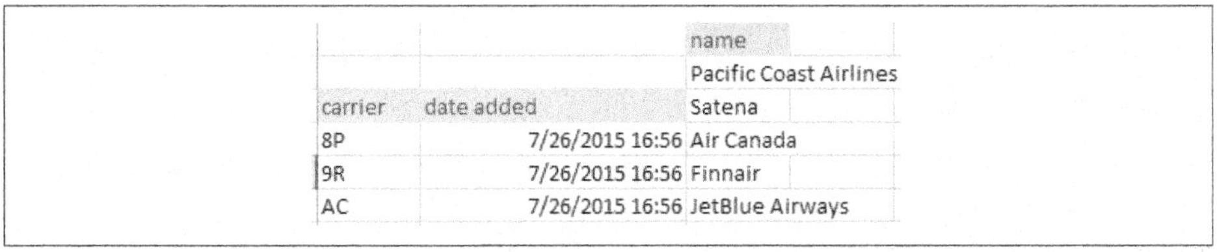

			name	
			Pacific Coast Airlines	
carrier	date added		Satena	
8P		7/26/2015 16:56	Air Canada	
9R		7/26/2015 16:56	Finnair	
AC		7/26/2015 16:56	JetBlue Airways	

Figure 6-3. Inserting rows into a sheet

Excel decides on the intended shift pattern based on the shape of the range given, but you can—and should—explicitly specify a shift parameter (xlShiftToRight or xlShiftToLeft) to ensure the intended result. For example, this code:

```
sheet.range("a1:b2").Insert xlShiftToRight
```

gives the result shown in Figure 6-4.

		carrier	date adde	name
		8P	########	Pacific Coast Airlines
9R	7/26/2015 16:56	Satena		
AC	7/26/2015 16:56	Air Canada		

Figure 6-4. Shifting the added rows to the right

In this example, Excel would decide to insert two columns, starting at column 2, and shift the others to the right:

```
sheet.range("b1:c26").Insert
```

Typically, though, insert operations involving whole rows and columns would use the Rows and Columns range property and the EntireRow and EntireColumn property:

```
Rows("1:2").EntireRow.Insert
Columns("B:C").EntireColumn.Insert
```

The Apps Script Spreadsheet service has specific methods for inserting rows and columns, which operate on the sheet object. It does not have the partial insertion and shift capabilities that VBA has:

```js
sheet.insertRows(1,2);
sheet.insertColumns(2,2);
```

Table 6-5 gives the VBA and Apps Script equivalents for inserting and deleting columns or rows.

Table 6-5. VBA and Apps Script insertion and deletion operations

Objective	VBA	Apps Script
Insert two rows at the top	Rows("1:2") .EntireRow .Insert	sheet.insertRows(1,2);
Insert two columns starting at column 2	Columns("B:C") .EntireColumn .Insert	sheet.insertColumns(1,2);
Insert three rows after row 5	Rows("5:7") .Offset(1) .EntireRow .Insert	sheet.insertRowsAfter(5,3);
Insert one column after column 1	Columns(1) .Offset(,1) .EntireColumn .Insert	sheet.insertColumnsAfter(1,1);
Delete four rows at the top	Rows("1:4") .EntireRow .Delete	sheet.deleteRows(1,4);
Delete three columns starting at column 2	Columns("B:D") .EntireColumn .Delete	sheet.deleteColumns(2,3);
Delete three rows after row 5	Rows("5:7") .Offset(1) .EntireRow .Delete	sheet.deleteRowsAfter(5,3);
Delete one column after column 1	Columns(1) .Offset(,1) .EntireColumn .Delete	sheet.deleteColumnsAfter(1,1);

Opening Other Sheets

So far the examples have focused on using the `ActiveSheet` property to specify which sheet to work on. This section will cover opening and iterating through other sheets in the spreadsheet.

Iterating All Sheets

In VBA, worksheets and charts (and a few other items) are kept together in a collection called Sheets. Collections named WorkSheets and Charts are also available for iteration through the specific sheet types.

This code will print the name and index (position of each sheet in the workbook):

```
VB  For Each sheet In Worksheets
        Debug.Print sheet.Name, sheet.Index
    Next sheet
```

Apps Script includes the same concept, but also has an Id—a value unique to a sheet—that remains constant even if the position or the name is changed:

```
JS  SpreadsheetApp.getActiveSpreadsheet().getSheets().forEach(function(sheet) {
        Logger.log(sheet.getName() + ":" + sheet.getIndex() + ":"
            + sheet.getSheetId() );
    });
```

Getting a Sheet by Name or Index

Because Sheets is a collection, we can access it either by index or by name like this in VBA:

```
VB  Debug.Print Sheets("lookup").Name
    Debug.Print Sheets(1).Name
```

In Apps Script, Sheets is an array, so to access its first element, use index [0]:

```
JS  var ss = SpreadsheetApp.getActiveSpreadsheet();
    Logger.log(ss.getSheetByName("lookup").getName());
    Logger.log(ss.getSheets()[0].getName());
```

Opening Other Workbooks

So far, the Apps Script examples have been operating on the current workbook, using a container-bound script. However, in both Apps Script and VBA you can open additional workbooks from within a script.

In the case of Apps Script, workbooks can be opened from a standalone script. These kinds of scripts mean you can write applications that orchestrate inputs from a whole range of sources.

Creating a Standalone Script

In Drive, create a new file of type Script. This will bring up the familiar IDE, but this time as a standalone project rather than one contained in a sheet.

Accessing Multiple Workbooks

In this example, there are two workbooks:

carrierLookup
:   A workbook with a list of carrier codes against airline names

updateCarrierLookup
:   A second workbook in the same format

The objective is to update carrierLookup with any airlines it doesn't yet know. carrierLookup has its data in a sheet called lookup (Figure 6-5).

carrier	name	Date added
LH	Lufthansa Airlines	7/26/2015 16:38
RJ	Royal Jordanian	7/26/2015 16:38
9R	Satena	7/26/2015 16:38
ZB	Monarch Airways	7/26/2015 16:38
CH	Bemidji Airlines	7/26/2015 16:38
BS	British International Helicopters	7/26/2015 16:38
NA	North American Airlines	7/26/2015 16:38
HW	North Wright Air	7/26/2015 16:38
WY	Oman Air	7/26/2015 16:38
8P	Pacific Coast Airlines	7/26/2015 16:38
AY	Finnair	7/26/2015 16:38
ON	Our Airline	7/26/2015 16:38
AC	Air Canada	7/26/2015 16:38
TX	Air Caraibes	7/26/2015 16:38
EN	Air Dolomiti	7/26/2015 16:38

Figure 6-5. The lookup sheet

updateCarrierlookup has its data in a sheet called updateLookup, shown in Figure 6-6.

carrier	name
AC	Air Canada
TX	Air Caraibes
EN	Air Dolomiti
7F	FirstAir
F9	Frontier Airlines
6E	Indigo
QF	Qantas Airways
B6	JetBlue Airways
XJ	Mesaba Airlines

Figure 6-6. The updateLookup sheet

Working with Multiple Workbooks

To work with multiple workbooks in VBA, you use the `Workbooks.open` method and the filename of the workbook you want to open.

Here are a few functions for opening an additional workbook and selecting a sheet in the current and new workbook:

```VB
'   /**
'    * update the carrier workbook with the contents of the update
'    * @param {string} carrierId the name of the update lookup book
'    * @param {string} carrierSheet the name of the carrier sheet
'    * @param {string} updateId the filename of the update lookup book
'    * @param {string} updateSheet the name of the update sheet
'    */
Private Sub update(carrierId As String, carrierSheet As String, _
    updateId As String, updateSheet As String)

    Dim us As Worksheet, cs As Worksheet

    ' open the carrier sheet
    Set cs = Workbooks(carrierId).Sheets(carrierSheet)

'    // open the update sheet
    Set us = openWorkbook(updateId).Worksheets(updateSheet)

'    // do the work

    doTheWorkBasic cs, us
    us.Parent.Close

End Sub
'   /**
'    * open a book given its filename
'    * @param {string} updateId the filename
'    * @return {Workbook} the workbook
'    */
Private Function openWorkbook(path As String) As Workbook
    Set openWorkbook = Workbooks.Open(path)
```

```vba
      End Function
```

It can be called like this:

```vba
VB  Public Sub doUpdate()
        update "carrierLookup.xlsx", _
            "lookup", _
            "c:/users/bruce/Documents/Excel/updateCarrierLookup.xlsx", _
            "updateLookup"
    End Sub
```

There is no module concept in Apps Script, but you can approximate VBA module behavior by using a namespace. It's not required, but it is good practice. (Namespaces were covered in Chapter 2.)

Apps Script uses `SpreadsheetApp.openById()` along with the unique id for the workbook. There are a couple of other ways of opening a workbook, but here is the ID method:

```javascript
JS  var Carrier = (function (carrier) {

      /**
       * open a book given its id
       * @param {string} id the id
       * @return {Spreadsheet} the workbook
       */
      carrier.openWorkbook = function (id) {
        return SpreadsheetApp.openById(id);
      };


      /**
       * update the carrier workbook with the contents of the update
       * @param {string} carrierId the id of the carrier lookup book
       * @param {string} updateId the id of the update lookup book
       * @param {string} carrierSheet the name of the carrier sheet
       * @param {string} updateSheet the name of the update sheet
       */
      carrier.update = function (carrierId, carrierSheet , updateId , updateSheet) {

        // open the carrier lookupsheet
        var cs = carrier.openWorkbook ( carrierId).getSheetByName(carrierSheet);

        // open the update sheet
        var us = carrier.openWorkbook ( updateId).getSheetByName(updateSheet);


        // do the work
        //.. to do

      };
```

```
      return carrier;

  })(Carrier || {});
```

It can be called like this:

JS
```
function doUpdate() {

  Carrier.update (
    '1f4zuZZv2NiLuYSGB5j4ENFc6wEWOmaEdCoHNuv-gHXo',
    'lookup',
    '1DsntVvvA1bIMKVSnvt1f7UKjV5Qz0DtSs8NiI7Kf21g',
    'updateLookup'
  );
}
```

Updating Sheets

One way to traverse data in VBA is by looking at the data directly in the worksheet cells. It's not the most efficient method, but probably the most common, as VBA has a good structure to enable this kind of access.

This VBA snippet implements the doTheWork function of matching and updating. Any items not in carrierLookup that are found in updateCarrierLookup will be added:

VB
```
' /**
'  * update the carrier sheet with items from the updatecarriersheet
'  * @param {worksheet} cs the carrier sheet
'  * @param {worksheet} us the update sheet
'  */
Private Sub doTheWorkBasic(cs As Worksheet, us As Worksheet)

    ' // in this example, the approach is simply to use column numbers
    Dim row As Range, cell As Range, _
        usDataRange As Range, csDataRange As Range, _
        usCarrierCol As Long, usNameCol As Long, _
        csCarrierCol As Long, csNameCol As Long, _
        csDateCol As Long


    Set usDataRange = us.UsedRange
    Set csDataRange = cs.UsedRange

    ' // get the data columns position
    usNameCol = getColPos(usDataRange, "name")
    usCarrierCol = getColPos(usDataRange, "carrier")
    csNameCol = getColPos(csDataRange, "name")
    csCarrierCol = getColPos(csDataRange, "carrier")
    csDateCol = getColPos(csDataRange, "date added")

    ' // check we found them all
```

```vba
    If (usNameCol = 0 Or usCarrierCol = 0 Or csNameCol = 0 Or _
      csCarrierCol = 0 Or csDateCol = 0) Then Exit Sub

    ' pass through the update worksheet
    Set usDataRange = usDataRange.Resize(usDataRange.Rows.Count - 1).Offset(1)
    Set csDataRange = csDataRange.Resize(csDataRange.Rows.Count - 1).Offset(1)

    For Each row In usDataRange.Rows
        Set cell = csDataRange.Resize(, 1).Offset(csCarrierCol - 1) _
          .Find(row.Cells(, usCarrierCol).Value)

        ' // add it
        If (cell Is Nothing) Then
            Set cell = csDataRange.Resize(1).Offset(csDataRange.Rows.Count)
            cell(1, csDateCol).Value = VBA.Now
            cell(1, csCarrierCol).Value = row.Cells(1, usCarrierCol).Value
            cell(1, csNameCol).Value = row.Cells(1, usNameCol).Value
            Set csDataRange = csDataRange.Resize(csDataRange.Rows.Count + 1)
        End If

    Next row

End Sub
'   /**
'    * get the column position of a piece of text
'    * @param {Range} theRange the range
'    * @param {string} text the string to match
'    */
Private Function getColPos(theRange As Range, text As String) As Long
    Dim cell As Range

    If (theRange.Rows.Count > 0) Then
        For Each cell In theRange.Rows(1).Cells
            If (VBA.LCase(cell.Value) = VBA.LCase(text)) Then
                getColPos = cell.Column - theRange.Column + 1
                Exit Function
            End If
        Next cell
    End If

    MsgBox ("could not find column heading " & text & " in " & _
      theRange.Worksheet.Name)
    getColPos = 0
End Function
```

Figure 6-7 shows the updated sheet, with some new airlines added at the end.

There is a problem with replicating this in Apps Script:

- It's generally discouraged to work with ranges one step at a time, as it's clumsy and not very efficient.

- There is no `Find` method for an Apps Script range. This may seem like an odd omission, but actually it ties in with the first point. Using `Find` encourages the cell-by-cell approach.

carrier	name	Date added
LH	Lufthansa Airlines	7/26/15 16:56
RJ	Royal Jordanian	7/26/15 16:56
9R	Satena	7/26/15 16:56
ZB	Monarch Airways	7/26/15 16:56
CH	Bemidji Airlines	7/26/15 16:56
BS	British International Helico	7/26/15 16:56
NA	North American Airlines	7/26/15 16:56
HW	North Wright Air	7/26/15 16:56
WY	Oman Air	7/26/15 16:56
8P	Pacific Coast Airlines	7/26/15 16:56
AY	Finnair	7/26/15 16:56
ON	Our Airline	7/26/15 16:56
AC	Air Canada	7/26/15 16:56
TX	Air Caraibes	7/26/15 16:56
EN	Air Dolomiti	7/26/15 16:56
7F	FirstAir	7/27/15 14:09
F9	Frontier Airlines	7/27/15 14:09
6E	Indigo	7/27/15 14:09
QF	Qantas Airways	7/27/15 14:09
B6	JetBlue Airways	7/27/15 14:09
XJ	Mesaba Airlines	7/27/15 14:09

Figure 6-7. The updated spreadsheet

Although most of this could be replicated in Apps Script, the `Find` portion would need to be implemented another way. In this case, it would be better to simply redo the solution in a more Apps Script–like manner.

While you could use tables and structured references in VBA and then use the table implementation in the VBA library, this very simple and efficient approach instead makes use of the JavaScript array methods for filtering and mapping and is a very reusable pattern for solving these kind of problems:

```
/**
 * update the carrier workbook with the contents of the update
 * @param {Sheet} cs the carrier sheet
 * @param {Sheet} us the update sheet
 */
carrier.doTheWorkBasic = function ( cs , us) {

  // get the data from both sheets
  var usData = us.getDataRange().getValues();
  var csData = cs.getDataRange().getValues();

  // get the headers, and clean the data
```

```
        var usHead = usData.shift();
        var csHead = csData.shift();

        // make headerobs so we know where the various columns are
        var usHeaderOb = makeHeaderOb (usHead);
        var csHeaderOb = makeHeaderOb (csHead);

        // find not already in the cs list and add to end, then map to same format
        var changes = usData.filter (function(d) {
          return  !csData.some(function(e) {
            return e[csHeaderOb.carrier].toString().toLowerCase() ===
              d[usHeaderOb.carrier].toString().toLowerCase();
          });
        })
        .map(function(d) {
            var row = [];
            row [csHeaderOb.carrier] = d[usHeaderOb.carrier];
            row [csHeaderOb.name] = d[usHeaderOb.name];
            row [csHeaderOb['date added']] = new Date ();
            return row;
        });

        // write that out
        if (changes.length) {
          cs.getRange(csData.length+2, 1 , changes.length ,
            changes[0].length).setValues(changes);
        }

        // this creates a mapping of column name to number
        function makeHeaderOb (head) {
          var idx = 0;
          return head.reduce(function(p,c) {
            p[c.toString().toLowerCase()] = idx++;
            return p;
          },{});
        }

    };
```

Showing Messages

MsgBox is normally used to display messages and get input in VBA. The Apps Script equivalent is accessed via the Browser service in the spreadsheet context, although you can also use HtmlService dialog boxes (which will be covered later).

Toast

Probably the most popular way to display quick informative messages is by using the toast method of the SpreadsheetApp. A toast is a small pop-up box that appears for a short time (customizable) in the bottom right of the spreadsheet. It's very simple to use.

This example is a general function to open and read the data in a sheet and report on its dimensions:

```js
function toastIt (sheetName) {

    var ss = SpreadsheetApp.getActiveSpreadsheet();

    // get the data
    var data = ss.getSheetByName(sheetName).getDataRange().getValues();

    // show results
    ss.toast(data.length + ' rows & ' + (data.length ? data[0].length : 0) +
        ' columns', 'Sheet ' + sheetName );

    return data;
}
```

It's invoked like this, and generates the toast shown in Figure 6-8:

```js
function tryToast () {
    toastIt ('lookup');
}
```

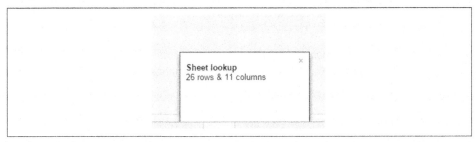

Figure 6-8. Generating a toast

Showing Messages with Buttons

VBA and Apps Script are very similar in how request dialogs are generated and displayed. Let's cover a couple of examples using VBA's `MsgBox` and Apps Script's `Browser.msgBox`.

Dialog with a simple OK button

The `MsgBox` in VBA can show a dialog with a default OK button as follows (which results in Figure 6-9):

```vb
MsgBox ("If at first you don't succeed, try, try again. Then quit." & _
    "There's no point in being a damn fool about it")
```

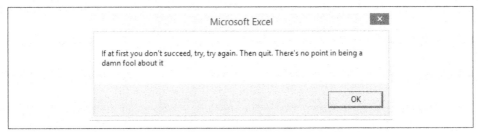

Figure 6-9. A dialog with a simple OK button created with VBA's MsgBox

Here is the equivalent in Apps Script using `Browser.msgBox` (with the result shown in Figure 6-10):

```
Browser.msgBox("If at first you don't succeed, try, try again. " +
    "Then quit. There's no point in being a damn fool about it");
```

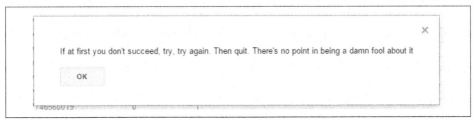

Figure 6-10. A dialog with a simple OK button created with Apps Script's Browser.msgBox

In these examples, the Browser service is being used for illustration. You can achieve fancier user interaction through the Spreadsheet UI, and even more complex interaction through the HTML service. Both are covered in Chapter 10.

Dialog with a title and buttons

In VBA you can create a dialog with a title and OK and Cancel buttons, as shown in Figure 6-11, like so:

```
If (MsgBox("I meant what I said and I said what I meant.", _
    vbOKCancel, "Doctor Seuss") = vbOK) Then
        ' do something
    End If
```

Figure 6-11. A VBA dialog with a title and OK and Cancel buttons

Here's the equivalent in Apps Script, with the result shown in Figure 6-12:

```
if(Browser.msgBox( "Doctor Seuss" ,
    "I meant what I said and I said what I meant.",
        Browser.Buttons.OK_CANCEL) === 'ok') {
    // do something
}
```

Figure 6-12. An Apps Script dialog with a title and OK and Cancel buttons

Getting Input

The InputBox and Browser.inputBox are also very similar, although as usual, VBA has many more options.

Create a dialog with an input box in VBA like so (resulting in Figure 6-13):

```
walkersKilled = InputBox("How many walkers have you killed ?", _
    "Rick's question number 1")
```

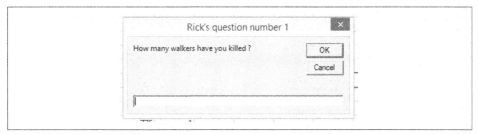

Figure 6-13. A VBA dialog with input box

And here is the Apps Script equivalent, resulting in Figure 6-14:

```
JS var walkersKilled = Browser.inputBox("Rick's question number 1",
        "How many walkers have you killed ?",Browser.Buttons.OK_CANCEL);
```

Figure 6-14. An Apps Script dialog with input box

Getting and Setting Properties

Being able to store persistent settings associated with a document lets you avoid asking the same question each time a workbook is opened.

Chapter 5 covered how and where settings can be stored in both Apps Script and VBA.

This example will use interactive data collected from a settings session to determine which files are needed for an application.

Document, User, or Script?

This example stores the data at the user level, meaning that the settings are specific to an individual user. In the example on opening multiple workbooks, the VBA version passed these parameters:

```
VB update "carrierLookup.xlsm", _
        "lookup", _
        "c:/users/bruce/Documents/Excel/updateCarrierLookup.xlsx", _
        "updateLookup"
```

And here's the Apps Script version:

```
JS Carrier.update (
        '1f4zuZZv2NiLuYSGB5j4ENFc6wEWOmaEdCoHNuv-gHXo',
        'lookup',
        '1DsntVvvA1bIMKVSnvt1f7UKjV5Qz0DtSs8NiI7Kf21g',
```

```
        'updateLookup'
    );
```

Building this into the application makes it very specific. If anything changes, the code will need to be modified. One option is to create a dialog to ask for these settings every time the application is run, but that would be tedious and error prone.

Another option is using the registry (VBA) and the Properties service (Apps Script). These properties will be stored against the application *carrier*.

Setting Properties in the Registry

VBA needs each property to be stored separately in the registry, but handled with a single custom type that looks like this:

```
VB  Public Type Properties
        carrierSheet As String
        carrierId As String
        updateSheet As String
        updateId As String
    End Type
```

It is probably not worth making a class out of this structure, but centralizing access to properties through getter and setter functions will avoid mistakes later:

```
VB  Const APP_NAME = "carriers"

    Public Function PropertiesSet(props As Properties) As Properties

        '// in the registry these are saved individually
        SaveSetting "gogas", APP_NAME, "carrierSheet", props.carrierSheet
        SaveSetting "gogas", APP_NAME, "carrierId", props.carrierId
        SaveSetting "gogas", APP_NAME, "updateSheet", props.updateSheet
        SaveSetting "gogas", APP_NAME, "updateId", props.updateId

        PropertiesSet = props

    End Function

    Public Function PropertiesGet() As Properties

        Dim props As Properties

        props.carrierSheet = GetSetting("gogas", APP_NAME, "carrierSheet")
        props.carrierId = GetSetting("gogas", APP_NAME, "carrierId")
        props.updateSheet = GetSetting("gogas", APP_NAME, "updateSheet")
        props.updateId = GetSetting("gogas", APP_NAME, "updateId")

        PropertiesGet = props

    End Function
```

The initial settings are applied thus:

```vb
Private Function setProperties()

    Dim props As Properties

    props.carrierId = "carrierLookup.xlsm"
    props.carrierSheet = "lookup"
    props.updateId = "c:/users/bruce/Documents/Excel/updateCarrierLookup.xlsx"
    props.updateSheet = "updateLookup"

    PropertiesSet props

End Function
```

Leading to the registry entry shown in Figure 6-15.

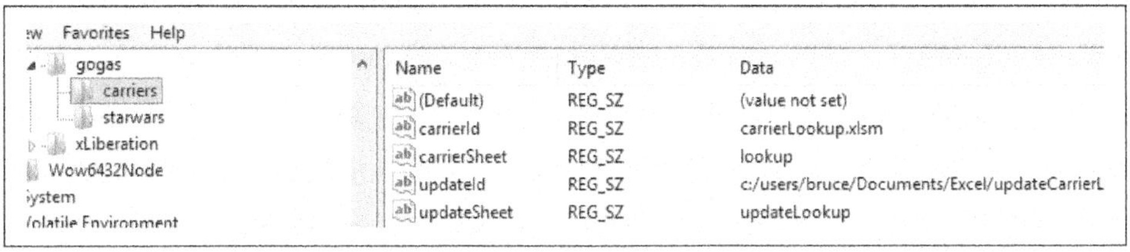

Name	Type	Data
(Default)	REG_SZ	(value not set)
carrierId	REG_SZ	carrierLookup.xlsm
carrierSheet	REG_SZ	lookup
updateId	REG_SZ	c:/users/bruce/Documents/Excel/updateCarrierL
updateSheet	REG_SZ	updateLookup

Figure 6-15. Storing application settings in the registry

Now that the persistent parameters for the application are stored in the registry, the update function can be simplified to expect the new Properties type:

```vb
' /**
'  * update the carrier workbook with the contents of the update
'  * @param {Properties} props the application properties
'  */
Private Sub update(props As Properties)

    Dim us As Worksheet, cs As Worksheet

    ' open the carrier sheet
    Set cs = Workbooks(props.carrierId).Sheets(props.carrierSheet)

    '   // open the update sheet
    Set us = openWorkbook(props.updateId).Worksheets(props.updateSheet)

    '   // do the work
    doTheWorkBasic cs, us

    us.Parent.Close

End Sub
```

You initiate the preceding like this:

```vb
Public Sub doUpdate()
    update PropertiesGet()
End Sub
```

Setting Properties Using the Properties Service

Implementing a similar approach using Apps Script's Properties service is straightforward.

It's generally a good idea to wrap up something like this in a function. That way, the names of the properties and the property store to use can be centralized rather than spread around any functions that might need them, just as in the VBA version.

As usual, this is implemented inside its own namespace, `Properties`:

```js
var Properties = (function (properties) {

    'use strict';

    var APP_NAME = 'carriers';
    /**
     * get the service to use
     * @return {PropertiesService}
     */
    properties.getService = function () {
        return PropertiesService.getUserProperties();
    };

    /**
     * get the properties for this app
     * @return {object|null} the properties
     */
    properties.get = function () {
      var prop = properties.getService().getProperty(APP_NAME);
      return prop ? JSON.parse(prop) : null;
    };

    /**
     * set the properties for this app
     * @param {object} props the properties for this app
     * @return {object} the properties
     */
    properties.set = function (props) {
      properties.getService().setProperty(APP_NAME, JSON.stringify(props));
      return props;
    };

    return properties;

})(Properties || {});
```

The properties are initially stored like this:

```vb
function setProperties() {
    Properties.set ( {
      carrier: {
        sheet:"lookup",
        id:"1f4zuZZv2NiLuYSGB5j4ENFc6wEWOmaEdCoHNuv-gHXo"
      },
      update: {
        sheet:"updateLookup",
        id:"1DsntVvvA1bIMKVSnvt1f7UKjV5Qz0DtSs8NiI7Kf21g"
      }
    })
  }
```

and retrieved like this:

```js
var props = Properties.get();
```

This also encourages the simplification of the `Carrier.update` function, which is now called like this:

```js
Carrier.update ( Properties.get() );
```

and simplified to this:

```js
/**
    * update the carrier workbook with the contents of the update
    * @param {object} props the properties
    */
   carrier.update = function (props) {

     // open the carrier lookupsheet
     var cs = carrier.openWorkbook ( props.carrier.id )
                  .getSheetByName( props.carrier.sheet );

     // open the update sheet
     var us = carrier.openWorkbook ( props.update.id)
                  .getSheetByName( props.update.sheet );

     // do the work
     carrier.doTheWorkBasic(cs, us);

   };
```

Changing Settings

Normally you change settings through a dialog of some kind. In VBA, it is likely to be a simple form, whereas in Apps Script, it's a little more complicated. Apps Script previously had a UI service that was a little like a VBA form. This was deprecated in 2014, however, and now the only way to create interactive dialogs is through the HTML service. This allows the creation of a very rich user interface, but it demands knowledge of CSS, HTML, and the Apps Script techniques to link server- and client-based JavaScript—all of which will be covered subsequently in dedicated chapters.

Custom Formulas

Custom formulas are intended to be invoked from a cell in a sheet. In Excel, they are known as *user-defined formulas* (UDFs). As with VBA, you must take care with what they do, as too much processing can slow down recalculation and sheet opening. Most custom formulas that simply manipulate sheet data are better done (and usually are) with regular worksheet functions, but these can quickly become syntactically complex and difficult to debug. For the sake of the examples in this section, let's assume that we are choosing to write custom formulas, regardless of whether there is an obvious alternative solution using worksheet functions.

Going back to the example data shown in Figure 6-16, our first function will capitalize the name parts where the carrier call sign matches the name. It's not really a proposition with much practical use, but it will illustrate a problem that is a potential candidate for a custom formula solution.

carrier	name
MY	Maya Airways
OZ	Asiana Airlines
OS	Austrian Airlines
UP	Bahamas Air
HG	Niki
HW	North Wright Air
ET	Ethiopian Airlines
MD	Air Madagascar
MK	Air Mauritius
9U	Air Moldova
KL	KLM Airlines
LX	Swiss
UA	United Airlines

Figure 6-16. Sample airline data

For example, United Airlines (UA) will stay as United Airlines, but Maya Airways (MY) will become Maya airways and Air Mauritius (MK) will become air Mauritius.

In each case, this formula will be entered in cell c2 and filled down:

VB `=capitalizeCallSign(A2,B2)`

Here's how our custom capitalization function looks in VBA:

VB
```
Function capitalizeCallSign(callSign As String, name As String) As String

    ' first split the name into components
    Dim nameComponents As Variant, result As String, com As String
```

```
    nameComponents = VBA.Split(name)

    Dim i As Long, pos As Long
    result = ""
    For i = LBound(nameComponents) To UBound(nameComponents)

        com = VBA.LCase(VBA.Left(nameComponents(i), 1))

        ' find the first letter of each name component in the call sign
        pos = VBA.InStr(1, VBA.LCase(callSign), com)

        ' add a separator
        If (i > 0) Then
            result = result & " "
        End If

        If (pos > 0) Then
            ' the starting letter is in the call sign - uppercase
            result = result & VBA.UCase(com)
        Else
            ' the starting letter is not in the call sign - lowercase
            result = result & VBA.LCase(com)
        End If

        ' the rest
        If (VBA.Len(nameComponents(i)) > 1) Then
            result = result & VBA.Mid(nameComponents(i), 2)
        End If
    Next i

    capitalizeCallSign = result
End Function
```

The result is shown in Figure 6-17.

Copy/Paste Port

Now let's do a copy/paste port of that custom formula to Apps Script, using the Apps Script VBA library.

Porting like this takes only a few moments, as only minor syntactical differences between the languages need to be dealt with:

```
function capitalizeCallSign(callSign, name ) {

    var nameComponents = VBA.Split(name);

    var result="";
    for (var i=0; i < nameComponents.length ;i++) {

        var com = VBA.LCase(VBA.Left(nameComponents[i], 1));
```

```
    //' find the first letter of each name component in the call sign
    var pos = VBA.InStr(1, VBA.LCase(callSign), com)

    //' add a separator
    if (i > 0) {
      result = result + " ";
    }


    if (pos > 0) {
      //' the starting letter is in the call sign - uppercase
      result = result + VBA.UCase(com);
    }
    else {
      //' the starting letter is not in the call sign - lowercase
      result = result + VBA.LCase(com);
    }

      //' the rest
    if (VBA.Len(nameComponents[i]) > 1) {
      result = result + VBA.Mid(nameComponents[i], 2)
    }
  }

  return result;
}
```

Native Port

Here's how I would have written this function from scratch in Apps Script:

```
JS  function nativeCapitalizeCallSign(callSign, name ) {

    return name.split(" ").map(function(d) {
      var com = d.slice(0,1).toLowerCase();
      return com[callSign.toLowerCase().indexOf(com) === -1 ?
        'toLowerCase' :
        'toUpperCase']() + d.slice(1);
    },[])
    .join(" ");
  }
```

It's more compact, but less immediately comprehensible.

Arguments to Custom Formulas

One big difference between Apps Script and VBA custom worksheet formulas is that
Apps Script range contents are always passed by value.

carrier	name	capitalized
MY	Maya Airways	Maya airways
OZ	Asiana Airlines	asiana airlines
OS	Austrian Airlines	austrian airlines
UP	Bahamas Air	bahamas air
HG	Niki	niki
HW	North Wright Air	north Wright air
ET	Ethiopian Airlines	Ethiopian airlines
MD	Air Madagascar	air Madagascar
MK	Air Mauritius	air Mauritius
9U	Air Moldova	air moldova
KL	KLM Airlines	KLM airlines
LX	Swiss	swiss
UA	United Airlines	United Airlines
US	US Airways	US airways
EQ	TAME	tAME
EJ	New England Airlines	new England airlines
DB	Brit Air	Brit air
WP	Island Air	island air
PM	Tropic Air	tropic air
RE	Aer Arann Express	aer arann Express
PX	Air Niugini	air niugini
SU	Aeroflot Russian Airline	aeroflot russian airlines
CZ	China Southern Airlines	China southern airlines
LH	Lufthansa Airlines	Lufthansa airlines
RJ	Royal Jordanian	Royal Jordanian

Figure 6-17. Result of applying the custom capitalization function in VBA

Consider these VBA custom functions:

```vb
Function theAddress(r As range) As String
    theAddress = r.Address
End Function
Function theValue(value As Variant) As Variant
    theValue = value
End Function
```

The range is passable to VBA:

```vb
=theAddress(c2) will give $C$2
```

but the value is also available by default:

```vb
=theValue(c2) will give Maya Airways
```

In Apps Script, the result will always be Maya Airways. You cannot pass a range from a worksheet to a custom formula.

Workaround

Let's say you have a function that gets the color of a given range and shows the color's value. To be able to access the color property, the function needs the range:

VB =getTheColor(A3) gives 781414

```
Function getTheColor(r As range) As Variant
    getTheColor = Hex(r.Interior.Color)
End Function
```

In Apps Script, A3 would always be passed as the value of A3, not its range. The address (and therefore the color attribute of that address) is never visible to the function.

As a workaround, the address could be passed as a string and converted to a range by the receiving function:

JS =getTheColor("A3");

```
function getTheColor(r) {
    return SpreadsheetApp.getActiveSheet().getRange(r).getBackground();
}
```

Performance

Executing Apps Script custom formulas can involve a round-trip to the server. As a result, the performance is poor compared to an equivalent Excel operation.

Timing functions

In order to simplify the process of timing functions, I'm using a helper function in this example. It's not important how it works for now (I include it in case you want to try it), but its purpose is to wrap a function in a timer, call the function with its passed arguments, and return the result plus the timing information:

JS
```
/**
 * takes a function and its arguments, runs it and times it
 * @param {func} the function
 * @param {...} the rest of the arguments
 * @return {object} the timing information and the function results
 */
function timeFunction () {

    var timedResult = {
      start: new Date().getTime(),
      finish: undefined,
      result: undefined,
      elapsed:undefined
    }
    // turn args into a proper array
    var args = Array.prototype.slice.call(arguments);
```

```
// the function name will be the first argument
var func = args.splice(0,1)[0];

// the rest are the arguments to fn - execute it
timedResult.result = func.apply(func, args);

// record finish time
timedResult.finish = new Date().getTime();
timedResult.elapsed = timedResult.finish - timedResult.start;

return timedResult;
}
```

Consider the Apps Script example from earlier, which capitalized the airline names based on whether their call signs matched some initials.

Instead of returning the result itself, this timer version of the function will return how long it took to calculate the result:

JS
```
function timeCallSign (callSign, name) {
    return timeFunction (nativeCapitalizeCallSign , callSign, name).elapsed;
}
```

It can be called from the worksheet like this:

VB `=timeCallSign(A2,B2)`

The results are surprising. I won't show them all, but the elapsed times are all 0–1 milliseconds (Figure 6-18).

Figure 6-18. Elapsed times for calculating the result of the custom capitalization function

The elapsed time between the earliest and latest calculation is over 1,500 milliseconds, yet the total time that functions are actually being executed is less than 25 milliseconds. This means that most of the elapsed time is not actually being spent executing functions. Figure 6-19 gives a visualization of what's happening (the dots are where the functions are being executed).

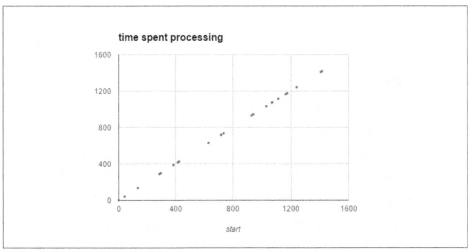

Figure 6-19. Graph of processing time for executing custom capitalization function

Improving performance with array formulas

In Excel, the explicit use of array formulas is not especially widespread. These formulas are fairly complex to figure out, difficult to debug, fiddly to enter, and fussy about the array dimensions. Nevertheless, they are a powerful feature when you're creating complex cell-based formulas. While this book is about VBA and Apps Script and not really focused on what you can do with worksheet formulas from the worksheet cells, the topic of custom formulas that provide array-based arguments and expect array-based answers certainly is in the scope of VBA and Apps Script, so this section will focus on that.

The majority of Excel built-in functions are not array-enabled, and I seldom come across custom functions written with arrays in mind in VBA.

In Apps Script, the array formula is much more commonly used, perhaps as a result of the relatively poor performance from which custom formulas suffer.

In both Apps Script and VBA, the normal way to implement the custom formula used in the timing experiment would be to enter the formula in one cell and fill down to copy to each cell in the result column.

Here is a version of that same formula, but modified to detect and return array results:

```
JS  function arrayCapitalizeCallSign(callSigns, names ) {

        // can handle either arrays or single arguments
        if ( !Array.isArray(callSigns) ) {
          return process (callSigns , names);
        }
```

```
    else {
      return callSigns.map (function (d,i) {
        return process (d[0], names[i][0]);
      })
    }


    // move out the processing to a function common arrays or single
    function process(callSign, name) {
      return name.split(" ").map(function(d) {
        var com = d.slice(0,1).toLowerCase();
        return com[callSign.toLowerCase().indexOf(com) === -1 ?
          'toLowerCase' : 'toUpperCase']() + d.slice(1);
      },[])
      .join(" ");
    }


  }
```

It can be called like this from the worksheet, without the need for any filling down:

VB `=arrayCapitalizeCallSign(A2:A,B2:B)`

The amazing result is that it runs in 6 milliseconds across all the data in one call, rather than the 1,500+ milliseconds it takes to call the function with each cell individually.

The lesson here is that if you do write Apps Script custom functions, always design them such that they can take array arguments and return array results if necessary.

Documentation and Autocomplete

A nice feature of VBA is that you get some level of autocomplete, in the sense that your custom function shows up in the list of known functions when a formula is in a cell. However, it doesn't prompt with the arguments or give any information on custom functions.

Using JSDOC, which was covered in Chapter 3, you can encourage custom functions to appear as autocomplete targets in sheet cells.

For example, adding the following JSDOC notation to the custom function pops up the autocomplete assistance shown in Figure 6-20 as you start to type the arguments for the function into the worksheet cell:

JS
```
/**
 * capitalize airline names where the first letter of a word is in a call sign;
 * @customfunction
 * @param {string} callSign the call sign
 * @param {string} name the airline name to be processed
 * @return {string} the airline name capitalized
 */
function capitalizeCallSign(callSign, name ) { ... }
```

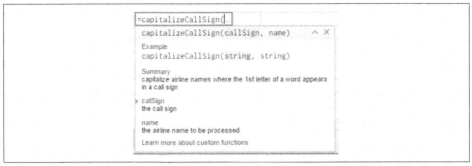

Figure 6-20. Adding autocomplete to our custom capitalization function

Adding Functions to Menus

I've always been confused about ribbons, menu bars, command bars, menus, submenus, shortcut menus, and toolbars in Excel. What are all these things, why do we need them all, and where exactly is the right place to add a link to my custom VBA function?

I did a quick count of just the command bars with VBA, and discovered there are 157 of them (apparently Excel 2016 has 159). If you want to try counting them yourself, here is the code:

```vb
Private Sub bars()
    Dim bar As CommandBar
    For Each bar In CommandBars
        Debug.Print bar.name
    Next bar
    Debug.Print CommandBars.Count
End Sub
```

Here is a simple way in VBA to add an item and subitem to execute a script:

```vb
Private Sub addToMenu()

    ' add the action item
    With CommandBars("Standard")
        If (testInCollection(.Controls, "Prettification")) Then
            .Controls("Prettification").Delete
        End If
        With .Controls.Add(msoControlPopup)
          .Caption = "Prettification"
          With .Controls.Add(msoControlButton)
              .Caption = "Code Box"
              .OnAction = "codePretty"
          End With
        End With
    End With
End Sub
```

```
End Sub
```

With Apps Script, there is only the custom menu, so it is fairly straightforward to both add and decide where to put script execution items. You can add the script execution item to the document menu by creating an onOpen trigger that will fire each time the document opens, like so (which results in Figure 6-21):

```js
function onOpen() {

    // set up a custom menu
    var ui =SpreadsheetApp.getUi();
    ui.createMenu('Prettification')
        .addItem('Code Box', 'codePretty')
        .addToUi();
}
```

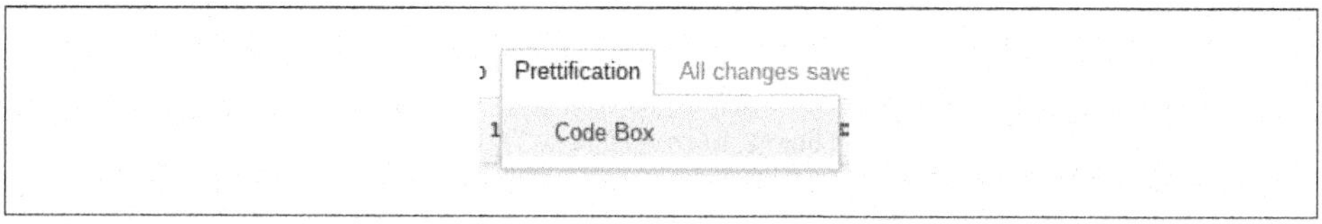

Figure 6-21. Adding a script execution item to the Apps Script custom menu

Tables

The Excel object model is extremely extensive, and the Sheets model doesn't come close in terms of richness. It does cover most important things, but one of the handy structures in Excel for which there is not a direct Sheets equivalent is the table. This is a contiguous range of cells that are considered together as a dynamic range (the dimensions of the table change as rows are added), and they contain various elements such as dynamic styling, totaling, sorting, and so on.

This section will look at a couple of ways to emulate the table structure with Apps Script.

Converting Values to an Object

It's very simple to convert a two-dimensional values array as retrieved from Sheets into an object array, using the column headers as the keys for each of the values in each row.

Consider this test:

```js
function testcvto() {

    // get the data from the range
    var range = SpreadsheetApp.getActiveSheet().getDataRange();
```

```
    // convert to an object and take a look at it
    Logger.log(JSON.stringify(VBA.convertValuesToObjects(range)));
}
```

You'll find the function VBA.convertValuesToObjects(range) in the Helpers section
of the VBA library:

JS
```
/**
 * get the data from a range and convert it into an array of key/value pairs
 * @param {Range} range a spreasheet range
 * @return {object[]} an array of objects, one element per row
 */
function convertValuesToObjects (range) {

  // get the data
  var data = range.getValues();
  // get the header row
  var headers = data.shift() ;

  // now create a dataOb
  return (data || []).map (function(row) {
    var cellIndex = 0;
    return row.reduce(function (p,c) {
      var key = headers[cellIndex++].toString();
      if (p.hasOwnProperty(key)) {
          throw 'duplicate header ' + key;
      }
      p[key] = c;
      return p;
    },{});
  });


}
```

Here's a snippet of the result from the test data sheet:

VB
```
[
    {
        "carrier": "MY",
        "name": "Maya Airways"
    },
    {
        "carrier": "OZ",
        "name": "Asiana Airlines"
    },
    {
        "carrier": "RJ",
        "name": "Royal Jordanian"
    }
]
```

This gives us only a small part of the functionality of tables and structured references,
but it is enough for certain application ports.

Emulating Tables in Apps Script

A table is recognizable in VBA through an object known as a `ListObject`. Each sheet has a collection of `ListObjects`, and creating a table is as simple as this:

```
Dim sheet As Worksheet
Set sheet = ActiveSheet
sheet.ListObjects.Add(xlSrcRange, sheet.UsedRange, , xlYes).name="airlineLookup"
```

This will convert the range of data in the active sheet to the result shown in Figure 6-22.

carrier	name
MY	Maya Airways
OZ	Asiana Airlines
OS	Austrian Airlines
UP	Bahamas Air
HG	Niki
HW	North Wright Air
ET	Ethiopian Airlines
MD	Air Madagascar
MK	Air Mauritius
9U	Air Moldova
KL	KLM Airlines
LX	Swiss
UA	United Airlines
US	US Airways
EQ	TAME
EJ	New England Airlines
DB	Brit Air
WP	Island Air
PM	Tropic Air
RE	Aer Arann Express
PX	Air Niugini
SU	Aeroflot Russian Airlines
CZ	China Southern Airlines
LH	Lufthansa Airlines
RJ	Royal Jordanian

Figure 6-22. Emulating a table in Apps Script

Using tables also gives you access to some fairly funky syntax for addressing a range and the data in a table (Microsoft calls this *structured references*). For example, this will give the range that references the name column of the table just created:

```
Debug.Print (sheet.range("airlineLookup[name]").Address)
result - $B$2:$B$26
```

ListObject

There is no such thing as a `ListObject` table in Sheets (there is a `DataTable` that can be used for creating charts, but that is an entirely different concept). However, it is pretty straightforward to emulate a `ListObject` using the `Collection` object previously created for the VBA library. In addition to the structured references that can be used in the spreadsheet itself, there are also built-in properties and methods for addressing the contents of the table, and it's these that the Apps Script implementation will mimic to approximate the `ListObject` in Sheets.

If you have written your VBA application to take advantage of the level of abstraction available from `ListObjects`, using this fill might save you a lot of conversion effort. Whether or not your VBA code uses tables today, this is quite a handy way to address data using column names (or numbers) rather than calculating ranges.

Creating a table reference

You create a table reference in VBA like so:

```
sheet.ListObjects.Add(xlSrcRange, sheet.UsedRange, , xlYes).name="airlineLookup"
Set listObject =  sheet.ListObjects.Item("airlinelookup")
```

And here's the equivalent using the Apps Script VBA library:

```
var listObject =  new VBA.ListObject (sheet.getDataRange() , 'airlineLookup');
```

Table ranges

Table 6-6 gives the range calculation equivalents from the VBA `ListObject` table and the Apps Script VBA library. They are pretty much identical.

Table 6-6. Calculating range using the VBA ListObject versus the Apps Script VBA library

Reference	VBA ListObject	Apps Script VBA library
Data part of the table	listObject.DataBodyRange	listObject.DataBodyRange;
Header part of the table	listObject.HeaderRowRange	listObject.HeaderRowRange;
The range of the header for column 1	listObject.ListColumns .Item(1).Range	listObject.ListColumns .Item(1).Range;
The range for the data part of the column called "name"	listObject.ListColumns .Item('name').DataBodyR ange	listObject.ListColumns .Item('name').DataBodyR ange;
The name of column 1	listObject.ListColumns .Item(1).Name	listObject.ListColumns .Item(1).Name;
The column number of the column with the header "carrier"	listObject.ListColumns .Item('carrier').Index	listObject.ListColumns .Item('carrier').Index;

Reference	VBA ListObject	Apps Script VBA library
The range for the data in row 10	listObject.ListRows .Item(10).Range	listObject.ListRows .Item(10).Range;

Getting data from a ListObject

So far we've looked at how to extract the range using structured references from a ListObject. Getting the data from that range is just a matter of using the range methods for the appropriate language.

Here's how to get range data in Apps Script:

```
JS   var data = listObject.ListRows.Item(10).Range.getValues();
```

And here's the VBA equivalent:

```
VB   data = listObject.ListRows.Item(10).Range.value
```

Clearly there is much more that can be done to develop this emulation, but the exposed Range object is enough to get started with most operations. The section "Other Resources" on page 417 specifies where to get this VBA library on GitHub.

ListObject JavaScript code

This code is part of the VBA library:

```
JS   /**
      * create a structured table from a range of data
      * @constructor ListObject
      * @param {Range} range the data range
      * @param {string} [name] the table name
      * @param {boolean} [hasHeaders=true] whether the table has headers
      * @return {ListObject} self
      */
      function ListObject (range , name , hasHeaders) {
        var self = this;
        hasHeaders_ = fixOptional (hasHeaders , true);

        // get the data from the range
        var range_ = range;
        var data_ = range_.getValues();
        // generate a unique name for the table if none given
        var name_ = name || 'table_'+new Date().getTime().toString(16);
        // get the header row
        var headers_ = hasHeaders_ ? data_.shift() : null;

        // get the header collection (using the VBA collection object)
        var numCols_ = range_.getNumColumns();
        self.ListColumns = new Collection();
        self.ListRows = new Collection();

        function reCalculate_ () {
```

```
      self.DataBodyRange =range_.offset(hasHeaders_ ?
        1 : 0, 0,  data_.length, numCols_) ;
      self.HeaderRowRange = hasHeaders_ ?
        range_.offset( 0, 0,  1, numCols_) : null ;

      for (var i=0; i < numCols_ ; i++) {
        self.ListColumns.Add ( {
          Index:i+1 ,
          Name:hasHeaders_ ? headers_[i] : 'Column'+(i+1).toFixed(0),
          Range:hasHeaders_ ? self.HeaderRowRange.offset(0,i,1,1) : null,
          DataBodyRange:self.DataBodyRange.offset(0,i,data_.length,1)
        }, hasHeaders_ ? headers_[i] : 'Column'+(i+1).toFixed(0) );
      }

      data_.forEach(function (d,i) {
        self.ListRows.Add ( {
          Index:i+1,
          Range:self.DataBodyRange.offset(i,0,1,numCols_)
        });
      });
    }
    reCalculate_();
    return self;
}
```

CHAPTER 7

The Document App

It's often said that we use only a small proportion of each Office application's capabilities, and only a minority of users are even aware of the more esoteric parts. The Word VBA implementation attempts to provide visibility to the majority of the extremely extensive object model, and much of its functionality is unused by many VBA developers. Docs targets only the most commonly used parts of Word and as a result, the Apps Script Document service has a much smaller footprint than VBA.

Word has a flat structure, and uses the range object as the principal interface for manipulation. A range is defined internally by its start and end character count address relative to the overall document. The Docs object model is a tree of elements that themselves can contain child elements, with these elements being the main interface. These different approaches mean that there is not as clear a mapping between Word and Docs platform components as there is with Excel and Sheets.

The VBA object model is somewhat muddled, because its flat nature includes some overlap and repetition, as illustrated by Figure 7-1.

The Apps Script model, shown in Figure 7-2, places the element as the main organizational driver.

This chapter will look at the Apps Script object model in some detail, and where possible, show the equivalent VBA approach.

Opening Documents

Just like the Spreadsheet app, a script can be container-bound (mainly for use with the current document), or standalone (for use with any document).

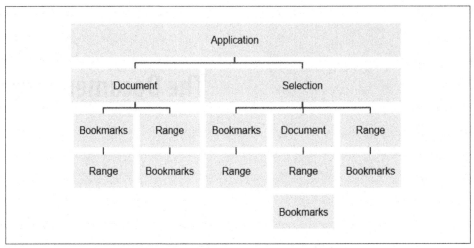

Figure 7-1. The VBA Word object model

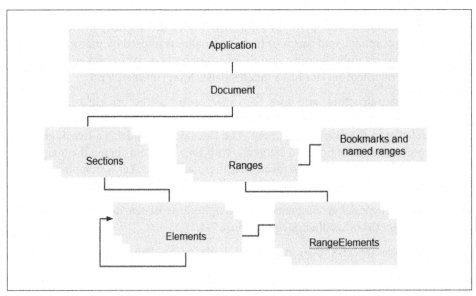

Figure 7-2. The Apps Script document object model

Docs can be opened by ID:

```
JS  var doc = DocumentApp.openById("12FszhEL-Sz-_AdTEWt7dRUUkZzqv_p4lyZFnpaL2uIo");
```

or by URL:

```
JS  var doc = DocumentApp.openByUrl(
            "https://docs.google.com/document/d " +
            "12FszhEL-Sz-_AdTEWt7dRUUkZzqv_p4lyZFnpaL2uIo/edit");
```

or by the currently open document:

```
JS  var doc = DocumentApp.getActiveDocument();
```

A VBA application is more likely to be container-bound, and applicable to the current document or other documents that are open under its control.

The active document is referenced like this:

```
VB  Dim doc As Document
    Set doc = ActiveDocument
```

and you can open other documents by referring to their path:

```
VB  Set doc = Documents.Open(
      "C:\Users\Bruce\Google Drive\books\going gas\report.docx", , True)
```

The Apps Script `getActiveDocument()` can take a significant time to execute, whereas the VBA `ActiveDocument` simply references an existing persistent structure.

Minimizing such calls in Apps Script is a good strategy.

Working with Elements

Apps Script includes the notion of an element, a little like the HTML DOM element, but more restrictive in structure. Elements are used to hold content, and are of one of the types listed in Table 7-1.

Table 7-1. Element types

Element type	Notes
BODY_SECTION	The container element for all of the document content aside from the header, footer, and footnotes.
DOCUMENT	The document root.
EQUATION	An element containing a mathematical equation.
EQUATION_FUNCTION	A mathematical equation.
EQUATION_FUNCTION_ARGUMENT	An argument to a mathematical equation.
EQUATION_SYMBOL	A symbol in a mathematical equation.
FOOTER_SECTION	The document section containing the footer elements.
FOOTNOTE	An element containing the elements that make up a footnote. At the time of writing, there is an issue with FOOTNOTE. See FOOTNOTE_SECTION.
FOOTNOTE_SECTION	An element that contains each footnote's contents. At the time of writing, there is an issue with the FOOTNOTE_SECTION; there is no method currently to retrieve it in Apps Script.
HEADER_SECTION	The document section that contains the header elements.
HORIZONTAL_RULE	An element that represents a horizontal line.
INLINE_DRAWING	An element containing a Google drawing.

Element type	Notes
INLINE_IMAGE	An element containing an image.
LIST_ITEM	An element containing a list item.
PAGE_BREAK	An element containing a page break.
PARAGRAPH	An element containing a paragraph.
TABLE	An element containing a table. These would contain table rows.
TABLE_CELL	An element containing a table cell. These would be children of a table row.
TABLE_ROW	An element containing table cell elements. These would be the children of table elements.
TABLE_OF_CONTENTS	This element is generally created automatically from the document content.
TEXT	The text content is contained within a text element. A typical parent of a text element would be a paragraph element.
UNSUPPORTED	These elements are inaccessible from Apps Script.

Traversing the Document

I'll use the document in Figure 7-3 for demonstration in the rest of this chapter.

We'll wrap the utilities created for these examples in their own namespace using this (by now) familiar pattern (these utilities can be found in the GitHub repository):

```
var DocUtils = (function myFunction(docUtils) {

    // code...
    return docUtils;

})(DocUtils || {});
```

This code traverses the document and prints a tree showing the relative relationship of each element:

```
function showElementsInDoc() {

    // get the current document
    var doc = DocumentApp.getActiveDocument();

    // display the tree recursively
    DocUtils.displayItems (doc.getBody());
    DocUtils.displayItems (doc.getHeader());
    DocUtils.displayItems (doc.getFooter());
}
```

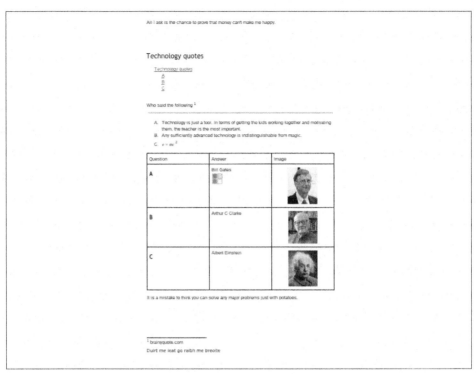

Figure 7-3. Sample document for chapter examples

This `displayItems` utility recursively examines elements and their children, indenting the result to illustrate its position in the document:

```js
docUtils.displayItems = function (elem, indent) {

  // default is no indentation
  indent = indent ||0;

  // get the element type
  var type = elem.getType();

  try {
    // not all elements can be cast as text
    var snip = elem.asText().getText().slice(0,10);
  }
  catch(err) {
    var snip = "..no extractable text..";
  }

  Logger.log (new Array(indent+1).join("-") + type + ":" + snip);

  // do any children and recurse
  if (elem.getNumChildren) {
```

```
    for (var i= 0; i < elem.getNumChildren() ; i++) {
      docUtils.displayItems ( elem.getChild(i) , indent +2);
    }
  }
}
};
```

Traversing in VBA

This VBA version shows collections of various types of elements accessible from a
Document object:

```
VB  Private Sub showElementsInDoc()
      Dim doc As Document, p As Paragraph
      ' get the active document
      Set doc = ActiveDocument

      ' display everything
      DocUtils.displayItems (doc.Paragraphs.item(1))

      ' the first table
      DocUtils.displayItems doc.Tables(1), doc.Tables(1)

      'the first image
      DocUtils.displayItems doc.InlineShapes(1), doc.InlineShapes(1)

      'the first list
      DocUtils.displayItems doc.Lists(1).ListParagraphs(1), _
        doc.Lists(1).ListParagraphs(doc.Lists(1).ListParagraphs.Count)

    End Sub
```

Generalizing the displayItems function in VBA is a little more challenging, because
it must deduce the container and child elements from their relative position, instead
of using recursive element hierarchy as Apps Script does:

```
VB  Private Sub showLog(elemRange As Range, Optional filter As Boolean = False, _
            Optional filterType As String)

      Dim elemType As String, containerType As String
      ' defaults
      elemType = getElemType(elemRange)
      If (filterType = elemType Or Not filter) Then
          containerType = "paragraph"
          If (elemRange.Information(wdWithInTable)) Then containerType = "table"
          Debug.Print containerType, elemType, _
              elemRange.start, elemRange.End, Left(elemRange.Text, 10)
      End If

    End Sub

    Private Function getElemType(elemRange As Range) As String
```

```
    getElemType = "text"
    If (elemRange.InlineShapes.Count > 0) Then getElemType = "inline_image"
End Function

Public Sub displayItems(startElem As Object, _
    Optional finishElem As Object, Optional filter As Boolean = False)

    ' using the start/finish range to determine whether it is in range
    Dim start As Long, finish As Long, doc As Document, filterType As String, _
        p As Paragraph

    Set doc = startElem.Parent

    ' paragraphs are passed as ranges by VBA
    If (TypeName(startElem) <> "Range") Then Set startElem = startElem.Range
    If (Not finishElem Is Nothing) Then
        If (TypeName(finishElem) <> "Range")
          Then Set finishElem = finishElem.Range End If

    start = startElem.start
    If (Not finishElem Is Nothing) Then finish = finishElem.End
    filterType = getElemType(startElem)

    For Each p In doc.Paragraphs
        ' if its inside, we can consider it as a child
        If (p.Range.start >= start And _
          (finish = 0 Or p.Range.End <= finish)) Then
            showLog p.Range, filter, filterType
        End If

    Next p

End Sub
```

Annotating the Document

Laying out the result of the displayItems function against the original document gives a clear picture of the Apps Script object model.

Figure 7-4 illustrates the body and heading.

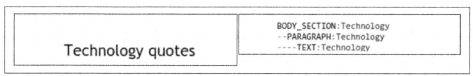

Figure 7-4. Document body and heading

Figure 7-5 shows the table of contents.

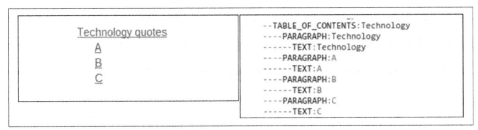

Figure 7-5. Document table of contents

Figure 7-6 demonstrates a paragraph in the document. A paragraph with no text element generates a blank line. The footnote is not properly accessible from Apps Script.

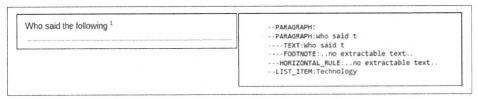

Figure 7-6. Document paragraph

Figure 7-7 depicts list items. The equation at item C generates a series of child elements.

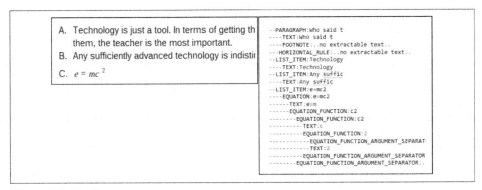

Figure 7-7. List items

As you can see in Figure 7-8, the table layout is very similar to <table>, <tr>, and <td> HTML tags.

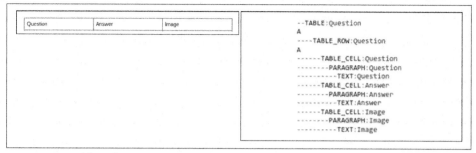

Figure 7-8. Table, table row, and table cell

Text, drawing, and image within cells of a table row are depicted in Figure 7-9.

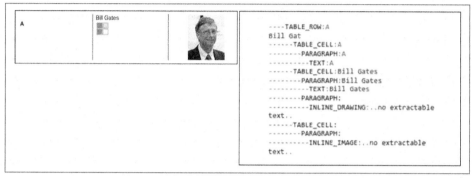

Figure 7-9. Inline images and drawings

The page header section, shown in Figure 7-10, can contain similar elements to the body section.

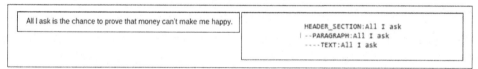

Figure 7-10. Header section

The page footer section, shown in Figure 7-11, can also contain similar elements to the body section.

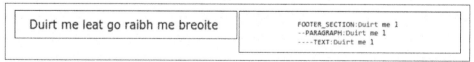

Figure 7-11. Footer section

Ranges

Ranges in Apps Script refer to some arbitrary selection in the document. A range can span multiple elements (and their children). An example of a range is the active selection, which can be obtained as follows:

```js
var selected = doc.getSelection();
```

VBA Range

A range in VBA is somewhat different, as it refers to a character position and length within a document. Every element, such as a paragraph, has an associated `Range` object.

The `Selection` object has a `Range` object, so the equivalent code in VBA is:

```vb
Dim selected as Range
    Set selected = Selection.Range
```

VBA Discontiguous Ranges

The Word UI allows the selection of multiple items into a single entity. The exposed object model doesn't have a suitable structure to support it, so it's likely that this was some kind of Word application refinement added at a later point. Examining the `Selection` object when multiple ranges are selected shows that it exposes information only on the final `Range` in the set.

The Apps Script model has a distinct advantage here, as the `Range` object is created from elements rather than positions, and multiple elements can be referenced by a single `Range`. In other words, you can't access a `Selection` containing multiple elements programmatically from VBA, but you can from Apps Script.

RangeElements

In Apps Script, a range is represented by an array of `RangeElements`. Using the `displayItems` function from the previous section (which shows a snippet of an element's contents), we can examine the active selection as follows:

```js
function showActiveSelection() {
    var doc = DocumentApp.getActiveDocument();
    DocUtils.showRange (doc.getSelection());
}
```

The showRange Utility

Here we use the `showRange` function to extract the `RangeElements` members of a `Selection` and then display the contents of the referenced `Elements` using the `displayItems` function:

```js
/**
 * given a range, extract the contents and show the element
 * @param {Range} selected the range
 */
docUtils.showRange = function (selected) {
  selected.getRangeElements().forEach(function(d) {
    docUtils.displayItems (d.getElement());
  });
};
```

The elements in the active selection are shown in Table 7-2.

Table 7-2. Elements in the active selection

Selection

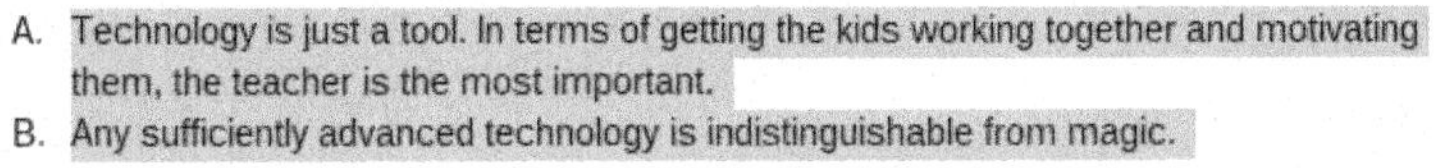

  A. Technology is just a tool. In terms of getting the kids working together and motivating them, the teacher is the most important.
  B. Any sufficiently advanced technology is indistinguishable from magic.

Range contents for this text

```
LIST_ITEM:Technology
--TEXT:Technology
LIST_ITEM:Any suffic
--TEXT:Any suffic
```

Partial RangeElements

Ranges may include partial elements. Consider the selection in Figure 7-12, which contains partial elements.

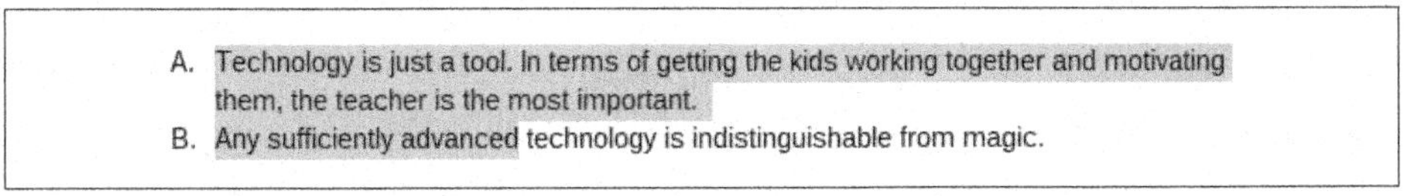

  A. Technology is just a tool. In terms of getting the kids working together and motivating them, the teacher is the most important.
  B. Any sufficiently advanced technology is indistinguishable from magic.

Figure 7-12. Selection containing partial elements

A small change to the `showActiveRange` utility function will signal that this is only a partial element, and where the text in scope begins and ends:

```js
/**
 * given a range, extract the contents and show the element
 * @param {Range} selected the range
 */
```

```
docUtils.showRange = function (selected) {
  selected.getRangeElements().forEach(function(d) {
    docUtils.displayItems (d.getElement(),0,d.isPartial(),
        d.getStartOffset(), d.getEndOffsetInclusive());
  });
};
```

A small change to the displayItems function will show the partial text of any elements not fully included in the selected range.

JS
```
/**
 * display elements and their children
 * @param {Element} elem the element
 * @param {number} [indent=0] number of characters to indent
 * @param {boolean} [partial=false] element is only partial
 * @param {number} [start] start of partial element
 * @param {number} [finish] finish of partial element
 */
docUtils.displayItems = function(elem, indent,partial,start,finish) {

    // default is no indentation
    indent = indent ||0;

    // get the element type
    var type = elem.getType();

    try {
      // not all elements can be cast as text
      var snip = elem.asText().getText().slice (
          partial ? start: 0, partial ? finish + 1 : 10);
    }
    catch(err) {
      var snip = "..no extractable text..";
    }

    Logger.log (new Array(indent+1).join("-") +
      type + ":" + snip + (partial ? '(partial)' : ''));

    // do any children and recurse
    if (elem.getNumChildren) {
      for (var i= 0; i < elem.getNumChildren() ; i++) {
        docUtils.displayItems ( elem.getChild(i) , indent +2);
      }
    }
};
```

Table 7-3 shows the results of selecting various partial elements.

Table 7-3. Result of selecting partial elements

Selection

> A. Technology is just a tool. In terms of getting the kids working together and motivating
> them, the teacher is the most important.
> B. Any sufficiently advanced technology is indistinguishable from magic.

Range contents for this text

```
LIST_ITEM:Technology
--TEXT:Technology
TEXT:Any sufficiently advanced(partial)
```

Selection

> Who said the following [1]
>
> _____
>
> A. Technology is just a tool. In terms of getting the kids working together and motivating
> them, the teacher is the most important.

Range contents for this text

```
TEXT:the following (partial)
FOOTNOTE:..no extractable text..
HORIZONTAL_RULE:..no extractable text..
TEXT:Tech(partial)
```

Note how a `RangeElement` containing a partial `TEXT` element excludes its parent element (`LIST_ITEM` and `PARAGRAPH` in the preceding examples) from the range. VBA does not have the concept of `RangeElements`, since a range in VBA is a simple start/finish structure:

RangeBuilder

You can create a range from a series of elements using the `RangeBuilder` class. This example will select each image in the document, make a range, and set it as the active selection:

```js
function showActiveSelection() {
    var doc = DocumentApp.getActiveDocument();
    showRange (doc.getSelection());
}

/**
 * finds all the images in a document and makes a range of them
 * @return {Range} the range with all the images
 */
function getAllTheImages (doc) {
```

```
    // gets all the images and builds a range
    return doc.getBody().getImages()
      .reduce(function(p,c) {
        return p.addElement (c);
      }, doc.newRange())
      .build();
  }
```

Using `showActiveSelection` to verify gives the following:

```
INLINE_IMAGE:..no extractable text..
INLINE_IMAGE:..no extractable text..
INLINE_IMAGE:..no extractable text..
```

VBA range collections

You cannot build a range consisting of disconnected elements, as with the Apps Script `RangeBuilder`. As a result, VBA developers use a variety of strategies such as arrays or collections to group multiple ranges.

Using an ordinary VBA collection means that the same functions for iterating over range-specific collections such as paragraphs can be used for collections of ranges, as in the following, where the `selected` argument can be a collection of paragraphs or simply an ordinary collection that happens to be full of ranges:

```
[VB]  Public Sub showRange(selected As Object)
          Dim item As Object

          ' this will show details of every item in a range or element collection
          For Each item In selected
              If (TypeName(item) = "Range") Then
                  showLog item
              Else
                  showLog item.Range
              End If
          Next item

      End Sub
```

Building partial element ranges

Creating a range with partial elements works similarly to displaying them. To illustrate, the following example creates a partial range everywhere the word *technology* is mentioned.

Finding text

The `body.findText` method is needed for this example. `findText` needs a search pattern (a regex, although `find` has only a partial regular expression support implementation), and returns a `RangeElement` describing where the match is in the document.

---

findText needs to be called successively to return each occurrence of text in a document, with the argument of the previous match to indicate where to start the search.

This loop will create an array of all matching RangeElements:

```js
var rangeElements = [],rangeElement=null;
while (rangeElement = body.findText(textPattern, rangeElement)) {
  rangeElements.push ( rangeElement );
}
```

Merging RangeElements

We can use the RangeBuilder class to make a range from each of the items found by findText:

```js
function textRangeTest() {
    var doc = DocumentApp.getActiveDocument();
    doc.setSelection(DocUtils.makeRangeFind(doc, "[tT]echnology"));
}
```

Here we use the makeRangeFind utility:

```js
/**
 * find all occurence of text in the document and make a range of it
 * @param {Document} doc the document
 * @param {string} textPattern a regex string
 * @return {Range} the range
 */
docUtils.makeRangeFind = function (doc, textPattern) {

  var body = doc.getBody();

  var rangeElement = null, build = doc.newRange();

  while (rangeElement = body.findText(textPattern, rangeElement)) {
    if (rangeElement.isPartial()) {
      build.addElement(rangeElement.getElement(),
        rangeElement.getStartOffset(), rangeElement.getEndOffsetInclusive());
    }
    else {
      build.addElement(rangeElement.getElement());
    }
  }

  return build.build();
};
```

Figure 7-13 shows the new active selection range, highlighting the found text.

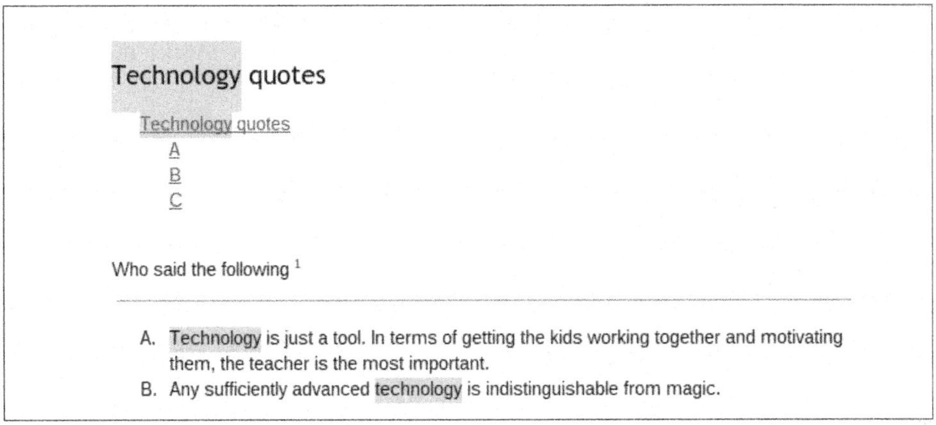

Technology quotes

Technology quotes
<u>A</u>
<u>B</u>
<u>C</u>

Who said the following [1]

_____

A. **Technology** is just a tool. In terms of getting the kids working together and motivating them, the teacher is the most important.
B. Any sufficiently advanced **technology** is indistinguishable from magic.

Figure 7-13. Highlighted the text found with findText

And here we confirm with `showActiveSelection`:

```
TEXT:Technology(partial)
TEXT:Technology(partial)
TEXT:Technology(partial)
TEXT:technology(partial)
```

VBA find

The `Range.Find` method in Word VBA is a fairly peculiar construction that dynamically adjusts the range of which it is a member as it goes along. I have always had some trouble coming to grips with its eccentricities, but it is the common method for finding text (and other properties).

Here is a VBA version of the `makeRangeFind` function. It returns a collection of qualifying ranges:

```vb
' /**
'  * find all occurence of text in the document and make a range of it
'  * @param {Document} doc the document
'  * @param {string} textPattern a string
'  * @return {Collection} all the ranges
'  */
Public Function makeRangeFind(doc As Document, textPattern As String) _
  As Collection
    Dim result As Collection, searchRange As Range
    Set result = New Collection

    With doc.Content
        .Find.Text = textPattern
        .Find.MatchCase = False
        While .Find.Execute
            result.Add doc.Range(.start, .End)
        Wend
```

```
    End With

    Set makeRangeFind = result
End Function
```

In this case then, the VBA ranges contained in the VBA collection are equivalent to the Apps Script `RangeElements` contained in the Apps Script range. The following searches for all occurrences of *technology* in the document:

```
VB  Private Sub rangeFinder()
        DocUtils.showRange _
            DocUtils.makeRangeFind(ActiveDocument, "technology")
    End Sub
```

with this result:

```
paragraph    text     0       10      Technology
paragraph    text     54      64      Technology
paragraph    text     217     227     Technology
paragraph    text     372     382     technology
```

Named Ranges

Ranges can be given names that persist in the document.

This snippet uses the find utility to create and name a range of all mentions of *Gates*:

```
JS  var doc = DocumentApp.getActiveDocument();
    var nr = doc.addNamedRange('bill gates',DocUtils.makeRangeFind(doc, "[gG]ates"));
```

It is possible to retrieve that range by name from the document. A named range has a unique ID (retrievable by `getId`), but there may be multiple ranges with the same name. `getNamedRanges` returns an array of matching names.

This snippet selects the first range with a matching range name, with the result shown in Figure 7-14:

```
JS  var doc = DocumentApp.getActiveDocument();
    doc.setSelection(doc.getNamedRanges('bill gates')[0].getRange());
```

Figure 7-14. Finding a named range

Named ranges can be retrieved by ID and removed as follows:

```
JS doc.getNamedRangeById('4abmsapby8h9').remove();
```

In VBA, a named range is a special use of the bookmark, and is illustrated in "Bookmarks" on page 177.

Setting a Cursor Using a Named Range

A named range can be used to set a cursor position. This snippet sets the cursor to the first named range in a document:

```
JS var rangeElement = doc.getNamedRanges()[0].getRange().getRangeElements()[0];
   doc.setCursor(doc.newPosition(rangeElement.getElement(),
                    rangeElement.getStartOffset()));
```

Position

A position class is returned by the getCursor method and indicates a specific position in the document. This example gets the current cursor and shows the element over which it positioned:

```
JS function getTheCursor() {
       var doc = DocumentApp.getActiveDocument();
       var position = doc.getCursor();
       // show the element we are in
       DocUtils.displayItems (position.getElement());
   }
```

Position provides a way of generating a dummy text element with the contents of its related element, shown here with its equivalent using the getElement method when the cursor is positioned over a regular text element:

```
JS Logger.log(position.getSurroundingText().getText());
   Logger.log(position.getElement().getText());
```

In VBA, a position is the same as a range, because they are defined in terms of their position within a document. You can retrieve the surrounding elements of a range by referencing its collection of elements:

```
VB Range.Paragraphs
```

Position Within Element

A position can refer to anywhere within an element. This snippet shows the character to which the position refers:

```
JS Logger.log(
       position.getSurroundingText().getText()
       .slice(position.getSurroundingTextOffset(),
```

```
            position.getSurroundingTextOffset()+1)
    );
```

Note that the position refers to the character just after the cursor icon. For example, the cursor position returned from "adva|nced" here will refer to *n*.

The `getOffset` method initially seems very similar to the `getSurroundingTextOff set` method. The difference between them becomes apparent when the active element is not a text element.

In Figure 7-15, the cursor is positioned at an inline image.

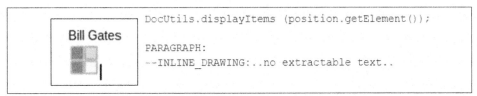

Figure 7-15. Cursor positioned at an inline image

This is not a text element, so `getSurroundingTextOffset` returns 0, and `getSurroun dingText` returns `''`:

```
getSurroundingTextOffset(); ///returns 0
getSurroundingText(); //returns ''
```

`getOffset` returns 1 when positioned at an inline image:

```
getOffset(); //returns 1
```

(The cursor is positioned just after the inline image.)

Setting the position

Aside from the position returned by `getCursor`, new positions can also be constructed. This snippet finds some text in the document and sets the cursor at that position:

```
var doc = DocumentApp.getActiveDocument();
var body = doc.getBody();
var rangeElement = body.findText('Einstein');
doc.setCursor(doc.newPosition(rangeElement.getElement(),
    rangeElement.getStartOffset()));
```

Creating a Selection

A useful operation is to create a selection based on the current cursor position, as shown in Figure 7-16.

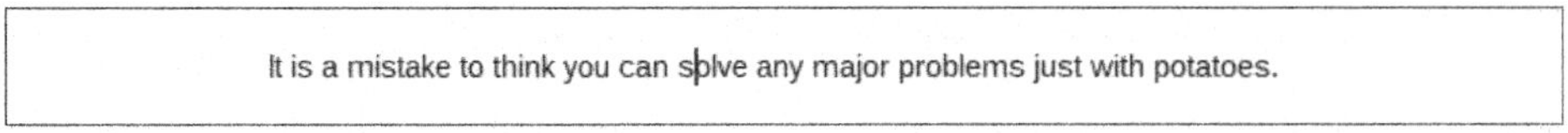

It is a mistake to think you can solve any major problems just with potatoes.

Figure 7-16. Creating a selection based on the current cursor position

This example sets the active selection to the complete element containing the current cursor position:

```
var doc = DocumentApp.getActiveDocument();
var position = doc.getCursor();
doc.setSelection(doc.newRange().addElement(position.getElement()).build());
```

and creates the selection shown in Figure 7-17.

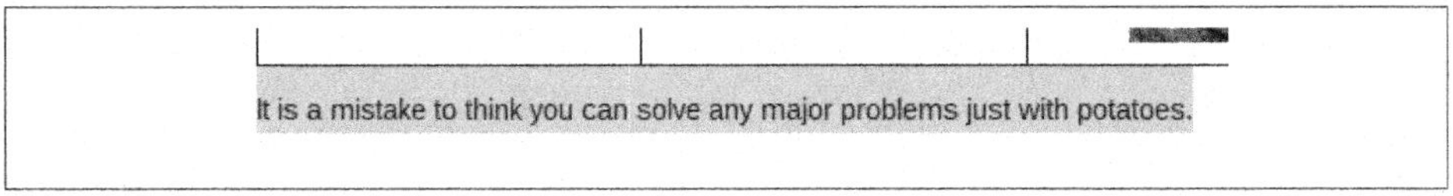

It is a mistake to think you can solve any major problems just with potatoes.

Figure 7-17. Selected text based on current cursor position

Creating a VBA Selection

The VBA version is a little more complex, as it has to look through all the paragraph ranges in the document to find one that fully encloses a given range:

```
Public Function getSurroundingElements(theRange As Range) As Collection
    Dim co As Collection, doc As Document, p As Paragraph
    Set co = New Collection
    Set doc = theRange.Parent

    For Each p In doc.Paragraphs
        If (theRange.start >= p.Range.start And theRange.End <= p.Range.End) Then
            co.Add doc.Range(p.Range.start, p.Range.End)
        End If
    Next p

    Set getSurroundingElements = co
End Function
```

Examining the result with showRange:

```
Private Sub getSurrounding()
    DocUtils.showRange getSurroundingElements(Selection.Range)
End Sub
```

gives this result:

```
paragraph     text           539          617          It is a mi
```

Applying the first matching element as the current selection:

VB `DocUtils.getSurroundingElements(Selection.Range)(1).Select`

gives the selection shown in Figure 7-18.

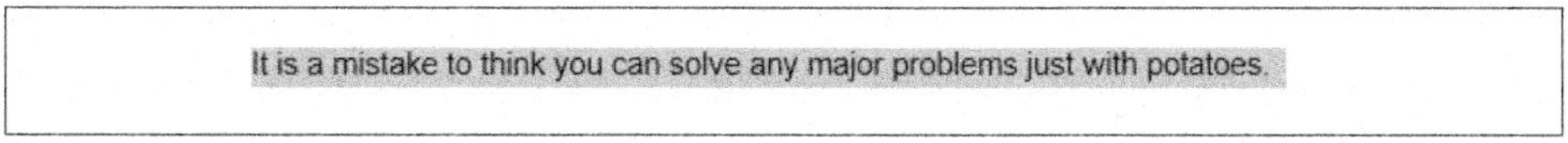

It is a mistake to think you can solve any major problems just with potatoes.

Figure 7-18. Result of applying the first matching element as the current selection

Inserting Text

The `position` class has a shortcut method for inserting text, as shown in Figure 7-19.

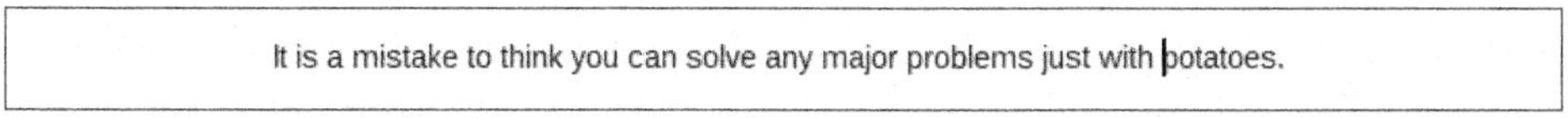

It is a mistake to think you can solve any major problems just with potatoes.

Figure 7-19. Inserting text

You can use `insertText` as follows:

JS `position.insertText('carrots or ');`

to create the result shown in Figure 7-20.

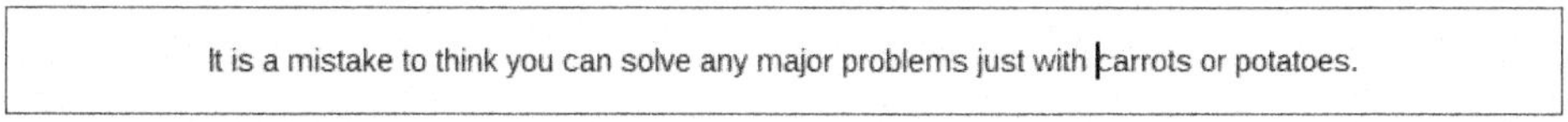

It is a mistake to think you can solve any major problems just with carrots or potatoes.

Figure 7-20. Result of using insertText

This is much less laborious than, but gives the same result as, the element's method for inserting text:

JS
```
position.getElement().asText().editAsText()
    .insertText(position.getOffset(), 'carrots or ');
```

These are equivalent to the following VBA:

VB `Selection.Range.InsertBefore "carrots or "`

Bookmarks

You can mark positions in a document with a bookmark. The following snippet creates a bookmark at the current position and displays its ID:

JS
```
var doc = DocumentApp.getActiveDocument();
var position = doc.getCursor();
var bookmark = doc.addBookmark(position);
Logger.log(bookmark.getId());
```

IDs

Each bookmark ID is unique within a document, and takes the format of the following example:

 id.riogj5sor008

VBA Bookmark Insert

In VBA, a bookmark is the same thing as a named range, except that it has no enclosed text. It does not have an ID, but does have a name that you assign (hence the equivalence with a named range).

This creates a bookmark at the current cursor and displays its name and position:

```
VB  Set b = doc.Bookmarks.Add("b1", Selection.Range)
    Debug.Print b.Name, b.Range.start, b.Range.End
```

resulting in:

```
b1              618             618
```

To make a bookmark into a named range (or *enclosing bookmark* in Word parlance), you need to assign the text to a range, then assign the range to a bookmark like this:

```
VB  Set r = Selection.Range
    r.Text = "carrots or "
    Set b = doc.Bookmarks.Add("b2", r)
    Debug.Print b.Name, b.Range.start, b.Range.End, b.Range.Text
```

which results in:

```
b2              615             626             carrots or
```

Bookmark Appearance

Bookmarks appear in the document as a blue image, as you can see in Figure 7-21.

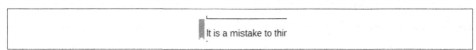

Figure 7-21. A bookmark

In Word, they appear as a marker that looks like a capital I.

Traversing Bookmarks

Bookmarks are not elements (they don't show up in document element traversal), but can be retrieved by the Documents getBookMarks method.

This snippet displays info on each of the bookmarks in a document:

```
doc.getBookmarks().forEach(function(d) {
    Logger.log('bookmark:'+d.getId());
    DocUtils.displayItems(d.getPosition().getElement());
});
```

giving this:

```
bookmark:id.fnaa1pxvsl1w
PARAGRAPH:It is a mi
--TEXT:It is a mi
```

The VBA version looks like this:

```
For Each b In doc.Bookmarks
        Debug.Print b.Name, b.Range.start, b.Range.End
Next b
```

Text Bookmarks

Bookmarks that are set at positions within a TEXT element (as opposed to their container element—which in the preceding case was a PARAGRAPH) still show in the document at the beginning of the container, as illustrated by Figure 7-22.

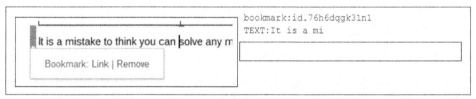

Figure 7-22. Bookmarks appear at the beginning of the container even when set within the TEXT element

In VBA, the bookmark marker always shows at the position of the bookmark.

Creating Links

Bookmarks can be used to create a shareable link that leads directly to a specific position in a document, as in this snippet:

```
doc.getBookmarks().forEach(function(d) {
    Logger.log(doc.getUrl() + '#bookmark=' + d.getId());
});
```

Because VBA refers to a local document, it has no equivalent.

Setting a Cursor Position

A bookmark can be used to set a cursor position.

This snippet sets the cursor to the first bookmark in a document:

```
var doc = DocumentApp.getActiveDocument();
doc.setCursor(doc.getBookmarks()[0].getPosition());
```

VBA cursor

```
doc.Bookmarks(1).Range.Select
```

Removing Bookmarks

Bookmarks are removed as follows:

```
doc.getBookmarks().forEach(function(d) {
    d.remove();
});
```

Here is the VBA equivalent:

```
For Each b In doc.Bookmarks
    b.Delete
Next b
```

Editing Text in Elements

Specific elements, such as TEXT or PARAGRAPH, inherit from the base Element class. The getElement function can return any of these, and it must be recast to allow manipulation. Each of these recast functions, such as asText, is of the format as *Type*.

Before manipulating text in an element, you must recast it as a TEXT element as in the following pattern, which exposes the editAsText method. This example shows how to insert text at a specific position:

```
position.getElement().asText().editAsText()
    .insertText(position.getOffset(), 'carrots or ');
```

VBA is rather more straightforward:

```
Selection.Range.InsertBefore "carrots or "
```

Finding and removing text also uses this recasting approach. This example finds some text and deletes it from the element:

```
var rangeElement = position.getElement().asText().findText('carrots or');
rangeElement.getElement().asText()
  .deleteText(rangeElement.getStartOffset(),
    rangeElement.getEndOffsetInclusive());
```

In VBA, for this task you'd probably use the find method with a replace argument of "", but using the makeRangeFind function created earlier makes this VBA snippet almost identical in structure to the Apps Script version:

```vb
Dim r As Range
For Each r In DocUtils.makeRangeFind(ActiveDocument, "carrots or")
    r.Delete
Next r
```

Adding Elements

Appending new elements to the document body is fairly straightforward, but inserting them is a little more complex.

Containers

As seen from traversing the example document, elements with content such as TEXT and INLINE_IMAGE are contained within other elements such as PARAGRAPH or LIST_ITEM. Unlike the HTML DOM, which has no limits on nesting and depth (aside from resources and practicality), the document object tree depth is limited. For example, PARAGRAPH cannot be inside another PARAGRAPH in the way that a <DIV> can be inside another <DIV>.

PARAGRAPH

This snippet creates both a paragraph and a text element and appends it to the end of the document:

```js
var doc = DocumentApp.getActiveDocument();
var body = doc.getBody();
body.appendParagraph('In chess, you should be as cool as a cucumber');
```

The result is shown in Figure 7-23.

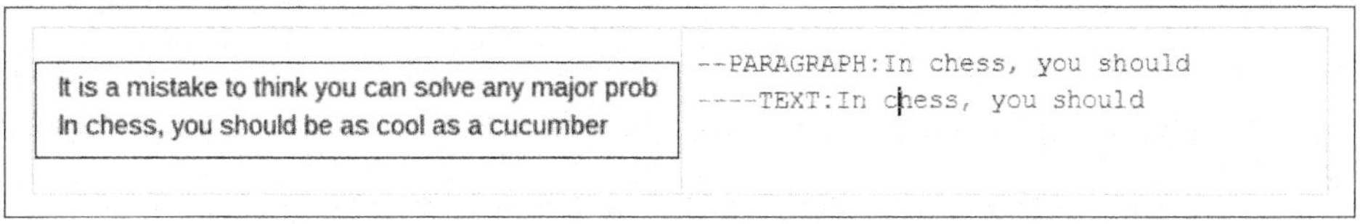

```
┌─────────────────────────────────────────────┬────────────────────────────────────┐
│                                              │ --PARAGRAPH:In chess, you should   │
│  It is a mistake to think you can solve any major prob │ ----TEXT:In chess, you should      │
│  In chess, you should be as cool as a cucumber        │                                    │
└─────────────────────────────────────────────┴────────────────────────────────────┘
```

Figure 7-23. Appending a paragraph and a text element to the end of the document

VBA appends a paragraph to the end of the document content like this:

```vb
ActiveDocument.Paragraphs().Add().Range.Text = _
    "In chess, you should be as cool as a cucumber"
```

Element childIndex

To be able to insert (as opposed to append) a new element, you need to know the index in the container element at which the element should be inserted. This snippet extracts all the elements in the body container, and shows their `childIndex` (which will match the loop index 0–10):

```js
var doc = DocumentApp.getActiveDocument();
var body = doc.getBody();
for (var num = body.getNumChildren(), i=0; i < num; i++) {
  Logger.log(body.getChildIndex(body.getChild(i)));
}
```

Strangely, it's not possible to directly get an element's `childIndex`. Instead, the `getChildIndex` of the element's parent is used as follows:

```js
elem.getParent().getChildIndex(elem);
```

With another slight update to the `DocUtils.displayItem`, the document structure can be shown with the `childindex` of each element:

```js
Logger.log (new Array(indent+1).join("-") +
    type + ":" + snip + (partial ? '(partial)' : '') +
    ' : index:' + elem.getParent().getChildIndex(elem));
```

Here's a snippet from the updated document tree, this time with indices shown:

```
------TABLE_CELL:Arthur C Clarke:index:1
--------PARAGRAPH:Arthur C Clarke:index:0
----------TEXT:Arthur C Clarke:index:0
------TABLE_CELL::index:2
--------PARAGRAPH::index:0
----------INLINE_IMAGE:..no extractable text..:index:0
```

VBA childIndex

While it's not an official property or one that is especially needed in VBA, finding the `childindex` of a particular range in a document is easy to do, and the approach provides some further insight into the nature of ranges in VBA for Word.

This snippet looks for the index of the first table in the document:

```vb
Debug.Print DocUtils.getChildIndex(ActiveDocument.tables(1).Range)
```

The `childIndex` function works by creating a new range from the beginning of the document to the end of the target range, and counting the paragraphs in between:

```vb
Public Function getChildIndex(elemRange As Range) As Long
    getChildIndex = elemRange.Parent.Range(0, elemRange.End).Paragraphs.Count
End Function
```

Inserting Elements

Besides needing to know the childindex, you need to know whether the parent of the current element can have elements inserted—in other words, whether it's a container element.

Let's say you want to insert a PARAGRAPH at the current position: there's a good chance that the cursor is on a TEXT element, contained within a PARAGRAPH.

However, the current position might be in a TABLE_CELL—or even more complicated, part of an EQUATION.

In any case, the child index required is not that of the TEXT element, but of the container object in which it is positioned.

The following code inserts a new paragraph just before the element at the current cursor position, using a new function implemented in the DocUtils namespace:

```js
function insertPara() {
    var doc = DocumentApp.getActiveDocument();
    var position = doc.getCursor();
    DocUtils.insertElement ('Paragraph', position.getElement(),
            'To be honest, I think bananas are a pathetic fruit.');
}
```

To generalize, the new element should be inserted at the closest parent that is capable of inserting an element. One approach would be to cater for each case by testing the element's parent type, but this could easily turn to spaghetti.

A simpler, more general approach that seems to work well is simply to check successive parents up the family tree until one is found that has an insert function available:

```js
/**
 * insert a element at the current element
 * @param {string} insertName function type (eg Paragraph);
 * @param {Element} elem elem at which to insert
 * @param {*} content the content to insert
 * @return {Paragraph} the inserted paragraph
 */
docUtils.insertElement = function( insertName, elem , content) {

  var functionName = 'insert' + insertName;

  // where to insert the paragraph-the first container element that can do it.
  for(var item = elem, parent; item && (parent = item.getParent()) &&
          !typeof parent[insertName] === 'function'  ; item = parent) {}

  if (!parent) throw 'cannot not insert ' + insertName;

  // insert the element
```

```
    return parent[functionName](parent.getChildIndex(item), content);

};
```

It's not so easy to generalize in VBA. You need to know what you are inserting. This example inserts a new paragraph at the current cursor:

VB
```
Private Sub insertPara()
    Selection.InsertParagraph
    Selection.Range.Text = _
        "To be honest, I think bananas are a pathetic fruit."
End Sub
```

Tables

A document TABLE element is a container that holds a collection of TABLE_ROWs, each of which itself holds a collection of TABLE_CELLs.

Appending a row to a table is straightforward:

JS
```
var doc = DocumentApp.getActiveDocument();
var body = doc.getBody();

// get the first table in the doc
var table = body.getTables()[0];

// append a row
var tableRow = table.appendTableRow();
```

The VBA equivalent is:

VB
```
Private Sub tables()
    Dim doc As Document, table As table, tableRow As Row
    Set doc = ActiveDocument

  ' get the first table
    Set table = doc.tables(1)

    ' append a table row
     Set tableRow = table.Rows.Add

  End Sub
```

In VBA, the correct number of cells is added automatically, but in Apps Script, a table is not a grid. Adding a row doesn't automatically add any cells. They have to be added individually:

JS
```
// append some cells.
tableRow.appendTableCell ('D.');
tableRow.appendTableCell ('B.F. Skinner');
```

with the result shown in Figure 7-24.

Inserting a TABLE_ROW is also straightforward; simply specify the TABLE_ROW to insert before:

```js
// insert a row
var tableRow = table.insertTableRow(2);

// append some cells.
tableRow.appendTableCell ('D.');
tableRow.appendTableCell ('B.F. Skinner');
```

Here's the equivalent in VBA:

```vb
' append a table row
Set tableRow = table.Rows.Add(beforerow:=table.Rows(3))

tableRow.Cells(1).Range.Text = "D."
tableRow.Cells(2).Range.Text = "B.F. Skinner"
```

```
----TABLE_ROW:D.B.F. Skinner : index:4
------TABLE_CELL:D. : index:0
--------PARAGRAPH:D. : index:0
----------TEXT:D. : index:0
------TABLE_CELL:B.F. Skinner : index:1
--------PARAGRAPH:B.F.       Skinner      :
index:0
----------TEXT:B.F. Skinner : index:0
```

Figure 7-24. Adding cells to a table

List Items

A LIST_ITEM has similar properties to a PARAGRAPH. Appending and inserting follow a similar pattern:

```js
function appendListItem() {
    var doc = DocumentApp.getActiveDocument();
    var body = doc.getBody();
    body.appendListItem(
      'The real problem is not whether machines think but whether men do.');
}
```

Inserting can use the generalized insertElement utility introduced in the PARAGRAPH section:

```js
function insertListItem() {
    var doc = DocumentApp.getActiveDocument();
    var position = doc.getCursor();
    DocUtils.insertElement ('ListItem', position.getElement(),
        'The real problem is not whether machines think but whether men do.');
}
```

and gives the result shown in Figure 7-25.

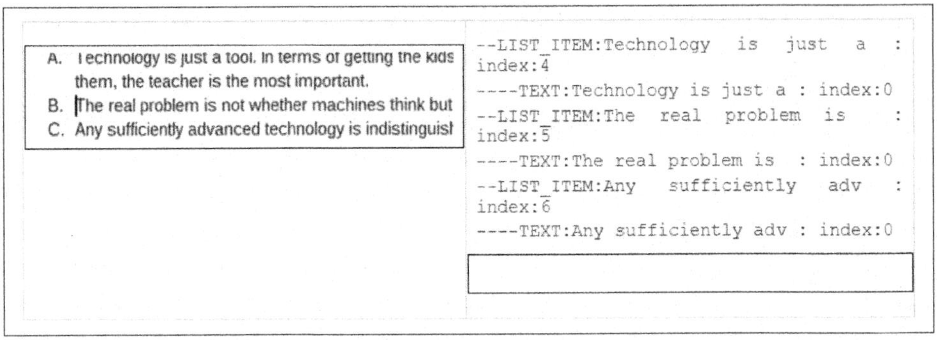

Figure 7-25. Inserting list items

Appending to an existing list in the middle of a document is just a matter of finding the list to be appended to, finding its index within its container, and inserting a new element just after:

```js
var doc = DocumentApp.getActiveDocument();
var body = doc.getBody();

// get all the list items
var items = body.getListItems();

// use the index of the last lisItem, and insert before the next
body.insertListItem(1+body.getChildIndex(items[items.length-1]),
    'The real problem is not whether machines think but whether men do.');
```

The preceding code gives the result shown in Figure 7-26.

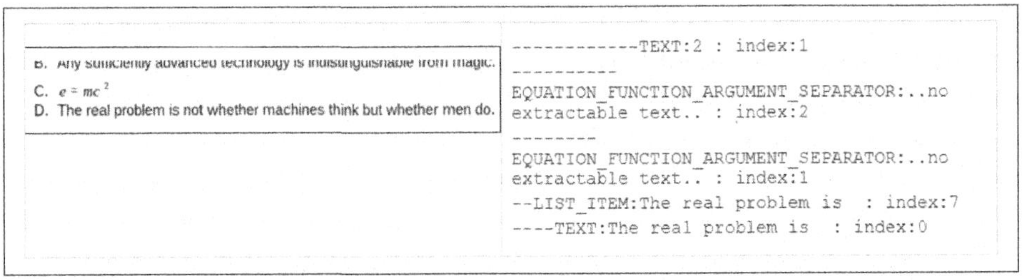

Figure 7-26. Appending to an existing list in the middle of a document

VBA ListParagraph

VBA doesn't have a specific list paragraph structure (although it does have an object called a `ListParagraph`). They seem to be simple paragraphs that have had `ListFormat` applied. You can return `ListParagraphs` using `.ListParagraphs`, and see them in separate lists by examining the collection returned by `Document.Lists`.

Here's the VBA equivalent of the preceding code, adding an item to a list:

```
Dim doc As Document,  r As Range, p As Range
Set doc = ActiveDocument

' the range of the last item in the first set of list items
Set r = doc.lists(1).ListParagraphs(doc.lists(1).CountNumberedItems).Range

' insert a paragraph after
Set p = doc.Range(r.End, r.End)
p.Text = "The real problem is not whether machines think but whether men do."

' this tells it to be a list element
p.Paragraphs.Format = r.Paragraphs.Format
```

Images

Revisiting the table example, here's how to add the row but include an INLINE_IMAGE read from a Google Drive file:

```
// append a row
var tr = table.appendTableRow();

// append some cells.
tr.appendTableCell ('D.');
tr.appendTableCell ('B.F. Skinner');

// get an image blob from Drive
var img = DriveApp.getFileById('0B92ExLh4POiZZ1oxR202aWxpOGM').getBlob();

// this will create an empty paragraph that we don't need
var td = tr.appendTableCell();
if (td.getNumChildren() > 0) {
  td.getChild(0).removeFromParent();
}

// now append the image
td.appendImage(img);
```

Using the same approach of expanding the table example to include an image in the third column, here is the VBA equivalent:

```
Dim doc As Document, table As table, tr As Row
Set doc = ActiveDocument

' get the first table
Set table = doc.tables(1)

' append a table row
Set tr = table.Rows.Add(beforerow:=table.Rows(3))

tr.Cells(1).Range.Text = "D."
```

```
tr.Cells(2).Range.Text = "B.F. Skinner"

' append an image
tr.Cells(3).Range.InlineShapes.AddPicture _
    ("C:\Users\Bruce\Google Drive\books\going gas\bfskinner.png")
```

Docs Automation Example

While writing this book (which I did using Docs), I discovered that the process of highlighting code was fairly tedious:

1. Create a one-cell table to receive the code.

2. Copy the code from the Script IDE.

3. Tidy it up to remove different levels of indentation.

4. Change the format to monospace.

About halfway through, I started to seriously reflect on the irony of continuing to do this in a book whose subject is Docs automation. The drawback, though, is that opening a large document takes quite a few seconds, and there is no way to keep a persistent handle open, but for smaller documents it works just fine.

There are a couple of other prettification steps, which I'll reveal in Chapter 10. Figure 7-27 shows the kind of transformation required.

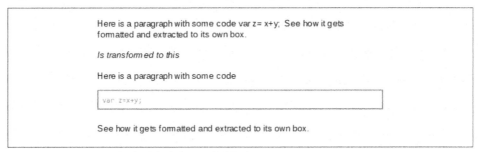

Figure 7-27. Process for highlighting code blocks

Selecting the Target Area

In Apps Script, it is possible to read the source code, which means you can copy from a container-bound script into a document. However, the UI for specifying the code snippet would be complicated, so this version of automation assumes that the target source code has already been copied into the document.

The target source code will either be a highlighted selection, or it will be the element at the current cursor position, invoked like this:

```js
var doc = DocumentApp.getActiveDocument();
var range = DocUtils.getTarget(doc);
```

The getTarget function is likely to be useful, so I've included it in the DocUtils namespace:

```js
/**
 * if there's an active selection then use that,
 * otherwise use the containing element of the cursor
 * @param {Document} doc the target document
 * @return {Range} the text range that needs to be dealt with
 */
docUtils.getTarget = function(doc) {

  // see if there is a current selection
  var selected = doc.getSelection();

  // otherwise create a range for the current element
  if (!selected) {

    // the current position
    var cursor = doc.getCursor();

    if (cursor) {

      // the element containing the current position
      var element = cursor.getElement();

      // now add that entire element to a new range
      if (element) {
        selected = doc.newRange().addElement(element).build();
      }
    }
  }
  return selected;
}
```

Here's how to set the target in VBA:

```vb
Set range = DocUtils.getTarget()
```

The previously written getSurroundingElements can be used to detect the element in which a given range is positioned:

```vb
'/**
' * if there's an active selection then use that,
' * otherwise use the containing element of the cursor
' * @return {Range} the text range that needs to be dealt with
' */
Public Function getTarget() As range
```

```
          If (Selection.range.End - Selection.range.start > 0) Then
              ' if the selection is active its range will be > 0 wide
              Set getTarget = Selection.range
          Else
              ' get the nearest surrounding element
              Set getTarget = getSurroundingElements(Selection.range)(1)
          End If
      End Function
```

Inserting the Table

As mentioned earlier, a one-cell table is used to hold the code. The insert position will
be before the beginning of the selected range. This can get messy because the beginning or end selection point could be in the middle of an element, which means splitting up the element's text.

This code pulls out the selected text, creates a one-cell table, moves the selected text
into that table, changes the font to monospace, and gets rid of as many leading spaces
as possible, while maintaining the block indentation:

```
function codePretty () {
    var doc = DocumentApp.getActiveDocument();
    // this will be either the current element or a selected range
    var range = DocUtils.getTarget(doc);
    var rangeElements = range.getRangeElements();

    var preText, postText;

    // the first element in the selection
    var startRE = rangeElements[0];
    var startElem = startRE.getElement();

    // if the selection starts on a partial element, we'll need to split it
    if (startRE.isPartial()) {
      var startText = startElem.asText().getText();
      if (startRE.getStartOffset() > 0) {
        preText = startText.slice(0,startRE.getStartOffset()-1);
      }
    }

    // the last element in the selection
    var finishRE = rangeElements[rangeElements.length-1];
    var finishElem = finishRE.getElement();

    // if the selection finishes on a partial element, we'll need to split it
    if (finishRE.isPartial()) {
      var finishText = finishElem.asText().getText();
      if (finishRE.getEndOffsetInclusive() < finishText.length  ) {
        postText = finishText.slice(finishRE.getEndOffsetInclusive()+1,
            finishText.length);
      }
```

```
  }

  // where the table will be inserted
  var tablePosition = startElem;

  // add the leading snippet of the range to exclude, and remove from original
  if(preText) {
    DocUtils.insertElement('Paragraph', startElem, preText);
    startElem.asText().editAsText().deleteText(0,preText.length-1);
    DocUtils.insertElement('Paragraph', tablePosition , '');
  }

  // add the trailing snippet of the range to exclude
  if(postText) {
    tablePosition = DocUtils.insertElement('Paragraph', startElem, postText);
    finishElem.asText().editAsText().deleteText(
      finishRE.getEndOffsetInclusive()+1- preText.length,
      finishElem.asText().getText().length-1);
  }

  // add the one cell table
  var table = DocUtils.insertElement('Table' , tablePosition);

  // add a separating paragraph
  if(postText) {
    DocUtils.insertElement('Paragraph', tablePosition, '' );
  }

  // create the table
  var td = table.appendTableRow().appendTableCell();

  // this will have created an unnecessary paragraph (no way around it)
  for(var i=0;i<td.getNumChildren();i++) {
    td.getChild(i).removeFromParent();
  };

  // deal with indentation - the minimum found is the amount to slice
  var indent = rangeElements.reduce(function(p,c) {
    var text = c.getElement().asText().getText();
    var preamble = text.length - text.replace(/^\s+/, "").length ;
    return p === -1 ? preamble : Math.min(p,preamble);
  },-1);

  // get original range elements, indent,
  // setting the font monospace & smaller size
  rangeElements.forEach(function(d) {
    td.appendParagraph(d.getElement().asText().getText()
      .slice(indent)).asText()
      .setFontFamily("Consolas").setFontSize(9);
  });

  // delete all of the original rangeelements
```

```
    rangeElements.forEach(function(d) {
      d.getElement().removeFromParent();
    });

  }
```

The VBA version of inserting the table is a little less complicated, as it deals in range positions only, and doesn't have to worry about partial elements:

```
VB  Public Sub codePretty()
        Dim doc As Document, range As range, tableStart As range, _
            table As table, text As String, p As Paragraph, preamble As Long, _
            indent As Long

        Set doc = ActiveDocument

        '// this will be either the current element or a selected range
        Set range = DocUtils.getTarget()

        '// split the line
        Set tableStart = doc.range(range.End, range.End)

        '//insert a table
        Set table = doc.tables.Add(tableStart, 1, 1)
        table.Borders.Enable = True

        '// deal with indentation - the minimum found is the amount to slice
        indent = -1
        For Each p In range.Paragraphs
            text = CStr(p.range.text)
            preamble = Len(text) - Len(LTrim(text))
            If (indent = -1 Or preamble < indent) Then
                indent = preamble
            End If
        Next p
        If (indent < 0) Then indent = 0

        '//copy the text, set the font, get rid of unnecessary leading space
        With table.Rows(1).Cells(1).range.Paragraphs
            For Each p In range.Paragraphs
                With .Add().range
                    .Font.Name = "Consolas"
                    .Font.Size = 9
                    text = Mid(CStr(p.range.text), indent + 1)
                    If (Right(text, 1) = vbCr) Then text = Left(text, Len(text) - 1)
                    .text = text
                End With
            Next p
        End With

        '// delete the original text
        range.Delete
```

```
End Sub
```

Adding to Custom Menu

We can add the code box to the document menu by creating an onOpen trigger as shown in Figure 7-28.

Figure 7-28. Adding the code box to the custom menu in Apps Script

Here's the Apps Script code (the result is shown in Figure 7-29):

```js
function onOpen() {

    // set up a custom menu
    var ui = DocumentApp.getUi();
    ui.createMenu('Prettification')
        .addItem('Code Box', 'codePretty')
        .addToUi();
}
```

```vb
Private Sub addToMenu()
    ' add the action item
    With CommandBars("Standard")
        If (testInCollection(.Controls, "Prettification")) Then
          .Controls("Prettification").Delete
        End If

        With .Controls.Add(msoControlPopup)
            .Caption = "Prettification"
            With .Controls.Add(msoControlButton)
                .Caption = "Code Box"
                .OnAction = "codePretty"
            End With
        End With

    End With
End Sub
```

Figure 7-29. Adding the code box to the custom menu in VBA

Attributes

In many ways, it would be nice if you could set text attributes in Docs using CSS markup to allow the kind of formatting possible with HTML. However, text attributes are set with dedicated methods, most of which have a VBA equivalent. An array of attributes is accessible at container level through a special get/set `Attributes` method, but to set text attributes, you need to cast the element with `asText`. A container element `getAttributes` will return an object containing each relevant attribute for that element.

This code gets the first element in a selection and gets its attributes:

```
var doc = DocumentApp.getActiveDocument();
var selection = doc.getSelection();
// get the first element
var element = selection.getRangeElements()[0].getElement();
Logger.log(JSON.stringify(element.getAttributes()));
```

`getAttributes` returns an object (in this case, from a LIST_ITEM), which can be modified with `setAttributes` as follows:

```
{"FONT_SIZE":null,"ITALIC":null,"HORIZONTAL_ALIGNMENT":null,"GLYPH_TYPE":{},
  "INDENT_END":null,"INDENT_START":36,"LINE_SPACING":null,"LINK_URL":null,
  "UNDERLINE":null,"BACKGROUND_COLOR":null,"INDENT_FIRST_LINE":18,
  "LEFT_TO_RIGHT":true,"SPACING_BEFORE":null,"HEADING":{},"SPACING_AFTER":10,
  "STRIKETHROUGH":null,"FOREGROUND_COLOR":null,"LIST_ID":"kix.1i8yhaqh4qzr",
  "BOLD":null,"NESTING_LEVEL":0,"FONT_FAMILY":null}
```

Text Attributes

These are the type of attributes returned from a TEXT element:

```
{"FONT_SIZE":null,"ITALIC":null,"STRIKETHROUGH":null,"FOREGROUND_COLOR":null,
  "BOLD":null,"LINK_URL":null,
  "UNDERLINE":null,"FONT_FAMILY":null,"BACKGROUND_COLOR":null}
```

Attributes are more often accessed through the following methods:

```
var text = element.asText();
if (text.isBold()) { // do something }
text.setItalic(true);
text.setFontSize(10);

// these three are equivalent
var color = text.getBackgroundColor();
var color = text.getAttribute("BACKGROUND_COLOR");
var color = text.getAttributes().BACKGROUND_COLOR;
```

Attribute Equivalence

Table 7-4 shows the VBA and Apps Script attribute comparisons.

Table 7-4. Attribute equivalence table

Apps Script (get/set)	VBA (applied to range)
BackgroundColor	.ParagraphFormat.Shading.BackgroundPatternColor
FontFamily	.Font.Name
FontSize	.Font.Size
ForegroundColor	.ColorIndex
LinkUrl	.Hyperlinks(1).Address[a]
TextAlignment	.ParagraphFormat.Alignment
Boolean (is/set)	
isBold	.Font.Bold
isItalic	.Font.Italic
isStrikethrough	.Font.Strikethrough
isUnderline	.Font.Underline[b]

[a] .Hyperlinks is a collection of hyperlinks in the Range, so the first test should be on Range.HyperLinks.Count to ensure there are some.

[b] Uses an Enum for different underline styles.

Partial Attributes

It is possible to have multiple values for the same attribute in a single element:

```js
// set the characters 3 and 4 only
text.setFontFamily (3,4, "Consolas");

// get the font family at character 3
var family = text.getFontFamily(3);
```

In VBA, you accomplish this by setting a range's start and end positions.

Attribute Indices

Apps Script includes a fairly peculiar method, `getTextAttributeIndices`, that returns a list of positions that text attributes change, but then it's up to you to figure out exactly which attribute is changing:

```js
element.asText().getTextAttributeIndices().forEach(function(d) {
    Logger.log (text.getForegroundColor(d));
});
```

`getTextAttributeIndices` returns a result like this:

```
null
#ff0000
null
#4a86e8
null
```

There is no VBA equivalent.

Gmail, Calendar, and Contacts Apps

Microsoft Outlook is a single client management service equivalent to the combined Google services of Gmail, Calendar, and Contacts.

In Apps Script, each of these services is independent and callable from any of the Apps platforms (Sheets, Docs, etc.). This makes automation of common workflow tasks simple and common across apps.

At first, this might seem rather more complicated, but within the Outlook object model, each service is an independent object in any case, and doesn't always follow the same paradigm.

Email Automation Exercise

The example in this chapter will bring together all these services into one workflow application implemented in VBA and in Apps Script. Although this is a fairly contrived example, it is designed to touch most of these services' components, and integrates with a few others covered in this book. Furthermore, this type of email-oriented workflow is fairly common and should be easily adaptable across subject domains.

The final script will be fairly long, so will not be reproduced in full in this chapter. However, it is included in the accompanying GitHub code repository as *gmailExample*. Code snippets in both VBA and Apps Script will be shown together to contrast the different approaches.

The services and capabilities you'll learn how to use during this exercise are listed in Table 8-1.

Table 8-1. Services and capabilities covered in this chapter

Service	Capability	Purpose
Gmail	Searching threads	Looking for threads that contain some text and fall within some time period
Gmail	Searching messages	Using regular expressions to search individual messages
Gmail	Labels	Using labels to mark threads when processed
Gmail	Starring	Adding and testing for starred messages
Gmail	Sending	Composing and sending complex messages
Drive	Parsing paths	Converting paths to Drive folder structures
Drive	Saving blobs to files	Saving Gmail attachments
Drive	Permissions	Assigning viewer rights to files and folders
Contacts	Creating	Creating contacts from emails
Contacts	Groups	Using contact groups to mark when contacts are processed
Calendar	Finding calendars	Searching for specific calendars
Calendar	Events	Searching for events by characteristic and date
Calendar API	Recurrence	Addressing individual events in a series
Calendar API	Patching	Patching events to automatically send invites

Scenario

The scenario here is that you work for a market research company that has been commissioned to collect material related to flights operated by specific airlines.

The informants are an initially unregistered set of people who learn about your study from an advertisement you've taken out in various in-flight magazines. They are asked to submit by email (which mentions their flight number and the term "flight club") any pictures or any other attachments they'd like to provide documenting their experience on the journey. By submitting material, they are recruited into a panel of respondents. The first time they are detected, they get invited to a regularly scheduled training course, sometime in the near future.

These attachments need to be stored in a directory structure by the informant's name and the flight number, either on Drive, or locally on the PC in the case of the Excel version.

The informants receive a confirmation of their upload and, in the Apps Script version, a link to the data they have provided.

Here is a summary of the process:

1. A scheduled task scans threads for messages that contain any reference that looks like a flight number operated by any of the airlines from the carrier lookup spreadsheet.

2. Settings are stored in the registry and Properties service.

3. Confirmation emails are sent to the informant. Multiple emails to the same informant are collapsed into one.

4. Attachments are stored locally or on Drive.

5. Threads are marked when processed so they are skipped the next time. Individual messages within a thread are starred to indicate they've been addressed. Unfortunately, it's not possible to label individual messages.

6. New informants are added to the Contacts service, and invited to a scheduled monthly initial briefing session via the Calendar service.

In real life, a more traditional (and robust) solution might involve databases or at least spreadsheets of respondents and their activities, along with some kind of UI for administration. However, this example is designed to show off the capabilities (and drawbacks) of the Gmail, Contacts, and Calendar services, as well as their relationship to their Office equivalents.

You'll see how it really is possible to build a viable workflow simply by relying on the built-in UI and labeling capabilities of these services.

Threads

Gmail threads are somewhat equivalent to Outlook conversations—groups of related messages that together make up an exchange.

In Outlook, the concept of conversations seems to be more of an afterthought (they were introduced in Outlook 2007), with messages tagged into conversations by means of a topic and presented as a conversation view. In Gmail, the thread forms part of the object model—in other words, messages are organized by threads.

This inability to deal with messages individually, but as part of a conversation, makes the implementation of the example application fairly complex, since most of the searching and labeling that's desirable at message level is implemented at thread level in Gmail. Threads are very effective for conversations in the Gmail UI, but they can get in the way of message-centric automation, as we'll see in this example.

Searching

Apps Script queries are performed at thread level, using the advanced Gmail search language—the same one used in the Gmail UI—to return a set of threads that match the query.

This snippet returns all threads that contain the text "flight data" since August 1, 2015, that are not marked with the label "flight-data-processed," and that are in the inbox:

```js
/**
 * get matching threads
 * @return {GmailThread[]} the threads
 */
threads.get = function () {

    return Utils.rateLimitExpBackoff (function () {
      // get all target threads
      return GmailApp.search("flight data" +
        " after:"+"2015/08/01" +
        " -label:" + "flight-data-processed" +
        " in:" + "inbox");
    });
};
```

This is a typical mail automation query and is similar to the one we'll use in the example application for this chapter. Exponential backoff is used to prevent rate limit problems.

The VBA version is a little different, because the equivalent of a label in Outlook is a category, and that can't be searched with the usual filtering mechanism.

The dates and inbox name are parameterized here, as they will shortly be in the Apps Script version:

```vb
Set result = New Collection

' get the specified folder to look in
Set outlookFolder = getFolder(Settings.getValue("THREADS.IN"))

' set up date filters
filter = "[ReceivedTime] > '" & _
    Format(Settings.getValue("THREADS.AFTER"), "ddddd h:nn AMPM") & "'"

' apply filters and get matching items
Set items = outlookFolder.items.Restrict(filter)
```

Getting the folder in which to search in VBA is also a little more convoluted:

```vb
' find a folder given a path
' will just bomb out if folder doesn't exist.
Private Function getFolder(path As String) As Outlook.folder

    Dim folder As Outlook.folder, splitPath As Variant, i As Long

    'the folder name components
    splitPath = VBA.Split(path, "/")

    'get the top-level folder
```

```
    Set folder = Session.GetDefaultFolder(olFolderInbox) _
        .parent.Folders(CStr(splitPath(0)))

    ' and any subfolders further down
    For i = LBound(splitPath) + 1 To UBound(splitPath)
        Set folder = folder.Folders.item(CStr(splitPath(i)))
    Next i

    Set getFolder = folder
End Function
```

Querying the message body

Despite being able to query the contents of all the messages in a thread to filter on only threads whose messages match some content query, you can't query individual messages directly from the GmailApp API.

Similarly, the body of an Outlook message is not queryable using the VBA restrict mechanism. In both cases, you must retrieve and examine each message individually.

Messages

Apps Script messages are accessed via their parent thread, and getMessages should be wrapped in exponential backoff:[1]

```
JS  var messages = Utils.rateLimitExpBackoff (function () {
        return c.getMessages();
    });
```

Message Filtering

In the example application, further searching is needed. We need to exclude messages that have already been dealt with (they will have been starred), as well as those that are too old to be in scope. We can do this by filtering the metadata of the data returned by getMessages:

```
JS  var messages = Utils.rateLimitExpBackoff (function () {
        return c.getMessages();
    })
    .filter(function(m) {
      return m.getDate().getTime() >
        new Date(Settings.THREADS.AFTER).getTime() && !m.isStarred();
    });
```

---

1 It's not clear if this is a rate-limited operation, but there is no harm in applying backoff just in case it is or becomes so in a future API update.

In VBA, on the other hand, body searching and category searching are done at the individual message level:

```vb
Set category = getLabel()
' do some further filtering on the body and categorize
For Each item In items
    ' can be other stuff than mail in a folder
    If (TypeName(item) = "MailItem") Then
        ' reclass to correct type
        Set mailItem = item
        ' if the mail contains the key phrase and is not categorized
        If (VBA.InStr(1, mailItem.categories, category.name) < 1 And _
            mailItem.FlagRequest <> Settings.getValue("THREADS.FLAG") And _
            (VBA.InStr(1, LCase(mailItem.Subject), _
                LCase(Settings.getValue("THREADS.PHRASE"))) > 0 Or _
            VBA.InStr(1, LCase(mailItem.Body), _
                LCase(Settings.getValue("THREADS.PHRASE"))) > 0)) Then
            result.add mailItem
        End If
    End If
Next item
```

Regular Expression Searching

The initial searching at thread level returns threads that match query attributes and the target text, but more complicated searching using regular expressions is available only at message level. The content of each message must be retrieved for filtering by potential flight numbers of target airlines.

Message body

Occasionally, complex emails (spammy stuff from LinkedIn, for example) will return content errors, so it's always wise to wrap this in a try/catch. It's not clear whether getPlainBody is (or will be one day) subject to Gmail rate limits, so by convention, wrapping potentially service-heavy calls in exponential backoff does no harm:

```js
messages.forEach(function(m) {
    try {
        // get the message content
        var content = Utils.rateLimitExpBackoff (function () {
            return m.getPlainBody();
        });
        // search the content...
    }
    catch (err) {
        // deal with the error...
    }
});
```

Searching the body. Search the content and the subject using the regular expression that looks for flight numbers as follows. If a match is found, then this message and various other attributes are added to the list of messages to be processed.

```
// see if there's a flight number here somewhere
// rx is a regular expression defining interesting flights
var found =  content ? (rx.exec(content) || rx.exec(m.getSubject())) : false ;

// store this message if it's got one
if (found) {
  p.push({
    flightNumber:found[0],
    message:m,
    carrier:found[1],
    name:lookup.filter(function(d){
        return d[Settings.HEADINGS.CODE].toLowerCase() === found[1]
    })[0][Settings.HEADINGS.NAME]
  });
}
```

Although it's not so commonly used, regular expression searching is possible in VBA too. In this case, qualifying flights are added to a KVPairs object, which is a little like the key/value pair paradigm in JavaScript:

```
For Each message In threads
        content = message.Body
        '// see if there's a flight number in the subject or the body
        '// rx is a regular expression describing interesting flights
        Set found = rx.Execute(message.Subject)
        If (found.Count = 0) Then Set found = rx.Execute(content)

        '// set up an object with useful kv pairs and add to the collection
        If (found.Count > 0) Then
            Set kv = New KVPairs
            kv.add "flightNumber", CStr(found.item(0))
            kv.add "message", message
            kv.add "name", findCarrierName(lookup, _
                CStr(found.item(0).SubMatches.item(0)))
            mobs.add kv
        End If

    Next message
```

Name Lookup

The name field of the object to be processed contains the name of the airline to which the flight code refers, as in the following example:

```
flightNumber: "BA128",
name: "British Airways"
```

The Carriers spreadsheet used in Chapter 6 was imported and converted to a standard object earlier in the application. Looking up the name based on the carrier code (found by the regex search) is a simple filter operation:

```
name:lookup.filter(function(d){
        return d[Settings.HEADINGS.CODE].toLowerCase() === found[1]
    })[0][Settings.HEADINGS.NAME]
```

An alternative approach would be to use the VBA library ListObject, created in a previous chapter, which would make the Apps Script solution very similar to the VBA one. VBA uses ListObject to scan for the airline name matching the airline code:

```
Private Function findCarrierName(lookup As ListObject, code As String) As String
    Dim r As Range

    For Each r In _
      lookup.ListColumns(Settings.getValue("HEADINGS.CODE")).Range.Cells
        If (VBA.LCase(r.value) = VBA.LCase(code)) Then
            findCarrierName = r.Offset(r.Column - _
                lookup.ListColumns(Settings.getValue _
                    ("HEADINGS.NAME")).Range.Column).value
            Exit Function
        End If
    Next r

    ' should never happen, as the regex was derived from this.
    Debug.Assert False

End Function
```

Body Errors

Some errors returned by getPlainBody can be ignored, as they are provoked by disfigured content in spammy messages. Here's how to ignore them:

```
catch (err) {
    // ignore the usual suspects
    if (okErrors.some (function (e) {
      return err.message.slice(0,e.length) !== e;
    })) throw new Error (err);
}
```

where okErrors is a static list of errors to ignore.

```
// These are nonthreatening errors from Gmail we'll just ignore.
var okErrors = [
    'Attachment content not recognized as string or binary.',
    'Invalid mime type'
];
```

Result Reduction

All of the preceding message processing is wrapped in a `reduce` operation. The final result is an array of messages that meet the criteria, along with lookup data about the flight and airline:

```js
match.messages = function (threads, lookup) {

    // get the regex for the allowable airlines
    var rx = new RegExp (getRegex(lookup) ,'gmi');
    // look at all the messages in all the threads
    return threads.reduce (function (p,c) {
      // process the messages and push interesting ones to p...
        return p;
  },[]);
};
```

The VBA equivalent is to push successful matches to a collection of qualifying messages:

```vb
If (found.Count > 0) Then
    Set kv = New KVPairs
    kv.add "flightNumber", CStr(found.item(0))
    kv.add "message", message
    kv.add "name", findCarrierName(lookup, _
        CStr(found.item(0).SubMatches.item(0)))
    mobs.add kv
End If
```

Generate a Regular Expression

The regular expression to find flight numbers is constructed from the list of known carrier codes derived from the Carriers spreadsheet.

```js
/**
 * make the regex for flight matching
 * @param {object} lookup the lookup data
 * @return {Regexp} the matching regex
 */
function getRegex (lookup) {

    // according to wikipedia, https://en.wikipedia.org/wiki/Airline_codes
    // a flight number looks like this
    // - xx(a)n(n)(n)(n)(a)
    // xx = the airline code
    // n - between 1 and 4 numeric codes
    // a - an operational optional code
    return '\\b(' +
        lookup.map(function(d) {
        return d[Settings.HEADINGS.CODE].toLowerCase();
      }).join("|") +
```

```
                ')([a-z]?)(\\d{1,4}[a-z]?)\\b';
        }
```

VBA iterates over the `ListObject` containing the spreadsheet data to extract the qualifying airline codes into a regular expression:

```VB
    '   /**
    '    * make the regex for flight matching
    '    * @param {ListObject} lookup the lookup data
    '    * @return {Regexp} the matching regex
    '    */
    Private Function getRegex(lookup As ListObject) As String

        Dim carrierList As String, r As Range
        carrierList = ""

        ' add each of the flight codes
        For Each r In lookup.ListColumns( _
                Settings.getValue("HEADINGS.CODE")).Range.Cells
            carrierList = carrierList + r.value + "|"
        Next r

        ' get rid of the trailing delimiter
        If (Len(carrierList) > 0) Then
          carrierList = Left(carrierList, Len(carrierList) - 1)
          End If

        getRegex = "\b(" & carrierList & ")([a-z]?)(\d{1,4}[a-z]?)\b"

    End Function
```

Attachments

Apps Script attachments are accessed via their parent message:

```JS
    messages.forEach (function(m) {
        // get the message attachments
        var attachments = Utils.rateLimitExpBackoff(function() {
          return m.getAttachments();
        });
        // do something with the attachments
    });
```

An attachment is already a blob, so saving it to Drive or otherwise processing it is straightforward:[2]

```JS
    var files = attachments.map(function(d) {
        return Utils.rateLimitExpBackoff(function() {
          return flightFolder.createFile(d);
```

---

2 A blob is an Apps Script data interchange object.

```
        });
    });
```

The VBA attachment object has a handy method for saving itself to a given local path:

VB
```
For Each attachment In attachments
        attachment.SaveAsFile (flightFolder.path & "\" & attachment.FileName)
    Next attachment
```

Organizing

It is possible that multiple messages qualify for processing in a single thread. Some may have a flight number but no attachments. In this case, the latest one that has attachments is the one that is processed. If there are no attachments, then an error email is sent to the informant.

Another scenario might be that there are submissions for multiple flight numbers in the same thread. In this case, each must be dealt with.

This function organizes the messages by thread and flight number, and adds any attachments to each message object. Using the thread ID and flight number as object keys also has the pleasant side effect of grouping related messages together:

JS
```
/**
 * organize the messages into threads/flightnumbers priority to attachments
 * @param {object[]} the filtered messages
 * @return {object} the organized messages
 */
match.organize = function (mobs) {

// there might be multiple messages for multiple flights in a thread
  return mobs.reduce (function(p,c) {

        // the message thread
        var threadId = c.message.getThread().getId();
        p[threadId] = p[threadId] || {};

        // the flight
        p[threadId][c.flightNumber] = p[threadId][c.flightNumber] || {};
        var ob = p[threadId][c.flightNumber];

        // mails with attachments get priority
        var attachments = Utils.rateLimitExpBackoff( function () {
          return c.message.getAttachments();
        });

        if ( (attachments && attachments.length) ||
            (!ob.attachments || !ob.attachments.length) ) {
          ob.attachments = attachments;
          ob.mob = c;
        }
```

```
        return p;
    },{});

};
```

We can achieve a similar (if more long-winded) result in VBA using the KVpairs object:

```vb
' /**
'  * organize the messages into threads/messages/flightnumbers
'  * giving priority to attachments
'  * @param {collection} the filtered messages
'  * @return {collection} the organized messages
'  */
Public Function organize(mobs As Collection) As KVPairs
    Dim threadId As String, mob As KVPairs, organizedMob As KVPairs, _
        message As Outlook.mailItem, ob As KVPairs, _
        attachments As Outlook.attachments

    Set organizedMob = New KVPairs

    For Each mob In mobs

        ' the original qualifying message
        Set message = mob.getValue("message")

        '  use the conversation ID
        threadId = CStr(message.ConversationID)

        ' create a new entry for this thread if it doesn't exist
        If (Not organizedMob.exists(threadId)) Then
            organizedMob.add threadId, New KVPairs
        End If

        ' create a new entry for this thread/flight combination
        ' if it doesn't exist
        If (Not organizedMob.getValue(threadId) _
                .exists(mob.getValue("flightNumber"))) Then
            organizedMob.getValue(threadId).add _
                mob.getValue("flightNumber"), New KVPairs
        End If

        ' this is where we'll add the details of this flight
        Set ob = organizedMob.getValue(threadId) _
          .getValue(mob.getValue("flightNumber"))

        ' get any attachments
        Set attachments = message.attachments

        ' messages with attachments take priority
        If (attachments.Count > 0 Or Not ob.exists("attachments")) Then
            ob.replace "attachments", attachments
            ob.replace "mob", mob
```

```
        End If

    Next mob

    Set organize = organizedMob

End Function
```

Recipients

Recipients can be retrieved from the message object. Normally a recipient address consists of two parts, like this:

```
Bruce Mcpherson <bruce@mcpher.com>
```

This code is useful to find the display name and the email address:

```js
var person =  getSplitEmail(m.message.getFrom());
```

And here is a function to split the address into a display name and email address:

```js
/**
 * get the from email and display name from a from field in Gmail app
 * @param {string} from the getFrom() data
 * @return {object} an object with email and display properties
 */
function getSplitEmail (from,def) {

  // the email address from gmailapp contains mixed email and display name
  return {
    email: Utils.getMatchPiece (/\<(.*)\>/ , from,'') ,
    display: Utils.getMatchPiece (/(.*)\s+\</, from,'')
  };
}
```

...which references a useful shared utility function for managing common regular expression matching operations:

```js
/**
 * execute a regex and return the single match
 * @param {Regexp} rx the regexp
 * @param {string} source the source string
 * @param {string} def the default value
 * @return {string} the match
 */
utils.getMatchPiece = function (rx, source, def) {
  var f = rx.exec(source);

  var result = f && f.length >1 ? f[1] : def;

  // special hack for boolean
  if (typeof def === typeof true) {
    result = utils.yesish ( result );
```

```
      }

      return result;
    };

    utils.yesish = function(s) {
      var t = s.toString().toLowerCase();
      return t === "yes" || "y" || "true" || "1";
    };
```

Split mail with VBA as follows:

VB
```
Private Function getSplitEmail(item As Outlook.mailItem) As KVPairs
    Dim person As KVPairs
    Set person = New KVPairs
    person.add "email", item.SenderEmailAddress
    person.add "display", item.SenderName
    Set getSplitEmail = person
End Function
```

Organizing by Recipient

With automation applications, it's sometimes necessary to roll up emails for the same recipient into a single message.

Attachments are added to a folder organized like this:

    ../username/flightnumber

The first time a user is encountered:

- The informant is invited to and booked on the next available scheduled briefing session.

- A folder is created, and the informant is given viewer access to it and will receive a separate invitation to visit it.

The input data is an object, one item per actionable message. `Object.keys(object)` returns an array of each key in an object—in this case, it will be the `threadId`, followed by the flight number—and the object might look like this:

```
[ {thread1:{ba123:{...message object...},ua777:{...message object...}},
  {thread2:{lh671:{...message object...},us7:{...message object...}} ]
```

Here is the function that consolidates the messages, deals with contacts, and sends the mails. (The Contacts service is discussed later in this chapter.) The `FilePaths` namespace contains some helpers to work with Drive and convert between traditional directory filepaths like */user/bruce/data/* and the Drive folder structure. (The namespace is covered in Chapter 9.)

Here's the code:

```js
/**
 * replies
 * @param {object} organized messages to process
 */
threads.send = function (mobs) {

  // things that need scheduling
  var emailsNeeded = [] ;

  // need to send an email confirming
  Object.keys(mobs).forEach (function(k) {
    // each flight within each thread
    Object.keys(mobs[k]).forEach (function(f) {

      var m = mobs[k][f].mob;
      var attachments = mobs[k][f].attachments;

      // get the name and email address
      var person =  getSplitEmail(m.message.getFrom());

      // add them to contacts
      var contact = Contacts.getContact( person.email, true ,
        Utils.getMatchPiece(/(.*)\s/,person.display),
        Utils.getMatchPiece(/\s+(.*)/,person.display));

      // if no attachments, it's a different workflow
      if (attachments && attachments.length ) {

        // if it's a new person, they won't have a folder yet
        var personFolder = FilePaths.getDriveFolderFromPath(
          Settings.PATHS.ARCHIVE + person.display);

        // do the workflow for a new person
        if(!personFolder) {
          var archiveFolder = FilePaths.getDriveFolderFromPath(
            Settings.PATHS.ARCHIVE);
          if (!archiveFolder) {
            throw new Error ('archive folder ' + Settings.PATHS.ARCHIVE +
              ' missing - please create it or change settings');
          }

          // create a folder and allow them to view it
          var personFolder = archiveFolder.createFolder(person.display);
          personFolder.addViewer (person.email);
        }

        // need to create a flight number folder if not existing
        var flightFolder =
          FilePaths.getDriveFolderFromPath(
            Settings.PATHS.ARCHIVE + person.display + "/" + m.flightNumber) ||
          personFolder.createFolder (m.flightNumber);
```

```
      // save them to Drive and get their file objects
      var files = attachments.map(function(d) {
        return Utils.rateLimitExpBackoff(function() {
            return flightFolder.createFile(d);
        });
      });

      emailsNeeded.push ({mob:m, person:person, files:files,
        folder:flightFolder,contact:contact});
    }
    else {
      // no attachments - still need an email to ask for one
      emailsNeeded.push ({mob:m, person:person,contact:contact});
    }
  });
});

// now deal with scheduled courses
Courses.organizeCourses(emailsNeeded);

// and with emails to be sent
// organize for only one consolidated email per person
sendEmails (emailsNeeded) ;

};
```

Formatting

Apps Script provides two methods of formatting the body of an email. If the recipient supports HTML, then the content provided in the options.htmlBody field is used; otherwise, the default body is used. This example is part of this chapter's exercise, and contains a different message for each HTML-enabled and non-HTML-enabled recipient mail client.

Table 8-2 lists each formatting item and its corresponding contents for this example.

Table 8-2. Items for formatting the body of an email

Item	Contains
m.message	A GmailMessage object
m.flightNumber	A flight code like ua928
m.name	An airline name like United Airlines
person.display	A recipient's name

This is the message an HTML-enabled client will receive:

Dear Bruce Mcpherson

Thank you for your email for United Airlines flight ua928

There were no files attached. Please try again, this time with the expected attachments

Organizing by recipient with VBA

In VBA, we need a slightly different approach, using categories and FlagRequests (VBA) in place of Labels and Starred (Apps Script), but it follows essentially the same principle:

```vb
Public Function send(mobs As KVPairs)
    Dim emailsNeeded As Collection, thread As KVPairs, flight As KVPairs, _
        threadKey As Variant, flightKey As Variant, mob As KVPairs, _
        attachments As Outlook.attachments, message As Outlook.mailItem, _
        person As KVPairs, attachment As Outlook.attachment, _
        personFolder As Object, kv As KVPairs, _
        archiveFolder As Object, flightFolder As Object

    Set emailsNeeded = New Collection

    For Each threadKey In mobs.getKeys
        Set thread = mobs.getValue(threadKey)
        For Each flightKey In thread.getKeys

            '// this should make it clearer where each item is coming from
            Set flight = thread.getValue(flightKey)
            Set attachments = flight.getValue("attachments")
            Set mob = flight.getValue("mob")
            Set message = mob.getValue("message")

            '// extract out the sender details
            Set person = getSplitEmail(message)

            '// all this is input to drive the email sending session
            Set kv = New KVPairs
            kv.add "mob", mob
            kv.add "person", person
            kv.add "contact", _
              Contacts_.getContact(person.getValue("email"), True, _
                person.getValue("display"), person.getValue("display"))

            '// if there are attachments, we need to save them
            If (attachments.Count > 0) Then
                Set archiveFolder = FilePaths_.getFolderFromPath( _
                  Settings.getValue("PATHS.ARCHIVE"), True)
                Set personFolder = _
                  FilePaths_.getFolderFromPath(archiveFolder.path & _
                    "\" & person.getValue("display"), True)
                Set flightFolder = _
```

```
                    FilePaths_.getFolderFromPath(personFolder.path & _
                        "\" & mob.getValue("flightNumber"), True)

                For Each attachment In attachments
                    attachment.SaveAsFile (flightFolder.path & "\" & _
                        attachment.FileName)
                Next attachment

                kv.add "files", attachments
                kv.add "folder", flightFolder

            End If

            ' all the details for emails to be added
            emailsNeeded.add kv, threadKey & "_" & flightKey


        Next flightKey
    Next threadKey

    '// now deal with scheduled courses
    Courses_.organizeCourses emailsNeeded

    '// send confirmation mails
    sendEmails emailsNeeded

    '//mark all as processed
    For Each thread In emailsNeeded
        Set message = thread.getValue("mob").getValue("message")

        ' check to see if this category is already known
        Dim cats As Variant, i As Long, cat As String
        cats = Split(message.categories, ",")
        For i = LBound(cats) To UBound(cats)
            If (cats(i) = Settings.getValue("THREADS.LABEL")) Then cat = cats(i)
        Next i

        ' add the category for the thread
        If (cat = vbNullString) Then
            ReDim cats(LBound(cats) To UBound(cats) + 1)
            cats(UBound(cats)) = Settings.getValue("THREADS.LABEL")
            message.categories = Join(cats, ",")
        End If

        ' flag the individual message
        message.FlagRequest = Settings.getValue("THREADS.FLAG")
        message.Save

    Next thread
```

Sending

Creating a new thread and sending a message is handled by the `GmailApp` class:

```js
GmailApp.sendEmail('bruce@mcpher.com',
    'about your flight data',
    'we got it'', {
      htmlBody: '<h1>We Got it!</h1> '
    });
```

The chapter example sends a single mail to each informant, rolling up the responses.

```js
/**
 * send emails after first summarizing them by unique individual
 * @param {object[]} emailsNeeded
 */
  function sendEmails (emailsNeeded) {

    // reduce to one item per person
    var organize = emailsNeeded.reduce(function(p,c) {
    // create an item indexed by contact
    var id = c.contact.getId();
    p[id] = p[id] || [];
    p[id].push(c);
    return p;
  },{});


    // then send
    Object.keys(organize).forEach(function(k) {
        var ob = organize[k];

        // each message received for one person
        var htmlBody = ob.reduce (function(p,c) {

          p += c.files ?
          '<p>You uploaded the following files for ' + c.mob.name +
          ' flight ' + c.mob.flightNumber + '</p>' +
            '<table><tr><th>Name</th><th>Folder</th></tr>' +
            c.files.map(function(d) {

                return '<tr>' +
                '<td><a href="' + d.getUrl() + '">' + d.getName() + '</td>' +
                '<td><a href="' +
                    c.folder.getUrl() + '">' + c.folder.getName() + '</td>'
              })
              .join('</tr>') + '</table>' :
              '<p>For ' + c.mob.name + ' flight ' + c.mob.flightNumber +
              'there were no files attached. Please resubmit,' +
              ' this time with the expected attachments</p>';
            return p;
        },'<h4>Dear ' + ob[0].person.display + '</h4>' +
          '<p>Thank you for your flight data submission<br></p>');
```

```
        // send the mail
        Utils.rateLimitExpBackoff(function() {
          GmailApp.sendEmail( ob[0].person.email,
            'your flight data submission' +
            'Thank you for your flight data submission. ' +
            'Please view this email on an HTML enabled device',{
            htmlBody:htmlBody,
            noReply:true
          });
        });

    });

    //mark all as processed
    emailsNeeded.forEach(function(e) {
        e.mob.message.getThread().addLabel(getLabel());
        e.mob.message.star();
    });
};
```

The type of email sent by this code is shown in Figure 8-1.

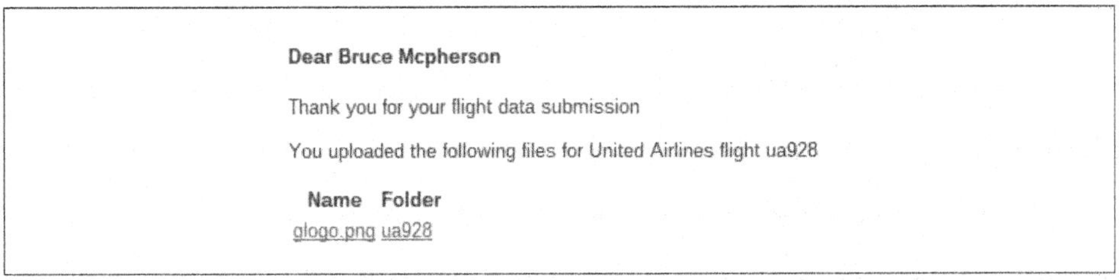

Dear Bruce Mcpherson

Thank you for your flight data submission

You uploaded the following files for United Airlines flight ua928

Name   Folder
glogo.png ua928

Figure 8-1. Email sent by Apps Script

Because both VBA and Apps Script can send HTML-formatted mails, the VBA code is similar. The only difference is that the links to the saved attachments and folders are not needed in VBA because they are created locally and not in the cloud, as they are with Drive:

```
VB  Private Function sendEmails(emailsNeeded As Collection)
        Dim organize As KVPairs, kv As KVPairs, _
          flight As Variant, flights As Collection, _
          thisPerson As Collection, key As Variant, htmlBody As String, _
          att As attachment, atts As attachments
        Set organize = New KVPairs

        '// reduce to one item per person
        For Each kv In emailsNeeded
            key = kv.getValue("person").getValue("email")
            If Not organize.exists(key) Then
                Set thisPerson = New Collection
                organize.add CStr(key), thisPerson
```

```
        Else
            Set thisPerson = organize.getValue(key)
        End If
        thisPerson.add kv, kv.getValue("mob").getValue("flightNumber")

Next kv

'// do the sending
For Each key In organize.getKeys
    Set flights = organize.getValue(key)

    htmlBody = "'<h4>Dear " & _
        flights(1).getValue("person").getValue("display") & _
            "</h4>" & "<p>Thank you for your flight data submission<br></p>"

    ' a line in the email for each flight
    For Each flight In flights
        ' type of message depends on whether there were files
        If flight.exists("files") Then

            htmlBody = htmlBody & _
                "<p>You uploaded the following files for " & _
                flight.getValue("mob").getValue("name") & " flight " & _
                flight.getValue("mob").getValue("flightNumber") & "</p>" & _
                "<table><tr><th>Name</th><th>Folder</th></tr>"

            ' list the files and the folder they are in
            For Each att In flight.getValue("files")
                htmlBody = htmlBody & "<tr>" & _
                    "<td>" & att.DisplayName & "</td>" & _
                    "<td>" & flight.getValue("folder").name & "</td></tr>"
            Next att
            htmlBody = htmlBody & "</table>"

        Else
            htmlBody = htmlBody & "<p>For " & _
                flight.getValue("mob").getValue("name") & _
                " flight " & _
                flight.getValue("mob").getValue("flightNumber") & _
                " there were no files attached." & _
                "Please resubmit, this time with the expected attachments</p>"
        End If

    Next flight

    With Outlook.Application.CreateItem(olMailItem)
        .To = key
        .Subject = "your flight data submission"
        .BodyFormat = olFormatHTML
        .htmlBody = htmlBody
        .send
    End With
```

```
          Next key
    End Function
```

Labels

Although Gmail does not organize threads by folder, it is possible to allocate labels to message threads. You can assign a thread multiple labels, and search on the presence (or absence) of a particular label. Marking a group of threads with a particular label is a good way to indicate that it has been addressed by some workflow process.

A label is more than just text. It has its own properties and methods, but it can be accessed by its name. This snippet checks to see if a label of a given name already exists, and creates it if not:

```js
/**
 * get a labels
 * @return {GmailLabel} the label
 */
function getLabel () {
  var label = GmailApp.getUserLabelByName('somelabel');
  return label || GmailApp.createLabel('somelabel');
}
```

A label can be assigned to a message's thread like this:

```js
message.getThread().addLabel(label);
```

The example application marks the thread with a label, and the individual messages that provoked an email with a star:

```js
//mark all as processed
emailsNeeded.forEach(function(e) {
    e.mob.message.getThread().addLabel(getLabel());
    e.mob.message.star();
});
```

VBA Categories

Categories in VBA can be used as a substitute for labels. The category (and label) is used to denote that a thread has already been processed so that it will be skipped in the future. VBA categories are a comma-separated list, so they are little more fiddly to deal with than labels in Apps Script. Here's how to get or create a category if it doesn't exist. Note that categories are local only, if your backend mail system is not Exchange (mine is Google Mail):

```vb
Private Function getLabel() As category
    Dim categories As Outlook.categories, category As category

    Set categories = Session.categories
    For Each category In categories
        If (category.name = Settings.getValue("THREADS.LABEL")) Then
```

```
        Set getLabel = category
        Exit Function
    End If
Next category

' create a new one
Set getLabel = categories.add(Settings.getValue("THREADS.LABEL"))

End Function
```

Calendar

CalendarApp is the service interface to the Google Calendars to which a user is subscribed. This will return the names of all your calendars:

```js
Logger.log(CalendarApp.getAllCalendars().map(function(calendar) {
    return calendar.getName();
}));
```

The example application references a calendar that should contain a series of events—briefing sessions for new informants. It is best to create a specific calendar for this purpose, which you can delete later. The informant is invited to the next available briefing session indicated in that calendar the first time they submit data to their repository (detected by the creation of their own personal folder).

Events

For this example, you will already have set up a recurring calendar event using the regular Calendar UI. The application will search by name for this event and add the contact as a guest if it's the first time the informant has been detected.

The Courses Namespace

The Courses namespace takes care of all the calendar interaction:

```js
var Courses = (function(courses) {
    'use strict';
    // ... the code for dealing with calendars
    return courses;
})(Courses || {});
```

Finding the course calendar works as follows:

```js
/**
 * get the course calendar
 * @return {Calendar} the calendar
 */
courses.getCalendar = function () {
    var calendars = CalendarApp.getCalendarsByName(
                    Settings.COURSES.FLIGHTS.CALENDAR);
```

```
    if (!calendars || !calendars.length) {
        throw new Error ('could not find course calendar ' +
Settings.COURSES.FLIGHTS.CALENDAR);
    }
    return calendars[0];
};
```

Dealing with recurring events in VBA is a little more complicated, so to avoid off-topic code, we'll assume the events are set up as a series of one-off (i.e., not recurring) events in the calendar whose name matches the flight calendar name setting. (In contrast, the Apps Script version can handle both types equally easily, as it can return a separate instance of each recurring event if required.) Here's the code:

VB
```
Public Function getCalendar() As folder
    Set getCalendar = Session.GetDefaultFolder(olFolderCalendar). _
        Folders(Settings.getValue("COURSES.flights.CALENDAR"))
End Function
```

Finding the next event

The idea here is to invite the informant to a briefing session not too close to now, but not too far in the future. These values are controlled by the number of days' values in the Settings property: DELAY and HORIZON. If DELAY were 7 and HORIZON were 100, this code would find the next recurring calendar event that's at least a week from now, but not more than 100 days in the future:

JS
```
/**
 * get the next course event
 * @return {CalendarEvent} the next available event
 */
courses.getNextEvent = function () {
  var now = new Date();
  var events = Utils.rateLimitExpBackoff(function() {
    return courses.getCalendar().getEvents (
      new Date(now.getTime()+Settings.COURSES.FLIGHTS.DELAY*60*60*24*1000),
      new Date(now.getTime()+Settings.COURSES.FLIGHTS.HORIZON*60*60*24*1000),
      {search:Settings.COURSES.FLIGHTS.NAME}
    );
  });
  return events && events.length ? events[0] : null;
};
```

By contrast, because VBA sorts the events on start date, it will return just the first event it finds that matches the date and name criteria:

VB
```
Public Function getNextEvent() As AppointmentItem
    Dim dateNow As Date, timeMin As Date, timeMax As Date, _
        restriction As String, events As items, _
        possibleEvents As items, e As AppointmentItem

    dateNow = now
```

```
    ' get all the events
    Set events = getCalendar().items
    events.IncludeRecurrences = True

    timeMin = DateAdd("d", dateNow, Settings.getValue("COURSES.FLIGHTS.DELAY"))
    timeMax = DateAdd("d", dateNow, Settings.getValue("COURSES.FLIGHTS.HORIZON"))

    ' set time filter
    restriction = "[Start] >= '" & _
        Format$(timeMin, "mm/dd/yyyy hh:mm AMPM") _
        & "' AND [End] <= '" & _
        Format$(timeMax, "mm/dd/yyyy hh:mm AMPM") & "'"

    ' apply filter and sort
    Set possibleEvents = events.Restrict(restriction)
    possibleEvents.Sort "[Start]"

    For Each e In possibleEvents
        ' filter on subject
        If (InStr(1, e.Subject, _
          Settings.getValue("COURSES.FLIGHTS.NAME")) > 0) Then
            Set getNextEvent = e
            Exit Function
        End If
    Next e

End Function
```

Adding guests

Adding the contact as a guest is straightforward once the event is found:

```js
/**
 * schedule an event
 * @param {Contact} contact the contact who needs scheduling
 * @return {CalendarEvent} the event
 */
courses.schedule = function (contact) {

  // get next available event
  var nextEvent = courses.getNextEvent();
  if (!nextEvent) throw new Error ('no events set up for course '
    + Settings.COURSES.FLIGHTS.NAME);

  // invite the contact to it
  Utils.rateLimitExpBackoff(function() {
    nextEvent.addGuest(contact.getEmails()[0].getAddress());
  });

  return nextEvent;
};
```

And it's equally straightforward in VBA. Sending appointment invites is even easier because it's automatic:

```vb
Public Function schedule(contact As ContactItem) As AppointmentItem
    Dim nextEvent As AppointmentItem

    ' get the next suitable event
    Set nextEvent = getNextEvent
    Debug.Assert Not nextEvent Is Nothing

    ' add attendees
    nextEvent.Recipients.add contact.Email1Address

    ' send invite
    nextEvent.send

    Set schedule = nextEvent
End Function
```

Email invites

Now we hit a limitation in this Apps Script service. Ideally, adding a guest should provoke an automatic invite to the guest as it does in VBA. At the time of writing, however, the Apps Script built-in Calendar service has no option to implement this behavior. So now we have a completed application that is able to schedule a meeting, but not inform the guest he is invited.

If you do want to send invites, there are (at least) three potential workarounds:

- You can set the event so that it sends reminders to guests up to four weeks in advance of the event date. One solution would be to modify the event to send reminders shortly after adding a guest. The problem here is that multiple guests would be added at different times and guests would receive multiple reminders (the first time about a meeting they know nothing about). Reminders can be modified like this:
  ```js
  event.addEmailReminder (6*24*60);
  ```
- An *ics* file is a standard format between email systems for calendar invites. It's quite a fiddly format, but nevertheless the application could create and attach an *ics* file to the mail to confirm receipt of the attachment, or in a separate construct. The drawback of this approach is that the invite would be an attachment rather than an official invite.
- Use the Advanced Calendar API, discussed next.

Advanced Calendar Service

The majority of the Apps Script services are built on top of APIs that can be accessed from a variety of languages through an SDK library. Many also have a JSON REST API for those languages or platforms that have no SDK support.

In many cases, the built-in Apps Script service implementation offers only a subset of the API's capabilities. For some services, Google provides a set of what it calls "advanced services" to enable access to some of these additional capabilities in the underlying APIs. Generally speaking, these mimic the capabilities of the JSON API, but are wrapped in a service that takes care of the authentication and HTTP challenges that accessing the JSON API directly would involve.

The Advanced Calendar service provides access to the event send notification option that is missing from the built-in Calendar service.

Enabling advanced services

As with all services, advanced services need to be enabled in your project. Actually, they need two kinds of enablement: in the project, and in the developers console. Both are accessible from the Resources menu, as shown in Figure 8-2.

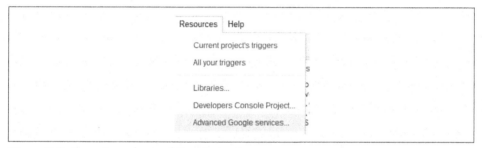

Figure 8-2. Accessing advanced Google services

First, enable the Calendar API in advanced Google services, as shown in Figure 8-3.

Figure 8-3. Enabling the Calendar API in advanced services

Then click the Google Developers Console link to enable it there. You'll see a list of all the Google APIs, a snippet of which is shown in Figure 8-4.

Figure 8-4. Google APIs

In the Google Apps APIs section, click the Calendar API link and enable it, as shown in Figure 8-5.

Figure 8-5. Enabling the Calendar API in the developers console

Advanced Google services will be covered in Chapter 14, but now the Calendar API is enabled for use in the Apps Script project, giving us full access to its capabilities.

Adding guests with the Calendar API

Now we can rewrite the `courses.schedule` function to use the advanced service, and automatically send an invite to the informant. CalendarApp and the Calendar API treat recurring events a little differently. CalendarApp returns an array of events, each with the same ID, the first of which is the recurring series event.

The Calendar API returns just the recurring series event. Behind the scenes, each individual event has an ID based on the recurring series event, but with a suffix of the individual event's start time in this format:

```
id_time
```

Specify this option to get a list of individual events associated with a recurring series:

```
singleEvents:true
```

Here's the code to find the next possible event:

```js
/**
 * get the next event using the advanced calendar service
 * @return {CalendarEvent} the first matching calendar event
 */
courses.getNextEvent = function () {

  var now = new Date().getTime();

  // find the first events for this course
  var events = Utils.rateLimitExpBackoff(function() {
    return Calendar.Events.list(courses.getCalendar().getId(),{
      q:Settings.COURSES.FLIGHTS.NAME,
      timeMin :new Date(now+Settings.COURSES.FLIGHTS.DELAY*60*60*24*1000)
        .toISOString(),
      timeMax : new Date(now+Settings.COURSES.FLIGHTS.HORIZON*60*60*24*1000)
        .toISOString(),
      singleEvents:true,
      orderBy:'startTime',
      maxResults:1
    });
  });
  return events && events.items.length ? events.items[0] : null;
};
```

And here's the updated scheduler, now using the Calendar API:

```js
/**
 * schedule an event using the advanced API
 * @param {Contact} contact the contact who needs scheduling
 * @return {CalendarEvent} the event
 */
courses.schedule = function (contact) {

  // get next available event
  var nextEvent = courses.getNextEvent();
  if (!nextEvent) throw new Error ('no events set up for course ' +
    Settings.COURSES.FLIGHTS.NAME);

  // get the event
  var event = Utils.rateLimitExpBackoff(function() {
    return Calendar.Events.get(courses.getCalendar().getId(), nextEvent.id);
  });

  // add attendee, creating attendees if none
  if (!event.attendees) {
    event.attendees = [];
  }
  event.attendees.push({email:contact.getEmails()[0].getAddress()});

  // patch the event with the new attendees
    return Utils.rateLimitExpBackoff(function() {
```

```
      return Calendar.Events.patch(
        event, courses.getCalendar().getId(), event.id, {
        sendNotifications: true
      });
    });
  };
```

CoursesAdvanced namespace

Because each of the courses versions are within namespaces, it's simple to change from one version to the other. The amended namespace is called `CoursesAdvanced` and is wrapped as follows:

```
var CoursesAdvanced = (function(courses) {
    'use strict';
    // ... the code ...
});
```

With the following small change in `Threads.send`, it now uses the advanced version.

From:

```
// now deal with scheduled courses
    Courses.organizeCourses(emailsNeeded);
```

to:

```
// now deal with scheduled courses
    CoursesAdvanced.organizeCourses(emailsNeeded);
```

Figure 8-6 shows the invite.

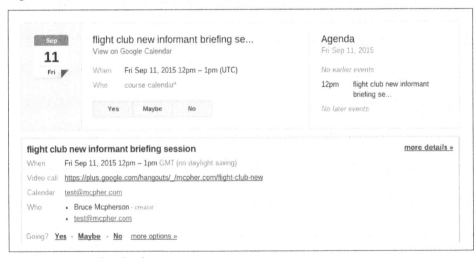

Figure 8-6. Completed informant invitation

Contacts

The ContactApp is the interface to the Contacts service. Here's how to get a contact by email address, or create it if the contact does not exist:

```js
var contact = getContact ("bruce@mcpher.com, true, "Bruce" , "McPherson");

/**
 * get a contact
 * @param {string} address the email address
 * @param {boolean} [create=false] create if it doesn't exist
 * @param {string} [givenName] given name to set if created
 * @param {string} [familyName] familyName to set if created
 * @return {Contact|null} the contact
 */
var getContact = function (address,create,givenName,familyName) {

  var contact = ContactsApp.getContact(address);
  // create it
  if (!contact && create) {
    contact = ContactsApp.createContact(givenName ,familyName, address);
  }
  return contact;
};
```

The VBA equivalent to the ContactApp is the folder that holds the contacts—in this case, the default contacts folder:

```vb
Public Function getContacts() As folder
    Set getContacts = Session.GetDefaultFolder(olFolderContacts)
End Function
```

Finding a contact by email address in VBA is a little more complicated, because there are three email fields in an Outlook ContactItem, each of which needs to be searched:

```vb
Public Function getContact(address As String, create As Boolean, _
        givenName As String, familyName As String) As ContactItem

    Dim contacts As folder, contact As ContactItem, restriction As String, _
        e As Outlook.ContactItem, matches As items

    Set contacts = getContacts()

    ' see if we know this person
    restriction = "[Email1Address] = '" & _
        address _
        & "' OR [Email2Address] = '" & _
        address _
        & "' OR [Email3Address] = '" & _
        address _
        & "'"
```

```
        Set matches = contacts.items.Restrict(restriction)

        ' just consider contact class
        For Each e In matches
            If e.Class = olContact Then
                Set contact = e
                Exit For
            End If
        Next e

        If contact Is Nothing And create Then
            ' add it
            Set contact = Application.CreateItem(olContactItem)
            With contact
                .Email1Address = address
                .FirstName = givenName
                .LastName = familyName
                .Save
            End With
        End If

        Set getContact = contact
End Function
```

ContactGroups

A contact can belong to multiple contact groups. Here's how to get a `ContactGroup` object (or create it if it doesn't exist), then assign it to a contact:

JS `getContactGroup ("some group", true).addContact(contact);`

```
    /**
     * get a contact group
     * @param {string} name name of the contact group
     * @param {boolean} [create=false] create if it doesn't exist
     * @return {ContactGroup|null} the contact group
     */
    var getContactGroup = function (name,create) {

      var group = ContactsApp.getContactGroup(name);

      // create it
      if (!group && create) {
        group = ContactsApp.createContactGroup(name);
      }

      return group;

    };
```

The contact group does not exist in VBA, but you can use a distribution list for similar functionality. Here is the VBA equivalent to the preceding code, using distribution lists:

```vb
Function getContactGroup(name As String, create As Boolean) As DistListItem
    Dim contacts As folder, group As DistListItem, _
        e As Object, o As DistListItem

    Set contacts = getContacts()

    ' just consider dl class
    For Each e In contacts.items
        If e.Class = olDistributionList Then
            Set o = e
            If o.DLName = name Then
                Set group = e
                Exit For
            End If
        End If
    Next e
    If group Is Nothing And create Then
        Set group = Application.CreateItem(olDistributionListItem)
        With group
            .DLName = name
            .Save
        End With
    End If
    Set getContactGroup = group
End Function
```

Contacts Namespace

As usual, the application code for dealing with contacts is wrapped inside a namespace:

```js
var Contacts = (function(contacts) {
    'use strict';

    /**
     * get a contact
     * @param {string} address the email address
     * @param {boolean} [create=false] create if it doesn't exist
     * @param {string} [givenName] given name to set if created
     * @param {string} [familyName] familyName to set if created
     * @return {Contact|null} the contact
     */
    contacts.getContact = function (address,create,givenName,familyName) {
        var contact = ContactsApp.getContact(address);

        // create it
        if (!contact && create) {
            contact = ContactsApp.createContact(
```

```
                givenName || Utils.getMatchPiece(/(.+)\@/,address,'unknown') ,
                familyName || Utils.getMatchPiece(/.+\@(.+)/,address,'unknown'),
                address);
        }

        return contact;

    };

    /**
     * get a contact group
     * @param {string} name name of the contact group
     * @param {boolean} [create=false] create if it doesn't exist
     * @return {ContactGroup|null} the contact group
     */
    contacts.getContactGroup = function (name,create) {

        var group = ContactsApp.getContactGroup(name);

        // create it
        if (!group && create) {
            group = ContactsApp.createContactGroup(name);
        }

        return group;

    };

    /**
     * check if a member of a group
     * @param {ContactGroup} group the contact group
     * @param {Contact} contact the contact
     * @return {boolean} whether contact is in group
     */
    contacts.isInGroup = function (group,contact) {
        // check if in
        return group ?
        contact.getContactGroups().some(function(d){
            return d.getId() === group.getId();}) :
            false;
    };

    return contacts;

})(Contacts || {});
```

The VBA contacts namespace is fairly similar, even though it uses distribution lists rather than contact groups:

```
VB  Option Explicit

    Public Function getContacts() As folder
        Set getContacts = Session.GetDefaultFolder(olFolderContacts)
```

```
End Function

Public Function getContact(address As String, _
    create As Boolean, givenName As String, _
        familyName As String) As ContactItem

    Dim contacts As folder, contact As ContactItem, restriction As String, _
        e As Outlook.ContactItem, matches As items

    Set contacts = getContacts()

    ' see if we know this person
    restriction = "[Email1Address] = '" & _
        address _
        & "' OR [Email2Address] = '" & _
        address _
        & "' OR [Email3Address] = '" & _
        address _
        & "'"

    Set matches = contacts.items.Restrict(restriction)

    ' just consider contact class
    For Each e In matches
        If e.Class = olContact Then
            Set contact = e
            Exit For
        End If
    Next e

    If contact Is Nothing And create Then
        ' add it
        Set contact = Application.CreateItem(olContactItem)
        With contact
            .Email1Address = address
            .FirstName = givenName
            .LastName = familyName
            .Save
        End With
    End If

    Set getContact = contact
End Function

Public Function getContactGroup ( _
        name As String, create As Boolean) As DistListItem
    Dim contacts As folder, group As DistListItem, _
        e As Object, o As DistListItem

    Set contacts = getContacts()

    ' just consider dl class
```

```
            For Each e In contacts.items
                If e.Class = olDistributionList Then
                    Set o = e
                    If o.DLName = name Then
                        Set group = e
                        Exit For
                    End If
                End If
            Next e

            If group Is Nothing And create Then
                Set group = Application.CreateItem(olDistributionListItem)
                With group
                    .DLName = name
                    .Save
                End With
            End If

            Set getContactGroup = group
        End Function

        Public Function isInGroup(group As DistListItem, _
            contact As ContactItem) As Boolean
            Dim i As Long, r As Recipient

            If Not group Is Nothing Then
                For i = 1 To group.MemberCount
                    Set r = group.GetMember(i)
                    If (r.address = contact.Email1Address _
                      Or r.address = contact.Email2Address _
                        Or r.address = contact.Email3Address) Then
                        isInGroup = True
                    End If
                Next i
            End If
            isInGroup = False
        End Function
```

Organizing Courses

The contact group is used from the example application to check whether someone
needs training, and to mark that they have been invited:

JS
```
/**
 * organize courses
 * @param {object[]} messages an array of objects containing contact info
 * @param {CalendarEvents[]} an array of the events invited to
 */
courses.organizeCourses= function  (messages) {

    // this is used to note whether they need a course
    var contactGroup = Contacts.getContactGroup (Settings.CONTACTS.GROUP, true);
```

```
      return messages.map(function(d) {

        // if not in the contact group already, they need a course
        if( !Contacts.isInGroup (contactGroup , d.contact) ) {
          var result = courses.schedule(d.contact);
          contactGroup.addContact (d.contact);
          return result;
        }
        return null;
      })

      // get rid of those that didnt get an invite
      .filter (function(d) {
        return d;
      });

  };
```

The VBA version creates a collection of contacts who need to be invited to courses:

```
VB  Public Function organizeCourses(messages As Collection) As Collection
      Dim kv As KVPairs, contactGroup As DistListItem, _
          result As AppointmentItem, invitees As Collection, _
          mailMessage As mailItem

      Set invitees = New Collection

      ' get the contact group or create it
      Set contactGroup = Contacts_.getContactGroup( _
          Settings.getValue("COURSES.CONTACTS.GROUP"), True)

      ' see what emails need to be sent
      For Each kv In messages
          ' if not in contact group, then need to be invited to a course
          If (Not Contacts_.isInGroup(contactGroup, kv.getValue("contact"))) Then
              Set result = schedule(kv.getValue("contact"))
              Set mailMessage = kv.getValue("mob").getValue("message")
              contactGroup.AddMember (mailMessage.Recipients(1))
              invitees.add kv
          End If
      Next kv
      Set organizeCourses = invitees

  End Function
```

Setting Up the Example

In Apps Script, it doesn't really matter whether everything is in one big script file or spread across multiple files, but as a general rule, it's good practice to keep each namespace separate.

In VBA, the module names each end with an underscore, as the IDE sometimes can't contextually distinguish a module name from a function name.

The full code for the application is in the GitHub repository. The code is organized into separate scripts, as shown in Figure 8-7.

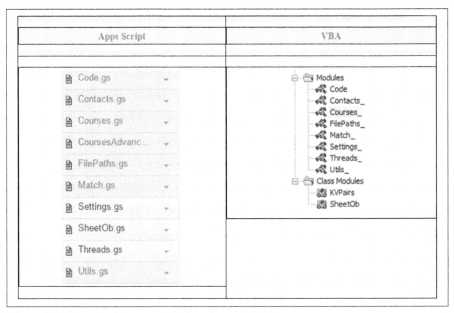

Figure 8-7. Apps Script versus VBA code organization

The Settings

The settings are stored in the Properties service (and the registry in VBA), but will need a one-off setting to initialize them. These should reflect your environment, as shown in Table 8-3.

Table 8-3. Settings stored in the Properties service

Setting	Purpose
LOOKUP	The ID and sheet name of the carrier lookup sheet. It's used to construct the airlines in scope of the example and to translate carrier codes to airline names.
THREADS	Any threads sent AFTER, containing PHRASE, in IN will be searched for likely flight codes generated from LOOKUP and labeled LABEL after processing.
HEADINGS	The name of the columns containing the interesting data in the sheet specified in LOOKUP.
PATHS	Any attachments extracted from in-scope emails will be saved to this Drive ARCHIVE. Make sure this folder path exists on your Google Drive.

Setting	Purpose
COURSES	A recurring event titled NAME needs to be set up in the Calendar named CALENDAR. Events at least DELAY and no more than HORIZON days from the date the first attachment is received will be assigned to informants for a briefing session.
CONTACTS	Informants will be added to GROUP when they have been assigned to a course.

Properties service

Here are the initial settings, which you can change as required.

```js
// one-off settings to get started

var SETTINGS_KEY = "gmailExample";

function setOneTimeProperties () {
  setProperties(oneTimeSettings);
}

function setProperties (props) {
  PropertiesService.getUserProperties()
    .setProperty(oneTimeSettings.KEY, JSON.stringify(props));
}

var oneTimeSettings = (function(settings) {
  'use strict';

  settings.KEY = SETTINGS_KEY;

  settings.LOOKUP = {
    ID: '19wbpUHwuIKbHaaIiylVSuG7lkK29uoAmYrTvTk_J2ho',
    NAME: 'lookup'
  };

  settings.THREADS = {
    AFTER:new Date("2015/08/01").toJSON(),
    LABEL:"flight club submissions",
    IN:"inbox",
    PHRASE:'"flight club"'
  };

  settings.HEADINGS = {
    CODE:'carrier',
    NAME:'name'
  };

  settings.PATHS = {
    ARCHIVE:'/books/going gas/gmailexample/archive/'
  };

  settings.COURSES = {
    FLIGHTS: {
```

```
      CALENDAR:'course calendar',
      NAME:'"flight club"',
      DELAY:21,
      HORIZON:100
    }
  };

  settings.CONTACTS = {
    GROUP:'flight club contacts'
  };

  // update the sheet
  return settings;

})(oneTimeSettings || {});
```

These setting are written once to the property store like this:

JS
```
function setOneTimeProperties () {
    setProperties(oneTimeSettings);
}

function setProperties (props) {
    PropertiesService.getUserProperties().setProperty(SETTINGS_KEY ,
        JSON.stringify(props));
}
```

And retrieved like this:

JS
```
var Settings = JSON.parse(
    PropertiesService.getUserProperties().getProperty(SETTINGS_KEY);
```

VBA registry

VBA can't easily handle JSON or XML without additional references and dependencies. I often use a custom class (KVPairs) to handle simple key/value pairs for this kind of application. The code for this is in the GitHub repository.

If you are accustomed to the same kind of approach in VBA, it's fairly straightforward to treat the Apps Script Properties service in a similar way to the registry. Here are the one-time settings in VBA:

VB
```
Public Sub setOneTimeProperties()
    setProperties oneTimeSettings()
End Sub


Private Sub setProperties(props As KVPairs)
    Dim kv As Variant

    ' write to registry
    For Each kv In props.getPairs()
        SaveSetting SETTINGS_KEY, "settings", VBA.CStr(kv(1)), kv(2)
```

```vb
        Next kv

    End Sub

    Public Function oneTimeSettings() As KVPairs

        Dim kv As KVPairs
        Set kv = New KVPairs

        kv.add "KEY", SETTINGS_KEY

        kv.add "LOOKUP.ID", "c:/users/bruce/Documents/Excel/updateCarrierLookup.xlsx"
        kv.add "LOOKUP.NAME", "lookup"

        kv.add "THREADS.AFTER", DateSerial(2015, 8, 1)
        kv.add "THREADS.LABEL", "flight club submissions"
        kv.add "THREADS.IN", "inbox"
        kv.add "THREADS.PHRASE", """flight club"""

        kv.add "HEADINGS.CODE", "carrier"
        kv.add "HEADINGS.NAME", "name"

        kv.add "PATHS.ARCHIVE", _
          "C:/Users/Bruce/Google Drive/books/going gas/gmailexample/archive/"

        kv.add "COURSES.FLIGHTS.CALENDAR", "course calendar"
        kv.add "COURSES.FLIGHTS.NAME", "flight club"
        kv.add "COURSES.FLIGHTS.DELAY", 21
        kv.add "COURSES.FLIGHTS.HORIZON", 100

        kv.add "COURSES.CONTACTS.GROUP", "flight club contacts"

        Set oneTimeSettings = kv
    End Function
```

These settings are stored as shown in Figure 8-8 in the Windows registry.

This is not too different from the Apps Script Properties service contents:

```vb
{
    "KEY": "gmailExample",
    "LOOKUP": {
        "ID": "19wbpUHwuIKbHaaIiylVSuG7lkK29uoAmYrTvTk_J2ho",
        "NAME": "lookup"
    },
    "THREADS": {
        "AFTER": "2015/08/10",
        "LABEL": "flight club submissions",
        "IN": "inbox",
        "PHRASE": "\"flight club\""
    },
    "HEADINGS": {
        "CODE": "carrier",
```

```
            "NAME": "name"
        },
        "PATHS": {
            "ARCHIVE": "/books/going gas/gmailexample/archive/"
        },
        "COURSES": {
            "FLIGHTS": {
                "CALENDAR": "course calendar",
                "NAME": "\"flight club\"",
                "DELAY": 21,
                "HORIZON": 100
            }
        },
        "CONTACTS": {
            "GROUP": "flight club contacts"
        }
    }
}
```

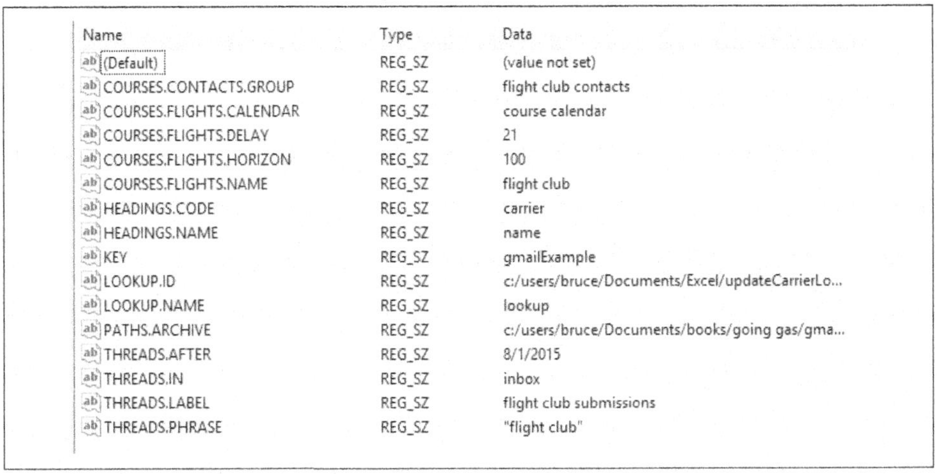

Name	Type	Data
(Default)	REG_SZ	(value not set)
COURSES.CONTACTS.GROUP	REG_SZ	flight club contacts
COURSES.FLIGHTS.CALENDAR	REG_SZ	course calendar
COURSES.FLIGHTS.DELAY	REG_SZ	21
COURSES.FLIGHTS.HORIZON	REG_SZ	100
COURSES.FLIGHTS.NAME	REG_SZ	flight club
HEADINGS.CODE	REG_SZ	carrier
HEADINGS.NAME	REG_SZ	name
KEY	REG_SZ	gmailExample
LOOKUP.ID	REG_SZ	c:/users/bruce/Documents/Excel/updateCarrierLo...
LOOKUP.NAME	REG_SZ	lookup
PATHS.ARCHIVE	REG_SZ	c:/users/bruce/Documents/books/going gas/gma...
THREADS.AFTER	REG_SZ	8/1/2015
THREADS.IN	REG_SZ	inbox
THREADS.LABEL	REG_SZ	flight club submissions
THREADS.PHRASE	REG_SZ	"flight club"

Figure 8-8. VBA settings in the Windows registry

Triggers

Using triggers in Apps Script ensures this entire process runs according to a schedule.

Apps Script Main Function

Any failures will be reported by email, but otherwise this will just run silently on Google's servers, quietly dealing with any emails that arrive:

```js
function trigger() {

  // open the sheet and get the carrier data
  var carrierData = new SheetOb().open(Settings.LOOKUP.ID,
    Settings.LOOKUP.NAME).getData();
```

```
// get all the potential threads
var threads = Threads.get();

// match for any likely flights
var mobs = Match.messages(threads, carrierData);

// organize matches to prioritize
var organized = Match.organize(mobs);

// generate emails and mark as processed
Threads.send (organized);

}
```

VBA Main Function

It is also possible to schedule this using either VBA's Application.run function or the Windows scheduler:

```vb
Option Explicit
Public Settings As KVPairs
Private Sub trigger()
    Dim carrierData As ListObject, sob As SheetOb, threads As Collection, _
        mobs As Collection, organized As KVPairs
    Set sob = New SheetOb

    ' get the settings from registry
    Set Settings = Settings_.getProperties()

    ' get the data
    Set carrierData = sob.sheetOpen(Settings.getValue("lookup.id"), _
        Settings.getValue("lookup.name")).getData()

    '  // get all the potential threads
    Set threads = Threads_.threadsGet

    ' // match for any likely flights
    Set mobs = Match_.messages(threads, carrierData)

    '// organize matches to prioritize
    Set organized = Match_.organize(mobs)

    '// send the mails
    Threads_.send organized

    '// close without saving workbook
    sob.getSheet().parent.Close False

End Sub
```

Scheduling

You can run the whole workflow unattended and regularly by using a trigger. Triggers are set up through the Resources menu, as shown in Figure 8-9.

Figure 8-9. Setting up a trigger

Figure 8-10 shows the workflow now set up to run once every 12 hours.

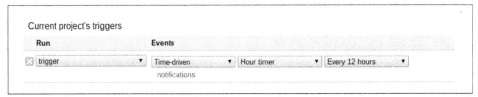

Figure 8-10. Scheduling the workflow to run every 12 hours

CHAPTER 9

Drive and DriveApp

Native Office and Docs files are accessed by services specifically for that purpose from within both VBA and Apps Script. There are times that you may need to access other kinds of files directly from your Apps Script or VBA application. With VBA, you can access the local client machine's filesystem to read and write supplementary files generated within the Office app.

Apps Script runs on Google servers so does not have access to the local client machine. Instead, these kinds of operations can be performed on Google Drive. However, if Drive client synchronization is enabled, reading and writing to Drive is essentially "accessing the client by proxy," as any files written to Drive are copied to the client and vice versa.

Drive can be accessed in three ways from Apps Script, as outlined in Table 9-1.

Table 9-1. Ways of accessing Google Drive from Apps Script

Interface	Description
DriveApp (Apps Script built-in service)	A simplified service for accessing the most commonly used capabilities through simple data structures
Drive (Apps Script advanced Google service)	Enables access to most of the Drive API capabilities, using the default (fairly complex) data structures.
Drive JSON API	Rest API to all of the Drive API features accessible via UrlFetchApp. OAuth 2.0 authentication required.

Microsoft OneDrive

OneDrive is similar to Drive, has a JSON API, and uses OAuth 2.0 for authentication. You can access OneDrive from Apps Script using UrlFetchApp, or from VBA using XMLHttp.

Chapter 15 includes an example of authenticating to OneDrive using OAuth 2.0.

You can also access Drive from VBA using `XMLHttp`, but this is outside the scope of this book.

Reading and Writing Files

There are a number of ways of writing and reading files from VBA. The one I prefer is the `Scripting.FileSystemObject`. Consider this test, which will write some text to a file, check if it exists, and read it back:

```VB
Function testFiles()

    ' write some things
    fileWrite "example.txt", "some text"

    ' check file exists
    Debug.Print fileExists("example.txt")

    ' read them back
    Debug.Print fileRead("example.txt")

End Function
```

VBA FileSystemObject

Here are some simple functions for handling text files using the filesystem object (for brevity's sake, without much error handling).

```VB
Function fileWrite(path As String, content As String)

    Dim file As Object, fso As Object

    ' late binding for filesystem
    Set fso = CreateObject("Scripting.FileSystemObject")

    ' open file for writing
    Set file = fso.OpenTextFile(path, 2, True)

    ' write it out
    file.write content

End Function

Function fileExists(path As String) As Boolean
    Dim fso As Object
```

```
    Set fso = CreateObject("Scripting.FileSystemObject")
    fileExists = fso.fileExists(path)
End Function
Function fileRead(path As String) As String
    Dim file As Object, fso As Object
    Set fso = CreateObject("Scripting.FileSystemObject")
    ' open a file
    Set file = fso.OpenTextFile(path, 1)

    ' check if file is empty
    If (file.AtEndOfStream) Then
        fileRead = ""
    Else
        fileRead = file.readAll()
    End If
    file.Close
End Function
```

Apps Script DriveApp Service

In Apps Script, the DriveApp service can be used to write to Google Drive in the same way as `Scripting.FileSystemObject` is used to write to the local Windows client. The next section will implement a `FileSystemObject` for the Apps Script VBA library with `fileRead`, `fileWrite`, and `fileExists` wrapper functions to handle simple text files, just like the ones just created for VBA.

Since Drive works in an inherently different way than `Windows.Scripting.FileSystemObject`, we can use these wrappers to harmonize the interface. Here's the previous test, ported to Apps Script through the DriveApp service wrapped in the `VBA.FileSystemObject`:

```
function testFiles() {

    // so that functions like DriveApp.getFiles() can be accessed
    var fs = new VBA.FileSystemObject (DriveApp);

    //write some things
    fs.fileWrite ("etest/example.txt", "some text");

    //check file exists
    Logger.log(fs.fileExists("etest/example.txt"));

    //read them back
    Logger.log(fs.fileRead("etest/example.txt"));

}
```

Paths in Drive

Drive has folders, of course, but the main ways it organizes files are by ID, parent, and children. A folder is a specific (MIME) type whose job is to hold references to children, which could be other folders or files. A file can appear in multiple folders simply by having multiple parents.

Drive files are mainly referenced by their ID as opposed to their path, even though most of us think mainly in terms of folder organization. To duplicate the Windows directory paradigm in Drive, we need a few helper functions that can unravel paths such as */goinggas/data/example.txt* by searching Drive for each folder in the path.

Splitting up the path.   This example will take a path and parse it into filename and folder path, then find and return the folder corresponding to the filepath. It uses regular expressions to do this. Although regular expressions are available from VBA, they are not as widely used as they are in JavaScript.

 Regular expressions have already cropped up a few times, but a deep discussion is outside the scope of this book. There are many tutorials out there if you want to look into them a little more.

```
/**
 * given a path like a/b/c.txt
 * extract the folder and return the folder and name
 * @param {string} path the path
 * @return {object} the DriveApp folder and file name {folder:..,fileName:..}
 */
function splitDrivePath (path) {

  // split the name up
  var folderMatch = path.match(/.*\//i);
  var fileMatch = path.match(/[^\/:*?"]*$/i);

  // get the folder
  return {
    folder : getDriveFolderFromPath(folderMatch ? folderMatch[0] : "/"),
    fileName : fileMatch ? fileMatch[0] : ""
  }
}
```

You'll notice this references another helper function, `getDriveFolderFromPath`, which is able to recursively travel through a Drive folder tree:

```
/**
 * given a path like a/b/c.txt
 * extract the folder
 * @param {string} path the path
 * @return {Folder} the DriveApp folder
```

```
  */
  function getDriveFolderFromPath (path) {
   return (path || "/").split("/").reduce ( function(prev,current) {
     if (prev && current) {
       var fldrs = prev.getFoldersByName(current);
       return fldrs.hasNext() ? fldrs.next() : null;
     }
     else {
       return current ? null : prev;
     }
   },DriveApp.getRootFolder());

  };
```

Apps Script reading and writing to Drive

Unlike the Windows filesystem, Drive allows multiple files of the same name to coexist in a folder (because their unique characteristic is their ID, not their name). This function:

```
folder.getFilesByName(someName);
```

returns a `FileIterator` object (as opposed to a single file), which is traversed thus:

```
while (iterator.hasNext()) {
    var file = iterator.next();
}
```

This method, `fileGet`, will traverse a path to find the parent folder, then return the `FileIterator` for the given name:

```
/**
 * check if file exists
 * path can include folder name - then get the file iterator
 * @param {string} path the path
 * @return {Iterator} a driveapp file iterator
 */
self.fileGet = function (path) {

  // get the folder and the filename
  var pathOb = splitDrivePath (path);

  // get the file
  return pathOb.folder ? pathOb.folder.getFilesByName(pathOb.fileName) : null;
};
```

fileExists. By applying `fileExists`, we can construct the first of the wrapper functions by testing if the iterator has anything in it:

```
/**
 * check to see if a file exists (the path can include folder name)
 * @param {string} path the path
 * @return {boolean} whether it exits
```

```
    */
    self.fileExists = function (path) {

      // get the files
      var iterator  = self.fileGet (path);

      // check if there were any
      return iterator ? iterator.hasNext() : false;

    };
```

fileRead.   Because multiple files could exist with the same name, the Windows behavior cannot be exactly duplicated. The `fileRead` function will pick the first file in the folder with a matching name, on the basis that the ported application from Windows would have only one file of that name in any case:

JS
```
/**
 * read content of a Drive file as a string given the path
 * @param {string} path the path
 * @return {string} the content
 */
self.fileRead = function (path ) {

  // see if the file exists and return its contents
  var iterator  = self.fileGet (path);

  // check if there were any
  return iterator && iterator.hasNext() ?
    iterator.next().getBlob().getDataAsString() : "";
};
```

fileWrite.   Drive uses the MIME type of a file to determine which application can handle it, and how to deal with it. For this simple case emulating Windows, leaving the MIME type undefined will work just fine.

Another wrinkle, again caused by the ability to have multiple files of the same name, is that to emulate the Windows behavior, we have to first check if there is a file of that name in the folder already and overwrite its contents, or otherwise create a new file:

JS
```
/**
 * write to a file (the path can include folder name)
 * then get the file iterator
 * normally we would set a MIME type,
 * but because this is from VBA porting, I'm leaving it blank for now
 * @param {string} path the path
 * @param {string} content the content
 * @param {MimeType} [mimeType] a Drive MIME type
 * @return {File} a driveapp file
 */
 self.fileWrite = function (path, content, mimeType ) {
```

```
  // see if the file exists
  var files = self.fileGet(path);

  // if it doesn't, you need to create it
  if (files.hasNext()) {
    var file = files.next();
    file.setContent(content);
  }
  else {
    var pathOb = splitDrivePath (path);
    var file = pathOb.folder.createFile(pathOb.fileName,content,mimeType);
  }

  return file;
}
```

VBA library FileSystemObject

The FileSystemObject is constructed like this:

```
var fs = new VBA.FileSystemObject(DriveApp);
```

but why pass the DriveApp object as an argument? Read on...

Drive authorization.   When code that accesses a Google service is run, Apps Script checks to see if it has been authorized to execute. This is a very important step, as it ensures that the user is always aware which resources are going to be accessed. Once the application is authorized, its scope is adjusted to automatically enable access to the required resource in the future.

For example, accessing the DriveApp results in the dialog shown in Figure 9-1.

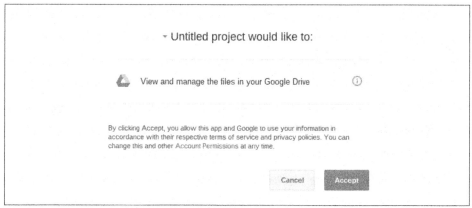

Figure 9-1. Authorizing DriveApp

The way that Apps Script decides whether to enter this dialog is fairly primitive. The application code and the code in any attached libraries are searched for references to any of the known services; if any are found (even in the comments), Apps Script seeks authorization.

Dependency-free VBA library. A design criteria for the VBA library for this book is that it should not provoke authorization dialogs for services that are not being used by a script using it. Had the library directly referenced `DriveApp`, then every script that linked to the library would be prompted for authorization to Drive (and any other services directly referenced in the library), *even though they did not use them*.

To get around this, I could have generated multiple libraries, one for every service. But by passing the `DriveApp` interface to the library, I ensure that it does not need any code that recognizably accesses the DriveApp service—which means that all the code for the Apps Script VBA library can be in one library, without prompting for unnecessary authorizations:

```js
var fs = new VBA.FileSystemObject(DriveApp);
```

It's important to understand that comments count as references. Apps Script can be provoked into generating a token scoped for a particular service simply by containing a reference to some service, even in a comment. If you do want to use the `VBA.FileSystemObject`, an authorization dialog is required, and the mention of `DriveApp` alone is not enough to provoke one.

You also need a mention of one of the `DriveApp` methods, even if it's in a comment. So you should construct the filesystem object as follows, including a comment like the one shown:

```js
function myFunction() {
    // so that functions like DriveApp.getFiles() can be accessed
    var fs = VBA.FileSystemObject(DriveApp);
}
```

The VBA.FileSystemObject code

Here is the full `VBA.FileSystemObject` code, as implemented in the VBA library:

```js
/**
 * create a filesystem object like the scripting.filesystemobject in windows
 * @constructor FileSystemObject
 * @param {driveApp} driveApp the driveapp service handle
 * @return {FileSystemObject} self
 */
function FileSystemObject (driveApp) {

    // the hosting script should pass the driveApp service
    // this avoids unnecessary authorization of the library if it's not used
    var driveApp_ = driveApp;

    var self = this;
```

```
/**
 * check if file exists (the path can include folder name),
 * then get the file iterator
 * @param {string} path the path
 * @return {Iterator} a driveapp file iterator
 */
self.fileGet = function (path) {

  //  get the folder  and the file name
  var pathOb = splitDrivePath (path);

  // get the file
  return pathOb.folder ? pathOb.folder.getFilesByName(pathOb.fileName) : null;

};

/**
 * check to see if a file exists (the path can include folder name)
 * @param {string} path the path
 * @return {boolean} whether it exits
 */
self.fileExists = function (path) {

  // get the files
  var iterator  = self.fileGet (path);

  // check if there were any
  return iterator ? iterator.hasNext() : false;

};

/**
 * read content of a Drive file as a string given the path
 * @param {string} path the path
 * @return {string} the content
 */
self.fileRead = function (path ) {

  // see if the file exists and return its contents
  var iterator  = self.fileGet (path);

  // check if there were any
  return iterator && iterator.hasNext() ?
     iterator.next().getBlob().getDataAsString() : "";

};

/**
 * write content to a file (the path can include folder name)
 * then get the file iterator
 * normally we would set a MIME Type,
```

```
   * but because this is from VBA porting, I'm leaving it blank for now
   * @param {string} path the path
   * @param {string} content the content
   * @param {MimeType} [mimeType] a drive mimetype
   * @return {File} a driveapp file
   */
self.fileWrite = function (path, content, mimeType ) {

  // see if the file exists
  var files = self.fileGet(path);

  // if it doesn't, you need to create it
  if (files.hasNext()) {
    var file = files.next();
    file.setContent(content);
  }
  else {
    var pathOb = splitDrivePath (path);
    var file = pathOb.folder.createFile(pathOb.fileName,content,mimeType);
  }

  return file;
}

/**
 * given a path like a/b/c.txt
 * extract the folder and return the folder and name
 * @param {string} path the path
 * @return {object} the driveApp folder and file name {folder:..,fileName:..}
 */
function splitDrivePath (path) {

  // split the name up
  var folderMatch = path.match(/.*\//i);
  var fileMatch = path.match(/[^\/:*?"]*$/i);

  // get the folder
  return {
    folder : getDriveFolderFromPath(folderMatch ? folderMatch[0] : "/"),
    fileName : fileMatch ? fileMatch[0] : ""
  };

}

/**
 * given a path like a/b/c.txt
 * extract the folder
 * @param {string} path the path
 * @return {Folder} the driveApp folder
 */
function getDriveFolderFromPath (path)  {
```

```
    return (path || "/").split("/").reduce ( function(prev,current) {
      if (prev && current) {
        var fldrs = prev.getFoldersByName(current);
        return fldrs.hasNext() ? fldrs.next() : null;
      }
      else {
        return current ? null : prev;
      }
    },driveApp_.getRootFolder());

  }

  return self;
}
```

CHAPTER 10

HTML Service

Apps Script is JavaScript code that executes on Google servers. It is also possible to construct and execute applications that execute in a browser on the PC, but under the control of and communicating with server-based Apps Script.

Why Client Execution?

Apps running on a server cannot have access to the client DOM or to local resources that can make a user experience compelling and immediate. Once client-side script is enabled, it's possible to create any kind of web application. Generally speaking, JavaScript will run on a local client more efficiently than it does on an Apps Script server and does not need to be limited and controlled as it does when executing in a shared-server environment.

The Downside

Earlier versions of Apps Script came with a UI service with which form controls such as text boxes and other interactive objects could be designed and deployed, in addition to a limited number of event handling capabilities to interact with the user. This capability was fairly basic, but it was also well integrated into Apps Script. The UI service has since been deprecated, and aside from the simplest interactions, the Apps Script frontend experience is now presented using the HTML service, running in a browser on the client.

This means that for any Apps Script application that needs anything more than rudimentary user interaction, the developer must now understand HTML and CSS in addition to JavaScript and the Apps Script services.

The interaction between Apps Script and the HtmlService class is asynchronous, and this adds another barrier layer of complexity for those not accustomed to writing web applications.

The VBA Connection

This book is mainly about migrating from VBA to Apps Script, and whereas VBA doesn't have this HTML service concept, it does have UserForms and events. To migrate these to Apps Script, the developer will need to master HtmlService.

HTML Service Varieties

The HTML service runs across three different presentation modes with minimal recoding required between them.

Web Apps

Another key feature of Apps Script is that Apps Script applications can be published as web apps. A web app reacts to HTTP GET and HTTP POST requests by passing them to Apps Script functions named doGet and doPost. You can publish any Apps Script project as a web app by including a doGet or doPost handler, and by using the HtmlService class to serve the result. Web apps are a powerful way to create full-screen web applications powered by Apps Script services and to access Apps data without the need for a separate server host.

Dialogs

HtmlService is presented in a modal dialog that is very much like a VBA form. User interaction is managed via HTML controls, handled by JavaScript, and rendered via the Apps Script HTML service. This is directly analogous to the controls created for user interaction in a VBA form and would be used to present or gather one-off data as part of an essentially server-side workflow.

The biggest difference in operation is that HtmlService runs in a completely different context (in the client browser) than the Apps Script (on a Google server) that provokes it. This means that we need special strategies to pass information between the calling Apps Script, HtmlService, any scripts called by the HtmlService class, and the entry point to the script after the HtmlService class has been executed.

Sidebars

Sidebars are presented as a 300-pixel sidebar to the right of the normal Docs, Spreadsheet, or Form page. The format is fairly inflexible and is the usual presentation format used in Google Add-ons. Sidebars are constructed in the same way as dialog-style

UI `HtmlService`, but would be used where continuous or repeated interaction is required between the apps and the sidebar content.

jQuery

JavaScript code intended to be run by `HtmlService` on the client browser is ordinary JavaScript with similar access to the DOM as a regular web application. There are some things that don't work as a result of `HtmlService` sanitization (to detect and block dangerous code), but nowadays these are few and far between. This means that it is possible to use various frameworks in order to create client applications. Google often uses jQuery in the examples in its developer site, but it is by no means mandatory.

There are opposing views about whether it is better to learn JavaScript before or after jQuery and other such frameworks. I'll leave that to others to make their case, and to you to make up your own mind. These examples use vanilla JavaScript (no jQuery or any other framework) in order to minimize the number of things you need to learn to get started. I recommend that your first choice should be whichever framework you already use or are familiar with (and that `HtmlService` supports).

Event Handling

VBA handles form events by creating procedures with a specific name in the context of the control whose event needs handling. When an event such as a change or click is triggered, the appropriate event handler is called. Quite often global variables are set with data received asynchronously through a control event.

Apps Script handles control events in the context of `HtmlService` by assigning callback functions to JavaScript events. All this takes place in the browser session, and there is no concept of global variables shared between the server and client sessions.

The purpose of controls in a UI is to collect or present variable data. The role of events is to be triggered in reaction to environmental or data changes. When the control data is needed only on the client side, it is not hard to orchestrate and manage workflow, but when the purpose of the `HtmlService` app is to collect variable data subsequently needed by a server-side function, we need a strategy for passing and persisting data in the server-side script. Figure 10-1 illustrates the HTML service data flow.

Templates

The HTML service provides a templating system that allows Apps Script functions to be executed and their result embedded in the HTML code being generated. Many people find this method easier than executing and handling variable data by asynchronous calls to Apps Script from within HtmlService. There will be examples of each approach in this chapter.

I seldom use templating (except to include source files when constructing the HTML code to be executed), but it's a personal choice and it certainly depends on the application. One key point is that Apps Script functions evaluated in templates at construction time will represent data at that point in time, and can't be used for interactive data interchange. Long-running functions in template evaluation can also lead to a poor user experience.

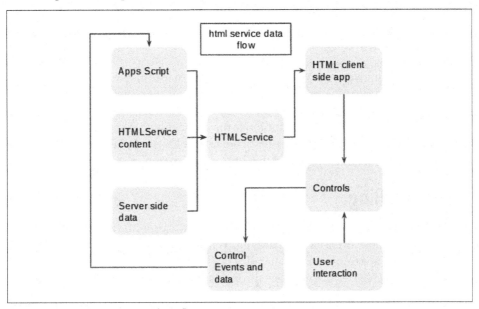

Figure 10-1. HTML service data flow

Structure

This simple example will construct a static drop-down selection list of carrier codes and airline names from the previously introduced Carriers spreadsheet using the template approach. For now it will just report which airline was chosen.

A simple sidebar HtmlService app at a minimum will probably have at least one Apps Script file and one HTML file. However, you will soon want to separate CSS from JavaScript from HTML in your client-based code, so let's start with the structure shown in Figure 10-2.

This structure will be used as outlined in Table 10-1.

Figure 10-2. Suggested structure for a simple HtmlService app

Table 10-1. Files used in this example and their purpose

File	Purpose
Code.gs	Apps Script containing server-side code and menu initialization
index.html	HTML file with the sidebar HTML code
main.js.html	JavaScript code to execute client side
styles.css.html	Style sheet for the app

In principle, this seems a lot more complicated than the equivalent VBA using the interactive form builder and events bound to controls on the form. In many ways it is indeed more complex, as there is a level of indirection (in addition to needing to know three different languages) that makes it hard to grasp at first.

On the other hand, using HTML for this kind of interaction can lead to much more familiar and usable interfaces than the type that can be achieved in the closed world of VBA forms. For the casual developer, it can be difficult to get started, and often becomes an inflection point in the learning process.

Installing the menu option

The sidebar will be kicked off with a menu option that looks like Figure 10-3.

We achieve this with a trigger that is run upon the user's opening the sheet to which this example is bound. When the menu item is selected, it will execute the function showCarriers. This code is in *Code.gs*, as it executes server-side:

```js
function onOpen(e) {
    SpreadsheetApp.getUi()
      .createMenu('carriers')
      .addItem('Choose carrier', 'showCarriers')
      .addToUi();
}
```

Figure 10-3. Sidebar menu option

Opening the sidebar

The showCarriers function is responsible for initiating the client-side sidebar session. It executes on the server, so is in *Code.gs*:

```js
/**
 * execute the HtmlService
 */
function showCarriers() {
  var ui = HtmlService.createTemplateFromFile('index.html')
    .evaluate()
    .setSandboxMode(HtmlService.SandboxMode.IFRAME)
    .setTitle('carriers select demo');

    SpreadsheetApp.getUi().showSidebar(ui);
}
```

This constructs an HTML app that can be executed on the client. The evaluate method takes care of any template substitution required by the template file, *index.html*.

The template

This is a complete HTML app that also includes styling (from the *style.css.html* file) and any required JavaScript (from *main.js.html*), in addition to templated data retrieved from the server during the evaluate method.

The result of executing JavaScript code contained within this substitution marker:

```
<?!= code  to be executed goes here ?>
```

is inserted as part of the evaluate process:

```js
<!DOCTYPE html>
<!-- styles -->
<?!= HtmlService.createHtmlOutputFromFile('styles.css').getContent(); ?>

<div class="content">
  <div class="block">

    <label for="code">Pick an airline</label>
    <select id="codes">

      <?!= getCarrierNames().map(function(d) {
```

```
        return "<option value="+d[0]+">("+d[0]+") "+d[1]+"</option>";
      }).join ('\n');
      ?>

    </select>

  </div>
  <div class = "block">
    <div id="chose"></div>
  </div>
</div>
<!-- javascript. -->
<?!= HtmlService.createHtmlOutputFromFile('main.js').getContent(); ?>
```

The templated items here are:

HtmlService.createHtmlOutputFromFile(*filename*).getContent
: Executes (on the server) an HtmlService method to include the contents of the given filename in the final HTML app. This is a common pattern to build a single app from multiple content files.

getCarrierNames *(in Code.gs)*
: Executes on the server and returns two columns of data with the carrier codes and names. Formatting each item as <option> HTML elements gives the content for a <select> element.

Here, getCarrierNames runs server-side and returns two columns of data from the active sheet in response to a client request:

```
/**
 * get the carrier names
 */
function getCarrierNames() {
  // get the data in the active sheet
  var sheet = SpreadsheetApp.getActiveSheet();

  // create a 2 dim area of the data in the carrier names column and codes
  return sheet.getRange(2, 1, sheet.getLastRow()-1 , 2)
    .getValues().reduce(function(p,c) {
      p.push(c);
      return p;
    },[]);
}
```

Stylesheet

CSS is used to lay out the contents of the sidebar. This example mainly uses the default Google styling, and includes a reference to an external Google stylesheet:

```
<!-- This CSS package applies Google styling; it should always be included. -->
<link rel="stylesheet"
```

```
      href="https://ssl.gstatic.com/docs/script/css/add-ons.css">

<style>
.content {
  padding:10px;
}
</style>
```

JavaScript. *main.js.html* contains JavaScript to be executed in the client browser. It simply listens for and reports on selection changes:

```
<script>
// the app
window.onload = function () {
  document.getElementById("codes").addEventListener ("change", function (e) {
    document.getElementById("chose").innerHTML = 'You chose ' + e.target.value;
  });
};
</script>
```

The result

The final drop-down selection list of carrier codes and airline names is shown in Figure 10-4.

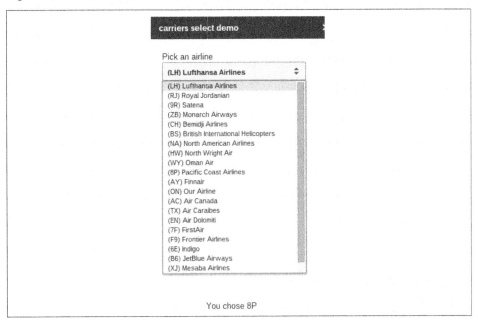

Figure 10-4. Resulting drop-down list of carrier codes and airline names

Controlling Apps Script from the Client

Using templates is a simple way to create static sites based on data Apps Script generates server-side. Generally, though, this is not enough. One reason for creating a UX is to collect and react to user instructions, which often results in some server-side activity following some client-side input.

The key to this is `google.script.run`, initiated from the client, but executed on the server. I'll illustrate in the next example—which is the previous example rewritten dynamically without HTML templating—but first let's cover a few more notes on namespaces.

Using Namespaces in HtmlService

The topic of namespaces, and the (now) familiar pattern of:

```js
var NS = (function(ns) {
    ... the code
    return ns;
})(NS||ns);
```

has been covered in various topics throughout this book.

With `HtmlService`, the level of abstraction involved makes the app fairly difficult to debug, and it can easily turn to spaghetti. I always recommend using namespaces, with short snippets of functionality that are incrementally tested. Another reason for using namespaces is to share code between server and client (but we'll come to that later).

This means that using many small scripts that are isolated from side effects may seem like overkill at first, but when an app starts to become in any way complex, the value of this approach will become apparent.

Table 10-2 shows a pattern I like to use for even the very simplest of apps. I recommend you develop the habit of doing the same, whether with this pattern or another of your own devising.

Table 10-2. Recommended pattern for organizing an HtmlService app

File	Purpose
Code.gs	Apps Script to initialize the app menu, the HtmlService orchestration, and small server-side tasks
index.html	The sidebar HTML—the client-side markup
main.js.html	JavaScript to wait for the DOM to load, then kick off the app initialization
app.js.html	Any application management, such as displaying error messages and storing global data and settings
client.js.html	Orchestration of communication between the client and the server

File	Purpose
render.js.html	Any dynamic DOM manipulation
styles.css.html	The stylesheet

Using `google.script.run` to communicate with the server to get the very latest data produces the updated app, organized into the pattern shown in Table 10-2, and with templating removed.

Multiple Menu Items

Code.gs now contains an additional menu item so that either the template or the `google.script.run` version can be selected:

```
function onOpen(e) {
    SpreadsheetApp.getUi()
      .createMenu('carriers')
      .addItem('Choose carrier', 'showCarriers')
      .addItem('use google.script.run', 'showCarriersRun')
      .addToUi();
}
```

The only difference is that `showCarriersRun` renders a different version of *index.html* that has had the templating removed:

```
function showCarriersRun() {
    var ui = HtmlService.createTemplateFromFile('indexRun.html')
      .evaluate()
      .setSandboxMode(HtmlService.SandboxMode.IFRAME)
      .setTitle('carriers select demo');

    SpreadsheetApp.getUi().showSidebar(ui);
}
```

indexRun.html

In *indexRun.html*, the templating is removed, there are a few more scripts included, and an element has been added in which to report errors:

```
<!DOCTYPE html>
<!-- styles -->
<?!= HtmlService.createHtmlOutputFromFile('styles.css').getContent(); ?>

<div class="content">
  <div class="block">

    <label for="code">Pick an airline</label>

    <select id="codes">
    </select>
```

```
    </div>
    <div class = "block">
      <div id="chose"></div>
    </div>
    <div class = "block">
      <div id="message" class="message"></div>
    </div>
  </div>
  <!-- javascript. -->
  <?!= HtmlService.createHtmlOutputFromFile('render.js').getContent(); ?>
  <?!= HtmlService.createHtmlOutputFromFile('client.js').getContent(); ?>
  <?!= HtmlService.createHtmlOutputFromFile('app.js').getContent(); ?>
  <?!= HtmlService.createHtmlOutputFromFile('mainRun.js').getContent(); ?>
```

mainRun.js

mainRun.js differs from the template version in that the work of the app has now been delegated to functions in the various namespaces. The purpose of this script now is to wait for the DOM to load, communicate with the server to get the data, build the options list, and wait for the user to make a selection, thus triggering a change event. I always recommend first writing what the app is supposed to do when working with a new concept.

The pattern shown next can be described as follows:

- *When* the DOM is finished loading,

  — ask Apps Script Server for some data; *then, when it has arrived,*

    — store it,

    — render it,

    — listen for changes,

    — and repeat.

JS
```
<script>
// the app
window.onload = function () {
  // kick off by getting data, and building page
  Client.getData (function (data) {

    // store the data
    App.globals.data = data;

    // render as options
    Render.build();

    // add any listeners
    App.listeners();

  });
```

```
};
</script>
```

It's important to note that data is retrieved asynchronously. JavaScript developers will be familiar with this kind of pattern, but it will be a little less intuitive for VBA (and indeed for Apps Script) developers. It is a very important concept and one that can cause confusion at first.

`Client.getData` is expecting a function to be passed to it that it will execute, but only when the data has actually been retrieved (as opposed to when it has been requested). In other words, the call to `Client.getData` will finish *before the data has actually been sent back*. In the most recent versions of JavaScript, this would be handled using *promises* (jQuery also includes the concept of deferred execution), but these are not implemented in every browser version, and you may not be using jQuery. Here, we use the traditional method of passing an anonymous function to be executed later to avoid having to learn yet another thing just to get started (although you should definitely take a look at promises and their benefits).

Client Namespace

The purpose of the client namespace is to retrieve data from the Apps Script servers, then execute some function passed to it when the data arrives.

google.script.run

`google.script.run` has these methods:

- `.withFailureHandle` (some function to execute on failure)
- `.withSuccessHandle` (some function to execute on success)
- `.yourFunctionNameToExecuteOnTheServer` (your function arguments)

and is the means by which any server code can be executed on the server under the control of the client. This is perhaps the most persuasive advantage of Apps Script Add-ons versus Microsoft Add-ins, and a key decision point if you are deciding between Office 365– and Google JavaScript–based automation solutions.

- With Google Add-ons, *any custom code* can be directed to execute server side.
- With Microsoft Add-ins, the *Office JavaScript API provides access to data structures* in the container document so you can access it "client-side," It does *not allow you to write custom functions* that operate "server-side." You are limited to *only the functionality that exists* in the JavaScript API.

JS
```
<script>
// all code for client-server communication
var Client = (function(client) {
```

```
      client.getData = function (successFunction) {

        // this executes a function asynchronously on the server
        // under control of the client
        google.script.run

          // this will be executed if it fails
          .withFailureHandler(function (err) {
            App.reportMessage (err);
          })

          // this will be executed if it succeeds
          .withSuccessHandler (successFunction)

          // this is what gets executed
          .getCarrierNames();
      };

      return client;

    })(Client || {});

    </script>
```

Render.js

The `Render.js` namespace is used to interact with the DOM—principally, to build the options based on the data retrieved from the server:

```
JS  <script>
    /**
     * anything to do with rendering happens here
     */
    var Render = (function (render) {

      /**
       * display the selection made on change
       * @param {object} e returned by change event
       */
      render.showChoice = function (e) {
        document.getElementById("chose").innerHTML = 'You chose ' + e.target.value;
      };

      /**
       * build selector
       */
      render.build = function () {

        // the select element is already in place
        var selector = document.getElementById ("codes");
```

```
      // add the options
      App.globals.data.forEach (function (d) {
        selector.appendChild(new Option ( "(" +d[0]+ ") " + d[1], d[0] ));
      });
    };

  return render;
})(Render || {});

</script>
```

App.js

The App.js namespace is used for tasks such as listening for events and reporting errors:

```
<script>
// app related globals
var App = (function(app) {

  /**
   * report a message
   * @param {string} message the message
   */
  app.reportMessage = function (message) {
    document.getElementById("message").innerHTML = message;
  };

  /**
   * any global stuff/settings is here
   */
  app.globals = {};

  /**
   * add listeners
   */
  app.listeners = function () {
    document.getElementById("codes").addEventListener ("change", function (e) {
      Render.showChoice(e);
    });
  };
  return app;
}) (App || {});
</script>
```

Dialog HtmlService

So far the focus has been on HtmlService presented as a sidebar. We can use exactly the same approach to present in a dialog style (much like a VBA form). We can achieve simple dialogs (like a prompt or message box) using the Browser service or the (fancier) App UI, without the use of any client-side HTML:

```js
function promptExample() {
    var ui = SpreadsheetApp.getUi();

    var result = ui.prompt('think of a number and enter it',
      ui.ButtonSet.OK_CANCEL);

    // see what we got
    var button = result.getSelectedButton();
    var value = parseInt(result.getResponseText(),10);

    if (button == ui.Button.OK) {
      ui.alert('Your number squared is ' + (value * value) );
    }

    else if (button == ui.Button.CANCEL) {
      ui.alert('ok - sorry for bothering you');
    }

    else if (button == ui.Button.CLOSE) {
      ui.alert('bye bye');
    }
}
```

This gives the result shown in Figure 10-5.

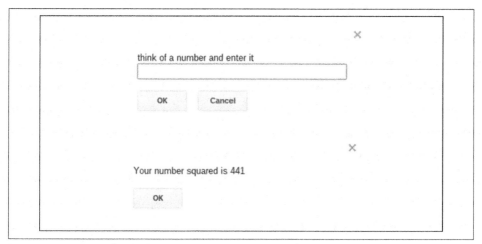

Figure 10-5. Using the Browser service to present in a dialog style

But for more complicated dialogs, we need to use HtmlService. Figure 10-6 shows the HtmlService app presented as a dialog instead of a sidebar.

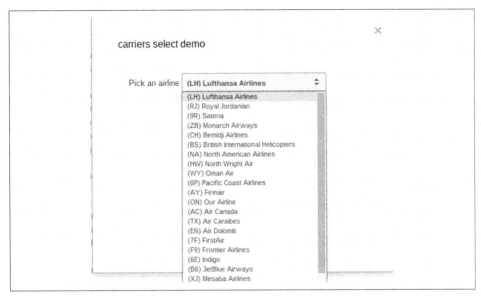

Figure 10-6. Presenting the HtmlService app as a dialog

The only coding difference between the sidebar and dialog mode is the use of the showModalDialog method:

```js
function showDialog() {
    var html = HtmlService.createTemplateFromFile('indexRun.html')
        .evaluate()
        .setSandboxMode(HtmlService.SandboxMode.IFRAME)
        .setWidth(400)
        .setHeight(300);
    SpreadsheetApp.getUi()
        .showModalDialog(html, 'carriers select demo');
}
```

Now both variations are shown as menu items, as you can see in Figure 10-7.

Figure 10-7. Showing sidebar and dialog mode as menu items

HtmlService Web Apps

You can create full-size web apps using HtmlService. Even though this example is container-bound, you can still publish it by including a doGet function in the code:

```js
function doGet(e) {
    return HtmlService.createTemplateFromFile('indexRun.html')
        .evaluate()
        .setSandboxMode(HtmlService.SandboxMode.IFRAME);
}
```

All the client-side code remains the same as it was for the sidebar and dialog versions. One change is needed for the server-side code. A container-bound script can still be published, but when it is being used as a web app it does not have access the concept of an active sheet, the following code will return null:

```
SpreadsheetApp.getActiveSheet()
```

To account for this, we need to specifically open the sheet that contains the input data, as shown here in the updated getCarrierNames:

```js
/**
 * get the carrier names
 */
function getCarrierNames() {
  // get the data in the active sheet
  var sheet = SpreadsheetApp.getActiveSheet();
  // if there is no sheet, then fallback to a specific sheet/spreadsheet
  // because we are executing as a webapp
  if (!sheet){
    sheet = SpreadsheetApp
      .openById('1f4zuZZv2NiLuYSGB5j4ENFc6wEWOmaEdCoHNuv-gHXo')
      .getSheetByName('lookup');
  }
  // create a 2 dim area of the data in the carrier names column and codes
  return sheet.getRange(2, 1, sheet.getLastRow()-1 , 2)
    .getValues().reduce(function(p,c) {
    p.push(c);
    return p;
  },[]);
}
```

The app is saved and published, as shown in Figure 10-8.

And now it can be accessed from any browser through the published link, as Figure 10-9 illustrates.

Figure 10-8. Saving and publishing the web app

Figure 10-9. Accessing the web app through the browser

VBA User Form

To contrast with VBA, this section will show the dialog-type UI implemented as a VBA form. The web app– and sidebar–style dialogs are not possible in VBA.

Create a User Form

VBA provides a visual tool to create forms, shown in Figure 10-10. In Apps Script, you need to code it with HTML. There was a visual UI tool for Apps Script when it first became available, but it was (like many Apps Script features) abandoned and deprecated.

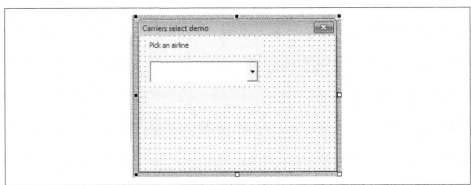

Figure 10-10. VBA's form creation tool

Initialize the Combo Box

An event can be assigned to a form initialize event. At that point, the latest values are assigned to the combo box from the values in the sheet, in the same way that Client.getData picked up the values from the SpreadsheetApp:

```vb
Private Sub UserForm_Initialize()
    ' set the select values
    Dim lst As ListObject, r As Range, combo As MSForms.ComboBox
    Set lst = ActiveWorkbook.Sheets("lookup").ListObjects.Item("lookupTable")
    Set combo = Me.Controls("codes")

    ' offset row
    Dim idx As Long
    idx = 0

    ' add to the option list
    For Each r In lst.ListColumns("carrier").DataBodyRange.Rows
        combo.AddItem "(" + r.Value + ") " + _
            lst.ListColumns("name").DataBodyRange.Offset(idx).Resize(1).Value
        idx = idx + 1
    Next r
End Sub
```

Listen for Changes

Assigning code to the change event of the combo box automatically sets up an event listener. When a change is detected, the selected value index is used to find the carrier code in the original data:

```vb
Private Sub Codes_Change()
    Dim lab As MSForms.Label, combo As MSForms.ComboBox
    Dim lst As ListObject, r As Range

    Set lst = ActiveWorkbook.Sheets("lookup").ListObjects.Item("lookupTable")

    ' called when combox box selection is changed
    Set combo = Me.Controls("codes")
    Set lab = Me.Controls("chose")

    ' set label to chosen value, but need to find it in the original data
    lab.Caption = "You chose " + _
        lst.ListColumns.Item("carrier"). _
          DataBodyRange.Resize(1).Offset(combo.ListIndex)


End Sub
```

The Form

As Figure 10-11 illustrates, the result is very similar to the Apps Script dialog version.

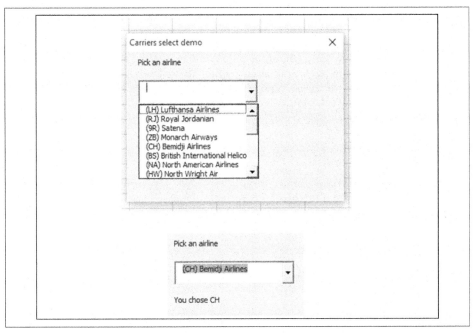

Figure 10-11. The final VBA user form

CHAPTER 11

Content Service

HtmlService can be used to render HTML content in response to HTTP requests to a published Apps Script web app. In this case, the Apps Script service is acting as web server. In addition to the web apps HTML capability, Apps Script can also serve up data as JSON (or JSONP), as well as XML and other formats. This allows you to create Apps Script apps that act as if they were a REST API, serving up processed data in response to query requests.

The Content Service

Just as with HtmlService, ContentService apps must be published as a web app, contain a doGet or doPost function to handle requests, and return results processed not by the HtmlService class, but by ContentService.

Where to Use the Content Service

It is possible to convert any script (even a container-bound one) into a published web app that can serve data through ContentService in response to HTTP queries, or content as HTML pages through HtmlService. These important capabilities mean that you can make visible the full power of scripting, and the data it can access, for consumption by a browser or some cooperating process.

The ContentService class can be used to expose Apps data such as spreadsheet content, calendar data, and JDBC database queries—in fact, anything processed with Apps Script can be published.

The Execution API was released recently, and you should consider it as an alternative when planning to use ContentService to create a private API to execute Apps Script functions. You can find out more in Chapter 17.

Types of Content

In addition to the content itself, a MIME type is attached to the data, which communicates information about the content and how it should be consumed. Applications use MIME types to advertise their capabilities, and operating systems and browsers use MIME types in content to launch applications that know how to service it.

Table 11-1 lists the types of content that can be signaled by MIME type from `Content Service`.

Table 11-1. MIME types and the types of content they signal

MIME type	Type of content and where to use
ATOM	Atom feeds for RSS content. Typically used for syndication of blog content such as Google Site pages.
CSV	CSV stands for comma-separated values, and is typically used to transfer tabular spreadsheet in a text format file.
ICAL	The ICAL format is used to communicate calendar appointment information between calendaring systems and would be used with calendar automation scripts.
JAVASCRIPT	This is a special kind of text MIME type used to signal that the content is to be treated as JavaScript code. The most common use of JAVASCRIPT is if response data is being returned as JSONP.
RSS	Another alternative for RSS format, used in the same places as ATOM would be used.
TEXT	For plain-text content.
JSON	JSON-formatted data. Note that if your data will be consumed by a client app running in a browser, you'll probably need to provide a callback with which to generate JSONP and use the JAVASCRIPT MIME type instead, since Apps Script web apps don't support CORS.
VCARD	Business card format. Would be used to interchange information from the Contacts service.
XML	XML format, if your consumer doesn't understand JSON.

Example

This chapter's example will reuse data and code from previous examples. The objective is to build a web app that will look up and return data for a given flight number.

Request

The request will be an HTTP GET, with a parameter of the flight number and an optional callback parameter to signal that JSONP is required, and a further optional parameter to indicate the format (XML or JSON). See Table 11-2.

Table 11-2. Parameters for our request

Parameter	Purpose	Default
flight	The flight number	N/A
format	XML or JSON	JSON
callback	Signal that JSONP is required	No callback

an example request might be:

```
https://the script url?flight=ua938&format=json&callback=abcfunction
```

Response

The expected JSON response to the preceding request is as follows:

```
{
    "status": "ok",
    "flight": "ua938",
    "name": "United Airlines",
    "carrier": "UA"
}
```

And here's the expected XML response:

```
<?xml version="1.0" encoding="UTF-8" ?>
<root>
    <status>ok</status>
    <flight>ua938</flight>
    <name>United Airlines</name>
    <carrier>UA</carrier>
</root>
```

Details

This example has been largely coded previously. We could use the previous example as a library and just execute it in place, but to make this a standalone example, we just copy forward the needed code.

When developing published scripts, where the parameters come from the URL and the output is not visible in the code, it's a good idea to populate the argument list from default values changeable inside the script, and to leave the actual publishing to the content service until the app is executing correctly, after which the example parameters can be removed.

Example | 275

With that in mind, the initial app looks like this:

```js
function doGet(e) {

    // set up defaults for debugging before publishing (these can be removed later)
    e = e || {};
    e.parameter = e.parameter || {};
    e.parameter.format = e.parameter.format || "json";
    e.parameter.flight = e.parameter.flight || "ua938";

    var result = getFlight (e);
    Logger.log(result);
}
```

doGet

The doGet function is executed when an HTTP GET request to a published web app is detected. As an example, a browser launches a GET request when a URL is entered into the address bar. The parameter (usually given the name e or eargs) is an object with various properties, the most interesting of which is parameter.

e.parameter contains properties corresponding to each parameter supplied in the command line.

The Settings

These are a subset of the settings used in the gmailExample introduced in Chapter 8 (since we are using the same lookup sheet), and follow the same pattern of using the Properties service to store the settings, but with a one-time setting function to populate it the first time it's used. The one-time setting function and references can be removed once the Properties service is populated:

```js
var SETTINGS_KEY = "contentsserviceexample";

function setOneTimeProperties () {
  setProperties(oneTimeSettings);
}

function setProperties (props) {
  PropertiesService.getUserProperties().setProperty(
      oneTimeSettings.KEY, JSON.stringify(props));
}

var oneTimeSettings = (function(settings) {
  'use strict';

  settings.KEY = SETTINGS_KEY;

  settings.LOOKUP = {
    ID: '19wbpUHwuIKbHaaIiylVSuG7lkK29uoAmYrTvTk_J2ho',
```

```
    NAME: 'lookup'
  };

  settings.HEADINGS = {
    CODE:'carrier',
    NAME:'name'
  };

  // update the sheet
  return settings;

})(oneTimeSettings || {});

// get them from prop service, or use the one-time setting function.
var Settings = JSON.parse(
    PropertiesService.getUserProperties().getProperty(SETTINGS_KEY) ||
    JSON.stringify(oneTimeSettings)) ;
```

SheetOb

This is exactly the same function as is used in the gmailExample, and its purpose is to
open a sheet, get its data, and create a JSON object of the data using the headings as
the object properties.

getFlight

The getFlight function uses the same technique with regular expressions to match
the given flight parameter against known airlines' flight number patterns. The flight
parameter value can be any piece of text that contains a flight number from an interesting airline somewhere in it:

JS `function getFlight(e) {`

```
  // get the carrier data
  var lookup = new SheetOb()
    .open(Settings.LOOKUP.ID, Settings.LOOKUP.NAME).getData();

  // get the regex based on the interesting airlines
  var rx = new RegExp (getRegex(lookup) ,'i');
  // match against the known airlines flight codes
  var found = rx.exec(e.parameter.flight);
  // store this message if it's got one
  if (found) {
    return {
      status:"ok",
      flight:found[0],
      carrier:found[1],
      name:lookup.filter(function(d) {
        return d[Settings.HEADINGS.CODE].toLowerCase()
          === found[1].toLowerCase();
      })[0][Settings.HEADINGS.NAME]
```

Example | 277

```
      };
    }
    else {
      return {
        status:'not found',
        flight:e.parameter.flight
      }
    }
  }
}
```

getRegex

getRegex is the same as in the gmailExample, and creates a regular expression of
valid carrier codes from the lookup sheet:

```js
/**
 * make the regex for flight matching
 * @param {object} lookup the lookup data
 * @return {Regexp} the matching regex
 */
function getRegex (lookup) {

  return '\\b(' +
    lookup.map(function(d) {
      return d[Settings.HEADINGS.CODE].toLowerCase();
    }).join("|") +
      ')([a-z]?)(\\d{1,4}[a-z]?)\\b';
}
```

Initial Result

Here's the result from the first attempt, using default parameters:

```
{
    "status": "ok",
    "flight": "ua938",
    "carrier": "ua",
    "name": "United Airlines"
}
```

and entering some invalid text gives an invalid result as expected:

```
{
    "status": "not found",
    "flight": "rubbish123"
}
```

JSONP

For security reasons, browser-based web apps are not allowed to receive JSON data
from a process that is not running in the same domain. This is called *cross-origin*

---

resource sharing. There is a technique involving client and server collaboration that securely enables this kind of interchange (CORS, which will be covered in Chapter 18), but ContentService (or more specifically the servers on which it runs), does not support this currently.

A workaround is to use JSONP. This is where the result returned from Con tentService is treated as if it is an external script (which is allowed to come from another domain), and the JSON data is an argument to the script, which processes the data returned.

The format of a JSONP response is:

```js
callbackName (thejsondata);
```

where callbackName is a client-side function that expects to receive and deal with data returned by the callback service.

You create JSONP (instead of JSON) data for use by ContentService by constructing a call to callbackName with the data as an argument, and setting a JAVASCRIPT MIME type instead of JSON. This example simulates a JSONP request, with a callback parameter specified:

```js
e.parameter.flight = e.parameter.flight || "us01";
e.parameter.callback = "someCallback"

var result = getFlight (e);

if (e.parameter.callback) {
  result = e.parameter.callback + '(' + JSON.stringify(result) + ');'
}
Logger.log(result);
```

Here's the result:

```js
someCallback({"status":"ok","flight":"us01","carrier":"us","name":"US Airways"});
```

XML

If you are working with VBA/Apps Script integration it may be preferable to use XML rather than JSON. Apps Script provides the XmlService class for converting to and from XML.

A few lines are added to doGet to detect and deal with requests that prefer XML:

```js
e.parameter.format = "xml";

// get the flight data
var result = getFlight (e);

// maybe xml is preferred
if (e.parameter.format.toLowerCase() === "xml") {
```

```
    if (e.parameter.callback) {
      result.status = "no callback possible for xml format";
    }
    result = makeXml (result);
  }
  else {
    // need a JSONP wrapper
    if (e.parameter.callback) {
      result = e.parameter.callback + '(' + JSON.stringify(result) + ');'
    }
  }
  Logger.log(result);
```

with this result:

```xml
<?xml version="1.0" encoding="UTF-8"?>
<root>
    <status>ok</status>
    <flight>us01</flight>
    <carrier>us</carrier>
    <name>US Airways</name>
</root>
```

makeXml

The makeXml function converts a simple JSON object to XML:

```js
/**
 * convert a json object to xml
 * @param {object} json a JSON object to be converted
 * @param {string} root [root="root"] element name
 * @return nicely formatting XML
 */

function makeXml (json, root) {
  root = root || "root";
  var rootElement = XmlService.createElement (root);

  // add each item in this one level object
  Object.keys(json).forEach (function (d) {
    var child = XmlService.createElement(d);
    child.setText(json[d]);
    rootElement.addContent(child);
  });

  // format it
  return XmlService.getPrettyFormat()
          .format(XmlService.createDocument(rootElement));

}
```

Publishing

The app is now ready to publish in this final version with the test values removed, ContentService enabled, and the MIME type appropriately selected:

```js
// content service web app
function doGet(e) {

  // set up defaults
  e = e || {};
  e.parameter = e.parameter || {};
  e.parameter.format = e.parameter.format || "json";

  // get the flight data
  var result = getFlight (e);
  var content,
      mime = e.parameter.callback ?
        ContentService.MimeType.JAVASCRIPT : ContentService.MimeType.JSON;

  // maybe XML is preferred
  if (e.parameter.format.toLowerCase() === "xml") {
    if (e.parameter.callback) {
      result.status = "no callback possible for xml format";
    }
    mime = ContentService.MimeType.XML;
    content = makeXml (result);
  }
  else {
    // need a JSONP wrapper?
    content = e.parameter.callback ?
        e.parameter.callback + '(' + JSON.stringify(result) + ');' : content;
  }
  // serve up as contentservice
  return ContentService.createTextOutput(content).setMimeType(mime);
}
```

Script Files

Here are the three script files in this app. *SheetOb* is directly copied from gmailExample, *Settings* is a subset of previous Settings namespaces, and *Code* is new.

Figure 11-1. Script files for the ContentService app

The Publishing Process

We first need to save a version of the script before we can publish it, as shown in Figure 11-2.

Figure 11-2. Saving a version of the script

The publishing process is launched via the Publish menu; choose "Deploy as web app," as shown in Figure 11-3.

Figure 11-3. Publishing the script

Permissions

A web app can be published to run as the script owner, or as the person accessing the script. If running as the script owner, it will be able to access resources belonging to the script owner; otherwise, it needs access to the executor's resources.

Additionally, the visibility of the script itself is adjustable. In this case, the web app needs read access to my spreadsheet with the carrier data (so it needs to execute as me), but I want anyone with the link to be able to run it, so I choose the publishing options shown in Figure 11-4.

Figure 11-4. Setting publishing options

This gives a fairly lengthy link (see Figure 11-5) that I can now distribute to whomever needs access to the app.

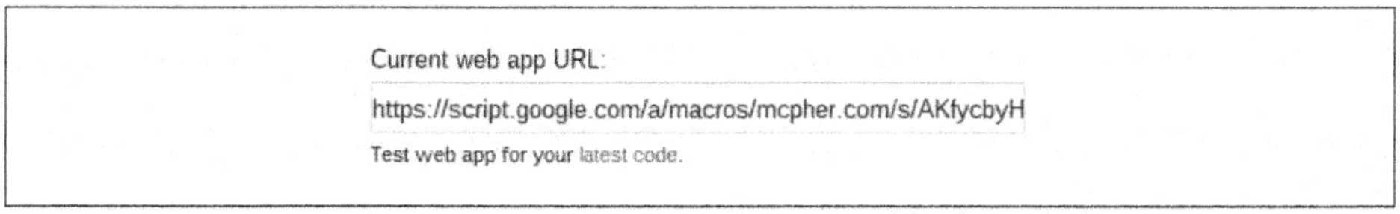

Figure 11-5. Getting the link to the web app for sharing with other users

Note that this link points to the production version of the app and will be associated with the version chosen in the previous dialog. You could also choose the "latest code" link, which points to the latest (potentially unsaved) code and is useful for testing development versions without bothering to save a version.

Now this app can be used, initially with a test using the browser:

*https://script.google.com/a/macros/mcpher.com/s/
AKfycbyHehh2LjOtDovKZQXTreZLPonau-KA1wL2xgKxK_2B83ENZ07m/exec?
flight=ua938*

with the result shown in Figure 11-6.

```
            {
                status: "ok",
                flight: "ua938",
                carrier: "ua",
                name: "United Airlines"
            }
```

Figure 11-6. Result of running the app through the browser

Delegation from VBA

There is no equivalent to the ContentService class in VBA, but apps implemented with ContentService provide a convenient means for VBA apps to communicate directly with Apps Script. As an example, the entire validation process of flight numbers in the VBA gmailExample can be completely delegated to this Apps Script web app. This is a huge advantage for porting a section at a time.

Using this approach, we no longer need to maintain the spreadsheet of airline code in Excel, even though the rest of the application stays in place in VBA. VBA makes a request to Apps Script, passing the email content as an argument. Apps Script validates and returns the lookup information with reference to its own workbook. Continuing this approach in other areas of the app, we can gradually delegate functionality to Apps Script through a series of small VBA changes.

With this approach, the VBA version no longer has to open a local spreadsheet, so the main function looks like this, using the MatchGAS_ module:

```
VB  Private Sub trigger()
        Dim threads As Collection, _
            mobs As Collection, organized As KVPairs

        ' get the settings from registry
        Set Settings = Settings_.getProperties()

        '  // get all the potential threads
        Set threads = Threads_.threadsGet

        ' // alternative for using GAS
        Set mobs = MatchGAS_.messages(threads)

        '// organize matches to prioritize
        Set organized = Match_.organize(mobs)

        '// send the mails
        Threads_.send organized

    End Sub
```

Querying Apps Script

This is a fairly simplistic implementation showing how an Apps Script function can be called to do some work on behalf of VBA. A few enhancements that might be needed are improved error handling, and some throttling to avoid hitting rate limitations when rapidly calling the Apps Script.

This example includes an additional setting in the `Settings_` module to refer to the published version of the Apps Script web app:

```VB
kv.add "GAS.URL", _
  "https://script.google.com/macros/s/ _
   AKfycbyHehh2LjOtDovKZQXTreZLPonau-KA1wL2xgKxK_2B83ENZ07m/exec"
```

The URL string is being used to pass the email content. In real life, those messages might be a little too long, and POST (with an equivalent implementation of `doPost`) on the Apps Script servicing app might be preferable to using GET, as a POST payload can be larger.

In this example, the decoded XML is converted to custom `KVPairs` simply because I find XML a little too laborious to work with:

```VB
' /**
'  * use GAS to check if there's any flight content
'  * @param {Mailitem} message the message
'  * @return {collection} the filtered messages
'  */
Private Function gasCheck(message As Outlook.mailItem) As KVPairs
    Dim hob As Object, combinedContent As String, root As Object, _
        doc As Object, kv As KVPairs, node As Object
    Set doc = CreateObject("MSXML2.DOMDocument")
    Set kv = New KVPairs

    ' avoid two calls by combining subject and body
    combinedContent = message.Subject & " " & message.Body

    ' set up a fetch
    Set hob = CreateObject("Msxml2.ServerXMLHTTP.6.0")

    'construct a query
    hob.Open "GET", Settings.getValue("GAS.URL") & _
        "?format=xml&flight=" & Utils_.encodeURI(combinedContent), False
    hob.send

    ' convert to XML element
    doc.LoadXML hob.responsetext
    Set root = doc.SelectSingleNode("root")

    ' replace this with some appropriate exception habdling
    Debug.Assert Not root Is Nothing
```

```
' load to a key/value pair structure
For Each node In root.ChildNodes
    kv.add node.nodename, node.Text
Next node

' return result
Set gasCheck = kv

End Function
```

Each message is played against the published Apps Script web app as follows, replacing the work previously done by VBA:

```
For Each message In threads

    ' ask apps script to do the work
    Set found = gasCheck(message)
    If (found.getValue("status") = "ok") Then

'       '// set up an object with useful kv pairs and add to the collection
        Set kv = New KVPairs
        kv.add "flightNumber", found.getValue("flight")
        kv.add "message", message
        kv.add "name", found.getValue("name")
        mobs.add kv
    End If

Next message
```

CHAPTER 12

Charts

In Excel, manipulating charts makes up a fairly large part of the VBA footprint. When Apps Script for Sheets first became available, a number of services, including charts, made use of the UIApp service to embed visualizations and create UIs. The UIApp was deprecated in 2014, and these services have partially or fully migrated to alternative solutions (`HtmlService`, for example), or have been deprecated themselves (UIApp builder).

There are two ways of creating charts in Sheets. One is to use the EmbeddedChart-Builder, and another is to use the charts available in the Google Visualization API (which can be used from `HtmlService`). As with all Google services, it's hard to predict which (if either) will be deprecated first, but given the reach of the Visualization API, and the continuing focus on Add-ons and other `HtmlService`-client-based capabilities, I would put my money on the Google Visualization API as the preferred way to create charts in the future.

Using the combination of the Google Visualization API and the `HtmlService` Dialog UI, you can create charts very much like the ones built by EmbeddedChartBuilder.

Chart Data

For these examples, I'll use Table 12-1, which shows US domestic passengers flown by each airline in 2014. There are 125 airlines in the dataset, but I'll concentrate on the top 10.

Table 12-1. US domestic passengers flown by each airline in 2014

Name	Passengers (000)	Carrier
Southwest Airlines Co.	126,746	WN
Delta Air Lines Inc.	106,424	DL
American Airlines Inc.	66,402	AA
United Air Lines Inc.	64,796	UA
US Airways Inc.	50,686	US
ExpressJet Airlines Inc.	27,968	EV
JetBlue Airways	26,466	B6
SkyWest Airlines Inc.	25,995	OO
Alaska Airlines Inc.	19,174	AS
Envoy Air	14,696	MQ

VBA Charts

Creating a bar chart from this data in Excel is very simple, and by default creates a very clean and readable result (Figure 12-1). In fact, Excel charts are generally superior to those produced by Sheets and offer a rich set of options for customization.

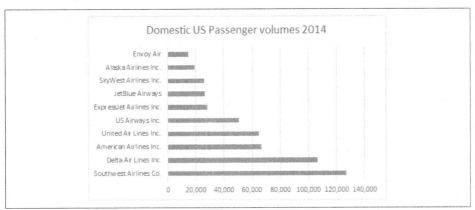

Figure 12-1. US air travel bar chart created in Excel

Code

The odd thing about an Excel bar chart is that it plots the data in the opposite order from the data order, but the code is extremely straightforward:

```vb
Public Sub build()
    Dim r As range, sht As Worksheet, cht As Chart
    Set sht = ActiveSheet
```

```
        sht.ChartObjects.Delete

        ' get the size of the data
        Set r = sht.UsedRange

        'create a chart & position it
        With r.Resize(1, 1).Offset(3, r.Columns.Count + 1)
            Set cht = sht.Shapes.AddChart2(, xlBarClustered, .Left, .Top).Chart
        End With

        ' set the chart type & data & options, first 2 columns & top 10
        With cht
            .SetSourceData r.Resize(11, 2)
            .HasTitle = True
            .ChartTitle.Text = "Domestic US Passenger volumes 2014"
        End With
End Sub
```

Sheets Charts

The same chart created in the Sheets UI looks like Figure 12-2. By default, the data is plotted in the same order as it appears on the sheet.

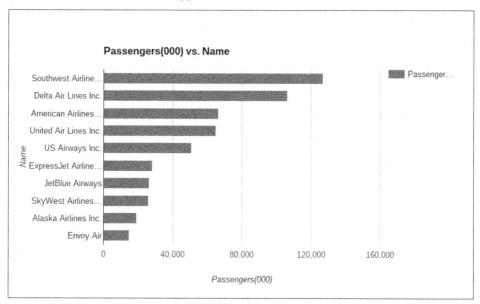

Figure 12-2. US air travel bar chart created in Sheets

Creating and formatting charts in Apps Script is generally more complex than it is using the VBA equivalent.

EmbeddedChartBuilder

The EmbeddedChartBuilder is comparatively simple to use in order to create default charts. This example creates a chart using Apps Script, and is roughly equivalent to the VBA and Sheets UI versions:

```js
function buildChart() {

    // get the sheet
    var sheet = SpreadsheetApp.getActiveSheet();
    // make a new chart, with top 10
    sheet.insertChart(
      sheet.newChart()
        .addRange(sheet.getRange(1,1, 11, 2))
        .setChartType (Charts.ChartType.BAR)
        .setOption('title' , 'Domestic US Passenger volumes 2014')
        .setPosition(3, sheet.getLastColumn()+1,0,0)
        .build()
    );
}
```

It gives the result shown in Figure 12-3.

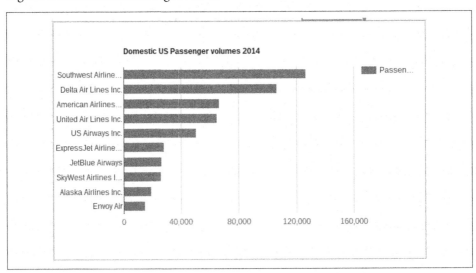

Figure 12-3. US air travel bar chart created in EmbeddedChartBuilder

setPosition

The setPosition(*startRow, startColumn, posX, posY*) line needs some explanation, as its omission leads to a confusing error message.

By default, the EmbeddedChartBuilder will position the chart over the first cell, but if there is data in that position (as there is likely to be), it will fail with an obscure message about the range being invalid. This refers to the position of the chart, not the data ranges added by the addRange method (assuming, of course, those are valid).

The setPosition method should be used to indicate a free position in the sheet at which to position the chart. posX and posY refer to the number of pixels to offset from the top left of the selected cell.

Types of Chart

You can create all of the charts listed in Table 12-2 by supplying the appropriate ENUM to the setChartType method.

Table 12-2. Types of chart that can be created through setChartType

ENUM	Chart type
Charts.ChartType.AREA	
Charts.ChartType.BAR	
Charts.ChartType.COLUMN	
Charts.ChartType.LINE	
Charts.ChartType.PIE	
Charts.ChartType.SCATTER	
Charts.ChartType.TABLE	

Visualization API

The documentation for the EmbeddedChartBuilder service refers to the Google Visualization (gViz) API documentation for details on chart options and settings. It is likely that it uses the gViz API behind the scenes. This API has a variety of charts that are not available directly from Apps Script, and can be used in any of the HtmlService presentation styles.

Figure 12-4 shows the chart as a dialog; Figure 12-5 shows it as a sidebar; and Figure 12-6 shows it as a published web app.

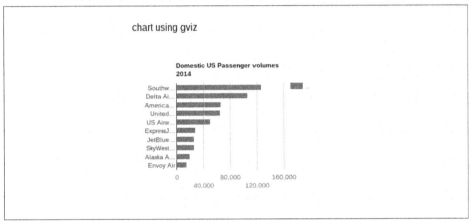

Figure 12-4. US air travel bar chart displayed as a dialog through the gViz API

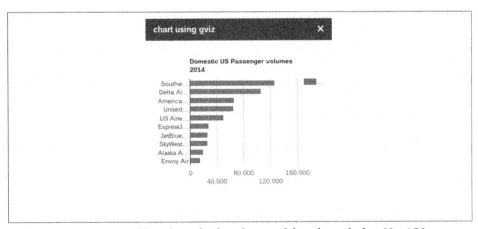

Figure 12-5. US air travel bar chart displayed as a sidebar through the gViz API

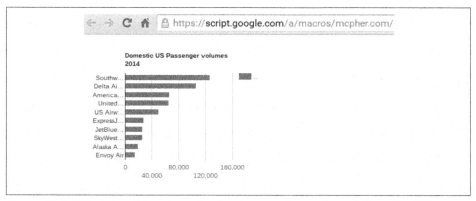

Figure 12-6. US air travel bar chart displayed as a web app through the gViz API

Google Visualization HtmlService App

To be able to create charts using the Visualization API, we first need to create an HtmlService app structure. The dialog style will emulate both VBA and the EmbeddedChartBuilder, but they can all be easily implemented by the same code. The script file structure should look like Figure 12-7 (the *embedded.gs* script contains the code for creating the chart using the EmbeddedChartBuilder, and the other scripts are for the HtmlService versions).

Figure 12-7. HtmlService chart app file structure

This will follow the familiar pattern introduced in Chapter 10. Many of the files in the pattern will need to be only slightly changed from that example, and some will need no changes at all.

code.gs

As usual, *code.gs* contains the code for initiating the HtmlService and for customizing the menu, which will now contain options for how to show the chart (See Figure 12-8).

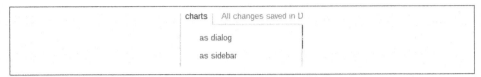

Figure 12-8. Menu options for displaying the chart

Aside from the menu changes, the function that returns the spreadsheet data to the client now simply returns all the data in the sheet, leaving the client code to figure out how much of it to use. This will allow for a future expansion—for example, the number of airlines to show could be user selectable in the HtmlService UI:

```js
'use strict';
function doGet(e) {
  return HtmlService.createTemplateFromFile('index.html')
      .evaluate()
      .setSandboxMode(HtmlService.SandboxMode.IFRAME);
}

function onOpen(e) {
  SpreadsheetApp.getUi()
    .createMenu('charts')
    .addItem('as dialog', 'showDialogChart')
    .addItem('as sidebar', 'showSideBarChart')
    .addToUi();
}
/**
 * get the getPassengerData
 */
function getData() {
  // get the data in the active sheet
  var sheet = SpreadsheetApp.getActiveSheet();

  // if there is no sheet, then fallback to a specific sheet/spreadsheet
  // because we are executing as a webapp
  if (!sheet){
    sheet = SpreadsheetApp
      .openById('1ZP7RAB7V6zr_oifR62xdLpY49FGOS7pnYuZHudT9LKg')
      .getSheetByName('Passengers');
  }
  // just return the whole dataset
  return sheet.getDataRange().getValues();
}
function showDialogChart() {
  var html = HtmlService.createTemplateFromFile('index.html')
      .evaluate()
      .setSandboxMode(HtmlService.SandboxMode.IFRAME)
      .setWidth(400)
      .setHeight(300);

  SpreadsheetApp.getUi()
```

```
      .showModalDialog(html, 'chart using gviz');

}

function showSideBarChart() {
  var ui = HtmlService.createTemplateFromFile('index.html')
    .evaluate()
    .setSandboxMode(HtmlService.SandboxMode.IFRAME)
    .setTitle('chart using gviz');


  SpreadsheetApp.getUi().showSidebar(ui);
}
```

index.html

The *index.html* file now includes a reference to the Google API so that the Google gViz code can be loaded, and an element that will be used as the container for the generated chart:

```
<!DOCTYPE html>
<!-- styles -->
<?!= HtmlService.createHtmlOutputFromFile('styles.css').getContent(); ?>

<div class="content">

  <div class = "block">
    <div id="chart"></div>
  </div>

  <div class = "block">
    <div id="message" class="message"></div>
  </div>

</div>
<!-- javascript. -->
<script type="text/javascript" src="https://www.google.com/jsapi"></script>

<?!= HtmlService.createHtmlOutputFromFile('render.js').getContent(); ?>
<?!= HtmlService.createHtmlOutputFromFile('client.js').getContent(); ?>
<?!= HtmlService.createHtmlOutputFromFile('app.js').getContent(); ?>
<?!= HtmlService.createHtmlOutputFromFile('main.js').getContent(); ?>
```

main.js

The google.load approach to loading libraries provides a method of setting a call-back to be executed when the modules are loaded and the DOM is ready. google.set LoadOnCallBack executes the same pattern as the previous HtmlService example:

```
<script>
// the app
google.load('visualization', '1.0', {'packages':['corechart']});
```

```
// wait for the viz lib to have loaded
google.setOnLoadCallback (function () {

  // kick by getting data, and building page
  Client.getData (function (data) {

    // store the data
    App.globals.data = data;

    // render the chart
    Render.build();

    // add any listeners
    App.listeners();

  });

});

</script>
```

client.js

The `Client` namespace is responsible for communicating with the server, using `google.script.run` to request the contents of the active sheet. The only change in *client.js* is the name of the server-side function to execute in *code.gs*:

```
<script>
// all code for client-server communication
var Client = (function(client) {

  client.getData = function (successFunction) {

    // this executes a function asynchronously on the server
    // under control of the client
    google.script.run

      // this will be executed if it fails
      .withFailureHandler(function (err) {
        App.reportMessage (err);
      })

      // this will be executed if it succeeds
      .withSuccessHandler (successFunction)

      // this is what gets executed
      .getData();
  };
  return client;

})(Client || {});
</script>
```

app.js

The `App` namespace takes care of the app housekeeping. This *app.js* script differs from the previous `HtmlService` example only in that there are no listened-for events:

```js
<script>
  // app-related globals
  var App = (function(app) {

    /**
     * report a message
     * @param {string} message the message
     */
    app.reportMessage = function (message) {
      document.getElementById("message").innerHTML = message;
    };

    /**
     * any global stuff/settings is here
     */
    app.globals = {};

    /**
     * add listeners
     */
    app.listeners = function () {

      // no listeners in this app

    };

    return app;
  }) (App || {});

</script>
```

render.js

The `Render` namespace still has the same function (updating the DOM), but is completely different than the previous example, as it is creating a chart using the gViz API. Building a chart consists of these simple steps:

1. Creating a visualization table to hold the data to be charted.

2. Adding columns and data to it (retrieved earlier in the `Client` namespace).

3. Setting up the formatting and content options and drawing the chart.

Here's the necessary code:

```js
<script>
  var Render = (function (render) {
```

```
render.build = function () {

  // the chart element is already in place
  var chartElem = document.getElementById ("chart");

  // Create a data table.
  var table = new google.visualization.DataTable();

  // get a copy of the data (top 10, first two columns) and the headings
  var heads = App.globals.data[0].slice();
  var rows = App.globals.data.slice(1,11).map(function(d) {
    return d.slice(0,2);
  });

  // add the headings
  table.addColumn('string', heads[0]);
  table.addColumn('number', heads[1]);

  // add the data
  table.addRows (rows);

  // Set chart options
  var options = {
    'title':'Domestic US Passenger volumes 2014',
    'width':280,
    'height':220
  };

  // show the chart
  var chart = new google.visualization.BarChart(chartElem);
  chart.draw(table, options);
};

  return render;
})(Render || {});

</script>
```

Other Chart Formats

Sheets and Apps Script have a long way to go to be able to produce charts with the same professionalism and ease as Excel and VBA. On the other hand, the Google Visualization API can produce a wide variety of charts in a number of different presentation media styles. It is even possible to create gViz charts embedded in an Excel user form, and certainly in an Excel Add-in using the Microsoft Office JavaScript API.

I have covered only one type of chart in this chapter, but the creation method is exactly the same (of course, some of the options differ) among chart styles; simply change the chart type value during the build process.

CHAPTER 13

Sites

Google Sites is a little like SharePoint, in that fairly complex sites and team sharing repositories can be created without too much effort. There is a template system to help you create a common look and feel and build pages with a specific function, such as uploading and downloading files.

Although Google Sites is largely designed for team collaboration and intranets, there are some large public websites with upward of 1,000 pages (mine is one of them).

Apps Script

A limited amount of automation can be introduced in a site through Apps Script, but more importantly, the Sites service enables you to automate the maintenance and creation of pages and content. This means that you can regularly and automatically update or access information from any Apps script, whether it is container-bound, triggered, an add-on, or otherwise.

Scripts can be container-bound to a site, but they can also be published web apps that are invoked from within a Sites page. In both cases, their utility is not what you would expect or hope for from a tool that you should be able to use to enhance a site's usability.

A site can help make a good container for the static content of a published standalone Apps Script web app.

Gadgets

Although gadgets are not related to sites per se, many sites have them as embedded miniature HTML/JavaScript apps, wrapped in XML. Developers often use gadgets, as they can be more flexible than embedded site Apps Script—you can essentially create a real app that runs in an iframe hosted by the Sites page.

There was a time when gadgets could be used to enhance your Google landing page, but this was deprecated some time ago. Gadgets in sites are still supported currently, but there may come a time when they are also deprecated.

Code Lockdown

Although it is possible to embed HTML in special HTML controls in Sites pages, these controls have limited usefulness. In regular pages, all HTML code is sanitized, and even styles cannot be defined. This leaves gadgets as the only real way to create interesting additions to standard Sites pages.

Advertising

Nowadays most sites have some form of advertising, usually enabled by Google AdSense. Google Sites initially had advertising enabled through a gadget where you could pick the style of ad to be displayed at that spot.

This capability was deprecated a year or so ago, so you can no longer add new ads to Sites pages, except by creating gadgets whose purpose is simply to show ads. However, these kinds of ads are likely to be against Google's terms of service, as they ban the use of iframes to display AdSense content.

There is now no proper way to display AdSense content on Google Sites, which reinforces the view that Google Sites is really only about internal team collaboration and not actually designed for public consumption.

VBA

Because there is no VBA equivalent (SharePoint does not provide any VBA automation), this chapter is simply an introduction to Sites.

The Future of Sites

There have been no real interesting developments in the SiteApp service for a number of years now, and various useful capabilities have either been deprecated or fallen behind other Googleverse developments, so either Sites is considered to be nonstrategic or there is some massive update in the works.

At the time of writing, I cannot recommend Sites as a good landing zone for SharePoint deployments, but I would not be surprised if there were soon some significant changes in the Sites platform.

CHAPTER 14

Advanced Google Services

What Are Advanced Google Services?

Google now provides a vast array of APIs, accessible from many platforms and often with software development kits (SDKs) in a variety of languages to make them as easy to use as possible. Figure 14-1 gives a snapshot of the currently available APIs.

Figure 14-1. Google APIs

Advanced Services Versus Google APIs

There are usually two ways to access these APIs:

- Using the language-specific SDK

- Via a REST API (normally JSON, but there are also some with XML capabilities)

The Google services, such as the Spreadsheet app, are built into Apps Script to enable easy access to the associated API, which you can also access through a language-specific library or by directly querying a JSON API. In principle, these services are doing the job that the language-specific SDK does in other platforms: simplifying access to the relevant parts of the underlying API.

Advanced services are integrated with Apps Script but do not have the same level of seamless integration as the built-in services. However, they give access to more features of the API. For example, the Drive app Apps Script service implements only part of the Google Drive web API, omitting certain features such as file revisions and custom properties.

Advanced services are more easily consumed and authenticated to than their equivalent JSON API, but sometimes are less capable.

In general, if a built-in service exists and provides the capabilities required, then it is the best choice. If an advanced service exists and does what you need, it will be easier to use than the equivalent REST JSON API.

The documentation for the advanced services can be sketchy. Almost always, you are referred to the underlying API detailed documentation, which is generally much more complex, and often more focused on Java or Go than JavaScript. Figure 14-2 shows an example of what you can expect from the Fusion Tables advanced services documentation (for which there is barely more than a page of specific detail).

Reference

For detailed information on this service, see the reference documentation for the Fusion Tables API. Like all advanced services in Apps Script, the Fusion Tables service uses the same objects, methods, and parameters as the public API.

Figure 14-2. Fusion Tables documentation

It's well worth looking at the API documentation, as it generally provides an opportunity for you to interactively try out the API and see what the resource representation objects look like.

Even if you need to resort to a JSON API, enabling the advanced service can help you generate an appropriately scoped access token for your application, and thus avoid having to create an OAuth 2.0 process.

Developers Console

All APIs are managed through the Developers Console. This is covered in more detail in Chapter 15, but using advanced services in Apps Script requires a trip to the Developers Console in order to enable the APIs required by the advanced service.

Normal services don't need this, and it has always been a bit of a mystery to me why enabling advanced services doesn't automatically enable the app on the console.

Enabling Advanced Services

The Resources menu option, shown in Figure 14-3, takes you to a dialog for enabling advanced services (Figure 14-4), which includes the comment "These services must also be enabled in the Google Developers Console."

Figure 14-3. The Resources menu option

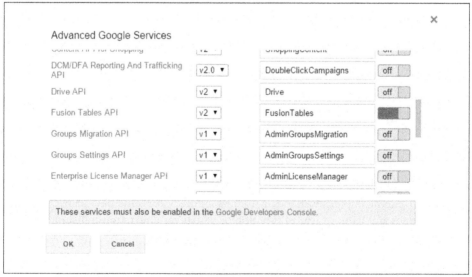

Figure 14-4. Dialog for enabling advanced services

In this example, I've enabled the Fusion Tables API, and now I need to also enable Fusion Tables in the Developers Console.

First, find the API, and click the result, as shown in Figure 14-5.

Figure 14-5. Finding the Fusion Tables API

Then enable it, as shown in Figure 14-6.

Figure 14-6. Enabling the Fusion Tables API

As shown in Figure 14-7, this provides access to some handy information on usage— of course there's none yet—and on quotas (Figure 14-8).

Fusion Tables Example

This example will create a Fusion table, copying from the sheet used in Chapter 11. The value of using namespaces in these examples should now be apparent.

The Settings and SheetOb namespaces created for the Content Service example in Chapter 11 can be copied over to (or used as a library for) this new project without many changes and without fear of function or global variable name collision.

The Quotas section of the Google Developer Console warned that there was a rate limit on this service, so we'll also need the exponential backoff code, which can be found in the Utils namespace of the gmailExample introduced in Chapter 8.

Figure 14-7. Usage information for the Fusion Tables API

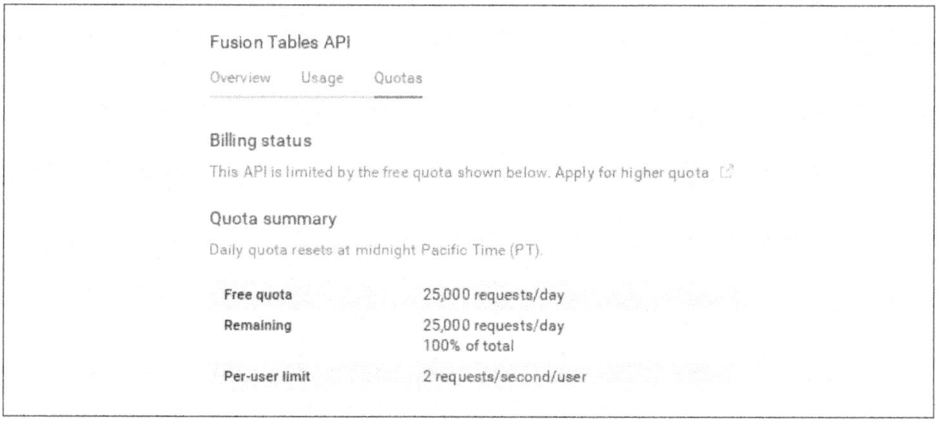

Figure 14-8. Quota information for the Fusion Tables API

Settings Namespace

The settings will be held in the Properties service (introduced in Chapter 5) and have a one-off initial setting. The spreadsheet setting defines the carrier code lookup reference sheet used in previous examples.

The new FUSION setting refers to the name to be used at the Fusion table's creation, and later will contain the Fusion table ID once it has been created:

```js
// one-off settings to get started
```

```
var SETTINGS_KEY = "advancedfusionexample";

function setOneTimeProperties () {
  setProperties(oneTimeSettings);
}

function setProperties (props) {
  PropertiesService.getUserProperties().setProperty(SETTINGS_KEY,
      JSON.stringify(props));
}

var oneTimeSettings = (function(settings) {
  'use strict';

  settings.KEY = SETTINGS_KEY;

  settings.LOOKUP = {
    ID: '1f4zuZZv2NiLuYSGB5j4ENFc6wEWOmaEdCoHNuv-gHXo',
    NAME: 'lookup'
  };

  settings.HEADINGS = {
    CODE:'carrier',
    NAME:'name'
  };

  settings.FUSION = {
    NAME:'carrierFusion',
    ID:''
  };
  // update the sheet
  return settings;

})(oneTimeSettings || {});

// get them from prop service, or use the one time setting function.
var Settings = JSON.parse(
    PropertiesService.getUserProperties().getProperty(SETTINGS_KEY))  ;
```

Copy Sheet to Fusion

This is the main function that gets the data from the sheet, creates a new Fusion table,
copies the data over, and records the new Fusion table's ID in Settings so that next
time it will use the same table:

```
// Copy data from spreadsheet to fusion table
function sheetCopy() {

  // get the sheet
   var sob = new SheetOb().open(Settings.LOOKUP.ID, Settings.LOOKUP.NAME);

  // get the fusion table or create it if we don't know it
```

```
if (!Settings.FUSION.ID) {
  Settings.FUSION.ID = Fusion.createTable (Settings.FUSION.NAME,sob).tableId;
}

// delete all data in the table
Fusion.clearData(Settings.FUSION.ID);

// insert the data from the sheet
Fusion.insertRows (Settings.FUSION.ID , sob);

// write back the settings with any updated stuff
setProperties (Settings);

}
```

Fusion Namespace

As usual, the features of the advanced service have been implemented in a simplified namespace. This code includes both the functions used in the example so far, plus a few others that could be needed for future examples:

```
// Handle fusion
var Fusion = (function (fusion) {

  /**
   * find all tables match name
   * @param {string} name the table name
   * @return {[object]} the tableId and name of tables that match
   */
  fusion.findByName = function (name) {

    var tables = Utils.rateLimitExpBackoff(function() {
      return FusionTables.Table.list({fields:"items(name,tableId)"});
    });

    // find the right one(s)
    return tables.items.filter(function(d) {
      return d.name === name;
    });
  };

  /**
   * do a query
   * @param {string} id the table id
   * @param {string} optSql the string after WHERE
   * @return {object} the result
   */
  fusion.query = function (id, where) {
    return Utils.rateLimitExpBackoff(function() {
      return FusionTables.Query.sqlGet(
        "SELECT * FROM " + id + (where ? " WHERE " + where : ''));
    });
```

```
};
/**
 * remove all the rows in a table
 * @param {string} id the table id
 * @return {object} the result
 */
fusion.clearData = function (id) {

  return Utils.rateLimitExpBackoff(function() {
    return FusionTables.Query.sql("DELETE FROM " + id);
  });

};

/**
 * insert data into a table
 * @param {string} id the table id
 * @param {SheetOb} sob the sheet object to insert
 * @return {Fusion} self
 */
fusion.insertRows = function (id,sob) {

  // generate a bunch of insert statements
  var inserts = sob.getData().map(function(d) {
    return 'INSERT INTO ' + id +
      ' (' + Object.keys(d).map(function(e) { return quote_(e); })
        .join(',') + ') ' +
        ' VALUES (' + Object.keys(d).map(function(e) {
          return quote_(d[e]); }).join(',') + ')';
  });

  // max quotas on the size of insert tables (500 lines, 1mb , 10000 cells)
  var MAX_CHUNKSIZE = 1024*1000,
    MAX_INSERTS = Math.min(500, Math.floor(10000 /
        Object.keys(sob.getHeaderOb()).length));

  // create arrays of chunks of insert sizes that don't break any rules.
  var toWrite = inserts.reduce (function (p,c) {
    if ( p.chunkSize + c.length > MAX_CHUNKSIZE ||
      p.chunks.length >= MAX_INSERTS-1) {
      p.inserts.push (p.chunks);
      p.chunks = [];
      p.chunkSize = 0;
    }
    p.chunks.push(c);
    p.chunkSize += c.length;
    return p;
  }, {chunks:[],chunkSize:0, inserts:[] });

  // now do the inserts
  if (toWrite.chunks.length) toWrite.inserts.push (toWrite.chunks);
  toWrite.inserts.forEach (function(d) {
```

```
        return Utils.rateLimitExpBackoff(function() {
          return FusionTables.Query.sql(d.join(';') + ';');
        });
    });

  };


  function quote_ (value) {
    return typeof value !== 'number' ? "'" + value.toString() + "'" : value;
  }

  /**
   * create table of a given name
   * @param {string} name the table name
   * @param {SheetOb} sob the sheetobject
   */
  fusion.createTable = function (name,sob) {

    // this needs some more work to generalize type detection.
    // for this example, it's fine as it should support string or number
    var columns = Object.keys(sob.getHeaderOb()).map (function(d) {
      return {
        name:d,
        type:sob.getData().reduce(function(p,c) {
          return p && p !== c[d] ? "STRING" : typeof c[d];
        }).toUpperCase() || "STRING"
      }
    });

    // set the column types
    var payload = {
      name:name,
      isExportable: true,
      columns:columns
    }

    // create the table
    return Utils.rateLimitExpBackoff(function() {
      return FusionTables.Table.insert(payload);
    });

  };

  return fusion;

})(Fusion || {});
```

Fusion Quotas

When you're inserting rows in a Fusion table, there are a number of limitations (over and above the daily quotas and rate limits) to keep in mind. Fusion tables are not really designed for SQL insertion, so some careful optimization is needed.

It is best to batch insertions, but there is a maximum number of insertions, cells, and string sizes. The `insertRows` method just shown takes care of balancing performance and living within Fusion quotas.

An alternative, and more reliable, approach for importing large amounts of data is to use the `FusionTables.Table.importRows` method.

Scripts Structure

For this example, `Settings` is copied from the Content Service example, with a few changes for the Fusion table parameters (Figure 14-9). `SheetOb` and `Utils` are copied with no changes, and `Fusion` and `Code` are the Fusion namespace and the main code, respectively.

Figure 14-9. Scripts structure

Currently Available Advanced Services

Each advanced service works in a similar way to the Fusion Tables example. Table 14-1 shows a list of the advanced services available at the time of writing.

Table 14-1. Currently available advanced services

Service	Purpose
Admin SDK	Manage Apps domains (administrators only)
AdSense	Manage ads and income in an AdSense account
Analytics	Manage Google Analytics activity, reports, and accounts
Apps Activity	Access file and Apps activity for an Apps domain
BigQuery	Execute and manage big query reports and data
Calendar	Access advanced Google Calendar services

Service	Purpose
Classroom	Manage students and courses in Google Classroom
Drive	Access Drive's advanced capabilities
Doubleclick	Manage double-click campaigns and reports
Fusion	Access Fusion tables
Google+	Access Google+ circles and posts
Google+ domains	Manage domain-wide Google+ circles and posts
Mirror	Interact with Google Glass
Prediction	Use the prediction API to train and execute prediction queries
Shopping	Manage accounts and product listings (Google merchants only)
Tasks	Manage Gmail tasks
URL shortener	Manage and create goo.gl short names
YouTube	Manage YouTube videos, playlists channels, and live events

CHAPTER 15

Authentication and Security

Google Apps has been designed from the start to ensure that only authorized processes and people have access to its resources. One of its key strengths—letting users access data from anywhere using any device—is also a potential weakness. This is not something that VBA is too concerned with, because local Office relies on Windows file and user protection and the files likely reside on a desktop or private network.

Apps takes a multilayered approach to security, with user-based identification tied to individuals by Google authentication, and role-based protection defined by permissions. Conversely, resources belonging to individual users are protected from unwelcome script access, as scripts require users to have explicit authorization to access private resources defined by scope.

Figure 15-1 shows how authentication and permission combine to grant a user authorization to access and operate on a resource in an agreed-upon way.

OAuth 2.0

When a user first attempts to access an Apps resource, they first need to provide proof of who they are. Like many providers, Google uses an authentication process called OAuth 2.0. This process, shown in Figure 15-2, is analogous to logging in, except that credential management is delegated to an identity provider (Google), and the authentication process is multistage, verified through the passing of tokens.

Coming to grips with the authentication process is often one of the most challenging tasks for those using APIs for the first time. If you are planning to use VBA to access Apps Script services directly, you'll need to use an OAuth 2.0 implementation to be able to do so.

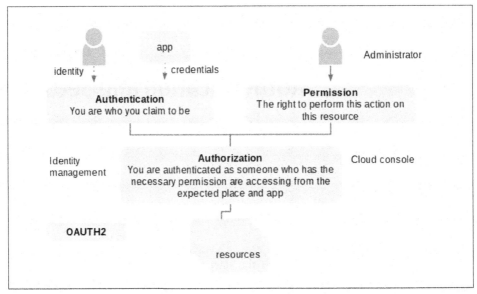

Figure 15-1. How authentication and permission work together to grant users access to resources

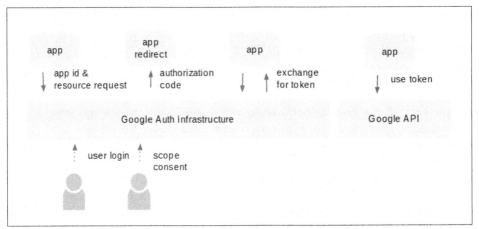

Figure 15-2. The OAuth 2.0 authentication process

If you are using Apps Script, most of this is handled automatically and behind the scenes for APIs that have an Apps Service interface. The others (and many non-Google APIs that use OAuth 2.0) need an Apps Script OAuth 2.0 library. There are implementations for both VBA and Apps Script, detailed in Appendix A and discussed in this chapter.

Setup

The setup process follows these steps:

1. An app profile is created in the Google Developers Console (in the case of Apps Script this is automatic), along with an execution domain (where the app will be run from) and a redirect URL (where the authorization code should be returned to).

2. The scopes (resources the app needs to access in order to operate) are defined in the Developers Console. This is also automatic for Apps Script.

3. The permissions (who is allowed to access the resource) are assigned to the document or script by the document owner.

Access

When an app is accessed:

1. The app requests an authorization code, which it can use to exchange for an access token. It provides secret data to match against that held in the Developers Console.

2. The user credentials profile (a cookie) is checked for an active logon, and to determine whether the requested resources have already been made accessible to the requesting app.

3. A login and authorization dialog are provoked if required.

4. If permissions are granted, the app receives an authorization code to the redirect URL.

5. The app makes another request, this time using the authorization code, and receives an access token (with a limited lifetime).

6. This access token is used in the header of requests to APIs. Requests with invalid access tokens or those that do not match the required scopes are rejected.

Refresh

In order to short-circuit this process, some OAuth 2.0 implementations return a refresh token along with the access token. When the access token expires, the app can get a new one simply by exchanging the refresh token (assuming it can also provide the secret data matching that held in the Developers Console).

Scopes

Scopes are used to define which resources an app needs to access, and tend to be set at a more granular level than, say, file types, because they can also define the type of access required (e.g., `drive` versus `drive.readonly`).

The scopes needed in Apps Script are detected automatically by the IDE, which scans the code in the scripts looking for references to particular services. The IDE knows which scopes are needed by services it recognizes, so it's able to create a service-to-scope mapping. Even commented-out code is considered during the scanning process. Running a script for the first time will provoke an authorization dialog like the one shown in Figure 15-3, granting the application permission to request access to these scopes.

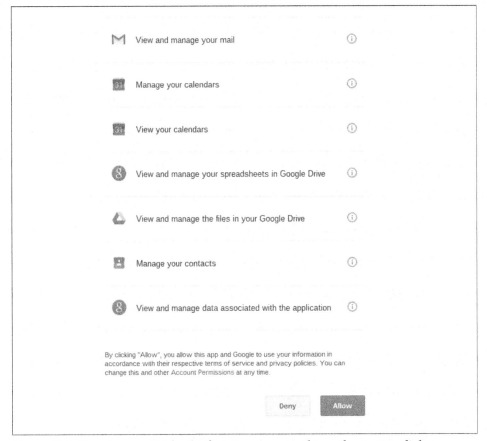

Figure 15-3. Running a script for the first time prompts this authorization dialog

The scopes accessed by a project can be found in the "Project properties" section, which looks like Figure 15-4 (from the gmailExample introduced in Chapter 8).

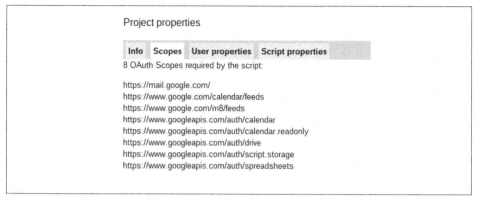

Figure 15-4. List of scopes accessed by a project

Limiting Scope to the Current Document

In the case of Docs, Sheets, and Forms, their scopes apply to all documents of that type. You can limit a script's authorized scope (useful for add-ons) to operate on only the currently active document by including the following JSDoc annotation in the script:

```
/**
 * @OnlyCurrentDoc
 */
```

If you're using libraries, it is possible that one of the referenced libraries contains such an annotation, which would also limit the main script to the currently active document. You can supersede this by including the following JSDoc annotation in the main script:

```
/**
 * @NotOnlyCurrentDoc
 */
```

Listing Authorized Apps

Just like other apps authorized to use your Google account for authentication, Apps Script apps can be found in the Google Account console (*https://myaccount.google.com/security*) (see Figure 15-5).

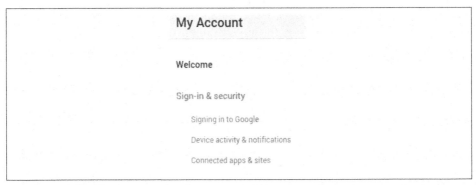

Figure 15-5. Google Account console

Figure 15-6 shows a portion of the list produced by the Manage Apps dialog of "Connected apps & sites." Names such as "executionapi" refer to the Apps Script project name. Giving your code projects meaningful names is a good habit to get into, particularly if you or a user needs to revoke access for some reason.

executionapi	Has some account access, including Google Docs, Google Drive
executionServer	Has access to Google Docs, Google Drive
expandcache	Has some account access, including Google Docs
extract script source	Has access to Google Drive
ezyPattern	Has some account access, including Fusion Tables (experimental), Google Docs, Google Drive
firebaseExample	Has some account access, including Fusion Tables (experimental), Google Docs
flightExec	Has access to Google Docs, Google Drive

Figure 15-6. Partial list of "Connected apps & sites"

Revoking Access

You can revoke access by clicking on a name and completing the REMOVE dialog, as shown in Figure 15-7. Again, giving projects meaningful names from the start can remove the detective work from this cleanup process.

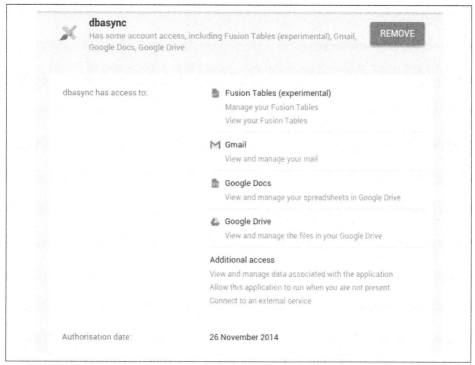

dbasync
Has some account access, including Fusion Tables (experimental), Gmail, Google Docs, Google Drive

REMOVE

dbasync has access to:

📋 **Fusion Tables (experimental)**
Manage your Fusion Tables
View your Fusion Tables

Ⓜ **Gmail**
View and manage your mail

📄 **Google Docs**
View and manage your spreadsheets in Google Drive

🔺 **Google Drive**
View and manage the files in your Google Drive

Additional access
View and manage data associated with the application
Allow this application to run when you are not present
Connect to an external service

Authorisation date: 26 November 2014

Figure 15-7. Revoking access

ScriptApp

The ScriptApp service provides visibility to various script properties associated with publishing, trigger, and authentication states.

The most useful is getOAuthToken, which returns the OAuth token for this script. Normally this is not needed, as the built-in services use it behind the scenes, but if the script is authorized with appropriate scopes, the same token can be used to access other APIs directly, avoiding the need to execute a complicated OAuth 2.0 process.

As an example, neither the DriveApp nor Advanced Drive Apps Script allow access to some of the script manipulation capabilities of the underlying Drive JSON API. The custom Drive JSON API library for Apps Script provides an interface to the full Drive

API, bypassing the Apps Script regular and advanced services. Details are in Appendix A.

Until this year, the only way to get an access token to enable this library was via an OAuth 2.0 custom implementation (EzyOauth2 is another custom library that handles OAuth 2.0, details of which can be found in Appendix A).

Nowadays, the active script's access token is available via:

```
ScriptApp.getOAuthToken()
```

As long as the script has enabled the Advanced Drive service, and it includes some code referencing the Drive service, the OAuth token associated with the script will have sufficient scope to be able to access the Drive JSON API.

You can now initialize the Drive JSON API library like this, reusing the current script's token, without it needing to go through its own OAuth 2.0 initialization process:

```
var dapi = new cDriveJsonApi.DriveJsonApi()
          .setAccessToken(ScriptApp.getOAuthToken());
```

Internally it uses the same access token in the header of a Fetch operation:

```
var result = UrlFetchApp.fetch( url , {
  headers: {authorization :"Bearer " + accesstoken}
});
```

Service Accounts

The normal OAuth 2.0 flow involves the user proving their identity using the Google authentication infrastructure. In some cases, especially server-based automation tasks, it makes more sense for the application to prove its identity rather than an individual.

This involves a different workflow—encryption and digital signing. Until recently, Apps Script did not have the capability to sign using the correct cipher, but now it can, which means that tasks not requiring human intervention can be coded to use a service account rather than a regular user account.

When a service account is used, claims are made via a JSON Web Token (JWT), which is digitally signed through this new Apps Script utility, where the value is the JWT and the key is derived from the service account credentials generated by the Google Developers Console entry associated with the app:

```
Utilities.computeRsaSha256Signature(value, key)
```

A walkthrough of the Developers Console credential creation process is shown later in this chapter.

Libraries

Creating your own OAuth 2.0 handler is outside the scope of this book. Appendix A references examples of open source libraries you can use for handling OAuth 2.0 within Apps Script. One is the open source EzyOauth2 library, and the other was created more recently by the Google engineering team (which can now also handle service accounts).

In addition, there is an open source VBA library for handling OAuth 2.0 from VBA, which will also be used for the examples in this chapter. The code for this library is in the book's GitHub repository.

Details of all these can be found in Appendix A.

OAuth 2.0 Example

In cases where APIs are not available through Apps Script (either directly or as an advanced service), OAuth 2.0 needs to be implemented as part of the script.

This example uses the cEzyOauth2 library to handle the authentication flow, but other libraries will work in a similar way. The Google API required for this demo is the Google Cloud Datastore, which is not directly accessible from Apps Script.

Creating the Cloud Console Project

All Google API access is controlled through the Developers Console (*https:// console.developers.google.com*).

Credentials

The first step is to create a project for the Apps Script application, and add credentials to obtain an OAuth 2.0 client ID (see Figure 15-8).

Figure 15-8. Adding credentials to a new project

As Figure 15-9 shows, we're creating a web app, and for now you can leave the "Authorized redirect URIs" and "Authorized JavaScript origins" sections blank. We'll come back and complete those later.

The redirect URL is used by OAuth 2.0 to call your application with the authorization code with which to apply for an access token. It will be related to the published address of the web app (which we don't yet know, as the app is neither written or published). For security, this project will respond only to the given address.

The JavaScript origin is the domain from which the initial authentication request is made, and will be `script.google.com`—the domain of the published app. Requests will be valid for this project only if they originate from the listed domain names.

Figure 15-9. Obtaining an OAuth 2.0 client ID

The response will be something like Figure 15-10 (the values shown are for illustration only).

Enabling the Datastore API

Multiple APIs can be enabled for a project if required, but in this case we just need to authorize the Datastore API (Figure 15-11).

Figure 15-12 shows the Datastore API after it's been enabled.

Figure 15-10. OAuth client response

Figure 15-11. Enabling the Datastore API

Figure 15-12. The enabled Datastore API

Scopes

As mentioned earlier, the scopes define the resources that this project will need to access. The easiest way to discover the scopes a particular API needs is to click "Explore this API" in the API enable screen, which leads to a page that describes its capabilities (Figure 15-13).

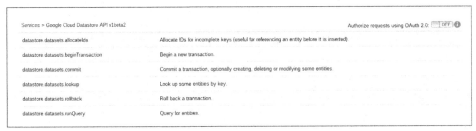

Services > Google Cloud Datastore API v1beta2   Authorize requests using OAuth 2.0: [Off] ⓘ

datastore.datasets.allocateIds	Allocate IDs for incomplete keys (useful for referencing an entity before it is inserted).
datastore.datasets.beginTransaction	Begin a new transaction.
datastore.datasets.commit	Commit a transaction, optionally creating, deleting or modifying some entities.
datastore.datasets.lookup	Look up some entities by key.
datastore.datasets.rollback	Roll back a transaction.
datastore.datasets.runQuery	Query for entities.

Figure 15-13. The Datastore API's capabilities

Turning on "Authorize requests using OAuth 2.0" shows the scopes associated with this API (Figure 15-14). You will need a subset of the scopes listed there, depending on which capabilities are needed by the app.

Select OAuth 2.0 scopes:

Scopes are used to grant an application different levels of access to data on behalf of the end user. Each API may declare one or more scopes. Learn more about OAuth 2.0

Google Cloud Datastore API declares the following scopes. Select which ones you want to grant to APIs Explorer.

☐ https://www.googleapis.com/auth/cloud-platform
View and manage your data across Google Cloud Platform services

☑ https://www.googleapis.com/auth/datastore
View and manage your Google Cloud Datastore data

☑ https://www.googleapis.com/auth/userinfo.email
View your email address

Add additional scopes (optional)

[Authorize] Cancel

Figure 15-14. Scopes associated with the Datastore API

Storing the credentials

Credentials should be kept secret and not directly written in code. The usual way to ensure their confidentiality is to use the Properties service and extract them when needed.

EzyOauth2 provides a way to store these kinds of credentials and scopes in a consistent way, and other OAuth 2.0 support libraries likely do the same. Details of where to get this library and how to use it are included in Appendix A.

This should be run once, then deleted (data is filed in the PropertiesService store):

```js
setAuthenticationPackage_ ({
    clientId : "1046843726xxxxxai5cknaa3.apps.googleusercontent.com",
    clientSecret : "CH1l3wW6lxxxR6iBvi",
```

```
        scopes : ['https://www.googleapis.com/auth/datastore',
                  'https://www.googleapis.com/auth/userinfo.email'],
        service: 'google',
        packageName: 'googleDatastore'
});
```

Finishing the app

EzyOauth2 manages the complete OAuth2 process, but it needs an authentication screen and a callback for what to do when the token is received. This screen can also be used to communicate the details of the redirect URL.

The callback function.   The callback function is called once an OAuth 2.0 access token has been received, and is the main executor of whatever the app is supposed to do. Because this app accesses the datastore, we can check if it will work by doing a simple query. I have an existing datastore to use for this.

This function uses the Datastore JSON API to query its contents, using the access token passed to it by the OAuth 2.0 process:

```js
/**
 * this is your main processing - will be called with your access token
 * @param {string} accessToken - the accessToken
 */
function doSomething (accessToken) {

  var options = {
    method: "POST",
    contentType : "application/json" ,
    muteHttpExceptions : true,
    headers: {
      "authorization": "Bearer " + accessToken,
    },
    payload:JSON.stringify({
      "query": {
      "kinds": [{"name":"polymerdbab"}]
      }
    })
  };

  var result = UrlFetchApp.fetch(
  "https://www.googleAPIs.com/datastore/v1beta2/" +
  "datasets/xliberationdatastore/runQuery"
   options);

  return HtmlService.createHtmlOutput (' it worked ' +
    accessToken + '<br>' + result.getContentText());

}
```

Notice another use of the HtmlService to communicate results as a web app.

The consent page. The consent page is required to initiate the OAuth 2.0 process. It will also display the redirect URL (which still needs to be set up in the cloud console):

```js
/**
 * tailor your consent screen with an html template
 * @param {string} consentUrl the url to click to provide user consent
 * @param {string} redirectUrl the url that redirect will happen on
 * @return {string} the html for the consent screen
 */
function constructConsentScreen (consentUrl,redirectUrl) {
  return '<p>Redirect URI to be added to cloud console is ' +
    redirectUrl + '</p><a href = "' + consentUrl +
      '">Click to authenticate to datastore</a> ';
}
```

The web app. The controlling process that pulls all this together is the doGet function of a published web app, which will execute in the browser. The mechanics of how it works is in the EzyOauth2 library, but a simple pattern like this should be used for all apps of this nature:

```js
/**
 * this is your web app
 * @param {object} web app param object
 * return {HtmlOutput}
 */
function doGet (e) {
  return doGetPattern(e, constructConsentScreen, doSomething, 'googleDatastore');
}
```

where:

constructConsentScreen
   Gets permission to start the OAuth 2.0 process. It executes this only if it does not already have an existing or refreshable access token. Because refresh token information is stored in the Properties service automatically, this will be shown only the first time the web app is run.

doSomething
   Is the main application that will receive the access token and do the work of the app.

'googleDataStore'
   Is the key that was used in the Properties store against which to store these project credentials.

The redirect URL. All that remains now is to set up the redirect URL (displayed on the consent screen) in the Developers Console:

1. Go through the publishing process as covered in previous chapters.

---

2. The `doGet` function will execute. Notice that there is not yet an access token available. The consent screen appears.
3. It will also (helpfully) show the redirect URL to enter into the Developers Console (see Figure 15-15). Do this (and save it) before consenting to authentication (see Figure 15-16).

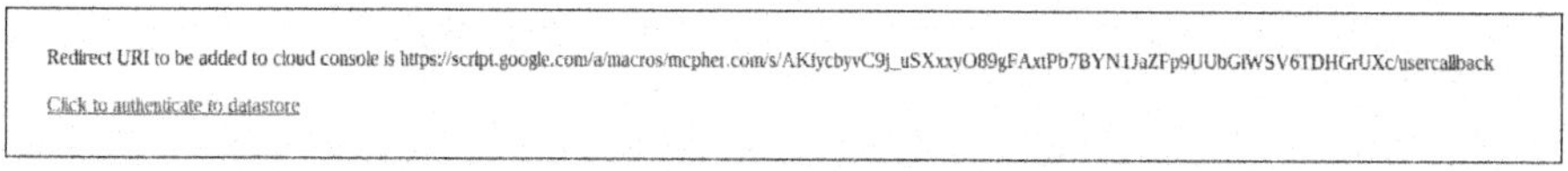

Redirect URI to be added to cloud console is https://script.google.com/a/macros/mcpher.com/s/AKfycbyvC9j_uSXxxyO89gFAxtPb7BYN1JaZFp9UUbGiWSV6TDHGrUXc/usercallback
Click to authenticate to datastore

Figure 15-15. The redirect URL to enter into the Developers Console

Client ID for Web application
Client ID
104684372 6255-0j8qlite6bsl7g0efdvip82ai5cknaa3.apps.googleusercontent.com
Client secret
CH1I3wW6lZofc0jX2OR6iBvi
Creation date
Sep 4, 2015, 11:59:01 AM
Name
datastore example
Authorized JavaScript origins
Enter JavaScript origins here or redirect URIs below (or both)
Cannot contain a wildcard (http://*.example.com) or a path (http://example.com/subdir).
https://script.google.com
http://www.example.com
Authorized redirect URIs
Must have a protocol. Cannot contain URL fragments or relative paths. Cannot be a public IP address.
https://script.google.com/a/macros/mcpher.com/s/AKfycbyvC9j_uSXxxyO89gFAxtPb7BYN1JaZFp9UUbGiWSV6TDHGrUXc/usercallback
http://www.example.com/oauth2callback
Save
Cancel

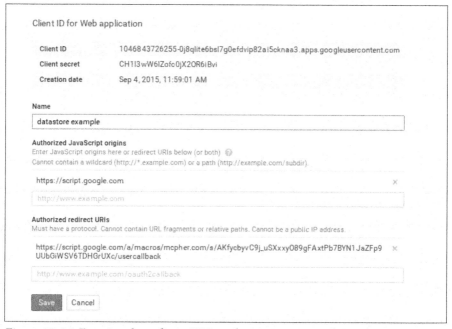

Figure 15-16. Entering the redirect URL and consenting to authentication

4. The application will now get a token via a conversation with the redirect URL, and then execute the `doSomething` function. Figure 15-17 shows a snippet of the result of retrieving some data from the datastore.

it worked ya29.5AF2E_lpaMEyRBiHxOpONZDTZgwVKBueGhckll5H8uV0qQAZ3OOYHEw-E9ZyXfK2x-JH
{ "batch": { "entityResultType": "FULL", "entityResults": [{ "entity": { "key": { "partitionId": { "datasetId": "s~xliberati
"networks.facebook.usage": { "stringValue": "seldom" }, "strain": { "stringValue": "strain99" }, "stuff.age": { "integerV

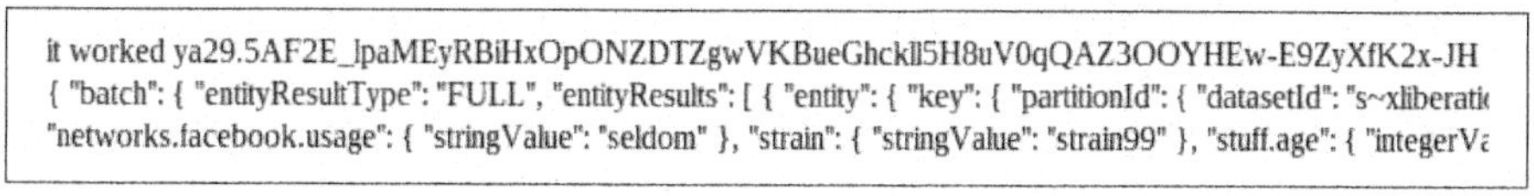

Figure 15-17. Partial result of retrieving data from the datastore

Accessing Other Oauth 2.0 Services

Many other services use OAuth 2.0 to manage resource access. The same library can be used to access them. The following example uses EzyOauth2 to access Microsoft OneDrive.

OneDrive Authentication

The Microsoft Applications Dashboard fulfills the same kind of role as the Google Developers Console, and all the same procedures associated with creating an application need to be followed.

Once you have all the information required, you need a one-off Properties service setup, just as with the Google API example, to store the credentials:

```js
setAuthenticationPackage_ ({
    clientId : "0xxxx3",
    clientSecret : "N-0xxxxEM",
    scopes : ["wl.signin","wl.basic","wl.offline_access","wl.skydrive_update"],
    service: 'live',
    packageName: 'onedrive'
});
```

Note the service name in this package is 'live'. For the Google API, it is 'google'. This directs the library to use the Microsoft Live OAuth 2.0 infrastructure rather than the Google one.

The EzyOauth2 library keeps a list of notable authentication endpoints and processes for a number of different providers (including Microsoft and Google), so there is no need for you to provide them.

Get consent

The process for getting consent is the same as for the datastore example but with the descriptions changed (see Figure 15-18):

```js
function constructConsentScreen (consentUrl,redirectUrl) {
    return '<p>Redirect URI to be added to microsoft application dashboard is ' +
        redirectUrl + '</p><a href = "' + consentUrl +
        '">Click to authenticate to Microsoft Live</a> ';
}
```

Redirect URI to be added to microsoft application dashboard is https://script.google.com/a/macros/mcpher.com/s/AKfy

Click to authenticate to Microsoft Live

Figure 15-18. Getting the redirect URL for Microsoft OneDrive

Access OneDrive

The code for the main app would be in the doSomething function. This example simply gets the OneDrive quota and space used (see Figure 15-19):

```js
function doSomething (accessToken) {

    var options = {
      method: "GET",
      headers: {
        authorization: "Bearer " + accessToken
      }
    };

    var result = UrlFetchApp.fetch(
        "https://apis.live.net/v5.0/me/skydrive/quota", options);
    return HtmlService.createHtmlOutput (' it worked ' + accessToken +
    '<br>' + result.getContentText());

}
```

> it worked
> EwBoAq1DBAAUGCCXc8wU/zFu9QnLdZXy+YnElFkAAdgDWYZKR
> { "quota": 1115617755136, "available": 1115613715013}

Figure 15-19. Retrieving the quota and space available

Other OAuth 2.0 Services

EzyOauth2 is capable of authenticating to many other services, such as SoundCloud, Podio, GitHub, Reddit, Shoeboxd, and others. Adding extra services is fairly trivial, and all apps follow exactly the same pattern of storing credentials, publishing, getting consent, receiving authorization, and executing.

OAuth 2.0 with VBA

Connecting to Apps Script web apps or Google APIs from VBA generally requires some kind of OAuth 2.0 authentication, unless the web app or API is public. Chapter 11 included an example of delegating work from VBA to an Apps Script web app. For the sake of the example, it was a public web app, but more realistically it would have been published with limited accessibility. This section will show how to access this web app from VBA using an open source VBA library that enables OAuth 2.0.

 As with many of the VBA libraries provided, a few changes to the Windows-specific HTTP access methods will be needed for this library to support Office for Mac.

Developers Console

Unlike with a web-based app, there is no way to call back a particular URL during the OAuth 2.0 process initiated by VBA. The cloud console provides for a special flow for what it terms "Other" application types (see Figure 15-20).

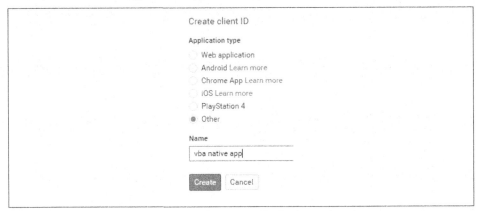

Figure 15-20. Creating a client ID for our VBA ("Other") application

The generated credentials have no origins or redirect URL, as you can see in Figure 15-21.

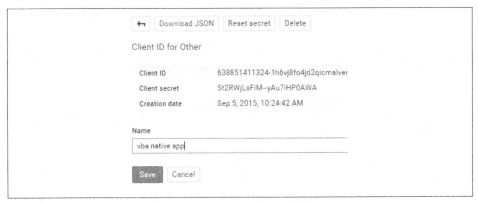

Figure 15-21. The VBA app has no origins or redirect URL

getGoogled

The custom cOauth2 class in VBA is fully featured to be able to access multiple OAuth 2.0 infrastructure endpoints, just like Apps Script EzyOauth2, but this example will use the default Google endpoints, because we will be accessing an Apps Script ContentService web app.

Getting started is straightforward once you have the necessary credentials and applications set up in the cloud console.

The getGoogled function initializes an entry for "drive" and passes the app credentials to be stored in the registry, just as the Apps Script library stored them in the Properties service:

```VB
With getGoogled("drive", , _
    "638851411324-1h6vj8fxxxxxadu.apps.googleusercontent.com", _
    "St2RWjLsxxxx0AWA")
End With
```

This flow uses a strange method for communicating with VBA using the browser bar URL. In any case, this process is handled behind the scenes by the cOauth2 class, which will also present the usual Google authorization dialog (and sign-in if required), as shown in Figure 15-22.

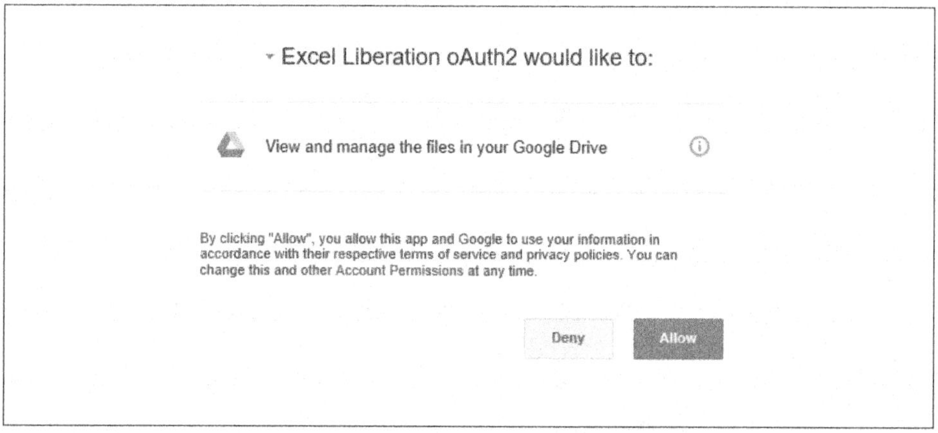

Figure 15-22. Google authorization dialog

Just as with Apps Script, the credentials are not needed and should not be present in the code after a one-off initialization. Future token refreshes will be handled automatically, and there will be no further need for any authorization dialogs from this user on this machine.

cOauth2 is aware of the scopes that "drive" represents and automatically includes them in the OAuth 2.0 dialog. In the future, tokens can be obtained as simply as this:

```VB
With getGoogled("drive")
    Debug.Print .authHeader
End With
```

The generated token is now ready to be used for HTTP access to the web app resource:

```
Bearer ya29.5QFrHw8wQsPWiHzy-76DZj98H6VRF8qB7674h7WA3IFEpJztBrJVU4zrkGFnioo1Eejf
```

Content Service with OAuth2

Now that there is a method for VBA to authenticate to a nonpublic script, a small change is all that is needed to instrument `ContentService` fetch with an access token.

Here is the updated `gasCheck` function with one extra line just before `hob.send`, where we use `getGoogled` to get an access token to use for protected script access:

```vb
' /**
'  * use gas to check if there's any flight content
'  * @param {Mailitem} message the message
'  * @return {collection} the filtered messages
'  */
Private Function gasCheck(message As Outlook.mailItem) As KVPairs
    Dim hob As Object, combinedContent As String, root As Object, _
        doc As Object, kv As KVPairs, node As Object
    Set doc = CreateObject("MSXML2.DOMDocument")
    Set kv = New KVPairs

    ' avoid two calls by combining subject and body
    combinedContent = message.Subject & " " & message.Body
    ' set up a fetch
    Set hob = CreateObject("Msxml2.ServerXMLHTTP.6.0")

    'construct a query
    hob.Open "GET", Settings.getValue("GAS.URL") & _
        "?format=xml&flight=" & Utils_.encodeURI(combinedContent), False

    ' add the access token
    hob.SetRequestHeader "Authorization", getGoogled("drive").authHeader
    hob.send

    ' convert to xml element
    doc.LoadXML hob.ResponseText
    Set root = doc.SelectSingleNode("root")

    ' replace this with some appropriate exception habdling
    Debug.Assert Not root Is Nothing

    ' load to a key/value pair structure
    For Each node In root.ChildNodes
        kv.add node.nodeName, node.Text
    Next node

    ' return result
    Set gasCheck = kv
End Function
```

The app is republished with a private setting, as shown in Figure 15-23.

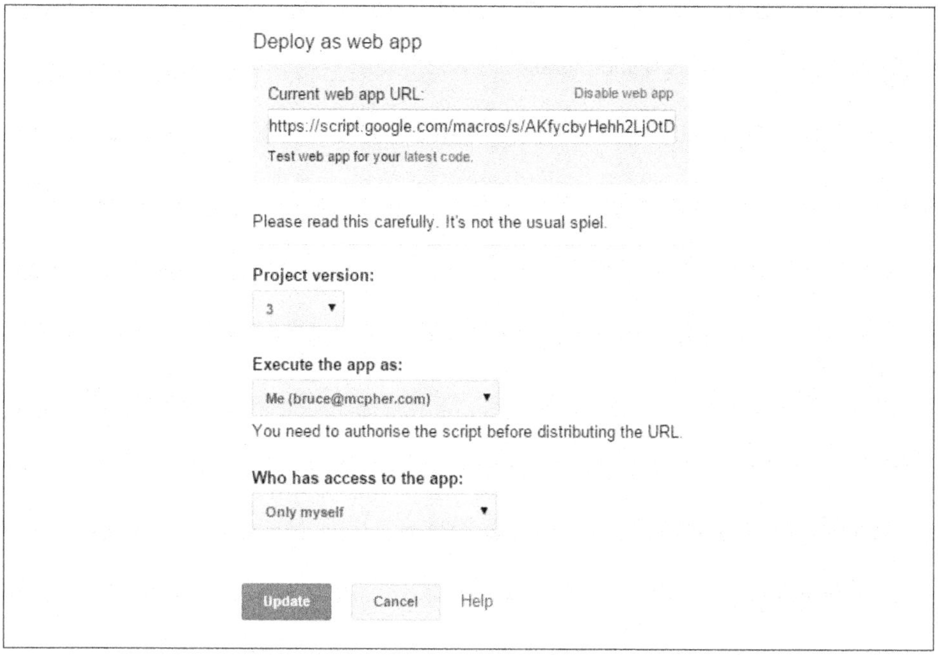

Figure 15-23. The republished app is now private

And now it can be accessed from VBA.

Other Kinds of Authentication

There are other kinds of authentication flows in use. Some (e.g., Firebase) are based on JSON Web Tokens (as are Google Service Accounts), and others (e.g., some Twitter services) use OAuth 1.0. There are still others that use basic authentication and digest authentication.

Basic Authentication

It happens less and less often nowadays, but when a website prompts for a username and password using the style of browser-generated dialog shown in Figure 15-24, it is generally executing a form of basic authentication.

You can automate basic authentication from both VBA and Apps Script by including a header that contains an encoded version of the username and password.

Here's how this looks in VBA:

```VB
oHttp.SetRequestHeader "Authorization", "Basic " + _
    Base64Encode(authUser + ":" + authPass)
```

And in Apps Script:

```
var result = UrlFetchApp.fetch (url, {
    headers:{
        authorization: Utilities.base64Encode(authUser + ":" + authPass)
    }
});
```

User Name:	
Password:	

Log In   Cancel

Figure 15-24. Basic authentication

JWT (JSON Web Tokens)

Google service accounts use JWT as the means by which to identify themselves, as do many other platforms.

What Is a JWT?

A JSON Web Token is a JSON object containing claims one party is making to another, signed by a shared secret known by both parties. It provides reassurances for the questions shown in Figure 15-25.

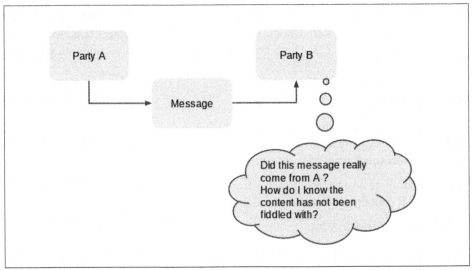

Figure 15-25. Questions that JWT addresses

A message consists of a header describing the signing encryption method, and claims (the items party A wishes to assert to party B). As shown in Figure 15-26, Parties A and B share a secret. Party A signs (encrypts using a key) with the shared secret as the key, and appends the signature to the message. Party B receives the message and applies the same secret to it. If the result is the same as the signed message sent by A, then B knows the message content is as A intended, and that it was indeed sent by A.

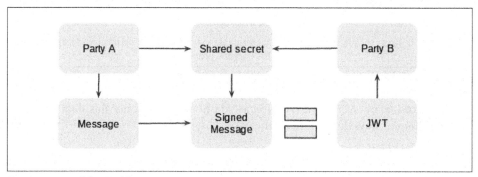

Figure 15-26. The JWT process

Firebase Authentication

Firebase is a real-time JSON database recently acquired by Google. It has a number of options for authentication, but this example will use a JWT to be consumed by Firebase.

A Firebase app has a secret key that is known by the developer and is stored by Firebase against the app. Firebase authenticates requests by comparing the signed JWT sent as part of the request against the result of resigning the request with the known shared key. If they match, Firebase knows that the request is coming from a reliable source and has not been tampered with.

JWT Format

Here's a function that will generate a JWT for Firebase. The final token has this structure:

```
message.base64(signedmessage)
```

where the message is:

```
base64(header).base64(claims)
```

Table 15-1 outlines the message components.

Table 15-1. Message components

Component	Property	Purpose
header	alg:"HS256"	The encryption method (Google service accounts use RS256)
	typ:"JWT"	Identifies this as a JWT
claims	iat:Math.floor(new Date().getTime()/1000)	The time now in seconds
	v:0	The version number
	d:{uid:"bruce"}	Any data to be passed to the security and rules processing on Firebase. This example is passing a user ID.

Firebase allows the d property in the claim to contain data that is accessible in the "Security and rules" section of the Firebase dashboard. Typically this data would be used in different ways depending on the passed user ID.

A JWT looks like this:

```
eyJhbGciOiJIUzI1NiIsInR5cCI6IkpXVCJ9.
eyJkIjp7InVpZCI6ImJydWNlIn0sImlhdCI6MTQ0MTY0NDgyNiwidiI6MH0.
xiqtUhmupdwzvhkmmkK_lnx2joenPLxG738qlZqiS9M
```

FirebaseAuth Namespace

The FirebaseAuth namespace can be used to create a JWT, and is used like this:

```
token_ = FirebaseAuth.generateJWT (data, secret);
```

The complete code is as follows:

```
var FirebaseAuth = (function (firebaseAuth) {

  /**
   * generate a jwt for firebase using default settings
   * @param {object} data the data package
   * @param {string} secret the jwt secret
   */
  firebaseAuth.generateJWT = function(data, secret) {

    var header = getHeader_ ();
    var claims = getClaims_ (data);
    var jwt = header + "." + claims;

    // now sign it
    var signature = Utilities.computeHmacSha256Signature (jwt, secret);
    var signed = unPad_ (Utilities.base64EncodeWebSafe(signature));

    // and that's the jwt
    return jwt + "." + signed;
  };
```

```
/**
 * generate a jwt header
 * return {string} a jwt header b64
 */
function getHeader_ () {

  return unPad_(Utilities.base64EncodeWebSafe(JSON.stringify( {
    "alg": "HS256",
    "typ": "JWT"
  })));
}

/**
 * generate a jwt claim for firebase
 * return {string} a jwt claims payload b64
 */
function getClaims_  (data) {

  return unPad_ (Utilities.base64EncodeWebSafe( JSON.stringify( {
    "d" : data || {},
    "iat": Math.floor(new Date().getTime()/1000),
    "v": 0
  })));
}

/**
 * remove padding from base 64
 * @param {string} b64 the encoded string
 * @return {string} padding removed
 */
function unPad_ (b64) {
  return b64 ?  b64.split ("=")[0] : b64;
}

return firebaseAuth;
})(FirebaseAuth || {});
```

This namespace will be used in Chapter 16 to access Firebase data.

Standardized OAuth 2.0 Process

As it becomes harder to protect privacy and data online, authentication schemes have become more and more complex to implement and use. OAuth 2.0 is certainly not easy if you're starting from scratch (neither is JWT), but with these kinds of libraries available in multiple platforms and languages, it becomes less of a science project and more of a simple process of following a series of steps.

Most providers are moving, or have already moved, to OAuth 2.0, and although their implementations differ in some of the details, the process is the same:

1. Register an app and get some credentials and a client ID using the provider's dashboard or console.

2. Declare where this app should run from.

3. Discover how to specify the resource scope requirement of the app.

4. Anticipate a multistep conversation of request, authentication, and access, potentially involving a user dialog.

5. Expect to deal with token refresh if the provider supports and allows it.

6. Find a way of protecting your app credentials.

Even though I've implemented a few of these in various platforms now, I'm still pleased (and a little amazed) when it all actually works.

CHAPTER 16

External APIs and Integration

Accessing external APIs, whether Google APIs or some other resource, is generally very easy. The Google infrastructure is super-fast, and accessing Internet services works at Google speed because Apps Script runs on that infrastructure. In previous examples, this kind of external data connectivity has been demonstrated a few times, but it's such a strong Apps Script capability that it's worth dedicating a few pages to it.

This chapter will demonstrate how to use the UrlFetchApp service to interact with:

A REST service
Get data and populate a spreadsheet with the results.

A NoSQL database
Use Firebase from Apps Script.

The UrlFetchApp service is somewhat equivalent to the VBA serverXMLHTTP object, but has a much simpler approach to headers and options.

REST API

This example will interact with the FAA (Federal Aviation Authority) API, to see if there are any current delays at selected US airports. Given an airport (IATA) code, this API returns data like this:

```
{
  delay: "false",
  IATA: "EWR",
  state: "New Jersey",
  name: "Newark International",
  weather:
  {
    visibility: 10,
```

```
    weather: "A Few Clouds",
    meta:
    {
      credit: "NOAA's National Weather Service",
      updated: "5:51 AM Local",
      url: "http://weather.gov/"
    },
    temp: "62.0 F (16.7 C)",
    wind: "Northeast at 4.6mph"
  },
  ICAO: "Kewr",
  city: "Newark",
  status:
  {
    reason: "No known delays for this airport.",
    closureBegin: "",
    endTime: "",
    minDelay: "",
    avgDelay: "",
    maxDelay: "",
    closureEnd: "",
    trend: "",
    type: ""
  }
}
```

In this sample, we'll start with a spreadsheet containing a list of airport codes and populate it with selected data returned from this API (see Figure 16-1).

IATA	Name	City	State	Weather	Temp	Delay	Reason	Max delay
EWR	Newark International	Newark	New Jersey	A Few Clouds	67.0 F (19.4 C)	FALSE	No known delays for this airport.	
IAH	George Bush Intercontinental/Houston	Houston	Texas	Patches Fog	75.0 F (23.9 C)	FALSE	No known delays for this airport.	
SEA	Seattle-Tacoma International	Seattle	Washington	Overcast	54.0 F (12.2 C)	FALSE	No known delays for this airport.	
ORD	Chicago OHare International	Chicago	Illinois	Partly Cloudy	72.0 F (22.2 C)	FALSE	No known delays for this airport.	
IAD	Washington Dulles International	Washington	District of Colum	Mostly Cloudy	66.0 F (18.9 C)	FALSE	No known delays for this airport.	
SAN	San Diego-Lindbergh Field	San Diego	California	A Few Clouds	68.0 F (20.0 C)	FALSE	No known delays for this airport.	
SFO	San Francisco International	San Francisco	California	Fair	56.0 F (13.3 C)	FALSE	No known delays for this airport.	
LAX	Los Angeles International	Los Angeles	California	Fair	66.0 F (18.9 C)	FALSE	No known delays for this airport.	
MIA	Miami International	Miami	Florida	Partly Cloudy	78.0 F (25.6 C)	FALSE	No known delays for this airport.	
CLE	Cleveland Hopkins International	Cleveland	Ohio	A Few Clouds	70.0 F (21.1 C)	FALSE	No known delays for this airport.	
PHX	Phoenix Sky Harbor International	Phoenix	Arizona	Mostly Cloudy	84.0 F (28.9 C)	FALSE	No known delays for this airport.	
JFK	John F Kennedy International	New York	New York	A Few Clouds	68.0 F (20.0 C)	FALSE	No known delays for this airport.	

Figure 16-1. Airport data source

Code

The IATA code from each row in the input sheet is used as a parameter to a request to the FAA API, and the result is mapped to existing columns in the sheet. A successful fetch will return a response code of 200 for this API. Anything else is an error, the most likely of which is a 404 if an invalid IATA code is given.

The use of the `muteHttpExceptions` option within `UrlFetchApp` prevents the fetch from throwing an error and leaves it to the code to handle.

Had this the FAA API response data object been single-level, it would have been a little easier to match up the incoming data to the output heading columns automatically, but instead the source and destination properties are explicitly defined.

Finally, the new data rows are written out, replacing the current values:

```js
function airportDelaysExample () {

    // the rest api endpoint
    var URL = 'http://services.faa.gov/airport/status/',
      APPEND= '?format=json';

    // get all the data, as usual using a sheetOb
    // but it's container bound so take the defaults
    var sob = new SheetOb().open();

    // pass through each row and do a query for each airport code
    var newData = sob.getData().map(function(d) {

      var row = {
        iata:d.iata
      };

      // overcome rate limiting
      var result = Utils.rateLimitExpBackoff ( function () {
        return UrlFetchApp.fetch(URL + d.iata.toUpperCase() + APPEND, {
          muteHttpExceptions:true
        });
      });

      // fill in the required fields
      if (result.getResponseCode() === 200 ) {
        var data = JSON.parse(result.getContentText());

        // simple data
        ['name','city','state','delay'].forEach(function(e) {
          row[e] = data[e];
        });

        // deeper levels
        row.weather = data.weather.weather;
        row.temp = data.weather.temp;
        row.reason = data.status.reason;
        row['max delay'] = data.status.maxDelay;
      }
      else {
        // report error
        row.name = 'error:' + result.getResponseCode();
      }
      return row;

    });
```

```
// write out the new data
sob.dump(newData);

}
```

Reuse

As usual, the example reuses functions created in previous examples:

SheetOb

Handles converting sheet data into JSON objects. It needs some new functionality, including the following:

- Ability to use the default (rather than a given) workbook and sheet.
- Ability to write out object data in the same order as the original, and clear any data left over in the sheet.

Utils

Includes various utilities, such as exponential backoff

open

Now supports defaults for the ID or sheetName to use the current workbook or sheet:

```js
self.open = function ( id, sheetName ) {
    var ss = id ?
      SpreadsheetApp.openById(id) : SpreadsheetApp.getActiveSpreadsheet();
    sheet_ = sheetName ?
      ss.getSheetByName(sheetName) : ss.getActiveSheet();
    return self;
};
```

dump

Converts a JSON object and writes it out to the sheet in the order of the current headings, omitting any properties not presently shown in the sheet:

```js
/**
 * write a new data object, where the headers match
 * @param {object} data
 * @return {SheetOb} self
 */
self.dump = function (data) {

    // map the new values
    var values = data.map(function(d) {

        return Object.keys(headerOb_).reduce(function(p,c) {
          p[headerOb_[c]] = d[c];
          return p;
```

```
    },new Array(Object.keys(headerOb_).length));
  });

  // clear the data from the sheet if necessary
  var dr = sheet_.getDataRange();
  if (dr.getNumRows() > values.length +1) {
    sheet_.getRange (values.length+1 , 1 ,
      dr.getNumRows() - values.length -1,
        dr.getNumColumns()).clearContents();
  }

  // write out the new values
  if(values.length) {
    sheet_.getRange (2,1, values.length,
      Object.keys(headerOb_).length).setValues(values);
  }

  // refresh this object
  self.refresh();

  return self;
};
```

Databases

Unlike VBA, which has Access, Apps Script has no native database. Some time after the initial release of Apps Script, ScriptDb was introduced, and provided a NoSQL schemaless datastore for each script. This was both useful and popular, but it was deprecated last year (to much outcry).

Although this leaves Apps Script without a native database, it does have a JDBC service that enables access to external MySQL, Microsoft SQL, Google SQL, and Oracle databases. However, the UrlFetchApp service enables access to any database that has a REST JSON API. This includes NoSQL-type databases such as MongoLab, Couch-Base, Parse, and Orchestrate; datastores such as Cloud DataStore and BigTable; and grids such as Fusion Tables.

One approach is to *abstract* the database (create a common interface) and provide a series of drivers that convert to and deal with the chosen database conversation. You can find an example of this—an open source Apps Script database abstraction library that supports about a dozen different backend databases—on my website (*http://www.mcpher.com*).

In fact, there is a wealth of database choices, but for the purposes of this example, I'll use Firebase—a real-time, NoSQL database recently acquired by Google.

Firebase

Firebase is a cloud database that stores data as JSON and synchronizes in real time to subscribed devices. It's a fairly unique approach, super-fast, and simple to use.

This example will repeat the exercise in the Fusion Tables example in Chapter 13—namely, populating Firebase with the airline carrier code to name lookup from a spreadsheet. It will use the `FirebaseAuth` namespace, covered in Chapter 15, for authentication.

Main Code

This simple structure reads the carrier codes sheet and copies it to a Firebase table:

```js
// Copy data from spreadsheet to fusion table
function sheetCopy() {

  // get the sheet
  var sob = new SheetOb().open(Settings.LOOKUP.ID, Settings.LOOKUP.NAME);

  // get the firebase table
  var firebase = new Firebase()
    .setRoot(Settings.FIREBASE.ROOT)
    .setToken(Settings.FIREBASE.AUTH, Settings.FIREBASE.SECRET);

  // delete all data in the table
  firebase.remove();

  // insert the data from the sheet
  sob.getData().forEach(function(d) {
    var result = firebase.put(d,'/'+d[Settings.HEADINGS.CODE]);
    if (!result.ok) throw result.response.getContentText();
  });

  // do a query to see what we have
  Logger.log(JSON.stringify(firebase.get().data));
}
```

Permissions

Permissions are controlled in the Firebase dashboard. For this app, I've set them for public (unauthenticated) reading but for writing only by me (Figure 16-2).

My user ID is encoded in the token used for authentication:

```js
.setToken(Settings.FIREBASE.AUTH, Settings.FIREBASE.SECRET);
```

where:

```
settings.FIREBASE = {
  SECRET:'EIk6x9iIYxxxxxxxxxxxx8oSnR78gh64cR3nOd',
```

```
      ROOT:'https://fiery-inferno-4685.firebaseio.com/carriers',
      AUTH:{uid:"bruce"}
    };
```

This ensures that only authenticated people with this UID can write, whereas anyone can read.

Settings

Settings here are very similar to the Fusion Tables example, except with a few Firebase-specific items. In this case, a Firebase app and database have been set up in the Firebase dashboard.

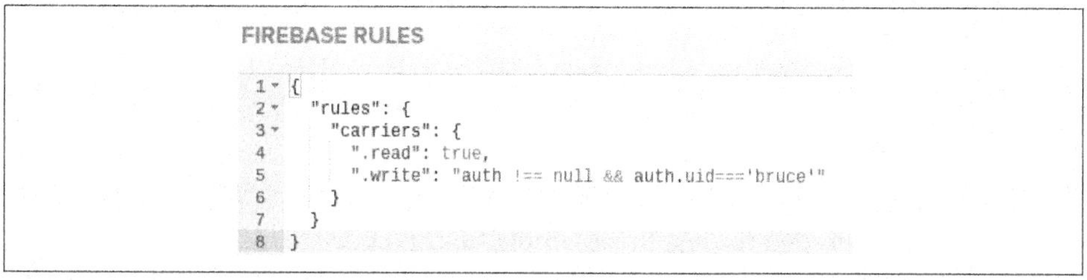

```
FIREBASE RULES

1 ▾ {
2 ▾    "rules": {
3 ▾      "carriers": {
4           ".read": true,
5           ".write": "auth !== null && auth.uid==='bruce'"
6         }
7       }
8 }
```

Figure 16-2. Setting permissions for public read access but write access only for me

As usual, they need a one-off setup to create the Properties service entry, after which the oneOffSettings function can be deleted:

```js
var SETTINGS_KEY = "firebasexample";

function setOneTimeProperties () {
  setProperties(oneTimeSettings);
}

function setProperties (props) {
  PropertiesService.getUserProperties().setProperty(SETTINGS_KEY,
      JSON.stringify(props));
}

var oneTimeSettings = (function(settings) {
  'use strict';

  settings.KEY = SETTINGS_KEY;

  settings.LOOKUP = {
    ID: '1f4zuZZv2NiLuYSGB5j4ENFc6wEWOmaEdCoHNuv-gHXo',
    NAME: 'lookup'
  };

  settings.HEADINGS = {
    CODE:'carrier',
    NAME:'name'
```

```
  };

  settings.FIREBASE = {
    SECRET:'EIk6x9iIY6xxxxxxxxxx8gh64cR3nOd',
    ROOT:'https://fiery-inferno-4685.firebaseio.com/carriers',
    AUTH:{uid:"bruce"}
  };

  // update the sheet
  return settings;

})(oneTimeSettings || {});

// get them from prop service, or use the one-time setting function.
var Settings = JSON.parse(
  PropertiesService.getUserProperties().getProperty(SETTINGS_KEY)) ;
```

Firebase Class

The Firebase class is a helper class for the Firebase Rest API. I've implemented more
methods than are needed for just this example, so this code should be fairly complete
for future use:

```
/**
 * firebase API
 * @constructor
 */
var Firebase = function () {

  var self = this, token_, root_;

  /**
   * set a token
   * @param {object} data the auth data
   * @param {string} secret the secret
   * @return {Firebase} self
   */
  self.setToken = function (data, secret) {
    token_ = FirebaseAuth.generateJWT (data, secret);
    return self;
  };

  /**
   * set a database
   * @param {string} root the database url
   * @return {Firebase} self
   */
  self.setRoot = function (root) {
    root_ = root;
    return self;
  };
```

```
/**
 * do a put (replaces data)
 * @param {string} putObject an object to put
 * @param {string} [childPath=''] a child path
 * @return
 */
self.put = function (putObject,childPath) {
  return payload_ ("PUT", putObject, childPath);
};

/**
 * do a delete
 * @param {string} [childPath=''] a child path
 * @return
 */
self.remove = function (childPath) {
  return fetch_ ( getPath_ (childPath), {method:"DELETE"});
};

/**
 * do a get
 * @param {string} [childPath=''] a child path
 * @return
 */
self.get = function (childPath) {
  return fetch_ ( getPath_ (childPath) );
};

/**
 * do a post (adds to data and generates a unique key)
 * @param {string} putObject an object to put
 * @param {string} [childPath=''] a child path
 * @return
 */
self.post = function (putObject,childPath) {
  return payload_ ("POST", putObject, childPath)
};

/**
 * do a patch (partially replaces an item)
 * @param {string} putObject an object to put
 * @param {string} [childPath=''] a child path
 * @return
 */
self.patch = function (putObject,childPath) {
  return payload_ ("PATCH", putObject, childPath);
};

/**
 * get the path given a child path
 * @param {string} [childPath=''] the childpath
 * @return {string} the path
```

```
    */
    function getPath_ (childPath) {
      return root_ + ( childPath || '' ) + '.json';
    }

    /**
     * do any payload methods
     * @param {string} putObject an object to put
     * @param {string} [childPath=''] a child path
     * @return
     */
    function payload_ (method, putObject,childPath) {

        return fetch_ ( getPath_ (childPath), {
          method:method,
          payload:JSON.stringify(putObject)
        });

    }

    /**
     * do a fetch
     * @param {string} url the url
     * @param {object} [options={method:'GET'}]
     * @return
     */
    function fetch_ (url, options) {

      // defaults
      options = options || {method:'GET'};
      if (!options.hasOwnProperty("muteHttpException")) {
        options.muteHttpExceptions = true;
      }

      // do the fetch
      var result = Utils.rateLimitExpBackoff (function() {
        return UrlFetchApp.fetch (url + "?auth=" + token_, options);
      });

      return {
        ok: result.getResponseCode() === 200,
        data: result.getResponseCode() === 200 ?
          JSON.parse(result.getContentText()) : null,
        response:result
      }
    };
    return self;
  };
```

Reuse

SheetOb and Utils can be copied as is from the Fusion Tables example (Chapter 13), and the FirebaseAuth namespace from the authentication examples (Chapter 15).

The final script structure looks like Figure 16-3.

Figure 16-3. Final Firebase script structure

Result

Here's a snippet from the firebase.get result:

```
{
    "6E": {
        "carrier": "6E",
        "date added": "2015-07-27T14:16:54.350Z",
        "name": "Indigo"
    },
    "7F": {
        "carrier": "7F",
        "date added": "2015-07-27T14:16:54.350Z",
        "name": "FirstAir"
    },
    "8P": {
        "carrier": "8P",
        "date added": "7/26/15 16:56",
        "name": "Pacific Coast Airlines"
    },
```

and from the Firebase dashboard (Figure 16-4).

Databases and Apps Script

The lack of a built-in database for Apps Script turns out to be not such a big deal after all. The ability to use UrlFetchApp to create powerful wrappers for JSON REST APIs means that all the modern cloud-based NoSQL JSON databases are easily consumable by Apps Script.

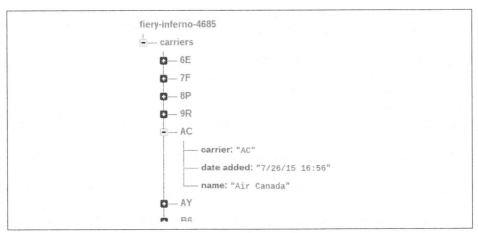

Figure 16-4. A snippet of the Firebase script from the Firebase dashboard

For those that prefer the traditional SQL approach, the JDBC service continues to provide access, and may be a better route for those looking for an easier migration from Access or SQL server. The authentication schemes for external services can become fairly complex, but using clean, proven, repeatable patterns makes this a surmountable hurdle.

CHAPTER 17

Execution API

The Execution API is a brand-new API that enables you to run Apps Script functions from other processes via JSON REST requests, or by using a library specific to your development language. It is unusual among Apps Script–related APIs in that it is not intended to be run from Apps Script (although it can be—for example, to enable splitting and parallel execution of workloads), but rather to provide access to Apps Script capabilities from other platforms.

I'm very impressed by the potential of the Execution API, and have eagerly anticipated its release. There are libraries, quickstarts, and developer tools available for a number of platforms, as well as the REST API, on which the VBA integration solution introduced in this chapter is based.

The Execution API has some similarity to `google.script.run`, whose function is to enable add-on/ `HtmlService` communication between client and server. This capability will greatly enhance the ability of mobile-based apps and add-ons to access Apps Script functionality.

Although probably not the purpose for which it was envisioned, the Execution API is also a powerful tool to enable incremental migration from Office (or anything else) to Apps, and this chapter will concentrate on the process and code needed.

As with all the code examples, you should adapt and enhance the error handling to match your house requirements if you choose to use any of it in your projects. Note that the provided VBA libraries are primarily focused on Office for Windows, and will not work on Office for Mac without some modification.

Chapter 11 showed a way to achieve this kind of capability using a published web app, but this is a much more complete solution.

What Is Incremental Migration?

The process of migrating assets and workflow from Office to Apps is fairly straight-forward (see Figure 17-1). Google has worked hard in providing Office compatibility within Google Drive for legacy assets, and the suite of applications within Apps is comparable in terms of core functionality.

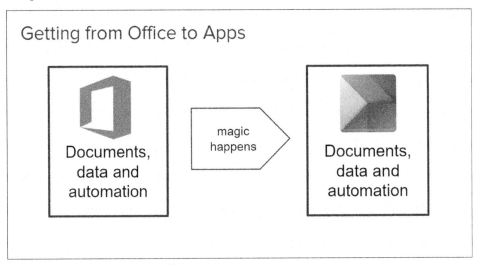

Figure 17-1. Migrating from Office to Apps

The "magic happens" step (Figure 17-2) is not so hard, as long as you don't have VBA automation and documents that are dependent on each other.

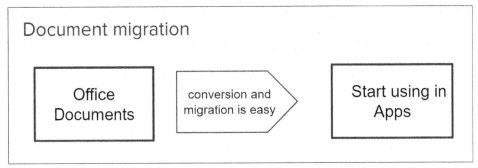

Figure 17-2. Document migration, aka where the "magic happens"

Sets of documents with dependencies that can be isolated can, of course, be migrated (Figure 17-3). It's more complicated as it usually involves coordinating processes and groups of people, but nevertheless, if a cutover period is tolerable and can be sched-uled and the dependencies are manageable, you can do it.

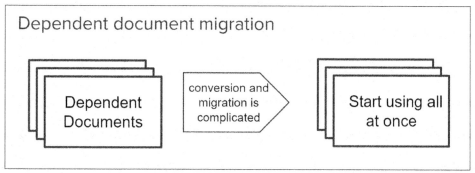

Figure 17-3. Dependent document migration

When there are documents, automated processes, and data that span multiple subject areas and migration timetables that cannot be coordinated, a different process is needed—one in which assets can be partially moved, and automation can be incrementally delegated.

Migration Process

Figure 17-4 shows an example of some VBA automation that accesses or maintains various Excel workbooks. The data and logic modules represent the pieces of VBA code that access the data or contain the business process logic for manipulating the data.

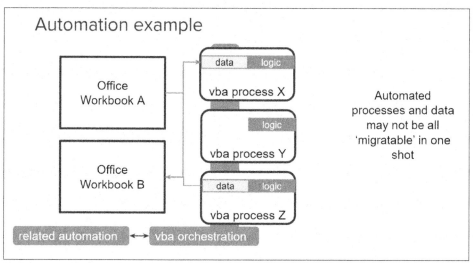

Figure 17-4. VBA automation for Excel workbooks

There may be various reasons that this entire process cannot be scheduled to happen all at once. Some examples could be:

- The workbooks(s) may be shared with a different subject group or process that is not ready to migrate.

- The automation may access databases or other resources that are not scheduled to move to Apps.

- There is no resource available to migrate the processing from VBA to Apps Script, but you need to move the workbooks to Sheets to support a subject group or process that has already moved.

The Execution API

The API shown in Figure 17-5 allows assets and automation to be migrated a chunk at a time.

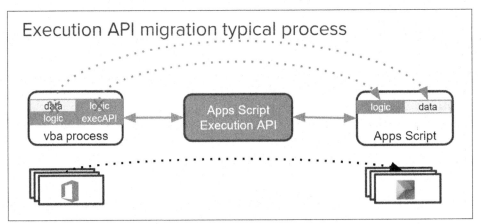

Figure 17-5. The Execution API migration process

For example:

- You can migrate workbooks to Sheets but still access them from VBA by simply substituting the data access code in VBA to delegate data access to Apps Script (see Figure 17-6).

- Some or all of the logic functions can be migrated to be executed by Apps Script, returning the result to VBA for orchestration. In the case of step 1 data from Google Sheet, Workbook A can be read or written in VBA Process X via the Apps Script Execution API. This can be extended in steps 3–5, where the logic used in the VBA processes is migrated and run as Apps Script processes.

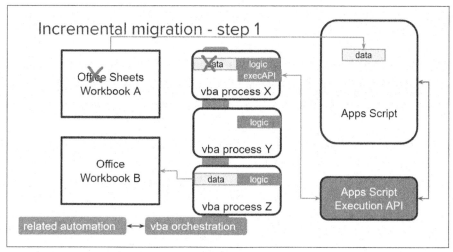

Figure 17-6. Step 1 of incremental migration

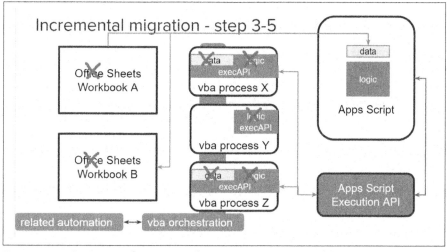

Figure 17-7. Steps 3–5 of incremental migration

Inventory for Execution API

To use the Execution API, you need various assets that are not naturally found in VBA (see Table 17-1). Some of the code for these will be covered in the following pages, and the complete code can be found in the GitHub repository.

The example workbook *executionAPI.xlsm* contains the VBA classes, examples, and modules required, and the Apps Script project exec contains the Apps Script code.

Table 17-1. Assets required for the Execution API

Asset	Purpose
Execution API	The Google API to execute Apps Script functions remotely
Executable examples	Apps Script examples of functions to be executed remotely
VBA examples	VBA examples of delegating to Apps Script
SheetExec (Apps Script)	An Apps Script function that can be used to manipulate sheets remotely
SheetExec (VBA)	The same function implemented to access Excel sheets
cExecuteApi	Execution API access library for VBA
cOauth2	Google OAuth 2.0 authentication library for VBA
cJavaScript	Later in the chapter, I'll show you how to implement JavaScript on Apps Script and run it locally on the PC directly from VBA, after retrieving the code from Apps Script using the Execution API. This is not strictly required for incremental migration, but it's handy for testing VBA that has been migrated to JavaScript in situ

Authentication and Access

As in previous chapters, authentication is handled through the VBA cOAuth2 class and the VBA wrapper function getGoogled. The project containing the scripts to be executed provides the scopes and the credentials, and can be accessed through its Developers Console entry, which is accessible from the Script Editor (see Figure 17-8).

Figure 17-8. Accessing the project from the Script Editor

Selecting the highlighted project will take you to its entry in the Developers Console, as shown in Figure 17-9.

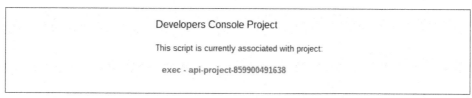

Figure 17-9. The project's entry in the Developers Console

And selecting the APIs option, as shown in Figure 17-10, will allow you to search for the Execution API.

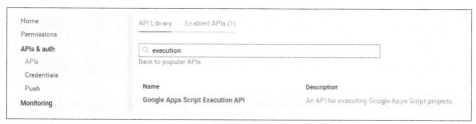

Figure 17-10. Searching for the Execution API

The Execution API needs to be enabled in the console for every project that will be accessed remotely. There is currently no way to programmatically enable the Execution API.

Figure 17-11. Enabling the Execution API in the console

Credentials

New credentials can be added from the Credentials option, as shown in Figure 17-12.

Figure 17-12. Adding new credentials

VBA doesn't use the same process for OAuth 2.0 conversations as a regular web app does, so when generating credentials, you'll need to select the "Other" option (Figure 17-13). If you are planning to create separate credentials for each VBA project, I recommend that you name them appropriately to help with housekeeping if you delete or modify the project at a later time.

Figure 17-13. Selecting the "Other" option when generating credentials

You'll need both the credentials and project key later (Figure 17-14).

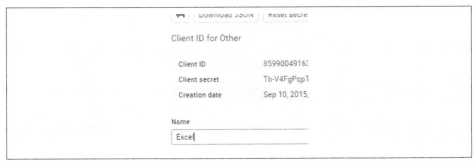

Figure 17-14. Viewing the credentials and project key

Publishing

As with a web app, you need to save and publish a version of the project, but this time using the "Deploy as API executable" publishing option, which is available from within the Script Editor (see Figure 17-15).

Figure 17-15. Deploying the project as an API executable

As shown in Figure 17-16, the API ID matches the project key in the project properties (and is the same key used when you access the API as a library).

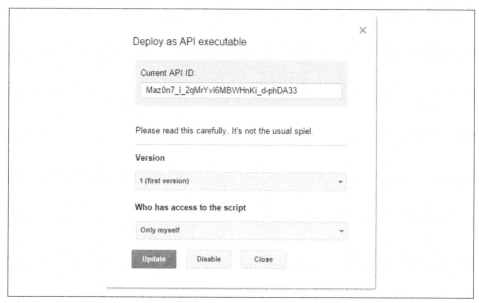

Figure 17-16. The API executable ID

Scopes

The API itself needs no particular scope (but a project needs to have at least one scope for Execution API eligibility). Instead, the authentication scopes are those required by the Apps Script project to be executed. In other words, the services included in the Apps Script project will be automatically added to the project properties Scopes list. For the example in this chapter, the `getGoogled` function uses the SpreadsheetApp service, and the only scope needed is spreadsheets (see Figure 17-17).

Figure 17-17. The only scope required for this project is spreadsheets

Getting Googled

Now you can set up the PC to be able to access this project, using cOAuth2 in VBA. This writes some information to the PC registry that is used behind the scenes for token management.

First, you need to add the project key to the known projects and define which scope(s) it needs:

1. Locate the addGoogleScope function in the cOAuth2 class.
2. Add this line with your project key (there are other standard entries there you can use as a reference):

```VB
Case "project key"
    .add "scope", _
        URLEncode("https://www.googleapis.com/auth/spreadsheets")
```

For first-time use, you need to provide the credentials. Because these credentials and scope are specific to the project being executed, I recommend using the project key to store the credentials against, as in the following example.

This should be run once, then deleted (it's not wise or necessary to keep credentials in code):

```VB
Private Function onceOff()

    getGoogled "...project key", , _
        "client id", _
        "secret"

End Function
```

That's it—now the project can be accessed by VBA.

JSON

VBA does not naturally support JSON, but to be able to use this API (and many others), we need to work with JSON. It's not just a question of encoding to and from

JSON, but also being able to navigate the structure of JavaScript-like objects, which is not straightforward in VBA.

In earlier chapters, I introduced the KVPairs class for VBA, which was a basic way of dealing with key/value pairs in VBA. But for this API, which needs to be able to convert to and from JSON, we'll need to use the cJobject class (which is in the example workbook).

I won't go into the details of this fairly complex and powerful class here, but full information is available at the Desktop Liberation site (*http://www.mcpher.com*) and the code is in the book's GitHub repository. However, to help you follow the examples and get a sense of how it works, here are a few basics.

Create a cJobject by parsing:

```VB
Set args = JSONParse( _
    "[{'id':'1f4zuZZv2NiLuYSGB5j4ENFc6wEWOmaEdCoHNuv-gHXo','sheetName':'lookup'}]")
```

Navigate a cJobect:

```VB
For Each job In args.children          ' navigate the array
    For Each prop In job.children       ' navigate the properties
        Debug.Print prop.key, prop.value ' print the key and the value
    Next prop
Next job
```

Convert a cJobect to JSON:

```VB
Debug.Print args.stringify
```

Access a property value in an array:

```VB
Debug.Print args.child('1.sheetName').value
```

Create a cJobject from scratch:

```VB
With arg.init (Nothing)
    .add "name", "Methuselah"
    .add "age",969
End With
```

SheetExec

We need a generic abstracted way of manipulating sheets from Apps Script, because we can't access the individual SpreadsheetApp methods. In previous chapters, this capability was provided by the SheetOb function, but we need something a little more versatile: SheetExec, which is in the GitHub repository and in the exec Apps Script project. There is also a VBA version in the *executionAPI* workbook. The JSON data produced by each platform is compatible so they can easily integrate.

I won't reproduce the code here, but Table 17-2 lists the methods. These would be used in the Apps Script code as a standard way to get and present data to the cooperating VBA process. I recommend always using `getData` and `setData` for data transfer.

Table 17-2. SheetExec methods

Method	Purpose
`open (id, sheetName)`	Given a sheet ID and sheet name, open a sheet.
`getSheet`	Get the sheet managed by this `SheetExec` instance.
`setLowerCase(lowerCase)`	Convert headings to lowercase when making objects out of sheet values.
`getValues(a1Range , attrib)`	Get the values in a sheet as a two-dimensional array. Optionally, you can specify a range and request an attribute other than values (e.g., `FontColors`).
`getData(a1Range , attrib)`	Get the data in a sheet as a one-dimensional array of key/value pairs using the headings row as properties. Optionally, you can specify a range and request an attribute other than values (e.g., `FontColors`).
`setValues(values , attrib,a1Range)`	Set the values in a sheet from a two-dimensional array. Optionally, you can specify a range and request an attribute other than values (e.g., `FontColors`).
`clearContent (a1Range)`	Clear the contents in a sheet. Optionally, you can specify a range.
`convertToObjects(values)`	Converts a two-dimensional array of values to a one-dimensional array of key/value pairs using the first row as the property names.
`convertToValues(dataOb)`	Converts to a two-dimensional array of values from a one-dimensional array of key/value pairs, inserting a first row of property names as headings.
`convertDatesToIso(dataOb)`	Converts data values from JavaScript dates (which can't be passed over the Execution API) to ISO dates.
`setData (dataOb, a1Range , attrib)`	Convert data to values and write to a sheet using the property keys as the headings. Optionally, you can specify a range and request an attribute other than values (e.g., `FontColors`).

Example Workflow Migration from Office

For this example, we'll use the assets built up in previous chapters—namely, the air carriers lookup sheet we used in the gmailExample introduced in Chapter 8. (The gmailExample considered an imaginary complex workflow process involving email, calendaring, file management, and spreadsheet logging and lookups.) In addition to using that example's carrier lookup sheet as a reference, this workflow will also maintain a sheet counting the number of times particular flight codes have been encountered.

The entire current process is orchestrated from Outlook and written in VBA, but it needs to be migrated to Google Apps Script. It is a 24/7 process, so incremental migration can help avoid disruption and double data maintenance. The workflow will continue to be orchestrated by VBA, but processes will gradually be delegated to Apps Script—the target platform.

The code follows the steps outlined in Table 17-3.

Table 17-3. Incremental migration process

Step	Details	Objective
Convert from workbook to sheet.	Migrate the data in the carrier lookup workbook from Excel to Sheets.	Sheets now becomes the master copy for this workbook.
Access Sheets data from VBA.	Generic Apps Script class (SheetExec) that VBA controls via the Execution API.	VBA stays in place but now accesses data directly from Sheets.
Access workbook data from VBA as JSON data.	An implementation of SheetExec for VBA.	This enables compatible data formats between VBA and Apps Script so they can be easily interchanged.
Migrate some logic from VBA to Apps Script.	Apps Script function to access Sheets data and process logic workload under the control of VBA via the Execution API.	After this step, VBA's role in this part of the workload is limited to providing input data and orchestrating results.
Migrate the rest of the data and logic workload to Apps Script.	Further expansion using these generic functions migrates the complete workload and remaining workbook to Apps.	After this step, VBA's role is simply to integrate with legacy systems remaining behind (in this case, Outlook) until they, too, are migrated.
Test JavaScript on PC.	Apps Script function that can return selected pieces of its own source code under control of VBA via the Execution API. A VBA function can run this locally using the Windows JScript engine.	This allows the testing of Apps Script code prior to any process or data migration.

Moving a Workbook to Sheets

The objective of this step is to replace the data access part of the VBA automation so that it refers to the workbook now converted to a sheet. The VBA cExecutionApi class coordinates communication with the Execution API, and in turn, the Apps Scripts functions to which the work is delegated.

VBA Code to Read a Sheet

This generic function returns all the data in any workbook/sheet, and the pattern is standard for all Execution API access from VBA. The project key is used both as part of the request and to access the OAuth 2.0 entry created by `getGoogled` earlier:

```vb
Private Function testSheetGet() As cJobject
    Dim api As cExecutionApi, execPackage As cJobject, args As cJobject

    '-- set up a run
    ' generic - get all the data on a given sheet from a given workbook
    Set args = JSONParse( _
        "[{'id':'1f4zuZZv2NiLuYSGB5j4ENFc6wEWOmaEdCoHNuv-gHXo', _
        'sheetName':'lookup'}]")


    Set api = New cExecutionApi
    Set execPackage = api _
        .setFunctionName("execGetData") _
        .setProject("MMo4EFhHV6wqa7IdrGew0eiz3TLx7pV4j") _
        .setDevMode(True) _
        .setArgs(args) _
        .execute

    ' see what we got
    Debug.Print JSONStringify(execPackage, True)

    ' clear up
    args.tearDown

    ' maybe useful for something else
    Set testSheetGet = execPackage
End Function
```

Here's a small snippet of what gets returned:

```vb
{
    "name":"execGetData",
    "done":true,
    "response":{
        "@type":"type.googleAPIs.com/google.apps.script.v1.ExecutionResponse",
        "result":[              {
            "carrier":"8P",
            "date added":"7/26/15 16:56",
            "name":"Pacific Coast Airlines"
        },
        {
            "carrier":"9R",
            "date added":"7/26/15 16:56",
            "name":"Satena"
        },
```

from the sheet shown in Figure 17-18.

carrier	name	date added
8P	Pacific Coast Airlines	7/26/2015 16:56
9R	Satena	7/26/2015 16:56
AC	Air Canada	7/26/2015 16:56
AY	Finnair	7/26/2015 16:56
B6	JetBlue Airways	
BS	British International Helicopters	7/26/2015 16:56
CH	Bemidji Airlines	7/26/2015 16:56
EN	Air Dolomiti	7/26/2015 16:56
F9	Frontier Airlines	
HW	North Wright Air	7/26/2015 16:56
LH	Lufthansa Airlines	7/26/2015 16:56
NA	North American Airlines	7/26/2015 16:56

Figure 17-18. Sheet from which results are returned

Apps Script Code to Read a Sheet

This is the function that Apps Script executes to read a sheet when invoked by the Execution API request. Note the function name and options match those passed from VBA:

```js
/**
 * given a sheet id and name, get the data converted to objects
 * @param {object} options args
 *    @param {string} id the sheet id
 *    @param {string} sheetName the sheetName
 * @return {[*]} the data
 */
function execGetData (options) {

  options = options || {};
  var exec = new SheetExec();
  var data = exec.sheetOpen(options.id, options.sheetName).getData();
  // need to convert any dates, as they are not transferrable
  return exec.convertDatesToIso(data);
}
```

VBA Code to Write Data to a Local Workbook

Perhaps the next step could be to write the retrieved data somewhere, or to otherwise process it. Because the SheetExec class is compatible on both VBA and Apps Script, the data transferred between them can be written directly to a workbook without intervention.

This executes the previous snippet (testGetSheet) to request data from the sheet from Apps Script, then uses the VBA SheetExec implementation to dump that data to a local Excel workbook:

```VB
Private Function writeDataToSheet()

    '' use the get data test to pick up current data from SHEETS
    Dim execPackage As cJobject, error As cJobject, sheetExec As cSheetExec

    ' do the reading test to get some data from sheets
    Set execPackage = testSheetGet

    ' make sure it worked
    If (isSomething(execPackage.childExists("error"))) Then
        '' test for error
        Debug.Print JSONStringify(execPackage, True)
        Debug.Assert False
    Else
        '' it was good
        '' copy the data to an Excel sheet
        Set sheetExec = New cSheetExec
        sheetExec.sheetOpen _ (, "fromGAS").clearContent.setData _
            execPackage.child("response.result")

    End If

    ' clear up
    execPackage.tearDown

End Function
```

VBA Code to Write to a Sheet from a Local Workbook

This example uses the VBA `SheetExec` class to read data from a local workbook, and sends it to Apps Script to be written to a given sheet. Note the use of the `cJobject.attach` method to add the data retrieved from the local workbook to the data property of the first argument required by the receiving Apps Script function.

```VB
Private Function testSheetSet()
    Dim api As cExecutionApi, execPackage As cJobject, _
        args As cJobject, sheetExec As cSheetExec

    ' set all the data to a given sheet from a given workbook
    Set args = JSONParse( _
    "[{'id':'1f4zuZZv2NiLuYSGB5j4ENFc6wEWOmaEdCoHNuv-gHXo', _
      'sheetName':'fromExcel'}]")

    ' this time get the data from the local Excel sheet, and add to arguments
    Set sheetExec = New cSheetExec
    args.children(1).add("data").attach _
      sheetExec.sheetOpen(, "dataSheet").getData

    ' do the API call
    Set api = New cExecutionApi
    Set execPackage = api _
```

```
        .setFunctionName("execSetData") _
        .setProject("MMo4EFhHV6wqa7IdrGew0eiz3TLx7pV4j") _
        .setDevMode(True) _
        .setArgs(args) _
        .execute

    ' see what we got
    Debug.Print JSONStringify(execPackage, True)

    ' clear this up
    args.tearDown

End Function
```

This produces a result like this, and of course the data is written to the selected sheet:

VB
```
{
    "name":"execSetData",
    "done":true,
    "response":{
        "@type":"type.googleAPIs.com/google.apps.script.v1.ExecutionResponse"
    }
}
```

Apps Script Code to Write to a Sheet from a Local Workbook

The data produced by the VBA implementation of `SheetExec` can be consumed without modification by the Apps Script version:

VB
```
/**
 * given a sheet id & name, set the given data
 * @param {object} options args
 *    @param {string} id the sheet id
 *    @param {string} sheetName the sheetName
 *    @param {boolean} clearFirst whether to clear first
 */
function execSetData (options ) {

    // maybe there are defaults
    options = options || {};

    var sheetExec = new SheetExec().sheetOpen(options.id, options.sheetName);

    // clear it ?
    if (options.clearFirst) sheetExec.clearContent();

    // write the data
    sheetExec.setData ( options.data );

}
```

Migrating Logic

The order in which the incremental migration takes place clearly depends on the environment, but let's assume that now the sheets have been moved, and it's time to move some of the logic (still currently performed in VBA, even though the data has been moved).

One of the tasks in this imaginary system is to automatically search incoming mail for content containing valid flight numbers from a selected list of airlines, and to process attachments and initiate email conversations when they are detected (Figure 17-19). Now it's time to move this logic to Apps Script.

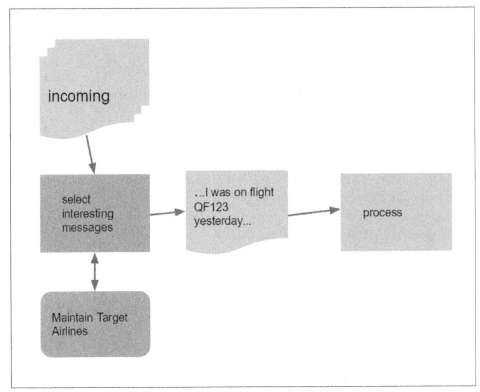

Figure 17-19. Logic we need to migrate from VBA to Apps Script

Using the Execution API, we can migrate the airline data and the selection process immediately to Google Apps, with only minimal changes to the VBA code. Other steps in the process can be migrated later, one piece at a time.

VBA Code to Initiate Logic on Apps Script

This snippet uses some simplified example data extracted from emails. The content is passed to Apps Script for processing, and the result should be equivalent to what the VBA version produced. The VBA logic can now be replaced with a call to the Execution API requesting that the Apps Script version processes the given test data:

```
VB  Private Function testFlights() As cJobject
        Dim api As cExecutionApi, execPackage As cJobject, args As cJobject

            '-- set up a run
            ' this one the sheet is known to the Execution API already
            ' the logic is in Apps Script

            Set args = JSONParse("[" & _
                "['scheduled to take LH123'," & _
                "'not an interesting XX123 airline number'," & _
                "'Going to AU on QF928 tomorrow']]")


            Set api = New cExecutionApi
            Set execPackage = api _
                .setFunctionName("executeMatch") _
                .setProject("MMo4EFhHV6wqa7IdrGew0eiz3TLx7pV4j") _
                .setDevMode(True) _
                .setArgs(args) _
                .execute

            ' see what we got
            Debug.Print JSONStringify(execPackage, True)

            ' clean up
            args.tearDown

            ' might need this later
            Set testFlights = execPackage
    End Function
```

Here is the result:

```
VB  {
        "name":"executeMatch",
        "done":true,
        "response":{
            "@type":"type.googleapis.com/google.apps.script.v1.ExecutionResponse",
            "result":[            {
                    "flight":"LH123",
                    "carrier":"LH",
                    "name":"Lufthansa Airlines",
                    "status":"ok"
                },
                {
```

```
            "flight":"not an interesting XX123 airline number",
            "status":"not found"
        },
        {
            "flight":"QF928",
            "carrier":"QF",
            "name":"Qantas Airways",
            "status":"ok"
        }
    ]
  }
}
```

Logic Code Delegated to Apps Script

Now both the lookup data and the logic are delegated to Apps Script in the following function. All that's needed is for VBA to pass over the text to be validated:

```
/**
 * @param {[string]} flightNumbers to check
 * @return {object} the result
 */
function execMatch (flightNumbers) {

  // get the sheet data
  var lookup = new SheetExec()
    .open(Settings.LOOKUP.ID, Settings.LOOKUP.NAME)
    .getData();

  // generate a regex for flightnumbers of each interesting airline
  var rx = new RegExp (getRegex(lookup) ,'gmi');

  return flightNumbers.map(function(flightNumber) {


    // match against given flight code
    var found = rx.exec(flightNumber);

  // return the airline code, name, and the flight number
    return found ?
      { status:"ok",
        flight:found[0],
        carrier:found[1],
        name:lookup.filter(function(d) {
          return d[Settings.HEADINGS.CODE].toLowerCase() ===
            found[1].toLowerCase();
        })[0][Settings.HEADINGS.NAME]
      } :
      { status:'not found',
        flight:flightNumber
      };
```

```
  });
}
/**
 * make the regex for flight matching
 * @param {object} lookup the lookup data
 * @return {Regexp} the matching regex
 */
function getRegex (lookup) {

  // in case the sender can't do JSON objects
  var ob = typeof lookup === typeof 's' ? JSON.parse(lookup) : lookup;

  return '\\b(' +
    ob.map(function(d) {
      return d[Settings.HEADINGS.CODE].toLowerCase();
    }).join("|") +
    ')([a-z]?)(\\d{1,4}[a-z]?)\\b';
}
```

VBA Orchestration

As the migration progresses, there is less and less happening in VBA, and its role is reduced to one of orchestration. In this example, all the data has moved to Sheets along with the logic. VBA still orchestrates the process and, based on the logic result, potentially makes some other changes or updates that are outside the scope of the process being migrated.

This case gets the results of matching as in the previous example; updates another worksheet (also in Sheets), incrementing the number of times a particular valid flight number is detected; and possibly enriches the worksheet with some data from another process.

VBA Process Orchestration Code

This example retrieves the flight validation results from `testFlights` as covered in the previous section, does some processing, and sends an array of flights to be logged by Apps Script in a different sheet:

```
VB Private Function testLog()
      Dim api As cExecutionApi, matchResults As cJobject, job As cJobject, _
          execPackage As cJobject, args As cJobject, sheetExec As cSheetExec


      ' does an update following a match - first do the match process
      Set matchResults = testFlights

      ' make sure it worked
      If (isSomething(matchResults.childExists("error"))) Then
          '' test for error
```

```
                Debug.Print JSONStringify(matchResults, True)
                Debug.Assert False
            Else

                '' only the data to add to an array
                Set args = New cJobject
                ' there's only one argument
                With args.Init(Nothing).addArray
                    '.. which is an array
                    With .add.addArray
                        '' maybe some more processing would happen here...
                        ''' here just filter on the good results
                        For Each job In matchResults.child("response.result").children
                            If (job.toString("status") = "ok") Then
                                .add.attach job
                            End If
                        Next job
                    End With
                End With

                ' do the API call
                Set api = New cExecutionApi
                Set execPackage = api _
                    .setFunctionName("execLog") _
                    .setProject("MMo4EFhHV6wqa7IdrGew0eiz3TLx7pV4j") _
                    .setDevMode(True) _
                    .setArgs(args) _
                    .execute

            End If


            ' see what we got
            Debug.Print JSONStringify(execPackage, True)

            ' clear this up
            args.tearDown

    End Function
```

Here's the result:

```
{
    "name":"execLog",
    "done":true,
    "response":{
        "@type":"type.googleAPIs.com/google.apps.script.v1.ExecutionResponse"
    }
}
```

Apps Script Logging Code

This example updates a log sheet with flights and the number of times they've been seen. If it's a new flight, it's added to the sheet.

```js
/**
 * this one increments a log with all the found flights
 * @param {object} results the results from an execmatch
 * @return {[object]} the data from the log
 */
function execLog (results) {

  // get the sheet data
  var sheetExec = new SheetExec().sheetOpen(Settings.LOG.ID, Settings.LOG.NAME);
  var log = sheetExec.getData();

  /// log the results
  results.forEach(function (d) {

    if (d.status === "ok") {
      // need to log
      var findLog = log.filter(function(f) {
        return f[Settings.LOG.HEADINGS.FLIGHT].toLowerCase() ===
          d.flight.toLowerCase();
      });

      // add if it's new
      if (!findLog.length) {
        var item = {};
        item[Settings.LOG.HEADINGS.FLIGHT] = d.flight;
        item[Settings.LOG.HEADINGS.COUNT] = 0;
        log.push(item);
      }
      else {
        var item = findLog[0];
      }

      // increment
      item[Settings.LOG.HEADINGS.COUNT]++;

    }
  });

  /// write the data (no need to clear)
  sheetExec.setData (log);

}
```

The log sheet looks like Figure 17-20.

flight	observations
LH123	5
QF928	4

Figure 17-20. Log sheet

Final Migration Steps

The ultimate objective is to migrate everything over to Apps (Figure 17-21), but there may be some circumstances (legacy databases and systems automation, for example), where automation needs to remain on VBA for some time.

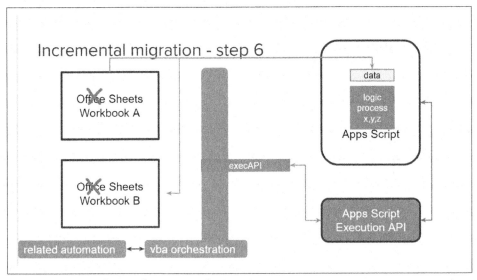

Figure 17-21. Final step of incremental migration

If this is the case, pay careful attention to quotas and timeouts. If the processes running on Apps Script become too long-running, or their results take too long to come back, they may need to be split into smaller chunks. Details of Apps Script quotas can be found in Chapter 4.

In any case, any incremental migration project needs as much planning and preparation as a straight cutover and should not be considered as the final operating model (Figure 17-22).

Testing JavaScript on the PC

Translated chunks of code can be hard to test outside the environment in which they were designed to reside. There comes a time when end-to-end tests are required, before any data has been migrated and before the system is complete.

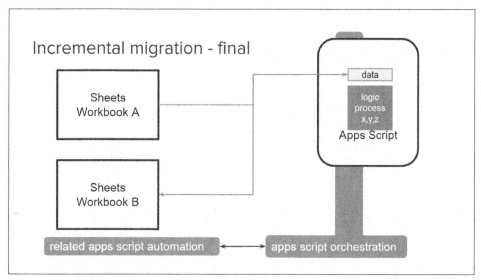

Figure 17-22. Incremental migration complete

Using the Execution API, you can retrieve code from Apps Script modules and run it on the PC under VBA's control and in place of the original VBA code. Not all code is suitable for this treatment, but pure logic code could be. Not only that, but the results can also be tested against the original VBA code in place.

This small demonstration is drawn from the example in this chapter. The purpose of this Apps Script function is to generate a regular expression based on the contents of the column of a lookup worksheet. At this early stage in the process, no data has been moved (it's still in Excel), and no other functions have been written in Apps Script.

Figure 17-23 illustrates the process of retrieving code and executing it locally.

VBA Code to Get Source Code from Apps Script

This is a generic VBA function to execute an Apps Script function to return some requested source code:

```
VB  Private Function getSource(args As cJobject) As cJobject
        Dim api As cExecutionApi, execPackage As cJobject


        ' do the API call
        Set api = New cExecutionApi
        Set execPackage = api _
            .setFunctionName("execGetSource") _
            .setProject("MMo4EFhHV6wqa7IdrGew0eiz3TLx7pV4j") _
            .setDevMode(True) _
            .setArgs(args) _
```

```
        .execute

    Set getSource = execPackage
End Function
```

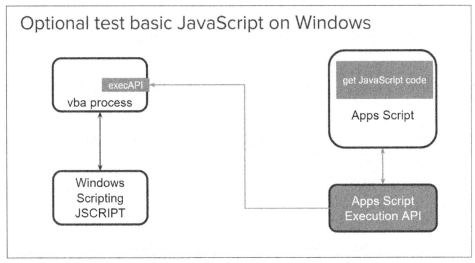

Figure 17-23. Retrieving code and executing it locally

Apps Script Code to Return Source Code

This function expects to be asked to return the source code of an array of modules
and optionally, an array of function names within modules. It's not perfect, as it's
clearly not a code parser, but it can find the common function constructs. If no function names are provided, it returns the whole module:

```js
/**
 * get any code -- doesn't handle {}() in comments or strings properly yet
 * @param {[object]} sourceToGet the source to get [{module:x, functions:[y]}]
 * @return {[object]} the result [{source:the source, module:x, functions:[y]}]
 */
function execGetSource (sourceToGet) {

  return sourceToGet.map(function(d) {
    var module = ScriptApp.getResource(d.module).getDataAsString();

    if (d.functions) {
      var source =  d.functions.reduce(function(p,c) {
        var match = new RegExp('\\b\\(?\\s*function\\s*' + c +
          '|var\\s+'+c+'\\s*=\\s*\\(?\\s*function','gm').exec(module);
        if (!match) {
          throw 'function ' + c + ' not found in module ' + d.module
        }

        // now find matching close {
```

```
    var depth, s = '', bracketStart = '{', bracketEnd = '}' ;

    module.slice (match.index).split('').some(function(r) {

      if (bracketStart == r) {
        depth = (typeof depth === typeof undefined ? 1 : depth +1);
      }
      if (bracketEnd == r) {
        depth = (typeof depth === typeof undefined ? undefined : depth -1);
      }
      s+=r;
      return depth ===0;
    });
    p += (s + '\n');
    return p;
  } ,'');
  return {module:d.module, functions:d.functions , source: source};
}
else {
  return {module:d.module, functions:d.functions , source: module};
}
});
```

```
}
```

Getting the Source and Testing Local Execution

This is the code to test local execution. After getting the required source code, it has to get the lookup data (still held locally in Excel at this stage), which is an argument to the JavaScript function running locally. Windows uses a fairly old JavaScript engine, so basic features are missing. The cJavaScript class can retrieve shim code to execute locally to modernize the engine, which you can see here. Finally, this code adds the source code retrieved by the Execution API from Apps Script and executes the new function, getRegex, with the argument of the lookup data retrieved from Excel:

```
VB  Private Function testLocalExecution()
      Dim js As New cJavaScript, result As Variant, lookup As cJobject, _
          execPackage As cJobject, job As cJobject, sheetExec As cSheetExec

      ' get the source code I need
      Set execPackage = getSource( JSONParse( _
        "[[{'module':'Settings'},{'module':'Executes','functions':['getRegex']}]]"))


      ' going to need the lookup data
      Set sheetExec = New cSheetExec

      ' here I'm passing the data from an Excel hosted data sheet
      ' at a later stage, the data could come from sheets instead
      Set lookup = sheetExec.sheetOpen(, "dataSheet").getData
```

```
        With js
            ' not really necessary first time in
            .clear

    ' here's a couple of polyfills to bring it more or less up to Apps Script levels
            .addUrl _
                "https://cdnjs.cloudflare.com/ajax/libs/json2/20150503/json2.min.js"
            .addUrl _
                "https://cdnjs.cloudflare.com/ajax/libs/es5-shim/4.1.7/es5-shim.min.js"

            ' my code
            For Each job In execPackage.child("response.result").children
                .addCode job.toString("source")
            Next job

            result = .compile.run("getRegex", lookup.stringify)

            Debug.Print result

        End With

        ' now we have the regex generated by the Apps Script code,
        ' pulled down to windows, and run locally
        ' it could be compared against the VBA version of the same thing
        ' to ensure the module is working okay

    End Function
```

Here is the result:

```
\b(8p|9r|ac|ay|b6|bs|ch|en|f9|hw|lh|na|on|qf|rj|tx|wy|xj|zb
    |zb)([a-z]?)(\d{1,4}[a-z]?)\b
```

Clearly this technique is not for all code, but it can provide a really useful comparative testing environment for early code conversions. Being able to test logic in the same environment at the same time has huge potential.

Execution API Potential

I've only scratched the surface of the Execution API's potential, but it's a huge development in opening up Apps Script. Even though it was probably not designed for this kind of use case, the Execution API provides an excellent basis for Apps Script delegation from VBA.

From a migration or even multiple platform coexistence perspective, using these kind of techniques can reduce or eliminate dual maintenance costs and errors, accelerate testing, and minimize the risks of the migration process.

CHAPTER 18

Office Add-Ins and Google Add-Ons

This chapter will look at extending Office and Google Apps using HTML web apps that run on the client and orchestrate server-side activities.

Add-Ons

Add-ons came to Google Drive in 2014. In Chapter 10, we used add-ons in the context of writing container-bound apps associated with a particular doc, sheet, or form. Add-ons allow these kinds of extensions to be published in a store and installed by a user so that they are available for all of the user's documents.

Coding add-ons is not much different from writing `HtmlService` custom menu extensions, although the process of publishing them is complicated.

Add-Ins

Excel users might be confused by the term *add-ins*, as it can also mean a companion workbook containing VBA code that can be executed by the main workbook, a COM add-in, or a VSTO add-in managed through the app's add-in manager. A little like a library in Apps Script, an add-in is one method used to distribute useful extension code for general use.

The Microsoft Office add-in nowadays refers to a completely different capability. Formerly called *Apps for Office*, now the tool is referred to as *Office Add-ins*. Add-ins use the JavaScript API for Office to access the Office object model, and execute HTML/JavaScript apps in an iframe associated with the container document.

The Same...

At first glance, add-ons and add-ins seem very much alike:

- Both run on the client and access data from the document on which they are operating.
- Coding is done in JavaScript and HTML.
- They are both published to a web store.
- Both dialog (content) and sidebar (taskpane) varieties are available.
- Both can be written for a number of the platform apps:
  - Office add-ins can be written for Outlook, Excel, SharePoint, PowerPoint, Project, Access (web), and Word.
  - Google add-ons are available for Sheets, Docs, and Forms.

...But Different

Their approach, however, is very different:

- Google add-ons can orchestrate any custom functions that run on the server from the client. This means that all Apps Script services are potentially available for a Google add-on.
- Microsoft add-ins provide access to the underlying data through an API whose functionality is limited to whatever the API is able to do. It's not possible to extend that functionality by orchestrating the running of custom macros.
- Microsoft has the concept of *binding* (when things change in the document, an event is fired in the add-in). Google add-ons have no binding capability and no event-driven push capability from the server.

The chapter implements Google add-on and Microsoft Office add-in solutions.

Add-On Example

This example will exercise many of the concepts covered throughout this book (and add a few new ones). The scenario is an add-on that will display the contents of a spreadsheet of major airports in the world using Google Maps in a sidebar (see Figure 18-1).

Although the subject is airports, we'll write the code to be easily customizable to other datasets—for example, restaurants with a type of food filter.

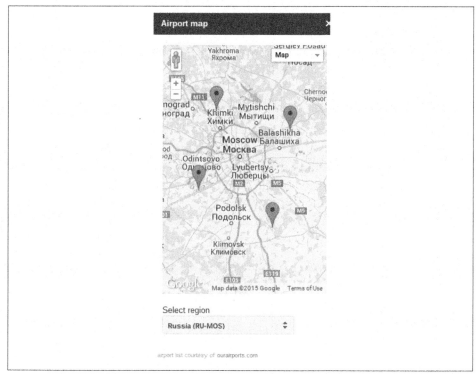

Figure 18-1. Add-on displaying major world airports using Google Maps

The Dataset

The sheet contains a list of large airports from the OurAirports.com public dataset, shown in Figure 18-2.

Each of these fields will be used either to display on the map or as a key to look up other APIs.

Capabilities

The add-on needs to be able to do all of the following:

- Provide drop-down selection of countries and regions. When selected, every airport in that region will be shown on the map.

- Adjust the map scaling so it comfortably displays all the selected airports, but without losing the regional context.

- Notice when changes in data have been made in the sheet and update the map input data with the changes.

- Automatically match the selected region to the current row on the sheet when the add-on is initiated and if the current row in the sheet changes (and settles down).
- Show the airport name when it's hovered over on the map, and an information window with the data fields when it's clicked.
- Adjust the center of the map to best show the information window and reposition it when the window is dismissed.
- Optimize data retrieval from the sheet so that data is transferred only if it has changed.
- Look up an external API to get the full country names (and other country information that could be shown in the information window with a later enhancement) and use them in the drop-down list.

name	latitude_deg	longitude_deg	elevation_ft	iso_country	iso_region	municipality	iata_code
Port Moresby Jacksons International Airport	-9.443380356	147.2200012	146	PG	PG-NCD	Port Moresby	POM
Keflavik International Airport	63.98500061	-22.60560036	171	IS	IS-2	Reykjavik	KEF
Prishtina International Airport	42.57279968	21.03580093	1789	KS	KS-U-A	Prishtina	PRN
Edmonton International Airport	53.30970001	-113.5800018	2373	CA	CA-AB	Edmonton	YEG
Halifax / Stanfield International Airport	44.88079834	-63.50859833	477	CA	CA-NS	Halifax	YHZ
Ottawa Macdonald-Cartier International Airport	45.32249832	-75.66919708	374	CA	CA-ON	Ottawa	YOW
Quebec Jean Lesage International Airport	46.79109955	-71.39330292	244	CA	CA-QC	Quebec	YQB
Montreal / Pierre Elliott Trudeau International Airport	45.47060013	-73.74079895	118	CA	CA-QC	Montreal	YUL
Vancouver International Airport	49.19390106	-123.1839981	14	CA	CA-BC	Vancouver	YVR
Winnipeg / James Armstrong Richardson International Airport	49.90999985	-97.23989868	783	CA	CA-MB	Winnipeg	YWG
London Airport	43.03559875	-81.15390015	912	CA	CA-ON	London	YXU
Calgary International Airport	51.11389923	-114.0199966	3557	CA	CA-AB	Calgary	YYC
Victoria International Airport	48.64690018	-123.4260025	63	CA	CA-BC	Victoria	YYJ
St. John's International Airport	47.61859894	-52.75189972	461	CA	CA-NL	St. John's	YYT
Lester B. Pearson International Airport	43.67720032	-79.63059998	569	CA	CA-ON	Toronto	YYZ
Houari Boumediene Airport	36.69100189	3.215409994	82	DZ	DZ-35	Algiers	ALG
Kotoka International Airport	5.6051898	-0.1667860001	205	GH	GH-AA	Accra	ACC
Nnamdi Azikiwe International Airport	9.006790161	7.263169765	1123	NG	NG-FC	Abuja	ABV
Akwa Ibom International Airport	4.8725	8.093	170	NG	NG-AK	Uyo	QUO
Murtala Muhammed International Airport	6.577370167	3.321160078	135	NG	NG-LA	Lagos	LOS
Tunis Carthage International Airport	36.85100174	10.22719955	22	TN	TN-11	Tunis	TUN

Figure 18-2. The OurAirports dataset

Apps Script Add-On

Let's start with the app implemented as a Google add-on. In principle, the client-side code written for the Google add-on will be directly transferrable to the Office add-in. However, the orchestration and data retrieval will be entirely different.

What You Will Learn

Given the lengthy list of requirements, there are a large number of new techniques to cover here, the main ones being:

- Simulate binding (detect changes in server-side data and position).
- Share the same code between server and client.

- Use cross-origin resource sharing (CORS) to circumvent issues related to accessing an external API from a client without needing to use JSONP.
- Use the Google Maps JavaScript API. More information on this API can be found in Appendix A.

The Namespaces

Figure 18-3 shows the scripts used in the project, most of which are namespaces.

Figure 18-3. Scripts used in this example

Even though the majority of the code is for client execution, you may notice that most of the scripts are in fact *.gs* files.

Sharing Code Between Client and Server

As a rule, I tend to write everything as if it will be shared between the server and client, even though it may be purely designed for one or the other. This has a number of advantages:

- Where appropriate, utility type JavaScript code needs to be written only once and used both server- and client-side.
- It gives access to the IDE to write both JavaScript and Apps Script. Editing an HTML type file does not give the same IDE support as editing a *.gs* file does.
- It enforces necessary discipline to avoid careless global variable execution and definition.

This is not the method Google uses in its code samples for HtmlService, and I've never seen any reference to it in any official documentation, but I find it to be a better pattern than using HTML type files to host scripts. Normally, you'd include code from HTML files in another by using this structure, repeated as many times as there are files to include. This also means that the files need <script> tags embedded in them (or around the scriptlet block):

```JS
<?!= HtmlService.createHtmlOutputFromFile(main.js).getContent(); ?>
```

requireGs

Instead, these two scriptlets in the *index.html* file will include the content from the HTML file (*main.js*), and the four Apps Scripts (App, Utils, Client, and Cors). <script> tags are automatically inserted, so there's no need to add them in the *.gs* files. I find this is more intuitive than the regular method:

```JS
<?!= requireJs(['main']); ?>
<?!= requireGs(['App','Utils','Client','Render','Cors']); ?>
```

The require functions run server-side, and are in the *Require.gs* script:

```JS
/**
 * given an array of .html filenames,
 * it will get the source and return them concatenated
 * for insertion into htmlservice
 * like this you can share the same code between client and server side,
 * and use the Apps Script IDE to manage your js code
 * @param {string[]} scripts the names of all the scripts needed
 * @return {string} the code inside script tags
 */
function requireJs (scripts) {
    return '<script>\n' + scripts.map (function (d) {
        return HtmlService.createHtmlOutputFromFile(d+".js").getContent();
    })
    .join('\n\n') + '</script>\n';
}


/**
 * given an array of .gs filenames, it will get the source
 * and return them concatenated for insertion into htmlservice
 * like this you can share the same code between client and server side,
 * and use the Apps Script IDE to manage your js code
 * @param {string[]} scripts the names of all the scripts needed
 * @return {string} the code inside script tags
 */
function requireGs (scripts) {
    return '<script>\n' + scripts.map (function (d) {
        return ScriptApp.getResource(d).getDataAsString();
    })
```

```
        .join('\n\n') + '</script>\n';
    }
```

index.html

As usual, the client-side app is defined by its *index.html* file. It doesn't have much in it—just a selector, a place to put messages, and a DIV to act as the map container.

It also includes the scripts and stylesheet from the project as well as the Google Maps API script:

```
<!DOCTYPE html>
<!-- styles -->
<?!= HtmlService.createHtmlOutputFromFile('styles.css').getContent(); ?>

<div class="content">
  <div id="map-canvas" class="block map"></div>
  <div class="block">
    <label for="region-select">Select region</label>
    <select id="region-select">
    </select>
  </div>
</div>

<div class = "block">
  <div id="message" class="message"></div>
</div>

<div class="block aside">
airport list courtesy of
  <a href="http://ourairports.com/data/">ourairports.com</a>
</div>
<!-- javascript. -->
<script src="https://maps.googleapis.com/maps/api/js?v=3.exp&signed_in=false">
  </script>
<?!= requireJs(['main']); ?>
<?!= requireGs(['App','Utils','Client','Render','Cors']); ?>
```

main.js

The *main.js* script waits for the DOM and the Maps API to be loaded, initializes any global data for the app, and does a one-off asynchronous call to the RESTCountries API to get useful data about countries that will be needed later.

The listener associated with the region selector is set up, and finally an asynchronous call is initiated to get some data back from the server:[1]

```js
// wait for the viz lib to have loaded
google.maps.event.addDomListener(window, 'load', function () {

    // hack the scroll bar
    // https://code.google.com/p/google-apps-script-issues/issues/detail?id=5164
    parent.document.getElementById('userHtmlFrame').style.overflowY = "hidden";

    // initialize the settings
    App.init();

    // get the countries from the API
    App.getCountries();

    // set up listeners
    App.listeners();

    // kick off by getting data, and building page
    Client.getData ();

});
```

styles.css

Mainly the styles are inherited from the standard add-on stylesheet. The size of the map is set to almost the width of the sidebar, and the height is designed to leave room for the region selector and message area.

Keeping custom styling to a minimum for add-ons helps maintain a consistency across add-on contributors:

```js
<!-- This CSS package applies Google styling; it should always be included. -->
<link rel="stylesheet"
    href="https://ssl.gstatic.com/docs/script/css/add-ons.css">

<style>
.content {
    padding:8px;
}

.message {
    color:red;
}
```

---

1 At the time of writing, there is a bug in the iframe setup of HTMLService. The symptom is an occasionally unnecessary vertical scroll bar. The hack mentioned in the code sample is a temporary workaround until Google fixes this.

```
.map {
  width:98%;
  height:390px;
}

.aside {
  font-size:.7em;
  color:gray;
}

td {
  padding:2px;
}

</style>
```

App Namespace

The app namespace is used to store global values and settings, and for housekeeping. It is always wise to include an init function that sets any parameter values rather than setting them directly, as this ensures that any scripts and the DOM are loaded before they're executed.

In this example, both elements from the DOM and Google Maps constants are referenced, with a guarantee that both will be available when init is executed:

```js
var App = (function (app) {

  'use strict';

  app.init = function () {
  // persistent client data
    app.globals = {
      sheet:{
        checksum:undefined,
        package:undefined,
        position:{}
      },
      polling:{
        interval:2000
      },
      divs: {
        mapCanvas:document.getElementById('map-canvas'),
        selector:document.getElementById('region-select'),
        message:document.getElementById('message')
      },
      countries: {
        url:'https://restcountries.eu/rest/v1/all',
        lookup:null,
        executed:false,
        interval:500
```

```
        },
        propertyNames: {
          region:'iso_region',
          arplat:'latitude_deg',
          arplon:'longitude_deg',
          title:'name',
          elevation:'elevation_ft',
          country:'iso_country',
          iata:'iata_code',
          municipality:'municipality'
        },
        map: {
          ob:null,
          options: {
           mapTypeId: google.maps.MapTypeId.ROADMAP,
           maxZoom:10
          },
          markers:[]
        }
    };
};

/**
* this gets data about all countries from an API
*/
app.getCountries = function () {

  // uses CORS
  Cors.request(
    function (response) {
      //success
      var data = JSON.parse(response.responseText);
      // make into a lookup
      app.globals.countries.lookup = data.reduce (function(p,c){
        p[c.alpha2Code.toLowerCase()] = c;
        return p;
      },{});
      app.globals.countries.executed = true;
    },
    function (response) {
      app.reportMessage ('failed to get country data ' + response.statusText);
      app.globals.countries.executed = true;
    },
    app.globals.countries.url,
    "GET");

};
/**
* report a message
* @param {string} message the message
*/
app.reportMessage = function (message) {
```

```
      app.globals.divs.message.innerHTML = message;
    };

    /**
     * add listeners
     */
    app.listeners = function () {

      app.globals.divs.selector.addEventListener ("change", function (e) {
        Render.map();
      });

    };

    return app;

  })(App || {});
```

Cors

The source data in the sheet contains a country code, but it does not contain the full name of the country. There is a very useful API, RESTCountries, that returns all kinds of information about countries that we could use to enrich this application. For the moment, only the full country name is of interest.

Accessing these kinds of APIs from a client-based application normally leads to cross-origin resource sharing (CORS) violations. JavaScript rules do not allow the retrieval of JSON data from domains other than the one doing the requesting. In the past, the usual way to get around this problem was to use JSONP (which was covered in earlier chapters), but nowadays more and more APIs are supporting CORS, including this one.

App.getCountries made a request to the API using CORS. The Cors namespace looks like this:

```
var Cors = (function (cors) {

  'use strict';

  // thanks to http://enable-cors.org/ for info on cors/html5

  /**
  *do a cors request
  *@param {function} callback the load callback
  *@param {function} errorCallback the error callback
  *@param {string}  url the url
  *@param {string} method the method (default GET)
  *@param {*} payload the optional payload
  *@return {object} the response
  */
```

```
cors.request = function (callback, errorCallback, url, method, payload) {

    // get the appropriate xhr
    var xhr = getXhr_ ();
    if (!xhr) throw 'cant do cors with this browser';

    // now we can go
    xhr.open(method || "GET", url, true);

    // set up callbacks
    xhr.onload = function(response) {
      // need to catch this, as it doesn't actually catch HTTP errors
      if (response.target.status < 200 || response.target.status >= 300) {
        errorCallback(response.target);
      }
      else {
        callback(response.target);
      }

    }
    xhr.onerror = function(response) {
      errorCallback(response.target);
    }

    // execute
    return xhr.send(payload);

    /**
    * get the correct xhr object for the browser being used
    * @return {XDomainRequest|XMLHttpReQuest} the xhr
    */
    function getXhr_() {

      // likely to be this, unless it's IE
      var xhr = new XMLHttpRequest();
      return isDefined_(xhr.withCredentials) ?
        xhr : (isDefined_(XDomainRequest) ? new XDomainRequest() : undefined);
    }

    function isDefined_(ob) {
      return typeof ob !== typeof undefined;
    }
  }
  return cors;
})(Cors || {});
```

Add-On Script

The role of the add-on script is to initialize the add-on, add it to the add-on menu, and kick off the HtmlService template evaluation and execution of *index.html*. It's just standard boilerplate:

```js
'use strict';
/**
 * Adds a custom menu with items to show the sidebar and dialog.
 *
 * @param {Object} e The event parameter for a simple onOpen trigger.
 */
function onOpen(e) {
  SpreadsheetApp.getUi()
      .createAddonMenu()
      .addItem('Show airport map', 'showMap')
      .addToUi();
}
/**
 * Runs when the add-on is installed; calls onOpen() to ensure menu creation and
 * any other initializion work is done immediately.
 *
 * @param {Object} e The event parameter for a simple onInstall trigger.
 */
function onInstall(e) {
  onOpen(e);
}
/**
 * Opens a sidebar.
 */
function showMap() {

  var ui = HtmlService.createTemplateFromFile('index.html')
      .evaluate()
      .setSandboxMode(HtmlService.SandboxMode.IFRAME)
      .setTitle('Airport map');

  SpreadsheetApp.getUi().showSidebar(ui);
}
```

When we run onOpen in the Script Editor to test our add-on, our Google Sheet container now includes our mapsExample menu under the Add-ons drop-down menu (Figure 18-4).

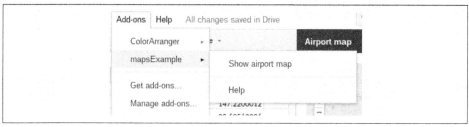

Figure 18-4. Acccessing mapsExample from the Add-ons menu

Reused Namespaces

Utils and SheetOb are carried forward with no change from previous examples. SheetOb runs on the server and transforms sheet data into a JSON object. Utils is a collection of useful snippets, some of which are used on both the server and the client.

Server Namespace

The role of the Server namespace (running on the server) is to respond to google.script.run requests from the client.

One of the app requirements was to optimize data transfers to the client. We do this using a checksum to determine whether the data has changed from the last data that was sent. Full data is sent only if there have been changes (see Figure 18-5).

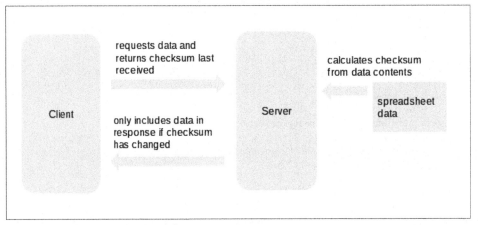

Figure 18-5. The Server.gs workflow

Server.gs implements this scheme:

```
var Server = (function(server) {
  'use strict;'

  server.getData = function (checksum) {

    // get data from activesheet
    var sob = new SheetOb().open();

    // calculate the data checksum
    var package = {
      data:sob.getData(),
      range:sob.getSheet().getDataRange().getA1Notation(),
      name:sob.getSheet().getName()
    }
```

```
    // calculate the checksum
    var newChecksum = Utils.checksum (package);
    var activeRange = sob.getSheet().getActiveRange();

    // return the data, null if the same as before
    return {
      package: checksum  === newChecksum ? null : package,
      position: {
        range:activeRange.getA1Notation(),
        row:activeRange.getRow(),
        column:activeRange.getColumn()
      },
      checksum:newChecksum
    }
  };

  return server;
})(Server || {});

// need to expose globally any functions to be called from the client;
function  getData (arg) {
  return Server.getData(arg);
}
```

Client Namespace

The Client namespace orchestrates the conversation with the server and detects and reacts to any data changes by recalculating the drop-down list.

Aside from data changes, position changes are also managed. If the cursor position in the spreadsheet has changed since the last communication, and the row it points to now contains a different region than previously, the map and selector are automatically adjusted to match the region at the current row:

```
/**
 * this is to run on the client
 * but I'm working with it as a .gs file
 */

// all code for client-server communication
var Client = (function(client) {

  /**
   * generic function to execute stuff on the server
   * @param {string} serverFunction the function to execute
   * @param {string} successFunction what to do when it succeeds
   * @param {*} serverArg arg to pass to the server
   */
  client.execute = function (serverFunction, successFunction, serverArg) {
```

```
    // this executes a function asynchronously on the server
    // under control of the client
    google.script.run

      // this will be executed if it fails
      .withFailureHandler(function (err) {
        App.reportMessage (err);
      })

      // this will be executed if it succeeds
      .withSuccessHandler (successFunction)

      // this is what gets executed
      [serverFunction](serverArg);

  };

  /**
   * get data from server
   * @param {function} [initFunction] call on successful if it's there.
   */
  client.getData = function () {

    // ask for data
    client.execute ( 'getData' , function (result) {

      // always store the latest checksum
      App.globals.sheet.checksum = result.checksum;

      // if the position has changed, but data has not,
      // we may need to change the selected item && re-map
      if (App.globals.sheet.position.row !==
      result.position.row && !result.package) {

        // change the selected option and redo and remap if necessary
        Render.selectionChanged(result.position);
        App.globals.sheet.position = result.position;

      }

      // if the checksum has changed,
      // then data.package is defined, store and update everything
      if (result.package) {
        App.globals.sheet.position = result.position;
        App.globals.sheet.package = result.package;

        // build the drop-down list and create map
        Render.build();

      }

      // schedule the next trip
```

```
      client.startPolling();

    },App.globals.sheet.checksum);
  }

  /**
   * trip to the server to look for updates
   */
  client.startPolling = function () {
    setTimeout(function(){
      client.getData();
    }, App.globals.polling.interval);
  };

  return client;

})(Client || {});
```

Binding

Data binding is not supported in Google add-ons, but Office add-ins do have binding capabilities. Binding is where client-side events are automatically triggered when a bound resource in the container document changes.

To simulate this in Apps Script, the client continuously polls the server, passing back the checksum of the data it knows about from the last poll. If the server script detects that the checksum of the current data is different from the checksum passed to it by the client, it sends updated data. It checks the current data content by reading it and calculating a checksum. Another approach, likely to be more appropriate for larger datasets, would be to monitor for onEdit changes and record these in the Properties service.

If the client detects the server has sent it some data, it processes the data anew. A similar process happens with the current cursor position, which is also passed to the client from the server. A change in cursor position or data contents provokes the client into potentially rendering a new map.

Render Namespace

Just as in previous HtmlService examples, the role of the Render namespace is to manage all operations that affect or are affected by the DOM. In this case, it handles the Google Maps rendering, markers, and information windows (a pop-up window usually associated with a marker), as well as user selection.

Back at the beginning of the app, a request was made to the external RESTCountries API to provide detail for all countries. This data is matched to the spreadsheet data to enrich it for selection and presentation. Because this was done asynchronously, there's a slight possibility that it hasn't yet finished.

Render.build, which builds the selector, won't execute until it sees that this request has completed. Thereafter, all map rerendering is done by triggering a change event on the region selector.

The region selector can then be built to include the full country names retrieved from the RESTCountry API, as shown in Figure 18-6.

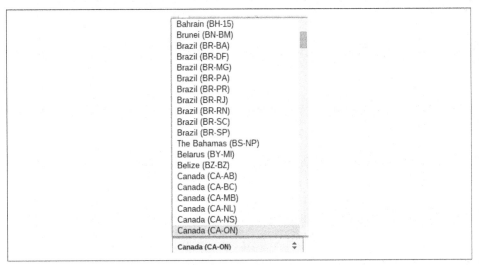

Figure 18-6. Including full country names retrieved from the RESTCountry API

fitBounds

If there is only one point to display on the map, Maps will zoom in close by default. This will lose the region and country context. If, on the other hand, a specific zoom value is chosen, it may not be big enough to show all airports in a selection or be too big to be appropriate for a small country.

The solution is to use fitBounds, along with maxZoom. fitBounds examines a collection of latitude/longitude points and makes a map just big enough to enclose them all. maxZoom is used to control the maximum zoom level allowed. With an appropriately chosen value for maxZoom, you can make any number of points fit without losing the intended context.

Another handy use of fitBounds is when an information window is dismissed. By default, Maps will reposition the map so that a marker's information window can be shown. By trapping the closeclick event on an information window, fitBounds can be used to recenter the map to its original position.

Figure 18-7 shows a map before, during, and after an information window is displayed.

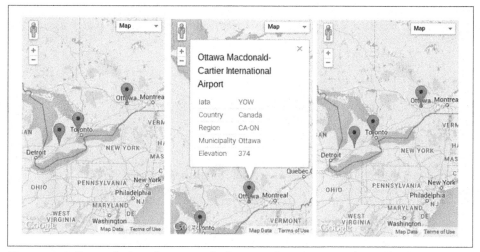

Figure 18-7. A map before, during, and after an information window is displayed

Render.js code

As usual, anything to do with DOM manipulation is isolated to the Render namespace (more information on the Google Maps JavaScript API, which is used in this code, can be found in the links in Appendix A).

```js
var Render = (function (render) {
  /**
   * render a map
   */
  render.map = function() {

    // do we need a new map?
    if (!App.globals.map.ob) {
      render.newMap();
    }
    var bounds = new google.maps.LatLngBounds();

    // clear previous markers
    App.globals.map.markers.forEach(function(d) {
      d.setMap(null);
    });
    App.globals.map.markers = [];

    //shortcuts
    var selectedregion = App.globals.divs.selector.value;
    var props = App.globals.propertyNames;

    App.globals.sheet.package.data.filter(function(d) {
      return d[props.region] === selectedregion;
    })
    .forEach (function (d) {
```

```
    // marker position
    var position = new google.maps.LatLng(d[props.arplat],d[props.arplon]);

    if (position) {
      // create a marker
      var marker = new google.maps.Marker({
        position: position,
        map:App.globals.map.ob,
        title:d[props.title]
      });

      // create a pop-up infowindow
      var infoWindow = new google.maps.InfoWindow({
       content: '<div>' +
         '<h1>' + d[props.title] + '</h1>' +
         '<table>' +
         '<tr><td>Iata</td><td>' + d[props.iata] + '</td></tr>' +
         '<tr><td>Country</td><td>' +
           countryText_(d[props.country]) + '</td></tr>' +
         '<tr><td>Region</td><td>' + d[props.region] + '</td></tr>' +
         '<tr><td>Municipality </td><td>' +
           d[props.municipality] + '</td></tr>' +
         '<tr><td>Elevation</td><td>' + d[props.elevation] + '</td></tr>' +
         '</table></div>'
      });

      // add an event to the marker
      marker.addListener('click', function() {
       infoWindow.open(App.globals.map.ob, marker);
      });

      // listen for the infowindow being closed, so map can be recentered
      google.maps.event.addListener(infoWindow,'closeclick',function(){
        infoWindow.close();
        App.globals.map.ob.fitBounds(bounds);
      });

      // resize the map
      bounds.extend(position);

      //remember the marker for later
      App.globals.map.markers.push(marker);

    }
  });

  // readjust the map size
  App.globals.map.ob.fitBounds(bounds);

};

/**
```

```
 * make new map
 */
render.newMap = function() {
  // create a map
  App.globals.map.ob = new google.maps.Map(
      App.globals.divs.mapCanvas, App.globals.map.options);
};

render.selectionChanged = function (position) {

  // if the default has changed, then redo
  var currentRow = position.row-2;

  var defaultRegion =
     App.globals.sheet.package.data[currentRow]
       [App.globals.propertyNames.region];

  // the select element
  if (defaultRegion === App.globals.divs.selector.value) return false;

  // i changed
  for (var i=0; i < App.globals.divs.selector.options.length; i++) {
    App.globals.divs.selector.options[i].selected =
      App.globals.divs.selector.options[i].value === defaultRegion;
  }

  // update the map
  render.map();
  return true;
}

/**
 * build selector
 */
 render.build = function () {

   // but can't do until the countries API is executed
   // waits a bit and tries again
   if (!App.globals.countries.executed) {
      setTimeout(function(){
        render.build();
     }, App.globals.countries.interval);
   }
   else {

     // the select element is already in place
     var props = App.globals.propertyNames;

     // add the options, but first reduce to one per region
     App.globals.sheet.package.data.filter(function(d,i,a) {
       return indexOfProps_ (a, props.region, d[props.region] ) === i;
     })
```

```
      .sort(function (a,b) {
        return a[props.region] > b[props.region] ? 1 :
          ( a[props.region] === b[props.region] ? 0 : -1 );
      })
      .forEach (function (d) {
          App.globals.divs.selector.appendChild(
            new Option ( countryText_ (d[props.country]) + ' (' +
              d[props.region] + ')', d[props.region] ));
      });

      // set the default
      render.selectionChanged(App.globals.sheet.position);
    }
  };

  function countryText_ (code) {
    return App.globals.countries.lookup &&
      App.globals.countries.lookup[code.toLowerCase()] ?
        App.globals.countries.lookup[code.toLowerCase()].name : code;
  }
  /**
   * a kind of indexof, but with property
   * @param {[*]} obs an array of objects
   * @param {string} property name to check
   * @param {*} value the value to check against
   * @return {number} the index of the first occurrence
   */
  function indexOfProps_ (obs , property, value) {
    for (var p =0 ; p < obs.length ; p++ ) {
      if (obs[p][property] ===  value) return p;
    }
    return -1;
  }

  return render;
})(Render || {});
```

Testing an Add-On

A container-bound custom menu function is fairly easy to test, because it forms part
of the associated document. However, there's a catch-22 for a standalone add-on: it
can't be installed unless it is published, but it can't be published until it is working and
has passed a quality test.

The IDE provides a way to associate an add-on with a document for the purposes of
testing (see Figure 18-8).

Figure 18-8. Associating an add-on with a document for testing

This leads to the document association dialog shown in Figure 18-9.

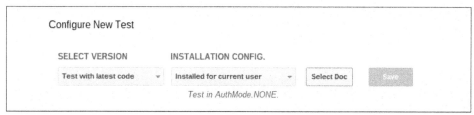

Figure 18-9. The document association dialog

This generates a URL that you can use to dry-run an add-on/document combination (see Figure 18-10).

Figure 18-10. Testing the add-on/document combination

Office Add-In

Naturally, Office has some starter apps demonstrating integration with Bing Maps as a solution to this kind of problem, and if you were solely using Office Add-ins it would be wise to use them. However, our objective here is to compare add-ins and add-ons, so this solution will use the same client-side code—namely, using Google Maps.

What You Will Learn

Add-ins are very different from add-ons, and there are peculiar omissions of some fundamental capabilities (which will probably drive you crazy), such as knowing where you are in a document, and finding out what data exists in the active sheet (or even knowing what the active sheet is).

On the other hand, Office Add-ins does have binding. This means that changes are detected in data and events fired in the client. It also has a very nice IDE.

Let's look at these items:

- How to use the Napa cloud IDE.
- How to set up binding and how to detect changes in data and cursor position.

The IDE

There are two ways to develop add-ins. One is to use Napa cloud, a web-based IDE, and the other is to use Visual Studio. In order to keep the comparison with Apps Script going, I'll use Napa cloud, which is close to the Apps Script IDE.

After signing in to Napacloudapp.com, you'll see any projects already developed, as shown in Figure 18-11.

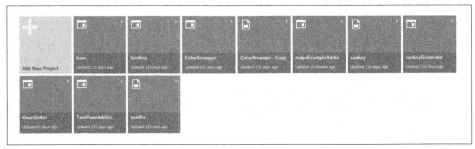

Figure 18-11. Projects already developed in Napa cloud

You'll also be able to create a new project (see Figure 18-12).

Figure 18-12. Adding a new project in Napa cloud

The example shown in Figure 18-13 is a taskpane add-in, which is the equivalent of the Apps Script sidebar app.

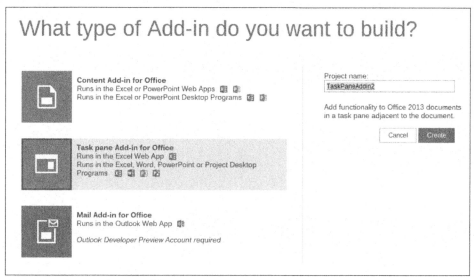

Figure 18-13. A taskpane add-in

Creating a project will generate a boilerplate structure (see Figure 18-14), most of which I'll discard, as this solution will leverage the patterns developed for the Apps Script version.

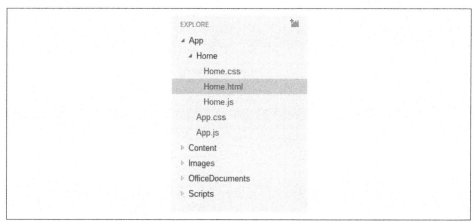

Figure 18-14. The boilerplate structure generated upon creating a new project

Figure 18-15 shows a snippet from the completed add-in.

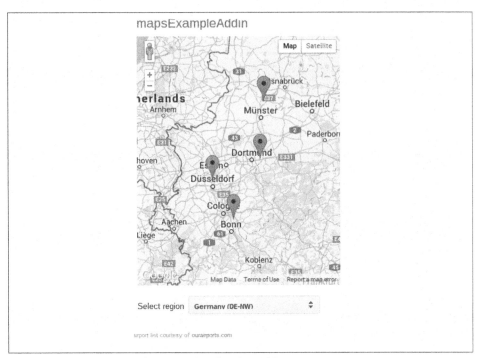

Figure 18-15. A snippet of the completed Office add-in

The data is held in an Excel table, as shown in Figure 18-16.

	A	B	C	D	E	F	
1	name	latitude_deg	longitude_deg	elevation_ft	iso_country	iso_region	municipalit
2	Port Moresby Jacksons International Airport	-9.443380356	147.2200012	146 PG		PG-NCD	Port Mores
3	Keflavik International Airport	63.98500061	-22.60560036	171 IS		IS-2	Reykjavik
4	Prishtina International Airport	42.57279968	21.03580093	1789 KS		KS-U-A	Prishtina
5	Edmonton International Airport	53.30970001	-113.5800018	2373 CA		CA-AB	Edmonton
6	Halifax / Stanfield International Airport	44.88079834	-63.50859833	477 CA		CA-NS	Halifax
7	Ottawa Macdonald-Cartier International Airport	45.32249832	-75.66919708	374 CA		CA-ON	Ottawa
8	Quebec Jean Lesage International Airport	46.79109955	-71.39330292	244 CA		CA-QC	Quebec
9	Montreal / Pierre Elliott Trudeau International Airport	45.47060013	-73.74079895	118 CA		CA-QC	Montreal
10	Vancouver International Airport	49.19390106	-123.1839981	14 CA		CA-BC	Vancouver
11	Winnipeg / James Armstrong Richardson International Airpo	49.90999985	-97.23989868	783 CA		CA-MB	Winnipeg
12	London Airport	43.03559875	-81.15390015	912 CA		CA-ON	London
13	Calgary International Airport	51.11389923	-114.0199966	3557 CA		CA-AB	Calgary
14	Victoria International Airport	48.64690018	-123.4260025	63 CA		CA-BC	Victoria
15	St. John's International Airport	47.61859894	-52.75189972	461 CA		CA-NL	St. John's
16	Lester B. Pearson International Airport	43.67720032	-79.63059998	569 CA		CA-ON	Toronto
17	Houari Boumediene Airport	36.69100189	3.215409994	82 DZ		DZ-35	Algiers
18	Kotoka International Airport	5.6051898	-0.166786	205 GH		GH-AA	Accra

Figure 18-16. Our add-in data in Excel

Structure

The Office module structure, shown in Figure 18-17, closely follows the Apps Script version. Where there is no change to the JavaScript code, the module names are the same as they were in Apps Script. Where there are some changes, they are renamed as *<modulename>Office*.

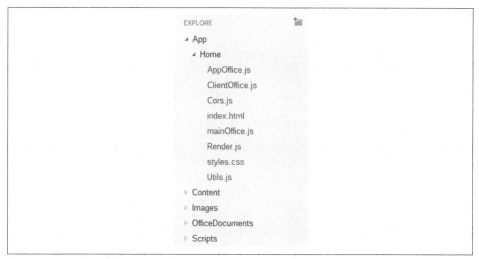

Figure 18-17. The Office module structure

So there are three changed files, plus a small change to *index.html*. All the others are directly copied from Apps Script.

Changing the start page

Because the boilerplate structure built by Napa cloud is not being used, we need to change the start page of the app from the default (see Figure 18-18).

index.html

index.html is very largely the same as the Apps Script version. Note that it needs to pull in the Office API:

```
<!DOCTYPE html>
<link href="../../Content/Office.css" rel="stylesheet" type="text/css" />
<link rel="stylesheet"
  href="https://ssl.gstatic.com/docs/script/css/add-ons.css">
<link rel="stylesheet" href="styles.css">
<div class="content">
  <div id="map-canvas" class="block map"></div>
  <div class="block">
    <label for="region-select">Select region</label>
    <select id="region-select">
    </select>
  </div>
</div>
```

```
<div class = "block">
  <div id="message" class="message"></div>
</div>

<div class="block aside">
airport list courtesy of
  <a href="http://ourairports.com/data/">ourairports.com</a>
</div>
<!-- javascript. -->
<script src="https://appsforoffice.microsoft.com/lib/1.1/hosted/office.js"
  type="text/javascript"></script>
<script src="https://maps.googleapis.com/maps/api/js?v=3.exp&signed_in=false">
  </script>
<script src="mainOffice.js"></script>
<script src="AppOffice.js"></script>
<script src="Utils.js"></script>
<script src="ClientOffice.js"></script>
<script src="Render.js"></script>
<script src="Cors.js"></script>
```

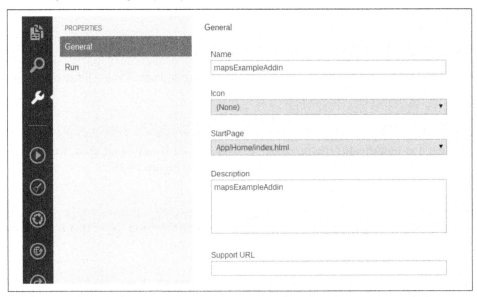

Figure 18-18. Changing Napa cloud's default start page

mainOffice.js

An additional wrapper is needed in *mainOffice.js*, because the Office API needs to be fully loaded before the app can start. Note also that the first data action is not to get the data, but to set up a binding to the data area so that changes can be detected:

```
JS  Office.initialize = function (reason) {

        // wait for the viz lib to have loaded
```

```
    google.maps.event.addDomListener(window, 'load', function () {

        // initialize the settings
        App.init();

        // get the countries from the API
        App.getCountries();

        // set up listeners
        App.listeners();

        // bind data
        Client.bind();

    });
};
```

App.js

There's very little difference between the Apps Script and Office code for *Apps.js*, so only a small section is shown here, prompted by a couple of Office limitations:

- The current position is difficult to figure out. Selection changes are detected through the binding event. This version will always start on the first row.

- Strangely it's not possible to detect which table is active, or to dynamically change a bound range that is not part of a table, so this version needs to rely on binding to a known, named table:

VB
```
sheet:{
    checksum:undefined,
    package:{},
    position:{
        row:2
    },
    tableName:'Table1',
    binding:undefined
}
```

Client.js

The biggest difference is in the client orchestration. There is no server to communicate with, only binding changes to react to:

JS
```
var Client = (function(client) {

    /**
     * set up binding to dataset
     */
    client.bind = function() {
```

```
    // add a named table as binding
    // don't know how to get the name of an active table so it's hardcoded
    Office.context.document.bindings.addFromNamedItemAsync(
      App.globals.sheet.tableName, Office.CoercionType.Table, {
        id: App.globals.sheet.tableName
      },
      function(asyncResult) {
        if (asyncResult.status === Office.AsyncResultStatus.Succeeded) {

          // store the binding object for later
          var binding = App.globals.sheet.binding = asyncResult.value;

          // get the first chunk of data
          client.getData();

          // add a data change handler
          binding.addHandlerAsync(
            Office.EventType.BindingDataChanged,
            function(e) {
              client.getData();
            });

          // add a selection change handler
          binding.addHandlerAsync(
            Office.EventType.BindingSelectionChanged,
            function(e) {

              // adjust position to match Apps Script row /col numbers.
              var position = {
                row: e.startRow + 2,
                column: e.startColumn + 1,
                columnCount: e.columnCount,
                rowCount: e.rowCount
              };

              // see if position has changed
              Render.selectionChanged(position);
              App.sheet.position = position;
            });

        }
        else {
          App.reportMessage('Error:', asynchResult.error.message);
        }
      });
};

/**
 * get data following a binding change event
 */
client.getData = function() {
  App.globals.sheet.binding.getDataAsync(function(asyncResult) {
```

```
      var headers = asyncResult.value.headers[0];
      var data = asyncResult.value.rows;

      // now convert to a more palatable format
      App.globals.sheet.package.data = data.map(function(row) {
        var col = 0;
        return row.reduce(function(p, c) {
          p[headers[col++]] = c;
          return p;
        }, {})
      });

      // use the changed data
      Render.build();

      // get to the right position
      Render.selectionChanged(App.sheet.position);
    });
  };

  return client;

})(Client || {});
```

Testing the Add-In

There is a nice dialog to create a new Excel workbook (see Figure 18-19), accessible from the OfficeDocuments link in the Napa cloud project sidebar.

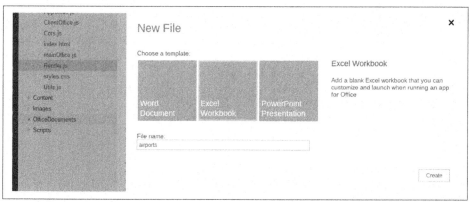

Figure 18-19. The New File dialog accessed from Napa cloud's OfficeDocuments link

Unfortunately that leads to a dead end, and does not create a file (Figure 18-20).

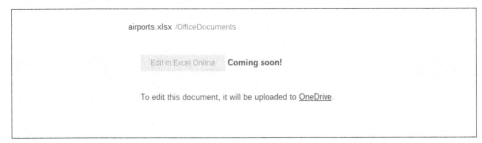

Figure 18-20. Excel editing capability is not enabled yet

Instead, go to OneDrive and create an *airports* workbook with the data from the Sheets version. You also need to convert the data in the first sheet to a table. The book resources on GitHub contain one already prepared to upload if you prefer.

Figure 18-21. Creating an airbooks workbook using the Sheets data

Now head over to the Properties area in Napa cloud, and you'll notice that the ability to add a file to the project is now enabled (Figure 18-22). The workbook you just created can be added to the project here.

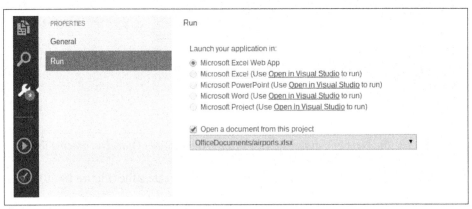

Figure 18-22. Uploading the airports workbook to Excel

Heading back to OneDrive and clicking on the *airports.xlsx* workbook magically opens it, with the add-in active (Figure 18-23). I have no idea how, but I'll definitely take it!

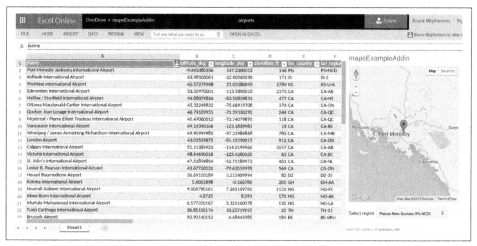

Figure 18-23. The add-in is now active

Result Comparison

Side by side, the Microsoft add-in renders better as it gives improved dimensions for the map. It allows a slightly wider sidebar than the Google add-on, whose maximum sidebar width is 300px (see Figure 18-24).

Because of the binding change events, the Office version seems much more responsive. The Apps Script version, relying as it does on polling and checking for changes, is bound to seem sluggish.

On the other hand, from a development perspective, the Office API is frustrating to work with. It gives the distinct impression of "not being finished," and looking over the past few years of blog and forum posts it hasn't changed much (aside from branding or name), nor has anything new been added for some time. This is in distinct contrast to the collection of Google APIs, which gain new or improved features regularly.

If you are coming from VBA, you may be tempted to favor the Office API, but there is not too much there that leverages existing knowledge. If you do choose the Office platform, make sure that it has the capabilities your app needs now, and for the future.

Despite its faults, I would generally favor and recommend the Apps Script add-on approach, unless Microsoft changes its energy and focus to make Office Add-ins a more complete platform.

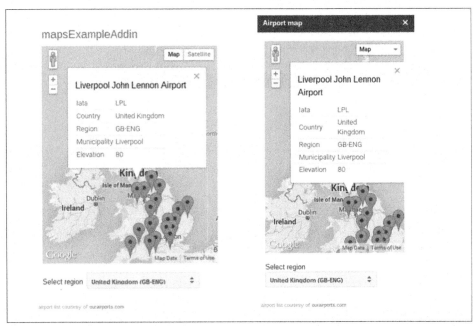

Figure 18-24. Microsoft add-in (left) versus Google add-on (right)

Further Exercises

Of course this is a pretty static dataset, so it probably doesn't need the change detection built into the app. However, with just few parameter changes and tweaks, this pattern can be easily applied to other, more dynamic datasets.

For an interesting exercise to bring together many of the techniques in this book, you might try:

- Using this dataset as a lookup either from a spreadsheet, a Fusion table, or some other kind of database previously covered.
- Using the modified add-on with your own dataset (e.g., the worldwide offices of the company you work for).
- Changing the behavior to plot airports in the sidebar within a certain distance of the currently selected data row in your dataset.

With these kinds of patterns already written, creating compelling apps that pull and visualize data from many different sources becomes an everyday undertaking.

Afterword

When I started this book in May 2015, I didn't expect it to be so long. I found the more I wrote, the more I felt the need to write. In fact, reaching the end has made me feel as if I've only just begun.

VBA has had 25 years to develop its comprehensive footprint. Apps Script is now about 6 years old. There are elements of VBA that will never be translatable to Apps Script, and there are definitely some parts that should be left far behind. On the other hand, there are some wonderful aspects of VBA that will be a great loss, not only for sentimental reasons, but also for their usability and affinity with the products with which they are associated.

Although the focus of this book has been mainly on transitioning from VBA to Apps Script (with some diversions along the way), my hope is that you have found something of value to help you on your journey, even if it started from somewhere other than Office.

My website and the communities mentioned will keep publishing and debating material related to this subject (and others). I highly recommend you keep the discussion going by following and joining the groups, and help me shape the content for the next book. With the speed of change in Google products, there will be plenty of new topics and migration strategies to cover.

Thanks for sticking with me all the way through!

Further Resources

There are many code snippets throughout this book, and they are presented to illustrate a point or a technique. Some of the apps can be reconstructed from the snippets given, but it may be easier to pick up the code for each of the completed apps from the companion GitHub repository. Each dataset and spreadsheet used is also in that same repository.

GitHub Repository

The repository can be found at *https://github.com/brucemcpherson/GoingGas.*

Repository Structure

Each set of material for each project is in a separate directory structure, organized as shown in Figure A-1 when cloned from Git.

If there is standalone Apps Script content for any topic, it will be in a subdirectory */gas/scripts* and the expanded source will be in */gas/<source>/<thenameofthescript>* as in Figure A-2.

When topics are container-bound, regardless of whether they are VBA or Apps Script, they will be in the *containerbound* folder.

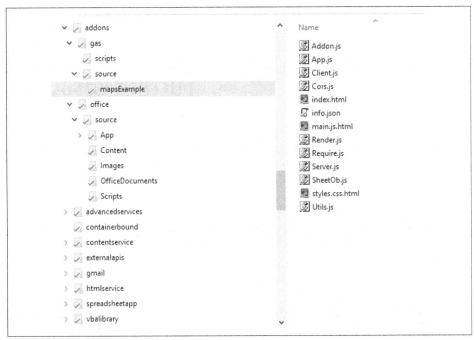

Figure A-1. Structure of a repository cloned from Git

Figure A-2. Directory structure for standalone Apps Script content

gscript Files

A gscript file is a pointer to the cloud-hosted script file, rather than the file itself. On GitHub it will look like Figure A-3.

Figure A-3. gscript file

When opened in GitHub, it will show the URL of the script (Figure A-4).

Figure A-4. Contents of the gscript file

Copy this into the browser bar to open. All the scripts are read-only. You should make a copy to play around with.

Other Resources

The following lists include some other resources referred to throughout the book.

Websites, blogs, and contact details:

- Desktop Liberation (*http://www.mcpher.com*), my site for info on VBA, Apps Scripts, and all things Google and Microsoft
- Desktop Liberation (*http://excelramblings.blogspot.com*), my companion blog for Google and Microsoft tips
- Twitter (*@brucemcpherson*)
- G+ (*+BruceMcpherson*)
- My O'Reilly profile (*http://www.oreilly.com/pub/au/6781*)

Communities:

- Google+ Google Apps Script (*http://bit.ly/gas-dev-comm*), a community for Apps Script developers
- Google+ Desktop Liberation (*http://bit.ly/dl-comm*), a community for discussion of Desktop Liberation site contents
- Google+ Going GAS (*http://bit.ly/going-gas-comm*), a community for readers of this book
- Google Developer Experts (*https://developers.google.com/experts*)
- Microsoft MVPs (*https://mvp.microsoft.com*)

Reference and utility sites:

- Apps Script Developers (*https://developers.google.com/apps-script*) (official Google reference site for Apps Script)
- Napa Cloud—Microsoft IDE (*https://www.napacloudapp.com/*)
- JavaScript API for Office (*http://bit.ly/js-api-office*)
- Google API Explorer (*http://bit.ly/api-explorer*)
- Google Developers Console (*https://console.developers.google.com*)

- Google Developers add-on reference (*http://bit.ly/google-addon*)
- Google Maps JavaScript API (*https://developers.google.com/maps/web/*)
- Mozilla Developer Network
  - JavaScript reference (*http://bit.ly/moz-dev-js*)
  - HTML reference (*http://bit.ly/moz-dev-html*)
  - CSS reference (*http://bit.ly/moz-dev-css*)
- Google Apps setup (*http://setup.googleapps.com/*)
- Managing Google domains with the Admin SDK (*http://bit.ly/admin-sdk*)

Data source references:

- Data-set about airports (*http://ourairports.com/data/*)
- Airport delay API (*http://services.faa.gov*)

Libraries (you can add them to your project, or copy the code and create your own):

VBA library
Key: `M6MGBNseI3rimhno7EClR5yz3TLx7pV4j`

Further reading and repositories:

- Drive JSON API for Apps Script
  - *http://bit.ly/drive-json-api*
  - *http://bit.ly/github-json-api*
- cJobject JavaScript equivalents for VBA
  - *http://bit.ly/cjobj-vba*
  - *http://bit.ly/github-cjobj*
- cJobject deep dive (*http://bit.ly/cjobj-deep-dive*)
- cEzyOAuth2 for Apps Script
  - *http://bit.ly/dl-ezy*
  - *http://bit.ly/github-ezy*
- OAuth 2.0 for Apps Script (*http://bit.ly/oauth2-gas*)

Keys and Credentials

Throughout the examples, there are various credentials and secrets. None of them will work because they are private to me, not to mention they've been disabled. Sharing code that needs authentication always means that you need to become familiar with how to get your own keys, and to substitute them in any code you clone or refactor.

Index

options.htmlBody field, 212

P

P-code (pseudocode), 3
paragraphs, creating, 181
parallel scripts, 104
payload limitations, 98
performance aids, 8
permissions, 313, 344
Polyfills, 5
project key, 358, 418
promises, 264
Properties service
  benefits and drawbacks of, 107, 109
  ContentService settings in, 276
  deleting from properties store, 112
  email settings in, 234
  Firebase settings, 345
  Fusion table settings in, 305
  getting started with, 108
  mitigating size limitations, 103
  property store versus Windows registry, 109
  reading the property store, 112
  selecting a property store, 108
  setting properties using, 140
  uses and types of property stores, 108
  writing to property store, 110
properties, getting/setting, 41, 137
prototype-based languages, 26
prototypes, 37
pseudoclasses, creating, 37

Q

queries, 199, 285
quota management
  avoiding service calls, 104
  daily limits, 97
  in shared-server environments, 8, 97
  limitations, 98
  rate limits, 100
  throttling, 100-104
  triggers, 99
  usage information, 304

R

Range class
  creating a range, 117
  getting values of a range, 118

offset function, 120
  reading attributes from ranges, 122
  reading/writing partial ranges, 122
  returning data ranges, 118
  returning selected data, 121
  writing attributes to ranges, 123
  writing values to ranges, 120
Range object, 166
Range.Find method, 172
RangeBuilder class, 169-173
RangeElements, 166
ranges
  building partial element ranges, 170
  finding text, 170
  in GAS, 166
  in VBA, 166
  invalid error message, 291
  merging RangeElements, 171
  named ranges, 173, 178
  RangeBuilder class, 169
  showRange utility, 167
  VBA discontinuous ranges, 166
  VBA find, 172
  VBA range collections, 170
rate limits, 8, 100, 200, 304
redirect URL, 322, 326
reduce method, 28, 205
reference loops, 59
refresh tokens, 315
registry access, 110
  (see also Windows registry)
regular expressions, 202, 205, 244
Render namespace, 265, 297, 395, 397
requireGs, 384
resources, 415-418
Resources menu, 240
REST API
  accessing Advanced Services via, 301
  Apps Script apps as, 273
  interaction through UrlFetchApp, 339-342
RESTCountries API, 389
Resume Next pattern, 85
Resume statements, 84
Right function, 69
role-based protection, 313
rows, inserting/deleting, 124, 184
RTrim function, 70

S

About the Author

Bruce Mcpherson is a veteran IT practitioner with 30+ years as CIO, Chief Architect, and many other roles—mainly in large global enterprises such as Motorola and Lucent. With expertise in each of Google, Microsoft, and Oracle technologies, his main interest is in integration.

For a number of years, he has been running a range of popular sites and blogs providing advice and assistance on transition connectivity.

Bruce is a Google Developer Expert (GDE) specializing in Apps Script and Google Drive.

Colophon

The animal on the cover of *Going GAS* is a spotted thick-knee (*Burhinus capensis*), also known as a spotted dikkop or Cape thick-knee. It is a member of the stone-curlew family, a group of birds found in arid or semi-arid habitats with open ground. The spotted thick-knee is native to central and southern Africa.

The term *dikkop* stems from Afrikaans for "thick head," but it is actually the protuberance around the ankles that gives these birds their name. They have long legs and the joint is positioned where a knee might be on a mammal, so the misnomer is understandable. Another prominent feature of this animal is its large, bright yellow eyes. The spotted thick-knee has speckled brown and white plumage that provides camouflage when it is resting on the ground during the day. It is nocturnal.

The thick-knee's diet is made up of insects, lizards, and small mammals, which it hunts on the ground and catches with quick stabs of its beak. They also nest on the ground, scraping a shallow hole in the earth and lining it with grass, feathers, and other material. Females typically lay two eggs. Mating pairs are monogamous and share responsibility for their young by taking turns incubating the eggs, guarding the nest, and bringing food back.

Many of the animals on O'Reilly covers are endangered; all of them are important to the world. To learn more about how you can help, go to *animals.oreilly.com*.

The cover image is from *Johnson's Natural History*. The cover fonts are URW Typewriter and Guardian Sans. The text font is Adobe Minion Pro; the heading font is Adobe Myriad Condensed; and the code font is Dalton Maag's Ubuntu Mono.

Have it your way.

Get even more for your money.

Join the O'Reilly Community, and register the O'Reilly books you own. It's free, and you'll get:

- $4.99 ebook upgrade offer
- 40% upgrade offer on O'Reilly print books
- Membership discounts on books and events
- Free lifetime updates to ebooks and videos
- Multiple ebook formats, DRM FREE
- Participation in the O'Reilly community
- Newsletters
- Account management
- 100% Satisfaction Guarantee

Signing up is easy:

1. Go to: oreilly.com/go/register
2. Create an O'Reilly login.
3. Provide your address.
4. Register your books.

Note: English-language books only

To order books online:
oreilly.com/store

For questions about products or an order:
orders@oreilly.com

To sign up to get topic-specific email announcements and/or news about upcoming books, conferences, special offers, and new technologies:
elists@oreilly.com

For technical questions about book content:
booktech@oreilly.com

To submit new book proposals to our editors:
proposals@oreilly.com

O'Reilly books are available in multiple DRM-free ebook formats. For more information:
oreilly.com/ebooks

O'REILLY®

CPSIA information can be obtained at www.ICGtesting.com
Printed in the USA
BVOW09s2058150216

436825BV00002B/2/P

9 781491 940464